STUDY GUIDE

JOSEPH CHINNICI · SUSAN WADKOWSKI

LIFE ON EARTH
Second Edition

AUDESIRK · AUDESIRK · BYERS

PRENTICE HALL, Upper Saddle River, NJ 07458

Senior Editor: Teresa Ryu
Project Manager: Karen Horton
Special Projects Manager: Barbara A. Murray
Production Editor: Jonathan Boylan
Supplement Cover Manager: Paul Gourhan
Supplement Cover Designer: PM Workshop Inc.
Manufacturing Manager: Trudy Pisciotti

ISBN 0-13-012684-5

Prentice-Hall International (UK) Limited, London
Prentice-Hall of Australia Pty. Limited, Sydney
Prentice-Hall Canada, Inc., Toronto
Prentice-Hall Hispanoamericana, S.A., Mexico
Prentice-Hall of India Private Limited, New Delhi
Prentice-Hall (Singapore) Pte. Ltd.
Prentice-Hall of Japan, Inc., Tokyo
Editora Prentice-Hall do Brazil, Ltda., Rio de Janeiro

CONTENTS

TO THE STUDENT – PLEASE READ

This Study Guide should be used with the textbook LIFE ON EARTH, second edition. The Study Guide is set up to help you learn the most from your non-majors biology course (and to earn the highest possible grade). However, working through the Study Guide is only a portion of the process. You should take advantage of the three interrelated elements of the course: the lectures, the textbook, and the Study Guide.

1. **Lecture**: Attend all lectures, be attentive in class, and take good and complete notes. Sitting toward the front of the class will help increase your ability to pay attention. You may want to tape the lectures as well. (Always get the instructor's permission to tape lectures.) On the evening after each lecture, recopy the notes into a more readable and organized from, relying on the textbook and Study Guide for help in understanding confusing and difficult topics and for filling in "gaps" in the notes. (A taped lecture helps here.) You'll be pleasantly surprised by how much you will learn and remember by simply rewriting and adding to class notes.

2. **Textbook**: Read the textbook chapters before they are covered in lecture. You will find the lecture more comprehensible since the terminology will be somewhat familiar. If you understand the lecture better, it will be less frustrating and more fun to go to class.

3. **Study Guide**: After reading the textbook and attending the lecture, use this Study Guide to help you prepare for the inevitable exams that go with college life. This Study Guide has a detailed overview of each chapter in the textbook, along with a set of review exercises and answers.

FORMAT OF THE STUDY GUIDE

This Study Guide is divided into 30 chapters, corresponding to the organization of the textbook. Each chapter has a similar format, consisting of:

1. A detailed **overview** of the material in the textbook, organized to allow you to gain additional understanding of the chapter and easily find answers to the review questions. All important concepts from the textbook are included in the overview, along with some helpful hints for remembering the material.

2. **Key terms and definitions** for that chapter. It has been suggested that the many new terms encountered in an introductory biology course equal the first course in a foreign language. Thus, the key terms and definitions will prove helpful in understanding the content of each chapter. Refer to them as often as needed.

3. A set of review exercises in a variety of formats, including: **thinking through the concepts**, which may include multiple choice, true/false, and fill-in questions, as well as the occasional crossword puzzle, concept maps, tables or diagrams; **clues to applying the concepts**, which are essay questions based on ideas covered in the chapter. These questions are designed to increase your ability to think critically about the concepts presented in the chapter. After reading the textbook, attending the lecture, rewriting your lecture notes, reviewing the Study Guide outline and exercises, and studying, you should be able to answer the review questions.

4. Answers to exercises. Refer to these after answering the review exercises. Looking at the answers before trying to answer them yourself can mislead you into thinking you know the answers when you may not. Use the answers provided in this guide to check your answers for accuracy, not to generate your answers.

HINTS FOR STUDYING

You should first learn the definitions of the key terms (and any others you are unfamiliar with). Then learn how those terms apply or are related to the topic covered. Try to keep in mind the big picture while you are learning the details of the process. While this can be difficult, it will increase your understanding.

Drawing diagrams of your own to outline a process will help increase your understanding, especially if you are a more visual learner. Some students use or devise their own mnemonic devices to help them remember terms or concepts in order. (For example: King Philip Came Over For Good Spaghetti is a great way to remember the taxonomic categories Kingdom, Phylum, Class, Order, Family, Genus, Species.) It doesn't matter how ridiculous it sounds, just so it works for you.

HINTS FOR DOING WELL IN CLASS AND ON LECTURE EXAMS

Nowadays, most colleges and universities have large sections of non-majors biology, and professors may determine grades by giving computer-graded "objective" examinations consisting of multiple choice, matching, and true/false questions. If this describes your course, (and even if it doesn't) the following hints may help improve your grades, even if you think you don't "test well" on **objective exams.**

1. **Learn the meaning of biological terms.** A listing of key terms with definitions appears after each chapter in the Study Guide. Learn the meaning of these words – they are often asked on objective exams.

2. **Answer questions you know first.** If you don't know the answer to a question, skip over it and come back to it later. Sometimes you will get a clue to the correct answer from other questions on the exam.

3. **Read all the choices** for multiple choice questions. Then, try to eliminate as many obviously incorrect choices as possible, and pick the choice that appears most correct from those remaining. If your professor says there is no penalty for guessing, answer every question.

   If you are sure that two or more choices are correct and another choice is "all of the above," that is usually the correct answer. (But be careful.)

   If part of a statement is false, the entire statement is false.

On essay exams, it is always a good idea to write down an outline. This will get your thoughts down on paper and you can reform them into a comprehensive paragraph. Your answer will be more precise and you will be less likely to leave out important points. Begin with a clear, concise introductory statement summarizing your answer. The rest of the answer should be long enough to answer the questions fully.

ACKNOWLEDGEMENTS

Our thanks go to the following individuals who were instrumental in bringing this project to reality. Sheri Snavely, Karen Horton and Teresa Ryu, from Prentice Hall, offered us the chance to review early drafts of the newly revised *Life on Earth* and then encouraged us to revise the study guide. Most importantly, Stephanie Hiebert spent many hours reviewing the content and accuracy of this supplementary text. It is a much better companion to the text due to her efforts. Of course, any remaining errors are solely our responsibility,

Susan Wadkowski would also like to thank Paige Akins, who suggested I take on this project, and Renee Minot. Due to Renee's skills at formatting and her software expertise, this truly became a partnership effort.

Chapter 1: An Introduction to Life on Earth

OVERVIEW

This chapter focuses on the characteristics of life and gives a brief overview of the vast diversity of living organisms. The authors introduce basic scientific principles as well as the scientific method. Finally, a brief introduction to the mechanism and evidence for evolution is presented.

1) What Are the Characteristics of Living Things?

Life has **emergent properties** (intangible attributes arising from the complex ordered interactions among the individual characteristics of living things). Life characteristics include (1) complexity based on highly organized **organic** (carbon-based) **molecules** (made up of **elements** with **subatomic particles**); (2) acquisition, conversion, and use of materials (**nutrients**) and **energy** (the ability to do work) from the environment (ultimately by **photosynthesis**, the making of sugar using solar energy) through **metabolism** (the chemical reactions needed to sustain life); (3) **homeostasis** (active maintenance of complex structure and internal environment); (4) growth involving conversion of environmentally-derived materials into specific molecules in the organism's body; (5) response to stimuli from the environment; (6) reproduction, using the information in molecules of **DNA** (**deoxyribonucleic acid**) called **genes**; and (7) the capacity for **evolution** making use of **mutations** (random changes in DNA structure) and, usually, **natural selection** (enhanced survival and reproduction of individuals with favorable inherited characteristics).

The hierarchy of life is (from least complex to most complex) as follows: subatomic particles, which are grouped into **atoms**, which are grouped into **molecules**, which are grouped into **organelles**, which are grouped into **cells** (the smallest unit of life, each with **plasma membrane**, **cytoplasm**, and **nucleus**), which are grouped into **tissues**, which are grouped into **organs**, which are grouped into **organ systems**, which are grouped into **organisms**.

2) How Do Scientists Categorize the Diversity of Life?

Based on the traits they exhibit (especially cell type, number of cells in each organism, and mode of nutrition and energy acquisition), organisms are classified into three major categories called **domains**: Bacteria, Archaea, and Eukarya. Bacteria and Archaea have single, simple (**prokaryotic**) cells lacking nuclei. Eukarya organisms each have one or more complex (**eukaryotic**) cells with nuclei and are divided into four **kingdoms**: Protista, Fungi, Plantae, and Animalia.

Bacteria, Archaea, and members of the kingdom Protista are mostly **unicellular**, while members of the kingdoms Fungi, Plantae, and Animalia are primarily **multicellular**, their lives depending on intimate cooperation among their cells. Members of different kingdoms have different ways of acquiring energy. Photosynthetic organisms (plants, some bacteria, and some protists) capture solar energy and use it to make sugars and fats; they are called **autotrophs** ("self-feeders"). Organisms that get energy from the bodies of other organisms are called **heterotrophs** ("other feeders"); these include many archaea, some bacteria, and all fungi and animals. Bacteria and fungi absorb predigested food molecules, while most animals eat chunks of food and break them down in their digestive tracts (ingestion).

3) What Does the Science of Biology Encompass?

A basic principle of modern biology is that living things obey the same laws of physics and chemistry that govern nonliving matter. There are three "scientific principles" (unproven assumptions) essential to biology: (1) **natural causality** (all earthly events can be traced to preceding natural causes); supernatural intervention has no place in science; (2) uniformity in time and space (natural laws do not change with time or distance; they apply everywhere and for all time); for example, scientists assume that gravity always has worked as it does today and works in the same way everywhere in the universe; and (3) common perception (the assumption that all humans individually perceive natural and aesthetic events through their senses in fundamentally the same way); however, our interpretation of such events (like *appreciation* of rock music or the *morality* of abortion) may differ.

The **scientific method** is how scientists study the workings of life. It consists of four interrelated operations:

(1) **observation**, the beginnings of scientific inquiry (for example, maggots appear on fresh meat left uncovered);

(2) **hypothesis**, a tentative testable explanation of an observed event based on an educated guess about its cause (for example, maggots appear on fresh meat left uncovered because flies land on the meat and lay eggs);

(3) **experiment**, a study done under rigidly controlled conditions based on a prediction stemming from the hypothesis (for example, if the fresh meat is covered with a fine gauze to keep the flies away, no maggots should appear in the meat). Simple experiments test the assertion that a single factor, or **variable**, is the cause of a single observation. Scientists design **controls** into their experiments, in which all variables remain constant. Controls are compared to experimental situations in which only the variable being tested is changed;

(4) **conclusion**, a judgment about the validity of the hypothesis, based on the results of the experiment (for example, maggots did not appear on the meat covered with gauze but did appear on fresh meat left uncovered in the same place at the same time. Thus, the hypothesis is supported by the results of the experiment).

Science is a human endeavor. Besides discoveries made by the scientific method, real scientific advances often involve accidents and acumen, lucky guesses, controversies between scientists, and the unusual insights of brilliant scientists. An example of "real science" was the accidental discovery of penicillin by Alexander Fleming.

When a hypothesis is supported by the results of many different kinds of experiments, scientists are confident enough about its validity to call it a **scientific theory**. Scientific conclusions must always remain tentative and be subject to revision if new observations or experiments demand it.

4) Evolution: The Unifying Concept of Biology

Evolution is the theory that present-day organisms descended, with modification, from preexisting forms; it is the unifying concept in biology. As proposed by the English naturalists Charles Darwin and Alfred Russel Wallace in the mid-1800s, evolution occurs as a result of three natural processes: (1) genetic variation among members of a **population**; (2) inheritance of variations from parents to offspring (we now know that inherited variations ultimately arise from gene mutations, changes in DNA structure); and (3) natural selection, the survival and enhanced reproduction of organisms with favorable variations (**adaptations**) in structure, physiology, or behavior that best meet the challenges of the environment. Ultimately, natural selection has unpredictable results because environments tend to change dramatically (for example, ice ages). What helps organisms survive today may be a liability tomorrow.

KEY TERMS AND CONCEPTS

Fill-In: Fill in the crossword puzzle on the bases of the following clues:

Across

2. A relatively stable combination of atoms.
5. The membrane-bound organelle of eukaryotic cells that contains the cell's genetic material.
8. A self-feeder, usually meaning a photosynthetic organism.
9. Any change in the proportions of different genotypes in a population from one generation to the next.
11. The smallest unit of life.
13. An organism that eats other organisms.
15. Two or more populations of different species living and interacting in the same area.
16. A structure, usually composed of several tissue types, that acts as a functional unit.

Down

1. A physical unit of inheritance.
2. What genes do when they undergo a genetic change.
3. A study done under rigidly controlled conditions based on a prediction stemming from the hypothesis.
4. A new major category of organisms, based on comparisons of cellular, molecular, and behavioral similarities and differences.
6. A judgment about the validity of a hypothesis, based on the results of an experiment.
7. In science, an explanation of natural events based on a large number of observations.
9. The ability to do work.
10. The cell's _____ membrane, encloses its contents.
12. The smallest particle of an element that retains all the properties of the element.
14. A molecule that encodes the genetic information of all living cells.

Key Terms and Definitions

adaptation: a characteristic of an organism that helps it survive and reproduce in a particular environment; also, the process of acquiring such characteristics.

atom: the smallest particle of an element that retains the properties of the element.

autotroph (aw´-tō-trof): "self-feeder"; normally, a photosynthetic organism; a producer.

biodiversity: the total number of species within an ecosystem and the resulting complexity of interactions among them.

biosphere (bī´-ō-sfēr): that part of Earth inhabited by living organisms; includes both living and nonliving components.

cell: the smallest unit of life, consisting, at a minimum, of an outer membrane that encloses a watery medium containing organic molecules, including genetic material composed of DNA.

community: all the interacting populations within an ecosystem.

conclusion: the final operation in the scientific method; a decision made about the validity of a hypothesis on the basis of experimental evidence.

control: that portion of an experiment in which all possible variables are held constant; in contrast to the "experimental" portion, in which a particular variable is altered.

creationism: the hypothesis that all species on Earth were created in essentially their present form by a supernatural being and that significant modification of those species–specifically, their transformation into new species–cannot occur by natural processes.

cytoplasm (sī´-tō-plaz-um): the material contained within the plasma membrane of a cell, exclusive of the nucleus.

deoxyribonucleic acid (dē-ox-ē-rī-bō-noo-klā´-ik; **DNA**): a molecule composed of deoxyribose nucleotides; contains the genetic information of all living cells.

domain: the broadest category for classifying organisms; organisms are classified into three domains: Bacteria, Archaea, and Eukarya.

ecosystem (ē´kō-sis-tem): all the organisms and their nonliving environment within a defined area.

element: a substance that cannot be broken down, or converted, to a simpler substance by ordinary chemical means.

emergent property: an intangible attribute that arises as the result of complex ordered interactions among individual parts.

energy: the capacity to do work.

eukaryotic (ū-kar-ē-ot´-ik): referring to cells of organisms of the domain Eukarya (kingdoms Protista, Fungi, Plantae, and Animalia). Eukaryotic cells have genetic material enclosed within a membrane-bound nucleus and contain other membrane-bound organelles.

evolution: the descent of modern organisms with modification from preexisting life-forms; strictly speaking, any change in the proportions of different genotypes in a population from one generation to the next.

experiment: the third operation in the scientific method; the testing of a hypothesis by further observations, leading to a conclusion.

gene: a unit of heredity that encodes the information needed to specify the amino acid sequence of proteins and hence particular traits; a functional segment of DNA located at a particular place on a chromosome.

heterotroph (het´-er-ō-trōf´): literally, "other-feeder"; an organism that eats other organisms; a consumer.

homeostasis (hōm-ē-ō-stā´-sis): the maintenance of a relatively constant environment required for the optimal functioning of cells, maintained by the coordinated activity of numerous regulatory mechanisms, including the respiratory, endocrine, circulatory, and excretory systems.

hypothesis (hī-poth´-eh-sis): the second operation in the scientific method; a supposition based on previous observations that is offered as an explanation for the observed phenomenon and is used as the basis for further observations, or experiments.

kingdom: the second broadest taxonomic category, contained within a domain and consisting of related phyla or divisions. This textbook recognizes four kingdoms within the domain Eukarya: Protista, Fungi, Plantae, and Animalia.

metabolism: the sum of all chemical reactions that occur within a single cell or within all the cells of a multicellular organism.

molecule (mol´-e-kūl): a particle composed of one or more atoms held together by chemical bonds; the smallest particle of a compound that displays all the properties of that compound.

multicellular: many-celled; most members of the kingdoms Fungi, Plantae, and Animalia are multicellular, with intimate cooperation among cells.

mutation: a change in the base sequence of DNA in a gene; normally refers to a genetic change significant enough to alter the appearance or function of the organism.

natural causality: the scientific principle that natural events occur as a result of preceding natural causes.

natural selection: the unequal survival and reproduction of organisms due to environmental forces, resulting in the preservation of favorable adaptations. Usually, natural selection refers specifically to differential survival and reproduction on the basis of genetic differences among individuals.

nucleus (cellular): the membrane-bound organelle of eukaryotic cells that contains the cell's genetic material.

nutrient: a substance acquired from the environment and needed for the survival, growth, and development of an organism.

observation: the first operation in the scientific method; the noting of a specific phenomenon, leading to the formulation of a hypothesis.

organ: a structure (such as the liver, kidney, or skin) composed of two or more distinct tissue types that function together.

organelle (or-guh-nel´): a structure, found in the cytoplasm of eukaryotic cells, that performs a specific function; sometimes refers specifically to membrane-bound structures, such as the nucleus or endoplasmic reticulum.

organic molecule: describing a molecule that contains both carbon and hydrogen.

organism (or´-guh-niz-um): an individual living thing.

organ system: two or more organs that work together to perform a specific function; for example, the digestive system.

photosynthesis: the complete series of chemical reactions in which the energy of light is used to synthesize high-energy organic molecules, normally carbohydrates, from low-energy inorganic molecules, normally carbon dioxide and water.

plasma membrane: the outer membrane of a cell, composed of a bilayer of phospholipids in which proteins are embedded.

population: all the members of a particular species within an ecosystem, found in the same time and place and actually or potentially interbreeding.

prokaryotic (prō-kar-ē-ot´-ik): referring to cells of the domains Bacteria or Archaea. Prokaryotic cells have genetic material that is not enclosed in a membrane-bound nucleus; they lack other membrane-bound organelles.

scientific method: a rigorous procedure for making observations of specific phenomena and searching for the order underlying those phenomena; consists of four operations: observation, hypothesis, experiment, and conclusion.

scientific theory: a general explanation of natural phenomena developed through extensive and reproducible observations; more general and reliable than a hypothesis.

species (spē´-sēs): all of the organisms that are potentially capable of interbreeding under natural conditions or, if asexually reproducing, are more closely related to one another than to other organisms within a given genus; the smallest major taxonomic category.

spontaneous generation: the proposal that living organisms can arise from nonliving matter.

subatomic particle: the particles of which atoms are made: electrons, protons, and neutrons.

tissue: a group of (normally similar) cells that together carry out a specific function; for example, muscle; may include extracellular material produced by its cells.

unicellular: single-celled; most members of the domains Bacteria and Archaea and the kingdom Protista are unicellular.

variable: a condition, particularly in a scientific experiment, that is subject to change.

THINKING THROUGH THE CONCEPTS

True or False: Determine if the statement given is true or false. If it is false, change the underlined word so that the statement reads true.

17. _____   Biology is <u>basically different from</u> other sciences.

18. _____   The basic assumptions of science <u>can</u> be proven.

19. _____   The conclusions of science are <u>permanent</u>.

20. _____   Science accepts only <u>natural</u> explanations for natural processes.

21. _____   Creationism <u>is not</u> a science.

22. _____   Organisms that produce their own food are <u>heterotrophic</u>.

23. _____   Bacteria are <u>eukaryotic</u> organisms.

24. _____   Prokaryotic forms <u>do not</u> possess distinct nuclei.

25. _____   Fungi are <u>autotrophic</u> organisms.

26. _____   Redi's experiments <u>supported</u> the theory that life can occur by spontaneous generation.

Matching: Classifying life.

27. _____   unicellular, movement by cilia or flagella   Choices:

28. _____   multicellular and autotrophic   a. Archea or Bacteria

29. _____   unicellular and prokaryotic   b. Protista

30. _____   multicellular, heterotrophic, and ingestive   c. Fungi

31. _____   multicellular, nonmotile, and photsynthetic   d. Plantae

32. _____   unicellular and eukaryotic   e. Animalia

33. _____   multicellular, heterotrophic, absorptive

34. _____   includes insects and mollusks

35. _____   has intimate relationships with animals

36. _____   may survive extreme conditions

Matching: Which scientific principle does each of the following violate?

37. _____   an anorexic woman sees herself as fat

38. _____   God created all life on Earth in six days

39. _____   a 6 foot man may look 10 feet tall to you

40. _____   miracles

41. _____   in biblical times, humans lived to be
900 years old

42. _____   gravity did not affect the dinosaurs as
much as it affects us

Choices:

    a. natural causality

    b. uniformity in time and space

    c. common perception

Multiple Choice: Pick the most correct choice for each question.

43. Which of the following are not
characteristics used to categorize
organisms into kingdoms?
   a.   types of cells present
   b.   numbers of cells present
   c.   presence or absence of cell walls
   d.   how the organisms acquire energy
   e.   how the organisms move
   f.   choices a and b
   g.   choices c and e
   h.   none of the above

44. What is the ultimate source of genetic
variation?
   a.   mutations in DNA
   b.   adaptations to a changing environment
   c.   natural selection
   d.   spontaneous generation
   e.   homeostasis

45. The basic difference between a prokaryotic
cell and a eukaryotic cell is that the
prokaryotic cell
   a.   possesses membrane-bound organelles
   b.   lacks DNA
   c.   lacks a nuclear membrane
   d.   is considerably larger
   e.   is in multicellular organisms

CLUES TO APPLYING THE CONCEPTS

This practice question is intended to sharpen your ability to apply critical thinking and analysis to biological concepts covered in this chapter.

46. Last summer, Zachary grew pepper plants in his garden and decided to use a new fertilizer called UltraGrow. He claims that his plants produced more peppers that were larger than those he had harvested the year before, and he credits the use of UltraGrow for the improvement. Scientifically speaking, has he proven the effectiveness of the fertilizer? How could he more validly test his hypothesis that UltraGrow works?

_____

_____

_____

_____

_____

_____

ANSWERS TO EXERCISES

17. false, essentially similar to	32. b
18. false, cannot	33. c
19. false, temporary	34. e
20. true	35. d
21. true	36. a
22. false, autotrophic	37. c
23. false, prokaryotic	38. a
24. true	39. c
25. false, heterotrophic	40. a
26. false, disproved	41. b
27. b	42. b
28. d	43. g
29. a	44. a
30. e	45. c
31. d	

46. Scientifically speaking, Zachary did not support his hypothesis that the fertilizer works. He did not perform a controlled experiment, meaning that there could be a number of reasons why he got more and larger peppers last year than the year before: differences in the amounts of sunlight, rainfall, and/or richness of the soil; differences in the types of seeds used; differences in plant pest activity each year; and perhaps others. What Zachary must do is plant two groups of pepper plants side by side at the same time. To test the effect of UltraGrow, only one factor (the amount of UltraGrow) must differ between the experimental (fed UltraGrow) and the control (not fed UltraGrow) plants. If there is a difference between the fruits produced by the experimental and the control plants, then Zachary may validly conclude that the fertilizer was responsible for the difference.

Chapter 2: Atoms, Molecules, and Life

OVERVIEW

This chapter focuses on matter and energy. The authors describe the structures of atoms and molecules and the three major types of chemical bonding. They also discuss important inorganic molecules, especially water. The chapter also focuses on the basic molecules that make up living things. The authors describe the structure, synthesis, and function of four types of large organic molecules: carbohydrates, lipids, proteins, and nucleic acids.

1) What Are Atoms and Molecules?

Atoms are the fundamental structural units of matter. Atoms contain a central dense nucleus (**atomic nucleus**) in which are found positively charged **protons** and uncharged **neutrons**. The **atomic number** of an atom is the number of protons in its nucleus, and this number is constant in all atoms of a particular type (for example, every hydrogen atom has one proton). An **element** is a substance containing the same kind of atoms and cannot be broken down or converted into another substance under ordinary conditions. Similar atoms that differ in the number of neutrons they possess are called **isotopes**.

Atoms also have negatively charged **electrons** that spin about the nucleus in paths called **energy levels** or **electron shells**. Up to two electrons are found in the energy level nearest the nucleus, while the next energy level may contain up to eight electrons. Electrically neutral atoms have equal numbers of protons and electrons (for example, a carbon atom has six protons and six electrons). Whereas the nuclei of atoms are stable and resistant to change, the electron shells are dynamic, and atoms interact with each other by gaining, losing, or sharing electrons.

Atoms react with other atoms when there are vacancies in their outermost electron shells. Stable atoms have completely filled or empty outer electron shells (like helium) while reactive atoms have partially filled outer shells (like hydrogen). An atom with a partially full outer electron shell is reactive and can become more stable through filling the outer shell by losing, gaining, or sharing electrons with other atoms. These electron interactions with other atoms create attractive forces called **chemical bonds**.

Charged atoms called **ions** interact to form **ionic bonds**. Atoms with almost full or almost empty outer electron shells will interact by gaining or losing electrons, respectively, forming charged ions that will attract each other (for example, sodium [Na^+] and chloride [Cl^-] ions), forming **molecules** by the formation of ionic bonds (NaCl is table salt). Ionic molecules tend to form crystals, although ionic bonds are relatively weak and easily broken.

Uncharged atoms can become stable by sharing electrons, forming **covalent bonds**. An atom of hydrogen has one electron in a shell that can hold two. Two hydrogen atoms each share an electron with the other, forming a molecule of hydrogen gas (H_2) held together by one covalent bond. Oxygen atoms need two electrons to fill their outer shells; thus, two oxygen atoms form a molecule of O_2 gas by forming two covalent bonds. Covalent bonds are relatively strong. Most biological molecules are held

Polar covalent bonds form when atoms share electrons unequally. A molecule having only one type of atom, like H_2 gas, is held together by a **nonpolar covalent bond** since each hydrogen nucleus exerts equal attraction on the shared electrons. In molecules made of different atoms, like water (H_2O), **polar covalent bonds** form because the oxygen nucleus has more protons than the hydrogen nuclei and exerts a greater attraction on the electrons, which spend more time orbiting the stronger nucleus. Thus, water is electrically neutral overall, but the oxygen end is more negatively charged than the hydrogen end; water is a polar molecule. Consequently, the negative end of one water molecule attracts the positive end of another, forming a **hydrogen bond**. Many other molecules in cells form hydrogen bonds.

2) Why Is Water So Important to Life?

Water interacts with many other molecules. Since water is a polar molecule, it can dissolve many other substances (it is a good **solvent**). Water will surround positive and negative ions, dissolving crystals of polar molecules. Water is attracted to and dissolves molecules containing polar covalent bonds (called **hydrophilic** molecules) such as sugars and amino acids. Uncharged and nonpolar molecules, like fats and oils, are **hydrophobic** and do not dissolve in water. Water can break apart into hydrogen ions (H^+) and hydroxyl ions (OH^-) ions. A volume of pure water contains equal amounts of these ions and is said to have a value of 7 on the **pH scale**. A solution with a H^+ concentration greater than the OH^- concentration is **acidic** and has a pH value less than 7. A solution with with a H^+ concentration less than the OH^- concentration is **basic** and has a pH value greater than 7. Each pH scale unit represents a 10-fold increase or decrease in the concentration of H^+ ions. **Buffers** like bicarbonate help organisms maintain a constant pH in their cells by accepting or releasing H^+ ions in response to small changes in pH.

Water moderates the effects of temperature changes because of its particular properties. It has high **specific heat** (it takes a lot of energy to raise the temperature of water) because of the hydrogen bonds between water molecules. It takes a great deal of heat to evaporate a molecule of water, leaving the remaining water cooler; and, since much energy is removed from water as it forms ice, it heats up its surroundings. These special properties of water come into play in natural systems, especially for fish living in lakes during sub-freeing temperatures. Since ice floats on cold liquid water, lakes remain liquid on the bottom in winter, allowing aquatic life to continue.

Also due to hydrogen bonding, water molecules stick together (**cohesion**), producing the **surface tension** at the surface of lakes and pools that allows light insects to walk on water. The cohesion of water allows trees to pull water from the roots up into the leaves.

3) Why Is Carbon So Important in Biological Molecules?

Organic molecules contain carbon and functional groups, and are made using a "modular approach." Organic molecules include a skeleton of carbon atoms, often with hydrogen atoms attached. Since each carbon can form four covalent bonds, molecules with many carbons can form complex shapes including chains, rings, and branches. Organic molecules also contain **functional groups** of atoms, including hydroxyl ($-OH$), carboxyl ($-COOH$), amino ($-NH_2$), phosphate ($-H_2PO_4$), and methyl ($-CH_3$) groups. These groups help determine the chemical properties of organic molecules. Cells use a "modular approach" in making large organic molecules by joining together many small **subunits** (for example, many **monomers** like sugar are joined to make a **polymer** like **starch**).

4) How Are Organic Molecules Synthesized?

Biological molecules are joined together or broken apart by adding or removing water molecules. Subunits are linked together to form large molecules by a chemical reaction called **dehydration synthesis**. One subunit loses a hydrogen ($-H$) and another loses a hydroxyl ($-OH$) group; the two subunits form a covalent bond linking them together, and the ($-H$) and ($-OH$) join to form water (H_2O). The reverse reaction is called **hydrolysis**: Water splits into ($-H$) and ($-OH$), and each covalently bonds to one or another subunit of a polymer, resulting in the breakdown of the polymer by removal of individual monomers.

5) What Are Carbohydrates?

Carbohydrates have carbon, hydrogen, and oxygen in an approximate ratio of 1:2:1. Carbohydrates are single **sugars** (like **glucose**) called **monosaccharides**, double sugars called **disaccharides**, or longer chains of sugars (like starch and **cellulose**) called **polysaccharides**. Carbohydrates (sugars and starch) are used to provide energy to cells or to provide structural support. Different monosaccharides have slightly different structures even though they contain the same types of atoms: Glucose, fructose, and galactose each have the molecular formula $C_6H_{12}O_6$.

    Disaccharides such as **sucrose** (table sugar), **lactose** (milk sugar), and **maltose** (made from starch) are used for short-term energy storage, especially in plants. Some polysaccharides are used for long-term energy storage in plants (starch) and animals (**glycogen**), while others provide structural support for plants (cellulose) and certain insects and fungi (**chitin**).

glucose   fructose   sucrose

dehydration synthesis

6) What Are Lipids?

Lipid molecules are insoluble in water and contain mainly carbons and hydrogens. Some lipids (**fats** and **oils**) store energy, some (**waxes**) form waterproof coatings on plants and animals, some (**phospholipids**) are found in cell membranes, and some (**steroids**) act as hormones .

    Oils, fats, and waxes contain only carbon, hydrogen, and oxygen. They contain **fatty acid** subunits and do not form ringed structures. Fats and oils form from **glycerol** and three fatty acid molecules through dehydration synthesis and are called **triglycerides**. Fats and oils store a much higher concentration of chemical energy than do carbohydrates and proteins. Fats are solid at room temperature because they contain fatty acids **saturated** with H, making them more compact. Oils are liquid at room temperature because they contain fatty acids **unsaturated** with H. The fatty acid chains in oils are kinky due to the presence of double covalent bonds; thus they are less compact. Waxes are chemically similar to fats.

    Phospholipids have water-soluble "heads" and water-insoluble "tails" and are found in high concentration in cell membranes. Phospholipids are similar to oils but one fatty acid "tail" is replaced by a phosphate "head" group attached to a polar, charged, functional group containing nitrogen. Thus, phospholipids have dissimilar ends: The "tail" is nonpolar and the "head" is polar. Steroids (like cholesterol, male and female sex hormones, and bile) have four rings of carbons with various functional groups attached.

7) What Are Proteins?

Proteins are polymers of **amino acids**. Depending on the sequences of amino acids in proteins, they may function as **enzymes** (controlling chemical reactions within cells) or as structural components (elastin or keratin), energy storage (albumin), transport (hemoglobin), cell movement (muscle proteins), hormones (insulin or growth hormone), antibodies to fight infection, or poisons (snake venom).

All amino acids have a the same basic structure: A central carbon bonded to an amino group ($-NH_2$), a carboxyl group ($-COOH$), a hydrogen, and a variable (or R) group that differs among the 20 types of amino acids and gives each its distinctive properties. Amino acids are joined to form protein chains by dehydration synthesis. The $-NH_2$ of one amino acid is joined to the $-COOH$ of another by a covalent bond called a **peptide bond**, resulting in a **peptide** molecule with two amino acids. More amino acids are added, one by one, until the protein is complete.

Proteins are highly organized molecules. Within a protein, the exact type, position, and number of amino acids bearing specific R groups determines the three-dimensional structure of the protein, which in turn determines its biological function.

8) What Are Nucleic Acids?

The genetic material is composed of **nucleic acids**, which are polymers of subunits called **nucleotides**. Each nucleotide has a five-carbon sugar (ribose in **RNA** or deoxyribose in **DNA**), a phosphate group, and a variable nitrogen-containing base. In addition to ribose and a phosphate group, **ribonucleic acid** (RNA) nucleotides contain either an adenine (A), a cytosine (C), a guanine (G), or a uracil (U) base. In addition to deoxyribose and a phosphate group, **deoxyribonucleic acid** (DNA) nucleotides contain either an A, a C, a G, or a thymine (T) base. Nucleotides are covalently bonded together into long chains to form DNA and RNA molecules. DNA is found in the chromosomes of all living things, and its sequence of bases provide the genetic information needed for cells to make specific proteins. RNA molecules are copied from DNA in the nucleus and move into the cytoplasm, where they direct the construction of proteins.

Other nucleotides (like the **cyclic nucleotide**, adenosine monophosphate) act as intracellular messengers. Some nucleotides (like **adenosine triphosphate** or **ATP**) have extra phosphate groups and carry energy from one place to another within cells. Some nucleotides (called **coenzymes**), usually in conjunction with vitamins, assist enzymes in their functions.

KEY TERMS AND CONCEPTS

Fill-In: From the following list of terms, fill in the blanks below. A term may be used more than once.

acidic	chemical bonds	hydrophilic	neutrons	protons
atomic number	covalent	hydrophobic	nonpolar	single covalent
atoms	electrons	ion	pH	specific heat
basic	energy levels	ionic	polar	triple covalent
buffers	hydrogen	ions		

(1)_____ contain a central dense nucleus in which are found positively charged

(2)_____ and electrically neutral (3)_____.

Atoms also have negatively charged (4)_____, which spin about the nucleus in paths

called (5)_____.

The (6)_____ of an atom is the number of protons present in its nucleus, and this number is constant for all atoms of a particular type.

Atoms enter into chemical reactions when there are vacancies in their outermost (7)_____.

(8)_____ are attractive forces between atoms due to interactions of their
(9)_____.

(10)_____ result when atoms lose or gain electrons. The attraction between a Na^+
(11)_____ and a Cl^- (11)_____ is called (12)_____ bonding.

Atoms that interact by sharing electrons form molecules by (13)_____ bonding. If two
atoms share one electron each, they form a (14)_____ bond; if two atoms share three
electrons each, they form a (15)_____ bond.

If two similar atoms share electrons, they form a (16)_____ covalent bond, but if
dissimilar atoms share electrons, as in water, they may form (17)_____ covalent bonds.

When two water molecules electrically attract each other, the attraction is called a
(18)_____ bond.

Charged molecules that attract water are called (19)_____ molecules, while uncharged
molecules that do not attract water are called (20)_____ molecules.

A solution with equal amounts of H^+ and OH^- (21)_____ has a (22)_____ of 7.

(23)_____ solutions have a pH that is less than 7, while (24)_____ solutions
have a pH greater than 7.

(25)_____ are important because they help maintain the pH of a cell at approximately 7.

Water moderates temperature changes because it has a high (26)_____ (a lot of energy is
needed to increase the temperature of water).

Fill-In: Complete the crossword puzzle with key terms, based on the following clues.

Across

27. The most common monosaccharide, with the formula $C_6H_{12}O_6$.
29. A triglyceride lipid that is solid at room temperature.
31. A water-insoluble organic molecule such as a wax.
35. Contains a phosphate group, a five-carbon sugar, and a nitrogen-containing base.
37. A chain made of at least two amino acids joined covalently.
38. A molecule with a central carbon joined to $-H$, $-NH_2$, $-COOH$, and a variable R group.
40. A molecule made of chains of amino acids, makes up enzymes and muscles.
41. A lipid coating that plants use to repel water.

Down

28. A polysaccharide used by fungi and some animals for structural support.
30. A disaccharide found in mammalian milk.
32. An organic molecule composed of many nucleotides.
33. A molecule that is liquid at room temperature.
34. A simple carbohydrate, such as a monosaccharide.
36. A protein catalyst that speeds up the rate of specific biological reactions.
38. A nucleotide with three phosphate groups for energy transfer.
39. Abbreviation for the genetic material.

Key Terms and Definitions

acid: a substance that releases hydrogen ions (H^+) into solution; a solution with a pH of less than 7.

acidic: with an H^+ concentration exceeding that of OH^-; releasing H^+.

adenosine triphosphate (a-den´-ō-sēn trī-fos´-fāt; **ATP**): a molecule composed of the sugar ribose, the base adenine, and three phosphate groups; the major energy carrier in cells. The last two phosphate groups are attached by "high-energy" bonds.

amino acid: the individual subunit of which proteins are made, composed of a central carbon atom bonded to an amino group ($-NH_2$), a carboxyl group ($-COOH$), a hydrogen atom, and a variable group of atoms denoted by the letter R.

atom: the smallest particle of an element that retains the properties of the element.

atomic nucleus: the central region of an atom, consisting of protons and neutrons.

atomic number: the number of protons in the nuclei of all atoms of a particular element.

base: a substance capable of combining with and neutralizing H^+ ions in a solution; a solution with a pH of more than 7.

basic: with an H^+ concentration less than that of OH^-; combining with H^+.

buffer: a compound that minimizes changes in pH by reversibly taking up or releasing H^+ ions.

calorie (kal´-ō-rē): the amount of energy required to raise the temperature of 1 gram of water by 1 degree Celsius.

carbohydrate: a compound composed of carbon, hydrogen, and oxygen, with the approximate chemical formula $(CH_2O)n$; includes sugars and starches.

cellulose: an insoluble carbohydrate composed of glucose subunits; forms the cell wall of plants.

chemical bond: the force of attraction between neighboring atoms that holds them together in a molecule.

chitin (kī´-tin): a compound found in the cell walls of fungi and the exoskeletons of insects and some other arthropods; composed of chains of nitrogen-containing, modified glucose molecules.

coenzyme: an organic molecule that is bound to certain enzymes and is required for the enzymes' proper functioning; typically, a nucleotide bound to a water-soluble vitamin.

cohesion: the tendency of the molecules of a substance to stick together.

compound: a substance whose molecules are formed by different types of atoms; can be broken into its constituent elements by chemical means.

covalent bond (kō-vā´-lent): a chemical bond between atoms in which electrons are shared.

cyclic nucleotide (sik´-lik noo´-klē-ō-tīd): a nucleotide in which the phosphate group is bonded to the sugar at two points, forming a ring; serves as an intracellular messenger.

dehydration synthesis: a chemical reaction in which two molecules are joined by a covalent bond with the simultaneous removal of a hydrogen from one molecule and a hydroxyl group from the other, forming water; the reverse of hydrolysis.

deoxyribonucleic acid (dē-ox-ē-rī-bō-noo-klā´-ik; **DNA**): a molecule composed of deoxyribose nucleotides; contains the genetic information of all living cells.

disaccharide (dī-sak´-uh-rīd): a carbohydrate formed by the covalent bonding of two monosaccharides.

double covalent bond: a covalent bond in which two atoms share two pairs of electrons.

electron: a subatomic particle, found in an electron shell outside the nucleus of an atom, that bears a unit of negative charge and very little mass.

electron shell: a region within which electrons orbit that corresponds to a fixed energy level at a given distance from the atomic nucleus of an atom.

element: a substance that cannot be broken down, or converted, to a simpler substance by ordinary chemical means.

energy level: the specific amount of energy characteristic of a given electron shell in an atom.

enzyme (en´zīm): a protein catalyst that speeds up the rate of specific biological reactions.

fat (molecular): a lipid composed of three saturated fatty acids covalently bonded to glycerol; solid at room temperature.

fatty acid: an organic molecule composed of a long chain of carbon atoms, with a carboxylic acid (COOH) group at one end; may be saturated (all single bonds between the carbon atoms) or unsaturated (one or more double bonds between the carbon atoms).

functional group: one of several groups of atoms commonly found in an organic molecule, including hydrogen, hydroxyl, amino, carboxyl, and phosphate groups, that determine the characteristics and chemical reactivity of the molecule.

glucose: the most common monosaccharide, with the molecular formula $C_6H_{12}O_6$; most polysaccharides, including cellulose, starch, and glycogen, are made of glucose subunits covalently bonded together.

glycerol (glis´-er-ol): a three-carbon alcohol to which fatty acids are covalently bonded to make fats and oils.

glycogen (glī´-kō-jen): a long, branched polymer of glucose stored by animals in the muscles and liver and metabolized as a source of energy.

hydrogen bond: the weak attraction between a hydrogen atom that bears a partial positive charge (due to polar covalent bonding with another atom) and another atom, normally oxygen or nitrogen, that bears a partial negative charge; hydrogen bonds may form between atoms of a single molecule or of different molecules.

hydrolysis (hī-drol´-i-sis): the chemical reaction that breaks a covalent bond by means of the addition of hydrogen to the atom on one side of the original bond and a hydroxyl group to the atom on the other side; the reverse of dehydration synthesis.

hydrophilic (hī-drō-fil´-ik): pertaining to a substance that dissolves readily in water, or to parts of a large molecule that form hydrogen bonds with water.

hydrophobic (hī-drō-fō´-bik): pertaining to a substance that does not dissolve in water.

hydrophobic interaction: the tendency for hydrophobic molecules to cluster together when immersed in water.

inorganic: describing any molecule that does not contain both carbon and hydrogen.

ion (ī´-on): a charged atom or molecule; an atom or molecule that has either an excess of electrons (and hence is negatively charged) or has lost electrons (and is positively charged).

ionic bond: a chemical bond formed by the electrical attraction between positively and negatively charged ions.

isotope: one of several forms of a single element, the nuclei of which contain the same number of protons but different numbers of neutrons.

lactose (lak´-tōs): a disaccharide composed of glucose and galactose; found in mammalian milk.

lipid (li´-pid): one of a number of organic molecules containing large nonpolar regions composed solely of carbon and hydrogen, which make lipids hydrophobic and insoluble in water; includes oils, fats, waxes, phospholipids, and steroids.

maltose (mal´-tōs): a disaccharide composed of two glucose molecules.

molecule (mol´-e-kūl): a particle composed of one or more atoms held together by chemical bonds; the smallest particle of a compound that displays all the properties of that compound.

monomer (mo´-nō-mer): a small organic molecule, several of which may be bonded together to form a chain called a polymer.

monosaccharide (mo-nō-sak´-uh-rīd): the basic molecular unit of all carbohydrates, normally composed of a chain of carbon atoms bonded to hydrogen and hydroxyl groups.

neutron: a subatomic particle that is found in the nuclei of atoms, bears no charge, and has a mass approximately equal to that of a proton.

nonpolar covalent bond: a covalent bond with equal sharing of electrons.

nucleic acid (noo-klā´-ik): an organic molecule composed of nucleotide subunits; the two common types of nucleic acids are ribonucleic acid (RNA) and deoxyribonucleic acid (DNA).

nucleotide: a subunit of which nucleic acids are composed; a phosphate group bonded to a sugar (deoxyribose in DNA), which is in turn bonded to a nitrogen-containing base (adenine, guanine, cytosine, or thymine in DNA). Nucleotides are linked together, forming a strand of nucleic acid, as follows: Bonds between the phosphate of one nucleotide link to the sugar of the next nucleotide.

nucleus (atomic): see *atomic nucleus*

oil: a lipid composed of three fatty acids, some of which are unsaturated, covalently bonded to a molecule of glycerol; liquid at room temperature.

organic: describing a molecule that contains both carbon and hydrogen.

peptide (pep´-tīd): a chain composed of two or more amino acids linked together by peptide bonds.

peptide bond: the covalent bond between the amino group's nitrogen of one amino acid and the carboxyl group's carbon of a second amino acid, joining the two amino acids together in a peptide or protein.

pH scale: a scale, with values from 0 to 14, used for measuring the relative acidity of a solution; at pH 7 a solution is neutral, pH 0 to 7 is acidic, and pH 7 to 14 is basic; each unit on the scale represents a tenfold change in H^+ concentration.

phospholipid (fos-fō-li´-pid): a lipid consisting of glycerol bonded to two fatty acids and one phosphate group, which bears another group of atoms, typically charged and containing nitrogen. A double layer of phospholipids is a component of all cellular membranes.

plaque (plak): a deposit of cholesterol and other fatty substances within the wall of an artery.

polar covalent bond: a covalent bond with unequal sharing of electrons, such that one atom is relatively negative and the other is relatively positive.

polymer (pah´-li-mer): a molecule composed of three or more (perhaps thousands) smaller subunits called *monomers*, which may be identical (for example, the glucose monomers of starch) or different (for example, the amino acids of a protein).

polysaccharide (pahl-ē-sak´-uh-rīd): a large carbohydrate molecule composed of branched or unbranched chains of repeating monosaccharide subunits, normally glucose or modified glucose molecules; includes starches, cellulose, and glycogen.

protein: an organic molecule composed of one or more chains of amino acids.

proton: a subatomic particle that is found in the nuclei of atoms, bears a unit of positive charge, and has a relatively large mass, roughly equal to the mass of the neutron.

radioactive: pertaining to an atom with an unstable nucleus that spontaneously disintegrates, with the emission of radiation.

ribonucleic acid (rī-bō-noo-klā´-ik; **RNA**): a molecule composed of ribose nucleotides, each of which consists of a phosphate group, the sugar ribose, and one of the bases adenine, cytosine, guanine, or uracil; transfers hereditary instructions from the nucleus to the cytoplasm; also the genetic material of some viruses.

saturated: referring to a fatty acid with as many hydrogen atoms as possible bonded to the carbon backbone; a fatty acid with no double bonds in its carbon backbone.

single covalent bond: a covalent bond in which two atoms share one pair of electrons.

solvent: a liquid capable of dissolving (uniformly dispersing) other substances in itself.

specific heat: the amount of energy required to raise the temperature of 1 gram of a substance by 1°C.

starch: a polysaccharide that is composed of branched or unbranched chains or glucose molecules; used by plants as a carbohydrate-storage molecule.

steroid: see *steroid hormone*.

steroid hormone: a class of hormone whose chemical structure (four fused carbon rings with various functional groups) resembles cholesterol; steroids, which are lipids, are secreted by the ovaries and placenta, the testes, and the adrenal cortex.

subunit: a small organic molecule, several of which may be bonded together to form a larger molecule. See also *monomer*.

sucrose: a disaccharide composed of glucose and fructose.

sugar: a simple carbohydrate molecule, either a monosaccharide or a disaccharide.

surface tension: the property of a liquid to resist penetration by objects at its interface with the air, due to cohesion between molecules of the liquid.

triglyceride (trī-glis´-er-īd): a lipid composed of three fatty-acid molecules bonded to a single glycerol molecule.

triple covalent bond: a covalent bond that occurs when two atoms share three pairs of electrons.

unsaturated: referring to a fatty acid with fewer than the maximum number of hydrogen atoms bonded to its carbon backbone; a fatty acid with one or more double bonds in its carbon backbone.

wax: a lipid composed of fatty acids covalently bonded to long-chain alcohols.

THINKING THROUGH THE CONCEPTS

Refer to the figure to the right to answer questions 42 through 45.

42. Which is more chemically stable?
    a) a sodium atom
    b) a sodium ion
    c) neither; they are equally stable

43. Which has the higher atomic number?
    a) a chlorine atom
    b) a chloride ion
    c) neither; they are equal

44. The type of chemical bond depicted in part (b) is a(n) _____ bond.

45. The structure shown in part (c) is a(n) _____.

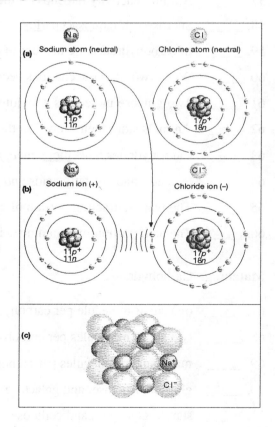

True or False: Determine if the statement given is true or false. If it is false, change the <u>underlined</u> word(s) so that the statement reads true.

46. _____ The smallest unit of matter in an element is the <u>molecule</u>.

47. _____ A positive unit in an atom is the <u>proton</u>.

48. _____ An electron is <u>heavier</u> than a proton.

49. _____ The number of protons in an atom determines its atomic <u>weight</u>.

50. _____ <u>Helium</u> is more likely to explode than <u>hydrogen</u>.

51. _____ Electrons close to the nucleus have <u>less</u> energy than those farther away from the nucleus.

52. _____ In salt, sodium and chlorine atoms attract each other by forming <u>covalent</u> bonds.

53. _____ The sodium atoms in salt tend to <u>take on</u> electrons.

54. _____ In a polar water molecule, the hydrogen region has a <u>positive</u> electrical charge.

55. _____ When atoms share electrons, they form <u>ionic</u> bonds.

56. _____ Electrons in a shell closer to the nucleus have <u>more</u> energy than those in a shell farther away.

57. _____ Atomic reactivity depends on the number of electrons in the <u>innermost</u> electron shell.

58. _____ Sucrose is a <u>monosaccharide</u>.

59. _____ In carbohydrates, the amount of carbon equals the amount of <u>hydrogen</u>.

60. _____ When two monosaccharides become a disaccharide, a water molecule is <u>added</u>.

61. _____ Two glucose molecules may join together to form a <u>polysaccharide</u>.

62. _____ Animals store their "food" in the form of <u>glycogen</u>.

63. _____ Carbohydrates have <u>more</u> energy per gram than fats.

64. _____ Fats are made of fatty acids and <u>cholesterol</u>.

65. _____ The water-attracting portion of a phospholipid is located <u>in the middle</u> of the cell membrane.

66. _____ The acid portion of an amino acid is the <u>NH_2</u> group.

Matching: Carbohydrates.

67. _____ one sugar molecule per carbohydrate

68. _____ two sugar molecules per carbohydrate

69. _____ many sugar molecules per carbohydrate

70. _____ glucose, fructose, and galactose

71. _____ starch, glycogen, and cellulose

72. _____ sucrose, lactose, and maltose

73. _____ ribose and deoxyribose

Choices:

a. disaccharide

b. monosaccharide

c. polysaccharide

Matching: Subunits making up large organic molecules.

74. _____ nitrogen bases

75. _____ amino acids

76. _____ glycerol

77. _____ phosphate group

Choices:

a. carbohydrates

b. nucleic acids

c. proteins

d. fats

Identification: Determine whether the following statements refer to **ionic**, **covalent**, or **hydrogen** bonds.

78. _____ two atoms share a pair of electrons

79. _____ one atom donates an electron and another atom accepts it

80. _____ it holds a crystal of salt together

81. _____ the attraction between the polar regions of molecules

82. _____ it results in atoms with unbalanced electrical charges

83. _____ it holds a molecule of water together

84. _____ the attraction between two water molecules

85. _____ the electrical attraction between oppositely charged atoms

86. _____ it holds most biological molecules together

87. _____ it can result in polar molecules

Matching: Specific carbohydrates.

88. _____ energy storage polysaccharide in plants

89. _____ plant cell wall component

90. _____ milk sugar

91. _____ found in insect skeletons

92. _____ most common sugar

93. _____ table sugar

94. _____ found in some nucleic acids

95. _____ energy storage polysaccharide in animals

Choices:

a. glucose

b. sucrose

c. lactose

d. deoxyribose

e. starch

f. glycogen

g. cellulose

h. chitin

Matching: Lipids.

96. _____   water-proofing substance for animals

97. _____   cholesterol

98. _____   liquid at room temperature

99. _____   contain all saturated fatty acids

100. _____   contain unsaturated fatty acids

101. _____   fatty acids contain kinks

102. _____   have hydrophilic and hydrophobic ends

103. _____   have four fused rings of carbon atoms

104. _____   a major component of cell membranes

Choices:

   a. fats

   b. oils

   c. waxes

   d. phospholipids

   e. steroids

Multiple Choice: Pick the most correct choice for each question.

105. The nucleus of an atom never contains
   a. protons
   b. neutrons
   c. electrons

106. Which of the following determines the atomic number of an atom?
   a. the number of electrons in its outermost energy level
   b. the total number of energy levels of electrons
   c. the arrangement of neutrons in the atomic nucleus
   d. the number of protons in the atomic nucleus

107. For an atom to achieve maximum stability and become chemically unreactive, what must occur?
   a. its outermost energy level must be filled with electrons
   b. the number of electrons must equal the number of protons
   c. sharing of electrons between atoms must occur
   d. ionization of atoms is required
   e. hydrogen bonds must form

108. Which of the following is an example of hydrogen bonding? The bond between
   a. O and H in a single molecule
   b. O of one water molecule and H of a second water molecule
   c. O of one water molecule and O of a second water molecule
   d. H of one water molecule and H of a second water molecule

109. How is the formation of ions explained?
   a. different atoms share electrons
   b. different atoms gain and lose electrons
   c. different atoms gain and lose protons
   d. different atoms share protons
   e. different atoms share neutrons

110. If a substance measures 7.0 on the pH scale, that substance
   a. has equal concentrations of H^+ and OH^- ions
   b. may be very acidic
   c. has a greater concentration of H^+ ions than of OH^- ions
   d. probably lacks OH^- ions
   e. may be very basic

111. A glass of lemon juice has a pH of 2, and a glass of grapefruit juice has a pH of 3. How much higher is the H^+ ion concentration in lemon juice than in grapefruit juice?
    a. 10 times as much
    b. two-thirds as much
    c. one and a half times as much
    d. one-tenth as much

112. As ice melts, it
    a. releases heat into its surroundings
    b. absorbs heat from its surroundings
    c. increases its property of cohesion
    d. increases its specific heat
    e. immediately vaporizes

113. What type of chemical reaction results in the breakdown of organic polymers into their respective subunits?
    a. dehydration synthesis
    b. oxidation
    c. hydrolysis

114. Which of the following reactions requires the removal of water to form a covalent bond?
    a. glycogen → glucose subunits
    b. dipeptide → two amino acids
    c. cellulose → glucose
    d. glucose + galactose → lactose
    e. triglyceride → 3 fatty acids + glycerol

115. What determines the specific function of a protein?
    a. the exact sequence of its amino acids
    b. the number of disulfide bonds
    c. having a hydrophilic head and a hydrophobic tail region
    d. having fatty acids as monomers
    e. the length of the molecule

Fill-In: Complete the following table.

Atom/Ion	Atomic number	Number of protons	Number of electrons	Number of electrons in the outermost energy level
hydrogen (H)	1	1	1	1
116. oxygen (O)	8		8	
117. carbon (C)		6		
118. chloride ion (Cl⁻)	17		18	

CLUES TO APPLYING THE CONCEPTS

This practice question is intended to sharpen your ability to apply critical thinking and analysis to biological concepts covered in this chapter.

119. Why are winter temperatures near a large lake often a few degrees warmer than in a land-locked city in the same state, while during the summer the reverse is true?

_____

_____

_____

_____

_____

_____

ANSWERS TO EXERCISES

1. atoms
2. protons
3. neutrons
4. electrons
5. energy levels
6. atomic number
7. energy levels
8. chemical bonds
9. electrons
10. ions
11. ion
12. ionic
13. covalent
14. single covalent
15. triple covalent

16. non polar
17. polar
18. hydrogen
19. hydrophilic
20. hydrophobic
21. ions
22. pH
23. acidic
24. basic
25. buffers
26. specific heat

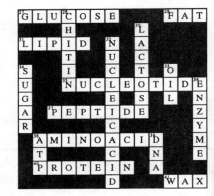

42. b
43. c
44. ionic
45 crystal
46. false, atom
47. true
48. false, lighter
49. false, number
50. false, hydrogen, helium
51. true
52. false, ionic
53. false, give up
54. true
55. false, covalent
56. false, less
57. false, outermost
58. false, disaccharide
59. false, oxygen
60. false, taken away

61. false, disaccharide
62. true
63. false, less
64. false, glycerol
65. false, on the edges
66. false, COOH
67. b
68. a
69. c
70. b
71. c
72. a
73. b
74. b
75. c
76. d
77. b
78. covalent
79. ionic

80. ionic
81. hydrogen
82. ionic
83. covalent
84. hydrogen
85. ionic
86. covalent
87. covalent
88. e
89. g
90. c
91. h
92. a
93. b
94. d
95. f
96. c
97. e
98. b

99. a
100. b
101. b
102. d
103. e
104. d
105. c
106. d
107. a
108. b
109. b
110. a
111. a
112. b
113. c
114. d
115. a

Atom/Ion	Atomic number	Number of protons	Number of electrons	Number of electrons in the outermost energy level
hydrogen (H)	1	1	1	1
116. oxygen (O)	8	8	8	6
117. carbon (C)	6	6	6	4
118. chloride ion (Cl^-)	17	17	18	8

119. During the winter, the water on the surface of the lake freezes into ice, giving off heat into the surrounding atmosphere. This raises the temperature around the lake in winter. During the summer, the water on the surface of the lake evaporates into the atmosphere, absorbing heat from the surrounding atmosphere. This lowers the temperature around the lake in summer.

Chapter 3: Energy Flow in the Life of a Cell

OVERVIEW

This chapter focuses on energy flow through the universe and particularly through living cells and organisms. The authors discuss the basic laws of thermodynamics and outline the basic types of metabolic reactions. They also explain how cells use enzymes to control chemical reactions.

1) What Is Energy?

Energy is the capacity to do work such as making molecules, moving them around, and generating light and heat. **Kinetic energy** is the energy of movement including light, heat, and electricity. **Potential energy** is stored energy, including chemical energy stored in the bonds of molecules.

The **laws of thermodynamics** define the basic properties and behavior of energy. The **first law** (conservation of energy) states that energy cannot be created or destroyed, although it can be changed from one form to another (the chemical energy in gasoline is converted to the heat and movement of cars, for instance). The **second law of thermodynamics** states that when energy is converted from one form to another, the amount of useful energy decreases. Spontaneous energy conversions in nature produce an increase in randomness and disorder, called **entropy**. Disorder spreads through the universe, and life alone battles against it by using energy from the sun to maintain orderliness within cells.

2) How Does Energy Flow in Chemical Reactions?

A chemical reaction converts **reactant** substances into **product** molecules. If the reactant energy is greater than the product energy, the reaction is **exergonic** (energy is released during the chemical reaction). For example, when sugar is heated with oxygen until it burns, chemical energy within the sugar molecules is released as heat and light (fire), and the molecules produced (carbon dioxide and water) have less energy.

If the product energy is greater than the reactant energy, the reactant is **endergonic** (energy is added to the reaction as it occurs). For example green plants use solar energy to make high-energy sugar and oxygen from low-energy water and carbon dioxide. Cells make complex biological molecules like proteins using endergonic reactions.

In a **coupled reaction**, an exergonic reaction provides the energy for an endergonic reaction. If the coupled reactions occur in different places within cells, the energy usually is transferred from place to place by energy-carrier molecules like ATP.

3) How Do Cells Control Their Metabolic Reactions?

Cell **metabolism** refers to the chemical reactions within cells; these reactions often occur in sequences called **metabolic pathways**. Cells regulate chemical reactions by using proteins called **enzymes**, which act as catalysts. Many of the chemical reactions required by the body can not take place at normal body temperatures. Therefore, most reactions are accelerated by supplying more **activation energy**, thus raising the temperature and speed of the molecules.

4) What Are Enzymes?

Enzymes act as **catalysts** by lowering the activation energy needed to begin exergonic chemical reactions. Due to its three-dimensional shape, a particular enzyme is very specific, catalyzing at most only a few types of reactions. The reactant molecule(s) (the **substrate**) fits into the **active site** region of an enzyme. The enzyme is not changed by the reaction it catalyzes. The activity of enzymes is influenced by their environment, such as pH, temperature, salt concentration, or the availability of **coenzyme** molecules (often vitamins) necessary to aid enzymes in interacting with reactants.

5) How Is Cellular Energy Carried Between Coupled Reactions?

During the breakdown of glucose (an exergonic reaction), its energy is transferred to reusable **energy-carrier molecules** for transfer to the muscle protein that uses energy to contract (endergonic reactions). **Adenosine triphosphate (ATP)** is the principal energy-carrier molecule. Energy from exergonic reactions is used to make ATP from **adenosine diphosphate (ADP)** and inorganic phosphate. ATP carries the energy to various cellular sites where energy-requiring reactions occur. The ATP then is broken down into ADP and inorganic phosphate, releasing energy to drive the endergonic reactions. Heat is released during these energy transfers, resulting in a loss of usable energy (an increase in entropy). Energy may be transported within a cell by other carrier molecules as well as by ATP. Some energy may be captured by electrons, which are taken by **electron-carrier** molecules to other parts of the cell to be released to drive endergonic reactions.

KEY TERMS AND CONCEPTS

Fill-In: From the following list of terms, fill in the blanks below. A term may be used more than once.

active site	energy	metabolic pathway
adenosine triphosphate (ATP)	entropy	metabolism
catalyst	enzyme	potential energy
coenzyme	exergonic	product
coupled reaction	first law of thermodynamics	reactant
endergonic	kinetic energy	second law of thermodynamics

(1)_____ This region of an enzyme binds substrates.

(2)_____ Any change in a system causes the amount of useful energy to decrease, and the amount of randomness and disorder (entropy) to increase.

(3)_____ This is the energy of movement.

(4)_____ This molecule is composed of ribose sugar, adenine, and three phosphate groups.

(5)_____ This is a protein that speeds up the rate of specific biological reactions.

(6)_____ This is a molecule resulting from a chemical reaction.

(7)_____ This is the sum of all chemical reactions occurring within a cell or organism.

(8)_____ A pair of reactions, one exergonic and one endergonic, are linked together so that the energy produced by one provides the energy needed for the other.

(9) _____ This is a chemical reaction requiring an input of energy to proceed.

(10) _____ This is the major energy carrier in cells.

(11) _____ This is a substance that speeds up a chemical reaction without itself being permanently changed in the process.

(12) _____ This is a molecule bound to an enzyme and required for the enzyme's proper functioning.

(13) _____ This is a measure of the amount of randomness and disorder in a system.

(14) _____ This type of a chemical reaction liberates energy and increases entropy.

(15) _____ Within a system, energy can be neither created nor destroyed.

(16) _____ This is stored energy, such as chemical energy in the bonds of molecules.

(17) _____ This is a molecule used up in a chemical reaction to form a product.

(18) _____ This is a sequence of chemical reactions within a cell.

(19) _____ Energy can be converted from one form to another.

(20) _____ This is the capacity to do work.

(21) _____ This includes light, heat, and mechanical movement.

Key Terms and Definitions

activation energy: in a chemical reaction, the energy needed to force the electron shells of reactants together, prior to the formation of products.

active site: the region of an enzyme molecule that binds substrates and performs the catalytic function of the enzyme.

adenosine diphosphate (a-den´-ō-sēn dī-fos´-fāt; **ADP**): a molecule composed of the sugar ribose, the base adenine, and two phosphate groups; a component of ATP.

adenosine triphosphate (a-den´-ō-sēn trī-fos´-fāt; **ATP**): a molecule composed of the sugar ribose, the base adenine, and three phosphate groups; the major energy carrier in cells. The last two phosphate groups are attached by "high-energy" bonds.

catalyst (kat´-uh-list): a substance that speeds up a chemical reaction without itself being permanently changed in the process; lowers the activation energy of a reaction.

coenzyme: an organic molecule that is bound to certain enzymes and is required for the enzymes' proper functioning; typically, a nucleotide bound to a water-soluble vitamin.

coupled reaction: a pair of reactions, one exergonic and one endergonic, that are linked together such that the energy produced by the exergonic reaction provides the energy needed to drive the endergonic reaction.

electron carrier: a molecule that can reversibly gain or lose electrons. Electron carriers generally accept high-energy electrons produced during an exergonic reaction and donate the electrons to acceptor molecules that use the energy to drive endergonic reactions.

endergonic (en-der-gon´-ik): pertaining to a chemical reaction that requires an input of energy to proceed; an "uphill" reaction.

energy: the capacity to do work.

energy-carrier molecule: a molecule that stores energy in "high-energy" chemical bonds and releases the energy to drive coupled endothermic reactions. In cells, ATP is the most common energy-carrier molecule.

entropy (en´-trō-pē): a measure of the amount of randomness and disorder in a system.

enzyme (en´zīm): a protein catalyst that speeds up the rate of specific biological reactions.

exergonic (ex-er-gon´-ik): pertaining to a chemical reaction that liberates energy (either as heat or in the form of increased entropy); a "downhill" reaction.

first law of thermodynamics: the principle of physics that states that within any isolated system, energy can be neither created nor destroyed but can be converted from one form to another.

kinetic energy: the energy of movement; includes light, heat, mechanical movement, and electricity.

laws of thermodynamics: the physical laws that define the basic properties and behavior of energy.

metabolic pathway: a sequence of chemical reactions within a cell, in which the products of one reaction are the reactants for the next reaction.

metabolism: the sum of all chemical reactions that occur within a single cell or within all the cells of a multicellular organism.

potential energy: "stored" energy, normally chemical energy or energy of position within a gravitational field.

product: an atom or molecule that is formed from reactants in a chemical reaction.

reactant: an atom or molecule that is used up in a chemical reaction to form a product.

second law of thermodynamics: the principle of physics that states that any change in an isolated system causes the quantity of concentrated, useful energy to decrease and the amount of randomness and disorder (entropy) to increase.

substrate: the atoms or molecules that are the reactants for an enzyme-catalyzed chemical reaction.

THINKING THROUGH THE CONCEPTS

True or False: Determine if the statement given is true or false. If it is false, change the underlined word(s) so that the statement reads true.

22. _____ Within a closed system, the amount of energy is <u>variable</u> over time.

23. _____ A fire <u>creates</u> energy.

24. _____ The <u>second</u> law of thermodynamics is concerned with entropy.

25. _____ Photosynthesis and similar reactions <u>decrease</u> entropy.

26. _____ Eventually, all molecules in the universe will become <u>randomly dispersed</u>.

27. _____ Reactions that release energy are <u>endergonic</u>.

28. _____ Enzymes <u>increase</u> the activation energy needed for chemical reactions to occur.

29. _____ ATP contains a <u>six-carbon</u> sugar.

30. _____ Conversion of ATP to ADP <u>releases</u> energy.

31. _____ In coupled reactions, the "downhill" reaction liberates <u>less</u> energy than the "uphill" reaction.

Matching: Chemical reactions.

32. _____ once started, these will continue by themselves

33. _____ these need activation energy to get started

34. _____ reactants have more energy than products

35. _____ photosynthesis is classed as this

36. _____ products have more energy than reactants

37. _____ energy is released from the reaction

38. _____ these usually involve energy-carrier molecules

39. _____ burning wood in a fireplace is classed as this

Choices:

a. exergonic reactions

b. endergonic reactions

c. both a and b

d. coupled reactions

Identification: Determine whether the following statements refer to **catalysts, enzymes**, or **both**.

40. _____ all are protein molecules

41. _____ these can speed up chemical reactions

42. _____ these are not changed in the reactions they affect

43. _____ generally, these are very specific as to the reaction they affect

44. _____ these cannot cause energetically unfavorable reactions to occur

45. _____ the activity of these can be regulated

Multiple Choice: Pick the most correct choice for each question.

46. Within a cell, metabolism is regulated in all the following ways *except*
    a. enzymes are precisely regulated
    b. several small steps are used to breakdown a molecule
    c. several small steps are used to synthesize a molecule
    d. enzymes are involved in many general reactions

47. The second law of thermodynamics states that
    a. light can be converted into heat
    b. within an isolated system, the total amount of energy remains constant
    c. energy always flows from an area of higher concentration to an area of lower concentration
    d. useful energy increases within an isolated system
    e. useful energy decreases within an isolated system

48. Which of the following statements about catalysts is <u>not</u> true?
    a. biological catalysts usually are enzymes
    b. catalysts increase activation energy requirements
    c. catalysts often increase the rate of reaction
    d. catalysts are not permanently altered during the reaction
    e. catalysts affect the amount of activation energy required in reactions

49. The statement that "energy is neither created nor destroyed" is part of
    a. entropy
    b. the first law of thermodynamics
    c. the second law of thermodynamics
    d. the regulation of enzyme activity

50. In exergonic chemical reactions
    a. reactants have more energy than products
    b. reactants have less energy than products
    c. reactants and products have equal amounts of energy
    d. energy is stored in the reactions
    e. enzymes are not necessary

51. When a muscle cell uses energy for contraction, what happens to ATP?
    a. it makes more ATP
    b. it enters a metabolic pathway
    c. it is hydrolyzed to ADP and inorganic phosphate
    d. a phosphate is added
    e. it is synthesized

52. Which is the most common short-term energy-storage molecule?
    a. glycogen
    b. fat
    c. sucrose
    d. adenosine triphosphate (ATP)

Refer to the figure below to answer questions 53 and 54.

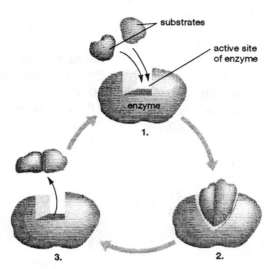

53. Which of the following statements are true?
   a. substrates enter an enzyme's active site in a random orientation
   b. while in the active site, substrates change their shape
   c. the active site changes its shape once the substrates are present
   d. products fit the active site just as well as substrates do
   e. enzymes are permanently changed during chemical reactions

54. If the figure depicts an endergonic reaction, which of the following statements are true?
   a. the substrates have more energy than the products
   b. the products have more energy than the substrates
   c. ATP could be produced from energy released by this reaction
   d. ATP could be used up to provide energy for this reaction
   e. the enzyme will be destroyed by the reaction

CLUES TO APPLYING THE CONCEPTS

This practice question is intended to sharpen your ability to apply critical thinking and analysis to biological concepts covered in this chapter.

56. When paper burns, it gives off both heat and light. Thus, the reaction is exergonic. Why, then, doesn't the paper that this book contains spontaneously burst into flames? If you touched the book with a burning match, you could set it on fire. What role does the energy supplied by the match play in this process?

_____

_____

_____

_____

_____

_____

ANSWERS TO EXERCISES

1. active site
2. second law of thermodynamics
3. kinetic energy
4. adenosine triphosphate (ATP)
5. enzyme
6. product
7. metabolism
8. coupled reaction
9. endergonic
10. adenosine triphosphate (ATP)
11. catalyst
12. coenzyme
13. entropy
14. exergonic
15. first law of thermodynamics
16. potential energy
17. reactant
18. metabolic pathway
19. first law of thermodynamics
20. energy
21. kinetic energy
22. false, constant
23. false, changes
24. true
25. true
26. true
27. false, exergonic
28. false, decrease
29. false, five-carbon
30. true
31. false, more
32. a
33. c
34. a
35. d
36. b
37. a
38. d
39. a
40. enzymes
41. both
42. both
43. enzymes
44. both
45. enzymes
46. d
47. e
48. b
49. b
50. a
51. c
52. d
53. b, c
54. b, d

55. The paper in this book doesn't spontaneously burst into flames because a sufficient amount of activation energy is not present to begin the intense exergonic reaction called burning. Holding a lit match to the paper would supply sufficient activation energy to begin the burning process. Often, as paper ages, it turns brown and becomes brittle. This occurs because the paper is reacting with oxygen in much the same way as in burning, except that the process is very slow due to insufficient activation energy.

Chapter 4: Cell Membrane Structure and Function

OVERVIEW

This chapter focuses on the characteristics and functions of cell walls and cell membranes. The authors discuss the transport of molecules across cell membranes, especially the processes of diffusion and osmosis. Cell connections and communication between cells also are discussed.

1) How Is the Structure of a Membrane Related to Its Function?

A **plasma membrane** surrounds a cell, protecting and isolating it while allowing it extensive communication with its surroundings. The basic structure of membranes is a **fluid mosaic** of proteins (which regulate exchange of substances and communication) floating within a double layer of phospholipids (which isolates the cell from its watery environment) and cholesterol (in animal cells).

Within membranes, phospholipids arrange themselves into a double layer, the **phospholipid bilayer**, with the hydrophilic heads forming the outer borders and the hydrophobic tails facing each other inside. Polar, water-soluble molecules (such as salts, amino acids, sugars) cannot pass through the phospholipid bilayer. Various proteins are embedded within or attached to the phospholipid bilayer to regulate the movement of molecules through the membrane and to communicate with the environment. Some proteins have carbohydrates attached, forming **glycoproteins**.

Transport proteins regulate the movement of water-soluble molecules through the plasma membrane. **Channel proteins** form pores to allow small molecules and ions (such as Ca^{++}, K^+, Na^+) to pass through. **Carrier proteins** bind molecules and, by changing shape, pass them across the membrane. **Receptor proteins** trigger cellular responses and/or communication between cells when certain molecules (hormones or nutrients) bind to them. **Recognition proteins** often are glycoproteins on the outer membrane surface of certain cells (immune system cells, for instance) and serve as identification tags and attachment sites for other cells and molecules.

2) How Are Substances Transported Across Cell Membranes?

Molecules in **fluids** move in response to **concentration gradients**, from regions of greater **concentration** to regions of lower concentration. Movement of molecules across membranes occurs by both **passive transport** (down the concentration **gradient** [high → low] by **diffusion**, requiring no cellular energy) and **active transport** (against the concentration gradient [low → high], requiring cellular energy). The greater the concentration gradient, the faster diffusion occurs, but diffusion cannot move molecules rapidly over long distances. In **simple diffusion**, water, dissolved gases, or lipid-soluble molecules pass freely through the phospholipid bilayer. In **facilitated diffusion**, molecules cross the membrane in a way that does not use energy; they are assisted by transport or receptor proteins embedded in the membrane.

Plasma membranes are **differentially permeable**, allowing some molecules to pass through, but not others. Diffusion of water across differentially permeable membranes is called **osmosis**. Extracellular fluids in animals usually are equal in water concentration (**isotonic**) to cellular fluids, so water diffuses equally into and out of cells. If the solution surrounding the cell is **hypertonic** in relation to the cell (that is, it has a lower concentration of water, or a higher concentration of dissolved molecules, than the cell has), water will leave the cell and the **cytoplasm** will shrink. If the solution is **hypotonic** to the cell (that is, it has a higher concentration of water, or lower concentration of dissolved substances, than the cell has), water will flow into the cell and the cytoplasm will expand. Under hypotonic conditions, certain animal cells utilize contractile vacuoles that pump the excess water out, and plant cells use central vacuoles which expand and allow those cells to become rigid.

Active transport uses energy to move substances against their concentration gradients into or out of cells. For example, brain cells use active transport to get rid of excess ions. Active transport proteins, often called "pumps," span plasma membranes and use energy (usually from breaking down ATP molecules) to transport molecules across the membrane against the concentration gradient.

Many cells acquire particles too large to pass through membranes. These particles aretaken into the cell by **endocytosis**. The cell uses energy to surround the substance with plasma membrane and pinches it off internally to form a **vesicle**). In **pinocytosis**, a small area of membrane pinches inward to surround extracellular fluid and buds off into the cytoplasm to form a tiny vacuole. In **receptor-mediated endocytosis**, depressed areas of membrane called coated pits contain many copies of a receptor protein. These proteins attach to specific extracellular molecules, and the coated pit deepens into a U-shaped pocket that pinches off into the cytoplasm forming a coated vesicle. In **phagocytosis**, cells (such as *Amoeba* and white blood cells) can ingest entire microorganisms or large molecules by extending sections of plasma membrane to form **pseudopods** that surround the object and enclose it within a food vacuole in the cytoplasm for digestion. Through **exocytosis**, cells eliminate unwanted materials (like digestive wastes) or secrete molecules (like hormones) into the extracellular fluid. A membrane-bound vesicle moves within the cytoplasm to the cell surface, where its membrane fuses with the plasma membrane, excreting the contents.

3) How Are Cell Surfaces Specialized?

In multicellular organisms, plasma membranes hold together clusters of cells and provide avenues through which cells communicate with their neighbors. **Cell walls** cover the outer surfaces of many cells (those of bacteria, plants, fungi, and some protists).. In protists, cell walls are made of cellulose, protein, or glassy silica. In plants they are made of cellulose and other polysaccharides, in fungi they are made of chitin, and in bacteria they are made of a chitin like material. Cell walls are strong yet porous, permitting easy passage of small molecules.

KEY TERMS AND CONCEPTS

Fill-In: From the following list of terms, fill in the blanks in the concept map below.

active transport	passive transport	proteins
carrier proteins	phagocytosis	receptor-mediated endocytosis
channel proteins	phospholipids	receptor proteins
cholesterol	pinocytosis	recognition proteins
differential permeability	plasma membrane	transport proteins
endocytosis		

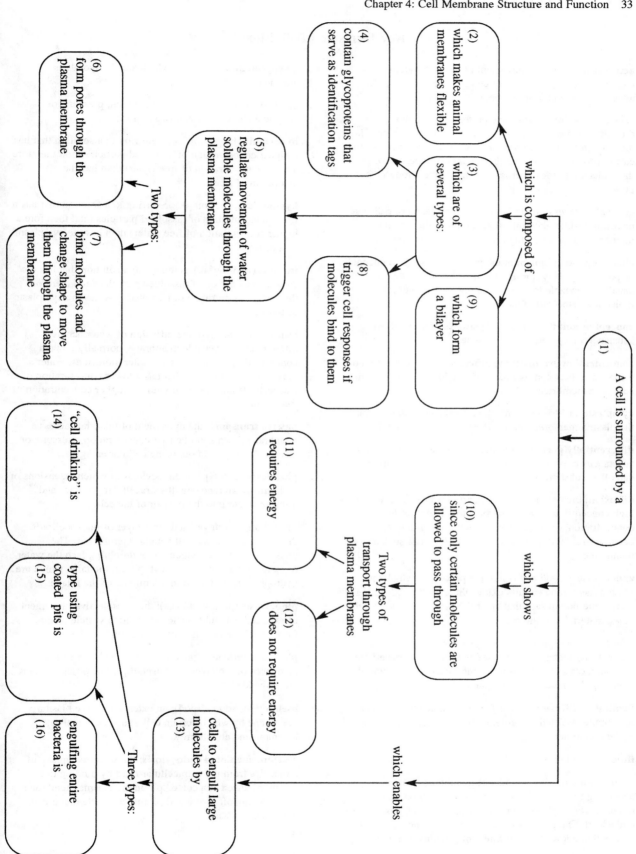

(1) A cell is surrounded by a

which is composed of

(2) which makes animal membranes flexible

(3) which are of several types:

(4) contain glycoproteins that serve as identification tags

(9) which form a bilayer

(8) trigger cell responses if molecules bind to them

(5) regulate movement of water soluble molecules through the plasma membrane

Two types:

(6) form pores through the plasma membrane

(7) bind molecules and change shape to move them through the plasma membrane

which shows

(10) since only certain molecules are allowed to pass through

Two types of transport through plasma membranes

(11) requires energy

(12) does not require energy

which enables

(13) cells to engulf large molecules by

Three types:

(14) "cell drinking" is

(15) type using coated pits is

(16) engulfing entire bacteria is

Key Terms and Definitions

active transport: the movement of materials across a membrane through the use of cellular energy, normally against a concentration gradient.

carrier protein: a membrane protein that facilitates the diffusion of specific substances across the membrane. The molecule to be transported binds to the outer surface of the carrier protein; the protein then changes shape, allowing the molecule to move across the membrane through the protein.

cell wall: a layer of material, normally made up of cellulose or cellulose-like materials, that is outside the plasma membrane of plants, fungi, bacteria, and some protists.

channel protein: a membrane protein that forms a channel or pore completely through the membrane and that is usually permeable to one or to a few water-soluble molecules, especially ions.

concentration: the number of particles of a dissolved substance in a given unit of volume.

concentration gradient: the difference in concentration of a substance between two parts of a fluid or across a barrier such as a membrane.

cytoplasm (sī´-tō-plaz-um): the material contained within the plasma membrane of a cell, exclusive of the nucleus.

differentially permeable: referring to the ability of some substances to pass through a membrane more readily than can other substances.

diffusion: the net movement of particles from a region of high concentration of that particle to a region of low concentration, driven by the concentration gradient; may occur entirely within a fluid or across a barrier such as a membrane.

endocytosis (en-dō-sī-tō´-sis): the process in which the plasma membrane engulfs extracellular material, forming membrane-bound sacs that enter the cytoplasm and thereby move material into the cell.

exocytosis (ex-ō-sī-tō´-sis): the process in which intracellular material is enclosed within a membrane-bound sac that moves to the plasma membrane and fuses with it, releasing the material outside the cell.

facilitated diffusion: the diffusion of molecules across a membrane, assisted by protein pores or carriers embedded in the membrane.

fluid: a liquid or gas.

fluid mosaic model: a model of membrane structure; according to this model, membranes are composed of a double layer of phospholipids in which various proteins are embedded. The phospholipid bilayer is a somewhat fluid matrix that allows the movement of proteins within it.

glycoprotein: a protein to which a carbohydrate is attached.

gradient: a difference in concentration, pressure, or electrical charge between two regions.

hypertonic (hī-per-ton´-ik): referring to a solution that has a higher concentration of dissolved particles (and therefore a lower concentration of free water) than has the cytoplasm of a cell.

hypotonic (hī-pō-ton´-ik): referring to a solution that has a lower concentration of dissolved particles (and therefore a higher concentration of free water) than has the cytoplasm of a cell.

isotonic (ī-sō-ton´-ik): referring to a solution that has the same concentration of dissolved particles (and therefore the same concentration of free water) as has the cytoplasm of a cell.

osmosis (oz-mō´-sis): the diffusion of water across a differentially permeable membrane, normally down a concentration gradient of free-water molecules. Water moves into the solution that has a lower concentration of free water from a solution with the higher concentration of free water.

passive transport: the movement of materials across a membrane down a gradient of concentration, pressure, or electrical charge without using cellular energy.

phagocytosis: a type of endocytosis in which extensions of a plasma membrane engulf extracellular particles and transport them into the interior of the cell.

phospholipid bilayer: a double layer of phospholipids that forms the basis of all cellular membranes. The phospholipid heads, which are hydrophilic, face the water of extracellular fluid or the cytoplasm; the tails, which are hydrophobic, are buried in the middle of the bilayer.

pinocytosis (pi-nō-sī-tō´-sis): the nonselective movement of extracellular fluid, enclosed within a vesicle formed from the plasma membrane, into a cell.

plasma membrane: the outer membrane of a cell, composed of a bilayer of phospholipids in which proteins are embedded.

pseudopod (sood´-ō-pod): an extension of the plasma membrane by which certain cells, such as amoebae, locomote and engulf prey.

receptor-mediated endocytosis: the selective uptake of molecules from the extracellular fluid by binding to a receptor located at a coated pit on the plasma membrane and pinching off the coated pit into a vesicle that moves into the cytoplasm.

receptor protein: a protein, located on a membrane (or in the cytoplasm), that recognizes and binds to specific molecules. Binding by receptor proteins typically triggers a response by a cell, such as endocytosis, increased metabolic rate, or cell division.

recognition protein: a protein or glycoprotein protruding from the outside surface of a plasma membrane that identifies a cell as belonging to a particular species, to a specific individual of that species, and in many cases to one specific organ within the individual.

simple diffusion: the diffusion of water, dissolved gases, or lipid-soluble molecules through the phospholipid bilayer of a cellular membrane.

transport protein: a protein that regulates the movement of water-soluble molecules through the plasma membrane.

vesicle (ves´-i-kul): a small, membrane-bound sac within the cytoplasm.

THINKING THROUGH THE CONCEPTS

True or False: Determine if the statement given is true or false. If it is false, change the underlined word(s) so that the statement reads true.

17. _____   As a cell increases in size, its surface area increases more rapidly than its internal volume.

18. _____   Red blood cells will burst when placed in fresh water.

19. _____   The water-loving portion of a compound is hydrophobic.

20. _____   The rate of diffusion is increased by decreasing the temperature.

21. _____   In diffusion, molecules move toward regions of higher concentration.

22. _____   More water will enter a cell if it is placed in a hypotonic solution.

23. _____   Solutions with higher salt concentrations than a cell are hypertonic when compared to the cell.

24. _____   Freshwater organisms deal with the tendency of their cells to gain water.

25. _____   Endocytosis is the movement of substances into cells.

26. _____   The movement of a solid substance into a cell is pinocytosis.

Identification: Determine whether the following statements refer to cell **walls** or cell **membranes**

27. _____   contain cellulose in plants

28. _____   isolate the cytoplasm from the external environment

29. _____   regulate the flow of materials into and out of cells

30. _____   contain chitin in fungi

31. _____   communicate with other cells

32. _____   are stiff, porous, and non living

33. _____   are described by the fluid-mosaic model

34. _____   has a lipid bilayer

Identification: Determine whether the following statements refer to **diffusion** or **osmosis**.

35. _____ effect of movement of all molecules down the concentration gradient

36. _____ effect of water moving down its concentration gradient across a differentially permeable membrane

37. _____ movement of O_2 into a cell and CO_2 out of a cell

38. _____ a cell expands when placed in pure water

39. _____ can cause cells to shrink

Matching: Effect of osmosis on cells.

40. _____ animal cells will expand

41. _____ animal cells will shrivel up

42. _____ red blood cells will burst

43. _____ celery will wilt

44. _____ lettuce leaves will become turgid (rigid, crisp) in fluid

45. _____ red blood cells will neither shrivel up nor swell up

Choices:

a. cells placed in hypotonic solution

b. cells placed in hypertonic solution

c. cells placed in isotonic solution

Multiple Choice: Pick the most correct choice for each question.

46. The hydrophobic tails of a phospholipid bilayer are oriented toward the
    a. interior of the plasma membrane
    b. extracellular fluid surrounding the cell
    c. cytoplasm of the cell
    d. nucleus of the cell

47. Molecules that permeate a plasma membrane by facilitated diffusion
    a. require the use of energy
    b. require the aid of transport proteins
    c. move from areas of low concentration to areas of high concentration
    d. do so much more quickly than those crossing by simple diffusion
    e. are water molecules

48. A molecule that can diffuse freely through a phospholipid bilayer is probably
    a. water-soluble
    b. positively charged
    c. nonpolar
    d. negatively charged
    e. a membrane-spanning protein

49. The preferential movement of water molecules across a differentially permeable membrane is termed
    a. facilitated diffusion
    b. osmosis
    c. active transport
    d. exocytosis
    e. a concentration gradient

50. If red blood cells are placed in a hypotonic solution, what happens?
    a. the cells swell and burst
    b. the cells shrivel up and shrink
    c. the cells remain unchanged in volume
    d. the cells take up salt molecules from the hypotonic solution
    e. the cells release salt molecules into the hypotonic solution

51. Solutions that cause water to preferentially enter cells by osmosis are called
    a. hypertonic
    b. isotonic
    c. hypotonic
    d. endosmotic
    e. exosmotic

CLUES TO APPLYING THE CONCEPTS

This practice question is intended to sharpen your ability to apply critical thinking and analysis to biological concepts covered in this chapter.

52. Suppose you are taking a cruise from San Francisco to Hawaii. About halfway there, the ship begins to sink and all passengers and crew board lifeboats and are floating around in the ocean waiting to be rescued. After several days, you are so thirsty that you bend over the side of your life boat and drink some of the seawater. Did you do a wise thing? Explain what you think will happen to your body within a few hours of drinking the ocean water, and explain the biological basis for your reactions.

_____

_____

_____

_____

_____

_____

_____

_____

_____

_____

_____

ANSWERS TO EXERCISES

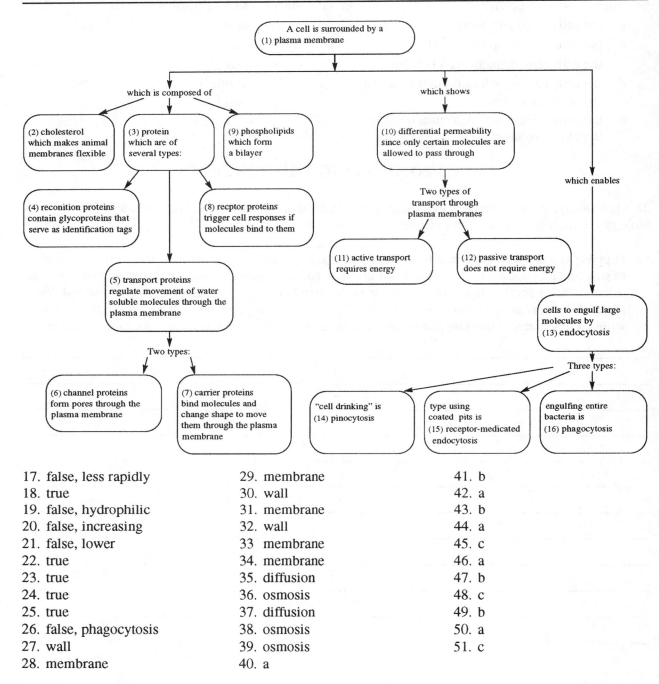

17. false, less rapidly
18. true
19. false, hydrophilic
20. false, increasing
21. false, lower
22. true
23. true
24. true
25. true
26. false, phagocytosis
27. wall
28. membrane

29. membrane
30. wall
31. membrane
32. wall
33 membrane
34. membrane
35. diffusion
36. osmosis
37. diffusion
38. osmosis
39. osmosis
40. a

41. b
42. a
43. b
44. a
45. c
46. a
47. b
48. c
49. b
50. a
51. c

52. Although you were thirsty and your cells craved water, drinking the salty seawater was unwise because seawater is hypertonic (has a higher concentration of salts) to cellular cytoplasm. So in your stomach, cells will begin to lose water by osmosis, since water flows through a selectively permeable membrane from regions of greater water concentration (the cytoplasm) toward regions of lesser water concentration (the seawater). Soon your stomach cells will have lost so much water that they will begin to die, causing you to go into convulsions and perhaps die.

Chapter 5: Cell Structure and Function

OVERVIEW

This chapter describes and compares prokaryotic and eukaryotic cells. The authors cover the organization of eukaryotic cells and emphasize the various organelles within these cells.

1) What Are the Basic Features of Cells?

In the 1850s, Virchow proclaimed, "All cells come from cells." Modern cell theory principles state that: (1) every organism is made of at least one cell; (2) cells are the functional units of life; and (3) all cells arise from preexisting cells. All cells obtain energy and nutrients from their environment, make molecules necessary for growth and repair, reproduce, get rid of wastes, and many interact with other cells.

The **plasma membrane** (phospholipid bilayer with embedded proteins) encloses the cell and mediates interactions between the cell and its environment. It (1) isolates the cytoplasm from the external environment, (2) regulates the flow of materials between the cytoplasm and its environment, and (3) allows interactions with other cells. **DNA (deoxyribonucleic acid)** determines cell structure and function and allows the cell to reproduce. In **eukaryotic** cells (plants, animals, fungi, and protists), DNA is found within the **nucleus** (a membrane-bound structure). In **prokaryotic** cells (bacteria), DNA is in a non-membrane enclosed space, the **nucleoid**. All cells contain **cytoplasm** (all material inside the plasma membrane and outside the nucleus or nucleoid). Cytoplasm includes water, salts, and organic molecules, and, in eukaryotic cells, contains various **organelles** (membrane-bound structures that perform distinct cell functions).

Cell function limits cell size. Most cells are small (1 to 100 micrometers in diameter) because they need to exchange nutrients and wastes through their plasma membranes mainly by diffusion, a slow process. Larger cells would have greater needs for exchange of molecules with the environment, but since they would have a smaller surface area to internal volume ratio than do smaller cells, diffusion would be too slow to meet their metabolic needs. Therefore, cells tend to remain small.

2) What Are the Features of Prokaryotic Cells?

Most prokaryotic cells are small (less than 5 micrometers long), with simple internal features (no nucleus or membrane-bound organelles). They contain **ribosomes** (made of **RNA [ribonucleic acid]** and proteins and on which protein synthesis occurs) and usually have a stiff cell wall. Photosynthetic bacteria have inner membranes containing light-capturing proteins and enzymes.

3) What Are the Features of Eukaryotic Cells?

Eukaryotic cells are larger than prokaryotic cells (typically more than 10 micrometers in diameter) and contain organelles and a cytoskeleton (a network of protein fibers for cellular shape and organization). The nucleus is the cellular control center, containing the genetic material (DNA). Nuclear components ar: (1) the **nuclear envelope** (two membranes riddled with pores to control flow of informational molecules), which separates nuclear material from the cytoplasm; (2) **chromatin** (DNA and associated proteins organized into **chromosomes**); and (3) one or more **nucleoli**, the sites of ribosome assembly.

Eukaryotic cells contain a complex system of internal membranes. The plasma membrane isolates a cell and allows selective interactions between a cell and its environment. The **endoplasmic reticulum (ER)** forms interconnected membrane-bound tubes and channels within the cytoplasm and is continuous with the nuclear membrane. Numerous ribosomes are embedded in **rough ER** (the site of protein synthesis) and **smooth ER** (the major site of lipid synthesis) lacks ribosomes. Proteins made by ribosomes in rough ER move through ER channels and accumulate in pockets that bud off to form **vesicles** (membrane-bound cytoplasmic sacs).

The **Golgi complex** (membranous sacs derived from ER) has three functions: (1) it separates out lipids and proteins obtained from the ER according to their destinations; (2) it chemically alters some molecules; and (3) it packages molecules into vesicles for transport. **Lysosomes** are cellular digestive centers that contain digestive enzymes to break down proteins, fats, and carbohydrates taken into cells as food. Lysosomes fuse with **food vacuoles**, and lysosomal enzymes then digest the food into small molecules. Lysosomes also digest defective organelles. The various parts of the membrane system can exchange membranous material with one another – for example, from ER to the Golgi complex to a vesicle, which fuses with plasma membrane.

Vacuoles (fluid-filled, membrane-bound sacs) serve many functions, including water regulation, support, and storage. **Central vacuoles**, found in plant cells, may: (1) collect cellular wastes; (2) store poisons that deter feeding animals; and (3) store sugars and amino acids for cellular use. (You may find it interesting that the central vacuole contents become hypertonic to cytoplasm and take in water through osmosis. The pressure of the expanding central vacuole stiffens the cell, providing support for nonwoody plant parts. Houseplants stiffen when watered and wilt when sufficient water is lacking.)

Mitochondria extract energy from food molecules and **chloroplasts** capture solar energy. Both organelles (1) are oblong, about 1 to 5 micrometers long; (2) are surrounded by a double membrane; (3) have DNA; and (4) make ATP. Mitochondria ("powerhouses of the cell", found in all eukaryotic cells) make ATP using energy stored in food molecules. **Anaerobic** (without oxygen) metabolism of sugar in the cytoplasm produces little ATP energy. Mitochondria use **aerobic** (with oxygen) metabolism to generate about 18 or 19 times as much ATP. The inner mitochondrial membrane loops back and forth to form deep folds (**cristae**) so that there are two regions: the **intermembrane compartment** between the outer and inner membranes, and the inner **matrix** region.

Chloroplasts (specialized **plastids**) are the sites of photosynthesis. Their inner membranes enclose a semifluid **stroma**. Stroma contains **thylakoids** (interconnected stacks of hollow membranous sacs containing **chlorophyll** and other pigments; a stack of thylakoids is a **granum**. Chlorophyll captures sunlight energy and transfers it to other molecules that in turn transfer it to ATP and other energy-carrier molecules. In the stroma, these energy molecules are used to combine carbon dioxide and water into sugars. Plastids store various types of molecules, including pigments and starch.

The **cytoskeleton** provides shape, support, and movement. It includes several types of protein fibers: thin **microfilaments**, medium-sized **intermediate filaments**, and thick **microtubules**. Cytoskeleton functions include (1) cell shape (especially in animal cells); (2) cell movement (through assembly, disassembly, and sliding of microfilaments and microtubules); (3) organelle movement (especially vesicles, by micro-filaments and microtubules); and (4) cell division (microtubules move chromosomes into daughter nuclei, and division of the cytoplasm in animal cells results from the contraction of a ring of microfilaments).

Cilia (short, with many per cell) and **flagella** (long, with few per cell) move cells or move fluid past cells. They are slender extensions of plasma membrane containing a ring of nine fused pairs of microtubules, with an unfused pair in the center of the ring (a "9 + 2" arrangement). The arrangement of microtubules is produced by a **centriole** located just beneath the plasma membrane.

KEY TERMS AND CONCEPTS

Fill-In: Fill in the names of the structures indicated in this diagram of an animal cell, identifying the following.

chromatin
cytoplasm
Golgi complex
lysosome
mitochondrion

nucleolus
nucleus
plasma membrane
rough endoplasmic reticulum
smooth endoplasmic reticulum

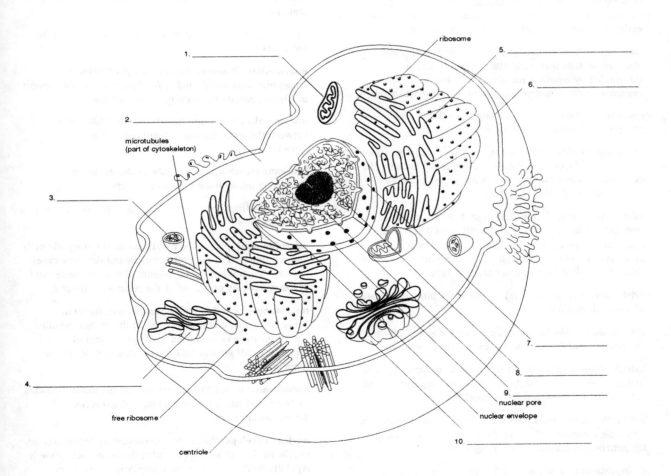

ribosome

1. _____

2. _____

microtubules
(part of cytoskeleton)

3. _____

4. _____

free ribosome

centriole

5. _____

6. _____

7. _____

8. _____

9. _____
nuclear pore

nuclear envelope

10. _____

Key Terms and Definitions

aerobic: using oxygen.

anaerobic: not using oxygen.

capsule: a polysaccharide or protein coating that surrounds the cell walls of some bacteria.

central vacuole: a large, fluid-filled vacuole occupying most of the volume of many plant cells; performs several functions, including maintaining turgor pressure.

centriole (sen´-trē-ōl): in animal cells, a short, barrel-shaped ring consisting of nine microtubule triplets; a microtubule-containing structure at the base of each cilium and flagellum; gives rise to the microtubules of cilia and flagella and is involved in spindle formation during cell division.

chlorophyll (klor´-ō-fil): a pigment found in chloroplasts that captures light energy during photosynthesis; absorbs violet, blue, and red light but reflects green light.

chloroplast (klor´-ō-plast): the organelle in plants and plantlike protists that is the site of photosynthesis; surrounded by a double membrane and containing an extensive internal membrane system that bears chlorophyll.

chromatin (krō´-ma-tin): the complex of DNA and proteins that makes up eukaryotic chromosomes.

chromosome (krō´-mō-sōm): in eukaryotes, a linear strand composed of DNA and protein, located in the nucleus of a cell, that contains the genes; in prokaryotes, a circular strand composed solely of DNA.

cilium (sil´-ē-um; pl., **cilia**): a short, hairlike projection from the surface of certain eukaryotic cells that contains microtubules in a 9 + 2 arrangement. The movement of cilia may propel cells through a fluid medium or move fluids over a stationary surface layer of cells.

crista (kris´-tuh; pl., **cristae**): a fold in the inner membrane of a mitochondrion.

cytoplasm (sī´-tō-plaz-um): the material contained within the plasma membrane of a cell, exclusive of the nucleus.

cytoskeleton: a network of protein fibers in the cytoplasm that gives shape to a cell, holds and moves organelles, and is typically involved in cell movement.

deoxyribonucleic acid (dē-ox-ē-rī-bō-noo-klā´-ik; **DNA**): a molecule composed of deoxyribose nucleotides; contains the genetic information of all living cells.

endoplasmic reticulum (en-dō-plaz´-mik re-tik´-ū-lum; **ER**): a system of membranous tubes and channels within eukaryotic cells; the site of most protein and lipid syntheses.

eukaryotic (ū-kar-ē-ot´-ik): referring to cells of organisms of the domain Eukarya (kingdoms Protista, Fungi, Plantae, and Animalia). Eukaryotic cells have genetic material enclosed within a membrane-bound nucleus and contain other membrane-bound organelles.

flagellum (fla-jel´-um; pl., flagella): a long, hairlike extension of the plasma membrane; in eukaryotic cells, it contains microtubules arranged in a 9 + 2 pattern. The movement of flagella propel some cells through fluids.

food vacuole: a membranous sac, within a single cell, in which food is enclosed. Digestive enzymes are released into the vacuole, where intracellular digestion occurs.

Golgi complex (gōl´-jē): a stack of membranous sacs, found in most eukaryotic cells, that is the site of processing and separation of membrane components and secretory materials.

granum (gra´-num; pl., **grana**): a stack of thylakoids in chloroplasts.

intermediate filament: part of the cytoskeleton of eukaryotic cells that probably functions mainly for support and is composed of several types of proteins.

intermembrane compartment: the fluid-filled space between the inner and outer membranes of a mitochondrion.

lysosome (lī´-sō-sōm): a membrane-bound organelle containing intracellular digestive enzymes.

matrix: the fluid contained within the inner membrane of a mitochondrion.

microfilament: part of the cytoskeleton of eukaryotic cells that is composed of the proteins actin and (in some cases) myosin; functions in the movement of cell organelles and in locomotion by extension of the plasma membrane.

microtubule: a hollow, cylindrical strand, found in eukaryotic cells, that is composed of the protein tubulin; part of the cytoskeleton used in the movement of organelles, cell growth, and the construction of cilia and flagella.

mitochondrion (mī-tō-kon´-drē-un): an organelle, bounded by two membranes, that is the site of the reactions of aerobic metabolism.

nuclear envelope: the double-membrane system surrounding the nucleus of eukaryotic cells; the outer membrane is typically continuous with the endoplasmic reticulum.

nucleoid (noo-klē-oid): the location of the genetic material in prokaryotic cells; not membrane-enclosed.

nucleolus (noo-klē´-ō-lus): the region of the eukaryotic nucleus that is engaged in ribosome synthesis; consists of the genes encoding ribosomal RNA, newly synthesized ribosomal RNA, and ribosomal proteins.

nucleus (**cellular**): the membrane-bound organelle of eukaryotic cells that contains the cell's genetic material.

organelle (or-guh-nel´): a structure, found in the cytoplasm of eukaryotic cells, that performs a specific function; sometimes refers specifically to membrane-bound structures, such as the nucleus or endoplasmic reticulum.

pilus: a hairlike projection made of protein and found on the surface of certain bacteria; often used to attach the bacterium to another cell.

plasma membrane: the outer membrane of a cell, composed of a bilayer of phospholipids in which proteins are embedded.

plastid (plas´-tid): in plant cells, an organelle bounded by two membranes that may be involved in photosynthesis (chloroplasts), pigment storage, or food storage.

prokaryotic (prō-kar-ē-ot´-ik): referring to cells of the domains Bacteria or Archaea. Prokaryotic cells have genetic material that is not enclosed in a membrane-bound nucleus; they lack other membrane-bound organelles.

ribonucleic acid (rī-bō-noo-klā´-ik; **RNA**): a molecule composed of ribose nucleotides, each of which consists of a phosphate group, the sugar ribose, and one of the bases adenine, cytosine, guanine, or uracil; transfers hereditary instructions from the nucleus to the cytoplasm; also the genetic material of some viruses.

ribosome: an organelle consisting of two subunits, each composed of ribosomal RNA and protein; the site of protein synthesis, during which the sequence of bases of messenger RNA is translated into the sequence of amino acids in a protein.

rough endoplasmic reticulum: endoplasmic reticulum lined on the outside with ribosomes.

slime layer: a polysaccharide or protein coating that some disease-causing bacteria secrete outside their cell wall.

smooth endoplasmic reticulum: endoplasmic reticulum without ribosomes.

stroma (strō´-muh): the semi-fluid material inside chloroplasts in which the grana are embedded.

thylakoid (thī´-luh-koid): a disk-shaped, membranous sac found in chloroplasts, the membranes of which contain the photosystems and ATP-synthesizing enzymes used in the light-dependent reactions of photosynthesis.

vacuole (vak´-ū-ōl): a vesicle that is typically large and consists of a single membrane enclosing a fluid-filled space.

vesicle (ves´-i-kul): a small, membrane-bound sac within the cytoplasm.

THINKING THROUGH THE CONCEPTS

True or False: Determine if the statement given is true or false. If it is false, change the underlined word so that the statement reads true.

11. _____ More primitive types of cells are called eukaryotic cells.

12. _____ The presence of large numbers of ribosomes is characteristic of rough endoplasmic reticulum.

13. _____ The majority of the hereditary material is found in the cytoplasm.

14. _____ Mitochondria are associated with the release of energy from sugar.

15. _____ Mitochondria are associated with the storage of energy in sugar.

16. _____ Lipid-producing enzymes are more common in rough endoplasmic reticulum.

17. _____ Animals store food in the form of starch.

18. _____ Animal cells are more likely than plant cells to have vacuoles.

19. _____ Higher plants lack ciliated or flagellated cells.

20. _____ Cilia are longer than flagella.

Identification: Determine whether the following statements refer to **eukaryotic** cells, **prokaryotic** cells, or **both**.

21. _____   lack a membrane-bound nucleus

22. _____   have many chromosomes with DNA and protein

23. _____   lack most cytoplasmic organelles

24. _____   are larger and more complex

25. _____   have nucleoid regions in the cytoplasm

26. _____   have DNA

27. _____   have flagella with a 9 + 2 structure

Identification: Determine whether the following statements refer to **mitochondria**, **chloroplasts**, or **both**.

28. _____   make ATP using energy

29. _____   capture sunlight energy to make sugar

30. _____   convert sugar energy into ATP energy

31. _____   have DNA

32. _____   have thylakoid membranes and semi-fluid stroma

33. _____   extract energy from food molecules

34. _____   found in plants

35. _____   have cristae membranes and semi-fluid matrix

36. _____   have chlorophyll

37. _____   function in photosynthesis

38. _____   function in cellular respiration

Identification: Determine whether the following statements refer to **cilia**, **flagella**, or **both**.

39. _____   microtubular extensions through the cell membrane

40. _____   are shorter and more numerous per cell

41. _____   have a 9 + 2 arrangement of microtubular pairs

42. _____   bend perpendicular to the cell membrane

43. _____   bend parallel to the cell membrane

44. _____   are used for food gathering and for movement

Fill-In: Fill in the names of the structures indicated in the following figure.

cristae   intermembrane compartment   outer membrane
inner membrane   matrix

45. _____

46. _____

47. _____

48. _____

49. _____

Matching: Organelles that manufacture or digest proteins and lipids.

50. _____   digest food particles

51. _____   interconnected membrane tubes and channels
             in the cytoplasm

52. _____   stacks of membranes in the cytoplasm

53. _____   made of RNA and proteins

54. _____   function in the nucleus

55. _____   membrane-bound vesicles

56. _____   "workbenches" for protein synthesis

57. _____   sort out various lipids and proteins

58. _____   may be rough or smooth in appearance

59. _____   sites of lipid synthesis

60. _____   large and small subunits are assembled in
             the nucleolus

61. _____   packages proteins and lipids into vesicles
             for transport out of the cell

62. _____   digest defective organelles

Choices:

a. ribosomes

b. endoplasmic reticulum

c. Golgi complexes

d. lysosomes

e. none of these

Multiple Choice: Pick the most correct choice for each question.

63. All cells possess all of the following *except*:
    a. cytoplasm
    b. genetic material
    c. nuclear membrane
    d. chromosome
    e. plasma (cell) membrane

64. Which of the following statements about mitochondria and chloroplasts is <u>not</u> true?
    a. both make ATP
    b. both capture solar energy and convert it into chemical energy
    c. both possess their own DNA
    d. both have a double membrane
    e. both probably evolved from bacteria long ago

65. Both prokaryotic and eukaryotic cells possess
    a. mitochondria
    b. chloroplasts
    c. a cytoskeleton
    d. ribosomes
    e. lysosomes

66. Which organelle extracts energy from food molecules and uses it to make ATP?
    a. mitochondrion
    b. chloroplast
    c. ribosome
    d. centriole
    e. nucleus

CLUES TO APPLYING THE CONCEPTS

These practice questions are intended to sharpen your ability to apply critical thinking and analysis to biological concepts covered in this chapter.

67. Why do cells seldom grow large enough to be seen without the aid of a microscope?

_____

_____

_____

_____

_____

68. Suppose you discovered a chemical that had all of the following effects on a cell: Cell growth slowed down, the movement of cilia slowed down, cell divisions occurred less frequently, proteins were made less often, and endocytosis occurred less often. Which of these organelles do you think the chemical affected most severely: lysosomes, the Golgi complex, or mitochondria? Briefly explain your answer.

_____

_____

_____

_____

ANSWERS TO EXERCISES

1. mitochondrion
2. cytoplasm
3. lysosome
4. smooth endoplasmic reticulum
5. rough endoplasmic reticulum
6. plasma membrane
7. nucleus
8. nucleolus
9. chromatin
10. Golgi complex
11. false, prokaryotic
12. true
13. false, nucleus
14. true
15. false, chloroplasts
16. false, smooth
17. false, plants
18. false, plant, animal
19. true
20. false, shorter
21. prokaryotic
22. eukaryotic

23. prokaryotic
24. eukaryotic
25. prokaryotic
26. both
27. eukaryotic
28. both
29. chloroplasts
30. mitochondria
31. both
32. chloroplasts
33. mitochondria
34. both
35. mitochondria
36. chloroplasts
37. chloroplasts
38. mitochondria
39. both
40. cilia
41. both
42. flagella
43. cilia
44. both

45. outer membrane
46. inner membrane
47. intermembrane compartment
48. matrix
49. cristae
50. d
51. b
52. c
53. a
54. e
55. d
56. a
57. c
58. b
59. b
60. a
61. c
62. d
63. c
64. b
65. d
66. a

67. Cells seldom grow this large because of two factors. First, a cell this size would have too much volume for the amount of surface area present, so not enough plasma membrane area would be present for the movement of molecules into and out of such a giant cell. Second, the time it would take for molecules deep inside of such a cell to move to the surface or vice versa would be extremely long and diffusion over relatively long distances is too slow to support life processes.

68. Mitochondria, because all the processes affected require energy and mitochondria are the chief organelles in which the energy in sugar is converted into cellular energy in the form of ATP molecules.

Chapter 6: Capturing Solar Energy: Photosynthesis

OVERVIEW

This chapter details the process of photosynthesis. The authors outline the light-dependent and light-independent steps of photosynthesis and present the two major ways in which plants trap carbon dioxide.

1) What Is Photosynthesis?

Starting with carbon dioxide and water, **photosynthesis** converts sunlight energy into chemical energy stored in the bonds of glucose and oxygen.

The overall reaction is $6\ CO_2 + 6\ H_2O + \text{light energy} \rightarrow C_6H_{12}O_6 + 6\ O_2$.

It occurs in plants, algae, and some bacteria. In plants, leaves and chloroplasts are adaptations for photosynthesis. Leaves obtain CO_2 from the air through adjustable pores in the epidermis called **stomata**. **Mesophyll** cells within leaves contain most of the chloroplasts. Vascular bundles (veins) carry water and minerals to the mesophyll cells and carry sugars to other plant parts.
    Photosynthesis consists of **light-dependent reactions** (chlorophyll in **thylakoid** membranes capture sunlight energy to split water and make O_2 and some ATP and NADPH energy-carriers) and **light-independent reactions** (**stroma** enzymes use chemical energy in ATP and NADPH to make glucose from CO_2).

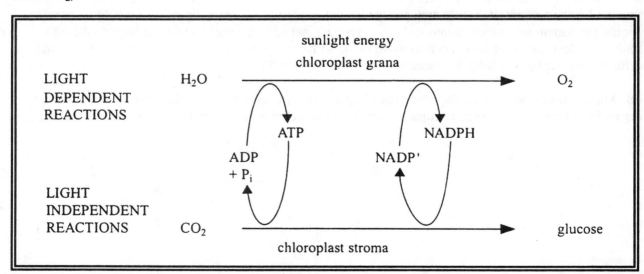

2) Light-Dependent Reactions: How is Light Energy Converted to Chemical Energy?

Light is first captured by pigments in chloroplasts. Wavelengths of light are composed of **photons** (individual packets of energy). Chloroplasts contain several pigments that absorb different wavelengths of light: **Chlorophyll** absorbs violet, blue, and red light but reflects green (this is why leaves are green), and **accessory pigments** (**carotenoids** which absorb blue and green but reflect yellow, orange, and red;

and **phycocyanins**, which absorb green and yellow but reflect blue and purple) absorb light energy and transfer it to chlorophyll.

Light-dependent reactions occur in clusters of molecules called **photosystems** (proteins including chlorophyll, accessory pigments, and electron-carrying molecules in the **thylakoids**). Each photosystem has two major parts: (1) a **light-harvesting complex** (about 300 pigment molecules that absorb light and pass the energy to a specific chlorophyll called the **reaction center**); and (2)an **electron transport system** (**ETS**, a series of electron-carrier molecules embedded in the thylakoid membrane). When the reaction center chlorophyll receives energy, one of its electrons enters the ETS and moves from one carrier to the next, releasing energy that allows ATP to be synthesized from ADP (through a hydrogen ion gradient in photosystem II) and NADP$^+$ to form NADPH (in photosystem I). Electrons from the ETS of photosystem II replenish those lost by the reaction center chlorophyll of photosystem I.

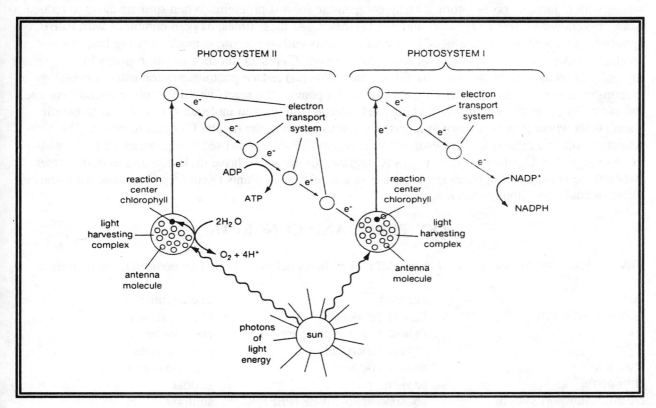

The splitting of water molecules maintains the flow of electrons through the photosystems. Electrons flow in one direction: from splitting water through the reaction center of photosystem II, through the ETS of photosystem II, to the reaction center of photosystem I, through the ETS of photosystem I, to NADPH.

3) Light-Independent Reactions: How Is Chemical Energy Stored in Glucose Molecules?

As long as sufficient ATP and NADPH are available, the light-independent reactions do not require sunlight. The **C$_3$** (three-carbon or **Calvin-Benson**) **cycle** captures carbon dioxide. It requires (1) CO$_2$ from the air; (2) the CO$_2$-capturing sugar, ribulose bisphosphate (RuBP); (3) stroma enzymes; and (4) energy from ATP and NADPH (from the light-dependent reactions). The three steps of the C$_3$ cycle are **carbon fixation** (CO$_2$ attaches to RuBP), making intermediate molecules using energy from ATP and NADPH, and regeneration of RuBP. Carbon fixed during the C$_3$ cycle is used to make glucose.

4) How Are Light-Dependent and Light-Independent Reactions Related?

Basically, the light-dependent reactions and the light-independent reations are related through the energy-carrier molecules ATP and NADPH. During the light-dependent reactions, ADP is energized to ATP and $NADP^+$ is energized to NADPH. ATP and NADPH travel to the stroma where they are required by the light-independent reactions. The light-independent reations use their energy, forming ADP and NADP+ again. The energy-carriers shuttle energy to the stroma and return to the thylakoids to be recharged.

5) Water, CO_2, and the C_4 Pathway.

For land plants, having leaves that are porous to CO_2 also allows water to evaporate. Large, waterproof leaves with adjustable pores (stomata) help compensate for this problem. When stomata close to reduce water loss, however, less CO_2 enters and less O_2 leaves. At these times, oxygen combines with RuBP (**photorespiration**), but no useful cellular energy results and no glucose is made. During hot, dry weather, plants may die due to lack of sufficient glucose. C_4 plants (those with chloroplasts in mesophyll and in **bundle-sheath cells** around the leaf veins) reduce photorespiration using a two-stage carbon-fixation process called the C_4 **pathway**. In C_4 plants, CO_2 reacts with PEP (phosphoenolpyruvate) instead of RuBP in the mesophyll, making oxaloacetate (four carbon molecules) that travels to bundle-sheath cells where it breaks down to release CO_2, thus allowing the regular C_3 cycle to occur. The remnant molecule returns to the mesophyllcells, where ATP energy is used to regenerate PEP. C_4 uses more energy than C_3. However, C_4 plants (crabgrass, for instance) thrive in deserts and in midsummer (when there is plenty of light energy but water is scarce) and C_3 plants (Kentucky bluegrass, for instance) thrive in cool, wet, cloudy climates.

KEY TERMS AND CONCEPTS

Fill-In: From the following list of terms, fill in the blanks below. A term may be used more than once.

ATP	gradient	photosynthesis
bundle-sheath cells	light-dependent	photosystem I
C_3	light-harvesting complex	photosystem II
C_4	light-independent	photosystems
chemical	oxaloacetic acid	reaction center
chlorophyll	oxygen	stroma
electron transport system	phosphoenolpyruvate (PEP)	sunlight
glucose	photorespiration	thylakoids

Starting with carbon dioxide and water, (1)_____ converts (2)_____ energy into (3)_____ energy stored in the bonds of glucose and oxygen.

Photosynthesis consists of (a) (4)_____ reactions [in which (5)_____ in thylakoid membranes captures sunlight energy to split water and make (6)_____ gas and some (7)_____ and NADPH energy-carriers] and (b) (8)_____ reactions [in which (9)_____ enzymes use chemical energy in ATP and NADPH to make (10)_____ from CO_2].

Light-dependent reactions occur in clusters of molecules called (11)_____ consisting of proteins including chlorophyll, accessory pigments, and electron-carrying molecules in the (12)_____.

Each photosystem has two major parts: (a) the (13)_____ (about 300 pigment molecules that absorb light and pass the energy to a specific chlorophyll called the (14)_____ and (b) the (15)_____ (series of electron carrier molecules embedded in the thylakoid membrane).

In (16)_____ ATP is synthesized from ADP through a hydrogen ion (17)_____. In (18)_____ $NADP^+$ becomes NADPH. Electrons from the electron transport center in (19)_____ replenish those lost by the reaction center chlorophyll of (20)_____.

Plants with chloroplasts in both mesophyll and (21)_____ around the leaf veins reduce (22)_____ using a two-stage carbon-fixation process called the (23)_____ pathway. In these plants, CO_2 reacts with (24)_____ instead of RuBP in the mesophyll, making (25)_____ (four carbon molecules) that travels to the (26)_____ cells, where it breaks down to release CO_2 thus allowing the regular (27)_____ cycle to occur. The remnant molecule returns to the mesophyll, where (28)_____ energy is used to regenerate (29)_____.

Key Terms and Definitions

accessory pigments: colored molecules other than chlorophyll that absorb light energy and pass it to chlorophyll.

bundle-sheath cell: one of a group of cells that surround the veins of plants; in C_4 (but not C_3) plants, bundle-sheath cells contain chloroplasts.

C_3 cycle: the cyclic series of reactions whereby carbon dioxide is fixed into carbohydrates during the light-independent reactions of photosynthesis; also called *Calvin-Benson cycle*.

C_4 pathway: the series of reactions in certain plants that fixes carbon dioxide into oxaloacetic acid, which is later broken down for use in the C_3 cycle of photosynthesis.

Calvin-Benson cycle: see *C_3 cycle*.

carbon fixation: the initial steps in the C_3 cycle, in which carbon dioxide reacts with ribulose bisphosphate to form a stable organic molecule.

carotenoid (ka-rot´-en-oid): a red, orange, or yellow pigment, found in chloroplasts, that serves as an accessory light-gathering molecule in thylakoid photosystems.

chlorophyll (klor´-ō-fil): a pigment found in chloroplasts that captures light energy during photosynthesis; absorbs violet, blue, and red light but reflects green light.

electron transport system: a series of electron carrier molecules, found in the thylakoid membranes of chloroplasts and the inner membrane of mitochondria, that extract energy from electrons and generate ATP or other energetic molecules.

granum (gra´-num; pl., **grana**): a stack of thylakoids in chloroplasts.

light-dependent reactions: the first stage of photosynthesis, in which the energy of light is captured as ATP and NADPH; occurs in thylakoids of chloroplasts.

light-harvesting complex: in photosystems, the assembly of pigment molecules (chlorophyll and accessory pigments) that absorb light energy and transfer that energy to electrons.

light-independent reactions: the second stage of photosynthesis, in which the energy obtained by the light-dependent reactions is used to fix carbon dioxide into carbohydrates; occurs in the stroma of chloroplasts.

mesophyll (mez´-ō-fil): loosely packed parenchyma cells beneath the epidermis of a leaf.

photon (fō´-ton): the smallest unit of light energy.

photorespiration: a series of reactions in plants in which O_2 replaces CO_2 during the C_3 cycle, preventing carbon fixation; this wasteful process dominates when C_3 plants are forced to close their stomata to prevent water loss.

photosynthesis: the complete series of chemical reactions in which the energy of light is used to synthesize high-energy organic molecules, normally carbohydrates, from low-energy inorganic molecules, normally carbon dioxide and water.

photosystem: in thylakoid membranes, a light-harvesting complex and its associated electron transport system.

phycocyanin (fī-kō-sī´-uh-nin): a blue or purple pigment that is located in the membranes of chloroplasts and is used as an accessory light-gathering molecule in thylakoid photosystems.

reaction center: in the light-harvesting complex of a photosystem, the chlorophyll molecule to which light energy is transferred by the antenna molecules (light-absorbing pigments); the captured energy ejects an electron from the reaction center chlorophyll, and the electron is transferred to the electron transport system.

stoma (stō´-muh; pl., **stomata**): an adjustable opening in the epidermis of a leaf, surrounded by a pair of guard cells, that regulates the diffusion of carbon dioxide and water into and out of the leaf.

stroma (strō´-muh): the semi-fluid material inside chloroplasts in which the grana are embedded.

thylakoid (thī´-luh-koid): a disk-shaped, membranous sac found in chloroplasts, the membranes of which contain the photosystems and ATP-synthesizing enzymes used in the light-dependent reactions of photosynthesis.

THINKING THROUGH THE CONCEPTS

True or False: Determine if the statement given is true or false. If it is false, change the underlined word(s) so that the statement reads true.

30. _____ Aerobic respiration probably evolved before photosynthesis.

31. _____ Chlorophyll molecules are associated with stroma.

32. _____ Glucose is synthesized in the grana.

33. _____ Blue is a more energetic wavelength of light than red.

34. _____ Leaves appear green because chlorophyll reflects green light.

35. _____ Light energy is first captured in photosystem I.

36. _____ As electrons are transferred from one carrier to another, they gain energy.

37. _____ Photosynthesis uses O_2 and produces CO_2.

38. _____ In the light-dependent reactions, chlorophyll captures sunlight energy and uses it to make glucose.

39. _____ The electron transport system is part of the light-dependent process of photosynthesis.

Identification: Determine whether the following statements refer to the light-**dependent** or the light-**independent** photosynthetic reactions.

40. _____ CO_2 is captured and converted into sugars

41. _____ light energy is converted into chemical energy of ATP and NADPH

42. _____ occurs in chloroplast grana

43. _____ uses chemical energy to make glucose

44. _____ uses chlorophyll, carotenoids, and phycocyanins to trap light energy

45. _____ Calvin-Benson, or C_3 cycle

46. _____ energy obtained from NADPH and ATP

47. _____ produces oxygen gas

48. _____ thylakoid membranes

49. _____ photosystems I and II

50. _____ carbon fixation occurs

51. _____ involves electron transport

52. _____ occurs in chloroplast stroma

53. _____ water is split into oxygen and hydrogen

Multiple Choice: Pick the most correct choice for each question.

54. Molecules of chlorophyll are located in the membranous sacs called
    a. cristae
    b. thylakoids
    c. stroma
    d. grana
    e. chloroplasts

55. A pigment that absorbs red and blue light but reflects green light is
    a. phycocyanin
    b. carotenoid
    c. chlorophyll
    d. melanin
    e. colored orange

56. Light-dependent photosynthetic reactions produce
    a. ATP, NADPH, and oxygen gas
    b. ATP, NADPH, and carbon dioxide gas
    c. glucose, ATP, and oxygen gas
    d. glucose, ATP, and carbon dioxide gas
    e. ADP, NADP, and glucose

57. Where does the oxygen gas produced during photosynthesis come from?
    a. carbon dioxide
    b. water
    c. ATP
    d. glucose
    e. the atmosphere

58. Carbon fixation requires which of the following?
    a. sunlight
    b. products of energy-capturing reactions
    c. high levels of oxygen gas and low levels of carbon dioxide gas
    d. water, ADP, and NADP

59. The immediate source of hydrogen atoms for the production of sugar during photosynthesis is
    a. ATP
    b. water
    c. NADPH
    d. glucose
    e. chlorophyll

CLUES TO APPLYING THE CONCEPTS

These practice questions are intended to sharpen your ability to apply critical thinking and analysis to biological concepts covered in this chapter.

60. Suppose you wanted to devise an experiment to determine whether the oxygen gas generated by photosynthesis came from oxygen molecules released from water or from carbon dioxide, each of which is broken down during photosynthesis. Briefly describe an idea you might have for such a study. Hint: You might want to use a radioactive isotope of oxygen in your study.

_____

_____

_____

_____

_____

61. Suppose you wanted to determine which color of light had the greatest effect on the amount of photosynthesis occurring in plants. How would you set up such an experiment? What variables would you use and what aspects would serve as controls?

_____

_____

_____

_____

_____

_____

ANSWERS TO EXERCISES

1. photosynthesis
2. sunlight
3. chemical
4. light-dependent
5. chlorophyll
6. oxygen
7. ATP
8. light-independent
9. stroma
10. glucose
11. photosystems
12. thylakoids
13. light-harvesting complex
14. reaction center
15. electron transport system
16. photosystem II
17. gradient
18. photosystem I
19. photosystem II
20. photosystem I
21. bundle-sheath cells
22. photorespiration
23. C_4
24. phosphoenolpyruvate (PEP)
25. oxaloacetate
26. bundle-sheath
27. C_3
28. ATP
29. phosphoenolpyruvate (PEP)
30. false, after
31. false, grana
32. false, stroma
33. false, less
34. true
35. false, photosystem II
36. false, lose
37. false, produces, uses
38. false, oxygen gas
39. true

40. independent	47. dependent	54. b
41. dependent	48. dependent	55. c
42. dependent	49. dependent	56. a
43. independent	50. independent	57. b
44. dependent	51. dependent	58. b
45. independent	52. independent	59. c
46. independent	53. dependent	

60. You could set up one study in which the plants received normal CO_2 and water containing radioactive oxygen (H_2O^*) and another study in which the plants received normal H_2O and carbon dioxide containing radioactive oxygen (CO_2^*). In each study, you would collect the oxygen gas and the sugars produced by photosynthesis and determine where the radioactive oxygen atoms show up.

61. After keeping a group of plants in the dark for several days, you could expose them, in separate experiments, to light from bulbs of different colors but equal intensities for equal amounts of time, keeping the plants equally watered and at constant temperatures. Then you could compare the amounts of oxygen gas each plant produced.

Chapter 7: Harvesting Energy: Glycolysis and Cellular Respiration

OVERVIEW

This chapter covers the processes of glycolysis and cellular respiration. The authors explain glycolysis and fermentation and discuss the role of mitochondria in converting the chemical energy of organic molecules, especially glucose, into the usable energy of ATP during aerobic respiration.

1) How Is Glucose Metabolized?

The chemical equations for glucose formation by photosynthesis and the complete metabolism of glucose are nearly symmetrical:

Photosynthesis:
$$6\ CO_2 + 6\ H_2O + \text{solar energy} \rightarrow C_6H_{12}O_6 + 6\ O_2 \uparrow$$

Complete glucose metabolism:
$$C_6H_{12}O_6 + 6\ O_2 \rightarrow 6\ CO_2 \uparrow + 6\ H_2O + \text{some chemical energy and much heat energy}$$

2) How Is the Energy in Glucose Harvested During Glycolysis?

In all living cells, the first step of glucose metabolism (**glycolysis**) proceeds the same in either the presence (aerobic) or absence (anaerobic) of oxygen. Glycolysis splits the six-carbon glucose into two, three-carbon molecules of **pyruvate**, and some released energy is used to make two ATP molecules. Under anaerobic conditions, **fermentation** occurs: The pyruvate is converted into lactate or ethanol in the cytoplasm. Under aerobic conditions, **cellular respiration** occurs: Pyruvate enters the mitochondria and is broken down into CO_2 and H_2O, generating 34 to 36 ATP molecules.

Glycolysis consists of two major steps: glucose activation (glucose is converted into fructose bisphosphate from energy provided by 2 ATP molecules) and energy harvest (4 ATP molecules are made, and NAD^+ is converted into NADH electron carriers using energy released when fructose bisphosphate is converted into pyruvate). When anaerobic conditions exist in animal muscle, fermentation occurs and pyruvate is used to produce lactate. During lactate fermentation, NAD^+ gains electrons and hydrogen ions while being converted to NADH. Lactate is toxic when concentrated, causing discomfort and fatigue. When oxygen is present again, lactate is converted into pyruvate, which enters cellular respiration. Anaerobic conditions in many microorganisms result in alcoholic fermentation: Pyruvate is converted into ethanol + CO_2, NAD^+ gains electrons and hydrogen ions while being converted to NADH. Alcoholic fermentation in yeast is useful in the brewing (ethanol) and baking (CO_2 makes bread rise) industries.

3) How Does Cellular Respiration Generate Still More Energy from Glucose?

During aerobic cellular respiration in the mitochondria of eukaryotic cells, pyruvate is converted into CO_2 and H_2O, plus many ATP molecules. The final reactions require oxygen because it is the final acceptor of electrons. Most ATP made during cellular respiration is generated by reactions catalyzed by enzymes in the mitochondrial **matrix**, by electron transport proteins in the inner membrane, and by the movement of hydrogen ions through ATP-synthesizing proteins in the inner membrane. The steps involved are as follows:

1. The pyruvate enters the mitochondrion by diffusion through pores.
2. Pyruvate + coenzyme A + NAD^+ → CO_2 + NADH + acetyl-Co A. The acetyl-CoA enters the **Kreb cycle** and is converted to two CO_2 molecules and one ATP, and donates energetic electrons to several electron-carrying molecules (three NADH and one $FADH_2$).
3. The electron carriers donate their energetic electrons to the **electron transport system (ETS)** of the inner mitochondrial membrane, where the energy is used to transport H^+ ions from the matrix to the **intermembrane compartment**, where electrons + H^+ + O_2 → H_2O.
4. In **chemiosmosis**, the H^+ ion gradient (high in the intermembrane compartment, low in the matrix) created by the ETS diffuses through channels in ATP-synthesizing enzymes located in the inner membrane. The flow of H^+ across the membrane produces energy that is used to create 32 to 34 molecules of ATP.
5. The ATP leaves the mitochondrion by diffusion and enters the cytoplasm.

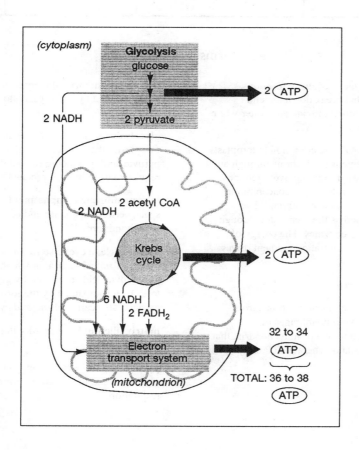

KEY TERMS AND CONCEPTS

Fill-In: Complete the following table.

Name of metabolic process:	Is oxygen necessary?	Part of a cell where it occurs:	Number of ATP molecules produced:	Types of molecules produced:
glycolysis	(1)	(2)	(3)	(4)
alcoholic fermentation	(5)	(6)	(7)	(8)
lactate fermentation	(9)	(10)	(11)	(12)
Krebs cycle	(13)	(14)	(15)	(16)
electron transport system and chemiosmosis	(17)	(18)	(19)	(20)

Key Terms and Definitions

cellular respiration: the oxygen-requiring reactions, occurring in mitochondria, that break down the end products of glycolysis into carbon dioxide and water while capturing large amounts of energy as ATP.

chemiosmosis: a process of ATP generation in chloroplasts and mitochondria. The movement of electrons through an electron transport system is used to pump hydrogen ions across a membrane, thereby building up a concentration gradient of hydrogen ions across the membrane. The hydrogen ions diffuse back across the membrane through the pores of ATP-synthesizing enzymes. The energy of their movement down their concentration gradient drives ATP synthesis.

citric acid cycle: see *Krebs cycle*.

electron transport system: a series of electron carrier molecules, found in the thylakoid membranes of chloroplasts and the inner membrane of mitochondria, that extract energy from electrons and generate ATP or other energetic molecules.

fermentation: anaerobic reactions that convert the pyruvic acid produced by glycolysis into lactic acid or alcohol and CO_2.

glycolysis (glī-kol´-i-sis): reactions, carried out in the cytoplasm, that break down glucose into two molecules of pyruvic acid, producing two ATP molecules; does not require oxygen but can proceed when oxygen is present.

intermembrane compartment: the fluid-filled space between the inner and outer membranes of a mitochondrion.

Krebs cycle: a cyclic series of reactions, occurring in the matrix of mitochondria, in which the acetyl groups from the pyruvic acids produced by glycolysis are broken down to CO_2, accompanied by the formation of ATP and electron carriers; also called *citric acid cycle*.

matrix: the fluid contained within the inner membrane of a mitochondrion.

pyruvate: a three-carbon molecule that is formed by glycolysis and then used in fermentation or cellular respiration.

THINKING THROUGH THE CONCEPTS

True or False: Determine if the statement given is true or false. If it is false, change the underlined word(s) so that the statement reads true.

21. _____ Aerobic forms of life evolved before anaerobic forms.

22. _____ Aerobic respiration uses O_2 and produces CO_2.

23. _____ Glycolysis requires oxygen in order to function.

24. _____ Glycolysis occurs in the mitochondria of a cell.

25. _____ Pyruvate is produced by glycolysis.

26. _____ The chemical energy in sugar is used to make O_2.

27. _____ When NADH becomes NAD^+, the hydrogens are used to make sugar.

28. _____ Lactate fermentation occurs when oxygen is abundant in muscle cells.

29. _____ When each pyruvate is completely broken down, six CO_2 molecules are released.

30. _____ Each glucose molecule releases enough energy to make 100 molecules of ATP.

Matching: Glucose metabolism.

31. _____ most of the ATP is made

32. _____ occurs only under anaerobic conditions

33. _____ occurs only under aerobic conditions

34. _____ occurs under either anaerobic or aerobic conditions

35. _____ glucose is split into 2 pyruvate molecules

36. _____ occurs in mitochondria

37. _____ produces lactate

38. _____ occurs in the cytoplasm

39. _____ produces CO_2 and ATP

40. _____ requires some ATP energy to get started

41. _____ produces ethanol

42. _____ involves acetyl-CoA

43. _____ involves Krebs cycle

44. _____ fructose bisphosphate is produced

Choices:

a. glycolysis

b. fermentation

c. both a and b

d. cellular respiration

Short Answer.

45. Explain, using chemical equations, how photosynthesis and aerobic cellular respiration are "complementary" processes.

Multiple Choice: Pick the most correct choice for each question:

46. During glycolysis, what provides the initial energy to break down glucose?
    a. ATP
    b. pyruvate
    c. NADH
    d. cytoplasmic enzymes
    e. mitochondria

47. At the end of glycolysis, where are the original carbons of the glucose molecule located?
    a. in six molecules of carbon dioxide
    b. in two molecules of NADH
    c. in two molecules of pyruvate
    d. in two molecules of citric acid

48. When oxygen is present
    a. most cells use aerobic cellular respiration
    b. most animal cells carry out lactate fermentation
    c. most bacteria and yeasts carry out alcoholic fermentation
    d. glucose is broken down to produce 2 ATP molecules
    e. mitochondria are less likely to function normally

49. The anaerobic breakdown of glucose is called
    a. artificial respiration
    b. glycolysis
    c. photosynthesis
    d. fermentation
    e. Krebs cycle

50. What happens when pyruvate is converted into lactate?
    a. the lactate enters the Krebs cycle
    b. the mitochondria are activated
    c. NAD^+ is regenerated for use in glycolysis
    d. pyruvate is oxidized
    e. oxygen gas is liberated

51. Oxygen is necessary for cellular respiration because oxygen
    a. combines with hydrogen ions to form water
    b. combines with carbon to form carbon dioxide
    c. combines with carbon dioxide and water to form glucose
    d. breaks down glucose into carbon dioxide and water
    e. allows glucose to be converted into pyruvate

CLUES TO APPLYING THE CONCEPTS

These practice questions are intended to sharpen your ability to apply critical thinking and analysis to biological concepts covered in this chapter.

52. Why can drowning, suffocation, or carbon monoxide poisoning lead to death?   The obvious initial response is that they prevent oxygen from reaching our cells, but go beyond that to explain why the lack of oxygen can cause death.

_____

_____

_____

_____

_____

_____

_____

_____

_____

_____

_____

_____

53. Some animals that live in deserts survive without drinking water. They eat food containing a little water, but most of the water they need is made within their cells and is called "metabolic water." From what you have read in this chapter, explain one way metabolic water is produced.

_____

_____

_____

_____

_____

_____

_____

_____

_____

ANSWERS TO EXERCISES

Name of metabolic process:	Is oxygen necessary?	Part of a cell where it occurs:	Number of ATP molecules produced:	Types of molecules produced:
glycolysis	(1) no	(2) cytoplasm	(3) 2	(4) ATP, NADH, pyruvate
alcoholic fermentation	(5) no	(6) cytoplasm	(7) 0	(8) CO_2, NAD^+, ethanol
lactate fermentation	(9) no	(10) cytoplasm	(11) 0	(12) NAD^+, lactate
Krebs cycle	(13) yes	(14) mitochondrial matrix	(15) 1 ATP per pyruvate	(16) CO_2, ATP, NADH, $FADH_2$
electron transport system and chemiosmosis	(17) yes	(18) inner mitochondrial membrance and intermembrane compartment	(19) 32 to 34	(20) H_2O, ATP, FAD, NAD^+

21. false, after
22. true
23. false, does not require
24. false, cytoplasm
25. true
26. false, ATP
27. false, water
28. false, absent

29. false, three
30. false, 36
31. d
32. b
33. d
34. a
35. a
36. d

37. b
38. c
39. d
40. a
41. b
42. d
43. d
44. a

45.
Photosynthesis
6 CO_2 + 6 H_2O + solar energy   → $C_6H_{12}O_6$ + 6 O_2 ↑
used in photosynthesis   made in photosynthesis
made in cell respiration   used in cell respiration

Aerobic cellular respiration
$C_6H_{12}O_6$ + 6 O_2 →   6 CO_2 ↑ + 6 H_2O + energy
made in photosynthesis   used in photosynthesis
used in cell respiration   made in cell respiration

46. a
47. c

48. a
49. b

50. c
51. a

52. Oxygen is the final electron acceptor in aerobic cellular respiration, receiving electrons and hydrogen ions from the electron transport chain and forming water. Without sufficient oxygen, the electrons and hydrogen ions clog up the electron transport chain, not allowing NADH and $FADH_2$ molecules to give off their electrons and hydrogen ions, and as cells run out of these molecules, mitochondria shut down. As a result, cells must rely on glycolysis and fermentation to produce very little ATP from glucose metabolism, and without sufficient energy from ATP, cells cannot continue functioning, and they die.

53. When oxygen combines with electrons and hydrogen ions at the end of the electron transport chain, metabolic water is produced. Some animals can use this cell-made water to help meet the water demands of their cells, and thus survive.

Chapter 8: DNA: The Molecule of Heredity

OVERVIEW

This chapter focuses on the molecular basis of inheritance, namely DNA. The authors describe the structure of DNA and explain how DNA replicates.

1) What Is the Composition of Chromosomes?

Eukaryotic **chromosomes** consist of long **DNA (deoxyribonucleic acid)** molecules complexed with proteins. They become visible within the nucleus during cell division. Nucleic acids consist of four types of smaller molecules called **nucleotides**. Each DNA nucleotide consists of a pentose sugar (S), deoxyribose, a phosphate group (P), and a nitrogen-containing **base** (B):

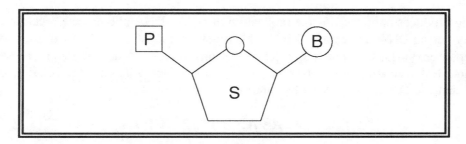

DNA nucleotides have four types of bases: adenine (A), thymine (T), guanine (G), and cytosine (C). The sequence of nucleotide bases in DNA can encode the vast amounts of information needed to make about 50,000 different proteins in human cells. A stretch of DNA just 10 nucleotides long can have more than a million possible sequences of the four bases ($4^{10} = 1,048,576$), and typical human DNA molecules are billions of nucleotides long.

2) What Is the Structure of DNA?

Chemical analysis showed that although the amounts of each of the four bases vary considerably from species to species, the DNA of any given species contains equal amounts of A and T and equal amounts of G and C. X-ray analysis showed that DNA is twisted into a helix (corkscrew shaped) and has repeating subunits. In 1953, Watson and Crick figured out that a DNA molecule consists of two strands twisted into a **double helix**, each made of a series of nucleotides: The phosphate group (P) of one nucleotide bonds to the sugar (S) of the next, forming a "backbone" of alternating P and S with the bases (B) sticking out:

$$-P\text{-}S -P\text{-}S -P\text{-}S -P\text{-}S -P\text{-}S -P\text{-}S -$$
$$\quad\ |\qquad |\qquad |\qquad |\qquad |\qquad |$$
$$\quad\ B\qquad B\qquad B\qquad B\qquad B\qquad B$$

In a DNA double helix, the backbones are on the outside (like uprights of a ladder) and the bases are paired up inside (like rungs of a ladder). Each rung is a **complementary base pair** (either A-T or G-C) held together by hydrogen bonds.

3) How Does DNA Replication Ensure Genetic Constancy?

Each chromosome consists of a long DNA molecule, together with proteins that help organize and fold up the DNA. DNA duplication (**replication**) produces two identical double helices of DNA. During DNA replication, the two DNA strands are separated and new strands are made from nucleotides with bases complementary to the parental strands. (New DNA = one parental strand + one new complimentary strand). DNA replication involves three steps, each controlled by enzymes: (1) the two original (parental) DNA strands unwind and separate from each other, using the enzyme DNA helicase; (2) using the enzyme **DNA polymerase**, each parental strand is used as a template for the new DNA strand. By connecting nucleotides in the order determined by the nucleotide sequence of the parental strand so that A pairs with T and G pairs with C, the new DNA strand is made. (The enzyme DNA ligase connects the nucleotides in the new strand.); and (3) parental and daughter complimentary strands wind together into double helices. This is **semiconservative replication** (one parental strand is conserved in each new double helix of DNA).

Proofreading produces almost error-free replication of DNA. DNA polymerases occasionally attach bases incorrectly during DNA replication (1 in 10,000 times), but most of these errors are corrected by several DNA repair enzymes, so completely replicated mammalian DNA has only about one error per billion base-pairs. Environmental forces (such as X-rays, ultraviolet radiation from the sun, and certain chemicals) also damage DNA, and inevitably some errors are overlooked.

KEY TERMS AND CONCEPTS

Fill-In: Fill in the crossword puzzle based on the following clues:

Across
2. Base that pairs with thymine in DNA.
4. Bases complementary to CT.
6. Complementary base sequence for TTAG.
10. Enzyme that connects the nucleotides in a newly made DNA strand.
11. Nitrogen-containing bases may have a _____-ringed or a double-ringed structure.
12. DNA replication is _____-conservative.
14. DNA has a double-_____ three-dimensional structure.
15. Complementary base sequence for CAATG.
16. What genes are made of.
18. Number of strands making up a DNA molecule.
20. New DNA strands are made using this enzyme.
22. The unit of heredity.
23. Base that pairs with guanine in DNA.

Down
1. Co-discoverer of the double helix structure.
3. Has a phosphate group, a sugar, and a nitrogen containing base.
5. Complementary base pair to TA.
7. DNA consists of the 5-carbon sugar deoxy_____.
8. An example is adenine.
9. The enzyme that unwinds DNA during replication.
13. Cell structure in the nucleus that contains genetic material.
15. Base that pairs with cytosine in DNA.
17. Number of different bases in a DNA molecule.
19. Co-discoverer of the double helix DNA structure.
21. Number of types of sugar molecules in DNA.

Key Terms and Definitions

base: in molecular genetics, one of the nitrogen-containing, single- or double-ringed structures that distinguish one nucleotide from another. In DNA, the bases are adenine, guanine, cytosine, and thymine.

chromosome (krō'-mō-sōm): in eukaryotes, a linear strand composed of DNA and protein, located in the nucleus of a cell, that contains the genes; in prokaryotes, a circular strand composed solely of DNA.

complementary base pair: in nucleic acids, bases that pair by hydrogen bonding. In DNA, adenine is complementary to thymine and guanine is complementary to cytosine; in RNA, adenine is complementary to uracil, and guanine to cytosine.

deoxyribonucleic acid (dē-ox-ē-rī-bō-noo-klā'-ik; **DNA**): a molecule composed of deoxyribose nucleotides; contains the genetic information of all living cells.

DNA polymerase: an enzyme that bonds DNA nucleotides together into a continuous strand, using a preexisting DNA strand as a template.

double helix (hē'-liks): the shape of the two-stranded DNA molecule; like a ladder twisted lengthwise into a corkscrew shape.

gene: a unit of heredity that encodes the information needed to specify the amino acid sequence of proteins and hence particular traits; a functional segment of DNA located at a particular place on a chromosome.

nucleotide: a subunit of which nucleic acids are composed; a phosphate group bonded to a sugar (deoxyribose in DNA), which is in turn bonded to a nitrogen-containing base (adenine, guanine, cytosine, or thymine in DNA). Nucleotides are linked together, forming a strand of nucleic acid, as follows: Bonds between the phosphate of one nucleotide link to the sugar of the next nucleotide.

replication: the copying of the double-stranded DNA molecule, producing two identical DNA double helices.

semiconservative replication: the process of replication of the DNA double helix; the two DNA strands separate, and each is used as a template for the synthesis of a complementary DNA strand. Consequently, each daughter double helix consists of one parental strand and one new strand.

THINKING THROUGH THE CONCEPTS

True or False: Determine if the statement given is true or false. If it is false, change the <u>underlined</u> word(s) so that the statement reads true.

24. _____   A molecule of DNA is <u>single</u>-stranded.

25. _____   DNA contains four types of <u>sugars</u>.

26. _____   Sugars found in DNA have <u>five</u> carbons each.

27. _____   DNA is found in cellular <u>chromosomes</u>.

28. _____   DNA contains sugars, bases, and <u>sulfur</u> groups.

29. _____   A DNA molecule contains <u>equal amounts of</u> A and T, <u>and of</u> C and G.

30. _____   The concentration of DNA is <u>constant</u> for different body cells of the same species.

31. _____   Adenine pairs with <u>guanine</u> in DNA.

32. _____   The duplication of DNA is called <u>fully</u>-conservative replication.

33. _____   The building blocks of nucleic acids are <u>amino acids</u>.

Matching: Complementary base pairs.

34. _____   complementary base to adenine (A)   Choices:

35. _____   complementary base to guanine (G)   a.   adenine (A)

36. _____   complementary base pairs in DNA   b.   cytosine (C)

37. _____   complementary base to cytosine (C)   c.   guanine (G)

38. _____   complementary base to thymine (T)   d.   thymine (T)

                                                          e.   A-T and G-C

                                                          f.   A-G and T-C

Identification: Determine whether the numbered structures refer to a **nucleotide**, a **deoxyribose**, a nitrogen containing **base** or a **phosphate group**.

39. _____

40. _____

41. _____

42. _____

43. _____

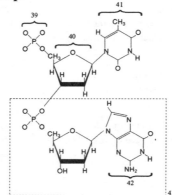

Multiple Choice: Pick the most correct choice for each question.

44. If amounts of bases in a DNA molecule are measured, we find that
    a. A = C and G = T
    b. A = G and C = T
    c. T = A and C = G
    d. no two bases are equal in amount
    e. all bases are equal in amount

45. Which of the following statements about DNA are <u>not</u> true?
    a. no sugar is present in the molecule
    b. hydrogen bonding is important
    c. it has a backbone of sugars and phosphates
    d. adenine pairs with the base uracil
    e. adenine pairs with the base thymine

46. The DNA of a certain organism has guanine as 30% of its bases. What percentage of its bases would be adenine?
    a. 0%
    b. 10%
    c. 20%
    d. 30%
    e. 40%

47. The correct general structure of a nucleotide is
    a. phosphate-ribose-adenine
    b. phospholipid-sugar-base
    c. phosphate-sugar-phosphate-sugar
    d. adenine-thymine and guanine-cytosine
    e. base-phosphate-sugar

48. The two nucleotide chains in a DNA molecule are attracted to each other by
    a. covalent bonds between carbon atoms
    b. hydrogen bonds between bases
    c. peptide bonds between amino acids
    d. ionic bonds between "R" groups in amino acids
    e. covalent bonds between phosphates and sugars

49. In the analogy of DNA as a twisted ladder, the rungs (steps) of the ladder are
    a. phosphate groups
    b. sugar groups
    c. paired nitrogen-containing bases
    d. oxygen-carbon double bonds

50. All the cells of a specific organism contain equal amounts of
    a. adenine and guanine
    b. guanine and cytosine
    c. adenine and cytosine
    d. thymine and cytosine

51. The sequence of subunits in the DNA backbone is
    a. –base–phosphate–sugar–base– phosphate–sugar–
    b. –base–phosphate–base–phosphate– base–phosphate–
    c. –phosphate–sugar–phosphate–sugar– phosphate–sugar–
    d. –sugar–base–sugar–base–sugar–base– sugar–base–
    e. –base–sugar–phosphate–base–sugar– phosphate–

52. Figuratively speaking, a double helix is comparable to
    a. a coiled rope
    b. stacked-up plates
    c. braided hair
    d. a twisted ladder
    e. tangled threads

CLUES TO APPLYING THE CONCEPTS

This practice question is intended to sharpen your ability to apply critical thinking and analysis to biological concepts covered in this chapter.

53. Instead of DNA being a double-stranded molecule, imagine it as a single-stranded molecule, such that each complete molecule of DNA consists of one chain of nucleotides. If DNA were single-stranded, describe how DNA replication could take place, using the same DNA polymerase enzyme that creates complimentary base pairing, so that exact copies of genes could be made. Would this type of replication be more efficient or less efficient than replication involving double-stranded DNA? Briefly explain.

_____

_____

_____

_____

_____

_____

_____

_____

_____

_____

_____

_____

_____

_____

_____

_____

ANSWERS TO EXERCISES

24. false, double
25. false, bases
26. true
27. true
28. false, phosphorus
29. true
30. true
31. false, thymine
32. false, semi
33. false, nucleotides
34. d
35. b
36. e
37. c
38. a

39. phosphate group
40. deoxyribose
41. base
42. base
43. nucleotide
44. c
45. d
46. c
47. e
48. b
49. c
50. b
51. c
52. d

53. Suppose a hypothetical single-stranded DNA molecule has the base sequence AAAAAAAAA. During replication, the DNA polymerase would make a complementary DNA molecule with the base sequence TTTTTTTTT. Then, the DNA polymerase would have to make a complementary copy of the TTTTTTTTT DNA molecule, which would be AAAAAAAAA, the same as the original gene. Then, the TTTTTTTTT molecule would have to be broken down, since it is not a normal DNA molecule for that organism. This scheme, in which two replications yield one new DNA molecule, is much less efficient than replication of a double-stranded DNA molecule, in which one round of semi-conservative replication yields two DNA molecules.

Chapter 9: Gene Expression and Regulation

OVERVIEW

This chapter covers how genes are expressed and regulated. The authors introduce the "one-gene, one-protein" hypothesis. They present the processes of transcription (information in DNA makes RNA) and translation (information in RNA makes protein) along with the three types of RNA and their functions. Transcriptional regulation of genes in eukaryotic cells is discussed, as are the effects of mutation.

1) How Are Genes and Proteins Related?

A **gene** is a segment of DNA with a nucleotide sequence specifying the amino acid sequence of a protein. There are thousands of genes per chromosome. In general, each gene contains the information, coded in its sequence of nucleotides, needed for making a specific sequence of amino acids, a protein. This generalization is called the **one-gene, one-protein hypothesis**. Some genes code for structural proteins or for types of **RNA (ribonucleic acid)**, but most code for enzymes.

Although eukaryotic DNA is in the nucleus, protein synthesis occurs on **ribosomes** in the cytoplasm. RNA molecules carry information from the DNA to the ribosomes. RNA differs from DNA in that it (1) is single-stranded; (2) has ribose sugar in its backbone; and (3) has uracil (U) instead of thymine. There are three types of RNA: **messenger RNA (mRNA)**, **transfer RNA (tRNA)**, and **ribosomal RNA (rRNA)**. Information from DNA is used to make proteins in a two-step process: **transcription** (DNA makes mRNA which will carry the genetic information to ribosomes in the cytoplasm), and **translation** (proteins are made at the ribosomes through interactions among mRNA, tRNA, and rRNA).

In the genetic code, base sequences stand for amino acids. The **genetic code** uses sequences of three consecutive bases in mRNA (called **codons**) to specify each amino acid. Since there are four types of bases in RNA and 20 types of amino acids in proteins, there are $4^3 = 64$ possible code words for proteins (for instance, UUU in mRNA = phenylalanine in a protein). The mRNA **start codon** is AUG, coding for the first amino acid in a protein. Three codons (UAG, UAA, UGA) are mRNA **stop codons** that signal that the protein's amino acid sequence is completed.

2) What Is the Role of RNA in Protein Synthesis?

Transcription copies only one (the **template strand**) of the two strands of DNA into mRNA. Only selected genes are copied. In a long DNA molecule, one strand may be the template strand for some genes, and the other strand may be the template strand for other genes. Transcription is a three-step process: (1) initiation (the enzyme **RNA polymerase** attaches to a short sequence of bases at the beginning of the genes, the **promoter** region); (2) elongation (RNA polymerase moves along the gene, synthesizing a single strand of RNA that is complementary to the template strand of DNA, base-pairing as usual except that RNA has uracil (U) instead of thymine); and (3) termination (RNA polymerase reaches the termination signal, a sequence of DNA bases that causes the RNA molecule to separate from the DNA and from the RNA polymerase, and causes the RNA polymerase to detach from the DNA).

The mRNA carries the code (base sequence) for protein synthesis from the nucleus into the cytoplasm through pores in the nuclear envelope. The mRNA binds to ribosomes, where the sequence of mRNA codons is translated into the sequence of amino acids in a protein. Each ribosome is composed of rRNA and proteins and has two subunits: The small subunit recognizes and binds mRNA and part of tRNA, and the large subunit has an enzymatic region for adding amino acids to the growing protein chain, as well as regions for binding tRNA. The tRNA molecules decode the mRNA codons into protein amino acids. Each tRNA binds to a free amino acid and delivers it to the ribosome. The amino acids are incorporated into proteins according to mRNA instructions. Each tRNA bears three exposed bases (the **anticodon**) that pair in a complementary manner to the mRNA codons that specify where the tRNA's amino acid is to be added to the protein chain. For example, the start codon (AUG) pairs with tRNA anticodon UAC, bringing in methionine to be the first amino acid in the protein.

Like transcription, translation has three steps: (1) initiation of protein synthesis, (2) elongation of the protein chain, and (3) termination. Initiation begins with the binding of protein "initiator factors" and an initiator tRNA to the small subunit of a ribosome. The small subunit then binds to an mRNA molecule and moves along it to the start codon. The large ribosomal subunit then binds to the small subunit, and the initiator tRNA binds to the first binding site of the large subunit. Elongation begins when a second tRNA recognizes and binds to the second mRNA codon and moves into the second binding site of the ribosome. A peptide bond forms between the first and second amino acids; the first amino acid detaches from the first tRNA, which then leaves the ribosome. The ribosome shifts the second tRNA into the first binding site and attracts a third tRNA into the second binding site. The third amino acid forms a peptide bond with the second amino acid; the second amino acid detaches from the second tRNA, which then leaves the ribosome. The ribosome shifts the third tRNA into the first binding site and attracts a fourth tRNA into the second binding site. This process continues until, near the end of the mRNA, a stop codon is reached. Enzymes then cut the protein off the last tRNA, releasing it from the ribosome.

3) How Do Mutations in DNA Affect the Function of Genes?

Mutations are changes in the sequence of bases in DNA, often through a mistake in base pairing during DNA replication. In a **point mutation**, a pair of bases becomes incorrectly matched. An **insertion mutation** occurs when one or more new nucleotide pairs are inserted into a gene. A **deletion mutation** occurs when one or more nucleotide pairs are removed from a gene. Deletions and insertions can have quite harmful effects on a gene because all the codons that follow the deletion or insertion will be misread.

Four types of effects may result from mutations: (1) the protein is unchanged; (2) the new protein is equivalent if the active site is unchanged and the rest of the molecule is changed in an unimportant way; (3) protein function is changed by an altered amino acid sequence; or (4) protein function is destroyed by a misplaced stop codon, resulting in a shortened protein chain.

Mutations provide the raw material for evolution. Mutation rates vary from 1 in 10,000 to 1 in 1,000,000 gametes. If mutations in gametes are not lethal, they may be passed on to future generations. Mutation is the source for genetic variation and thus is essential for evolution.

4) How Are Genes Regulated?

Most cells in the body have identical DNA (60,000 to more than 100,000 genes) but they do not use all the DNA all the time. Gene expression changes over time, and an organism's environment can determine which genes are translated.

Eukaryotic cells may (1) regulate the transcription of individual genes, through the action of regulatory proteins such as steroid hormones; (2) regulate the transcription of regions of chromosomes with several genes, by condensing those regions into compact DNA that is inaccessible to RNA polymerase; or (3) inactivate an entire chromosome with thousands of genes, such as one of the X chromosomes in mammalian females to form a **Barr body**. Which X chromosome is inactivated in any cell is random, but all its daughter cells will have the same inactive chromosome. For example, the separate patches of orange and black fur in female calico cats are due to fur-color genes on the X chromosome active in those cells.

KEY TERMS AND CONCEPTS

Fill-In: From the following list of terms, fill in the blanks below.

anticodon	mutation	start codon
codon	one-gene, one-protein hypothesis	stop codons
deletion mutations	point mutation	transcription
genetic code	ribosome	transfer RNA
insertion mutations	RNA polymerase	translation
messenger RNA		

The (1)_____ is the amino acid meanings of all the codons, each of which directs the incorporation of an amino acid during protein synthesis.

The enzyme that catalyzes the covalent bonding of free RNA nucleotides into a continuous strand, using the sequence of bases in DNA as a template, is called (2)_____.

The hypothesis that each gene encodes information (as a sequence of bases) needed for making one specific protein (amino acid sequence) is the (3)_____ .

A(n) (4)_____ is a sequence of three nucleotides in transfer RNA that is complementary to the three nucleotides in messenger RNA.

The process in which a sequence of nucleotide bases in mRNA is converted into a sequence of amino acids in a protein is called (5)_____.

The mRNA (6)_____ is AUG, coding for the first amino acid in a protein. Three codons (UAG, UAA, UGA) are mRNA (7)_____, signals that the protein's amino acid sequence is completed.

A molecule of (8)_____ is a strand of nucleotides, complementary to the DNA of a gene, that conveys genetic information to ribosomes to be used to sequence amino acids during protein synthesis.

(9)_____ is the synthesis of an RNA molecule from a DNA template.

A change in the base sequence of DNA is a(n) (10)_____.

A molecule that binds to a specific amino acid and has a set of three nucleotides complementary to the codon for that amino acid is known as (11)_____.

In a (12)_____, a pair of bases becomes incorrectly matched; (13)_____ occur when one or more new nucleotide pairs are added into a gene; (14)_____ occur when one or more nucleotide pairs are removed from a gene.

A(n) (15)_____ is a sequence of three nucleotides of mRNA that specifies a particular amino acid to be incorporated into a protein.

An organelle with two subunits, each composed of RNA and protein, that serves as the site of protein synthesis is a (16)_____.

Key Terms and Definitions

androgen insensitivity: a rare condition in which an individual with XY chromosomes is female in appearance because the body's cells don't respond to the male hormones that are present.

anticodon: a sequence of three bases in transfer RNA that is complementary to the three bases of a codon of messenger RNA.

Barr body: an inactivated X chromosome in cells of female mammals, which have two X chromosomes; normally appears as a dark spot in the nucleus.

codon: a sequence of three bases of messenger RNA that specifies a particular amino acid to be incorporated into a protein; certain codons also signal the beginning or end of protein synthesis.

deletion mutation: a mutation in which one or more pairs of nucleotides are removed from a gene.

gene: a unit of heredity that encodes the information needed to specify the amino acid sequence of proteins and hence particular traits; a functional segment of DNA located at a particular place on a chromosome.

genetic code: the collection of codons of mRNA, each of which directs the incorporation of a particular amino acid into a protein during protein synthesis.

insertion mutation: a mutation in which one or more pairs of nucleotides are inserted into a gene.

messenger RNA (mRNA): a strand of RNA, complementary to the DNA of a gene, that conveys the genetic information in DNA to the ribosomes to be used during protein synthesis; sequences of three bases (codons) in mRNA specify particular amino acids to be incorporated into a protein.

mutation: a change in the base sequence of DNA in a gene; normally refers to a genetic change significant enough to alter the appearance or function of the organism.

one-gene, one-protein hypothesis: the prem-ise that each gene encodes the information for the synthesis of a single protein.

point mutation: a mutation in which a single base pair in DNA has been changed.

promoter: a specific sequence of DNA to which RNA polymerase binds, initiating gene transcription.

ribonucleic acid (rī-bō-noo-klā´-ik; **RNA**): a molecule composed of ribose nucleotides, each of which consists of a phosphate group, the sugar ribose, and one of the bases adenine, cytosine, guanine, or uracil; transfers hereditary instructions from the nucleus to the cytoplasm; also the genetic material of some viruses.

ribosomal RNA (rRNA): a type of RNA that combines with proteins to form ribosomes.

ribosome: an organelle consisting of two subunits, each composed of ribosomal RNA and protein; the site of protein synthesis, during which the sequence of bases of messenger RNA is translated into the sequence of amino acids in a protein.

RNA polymerase: in RNA synthesis, an enzyme that catalyzes the bonding of free RNA nucleotides into a continuous strand, using RNA nucleotides that are complementary to those of a strand of DNA.

start codon: a codon in messenger RNA that signals the beginning of protein synthesis on a ribosome.

stop codon: a codon in messenger RNA that stops protein synthesis and causes the completed protein chain to be released from the ribosome.

template strand: the strand of the DNA double helix from which RNA is transcribed.

transcription: the synthesis of an RNA molecule from a DNA template.

transfer RNA (tRNA): a type of RNA that binds to a specific amino acid by means of a set of three bases (the anticodon) on the tRNA that are complementary to the mRNA codon for that amino acid; carries its amino acid to a ribosome during protein synthesis, recognizes a codon of mRNA, and positions its amino acid for incorporation into the growing protein chain.

translation: the process whereby the sequence of bases of messenger RNA is converted into the sequence of amino acids of a protein.

Werner syndrome: a rare condition in which a defective gene causes premature aging; caused by a mutation in the gene that codes for DNA replication/repair enzymes.

THINKING THROUGH THE CONCEPTS

True or False: Determine if the statement given is true or false. If it is false, change the underlined word(s) so that the statement reads true.

17. _____   Genes are made of <u>RNA</u> in human cells.

18. _____   <u>Transfer RNA</u> carries amino acids to the ribosomes.

19. _____   Protein synthesis occurs in the <u>ribosome</u>.

20. _____   Messenger RNA is <u>double</u>-stranded.

21. _____   Messenger RNA is manufactured in the <u>cytoplasm</u>.

22. _____   The triplets of bases in messenger RNA are called <u>anticodons</u>.

23. _____   Proteins are made during <u>transcription</u>.

24. _____   Proteins contain many <u>nucleotide</u> subunits.

25. _____   Barr bodies are found in normal mammalian <u>females</u>.

26. _____   Barr bodies are <u>active</u> X chromosomes found in mammals.

Matching: Types of RNA molecules.

27. _____   has anticodons   Choices:

28. _____   deciphers the genetic code   a.   mRNA

29. _____   carries the genetic code   b.   tRNA

30. _____   picks up and transports amino acids   c.   rRNA

31. _____   part of ribosomes

32. _____   has codons

33. _____   recognizes a mRNA codon

34. _____   fits into binding sites in ribosomes

Identification: Determine whether the following statements refer to **transcription** or **translation**.

35. _____ information from DNA makes RNA

36. _____ information from RNA makes protein

37. _____ occurs in the nucleus of eukaryotic cells

38. _____ occurs in the cytoplasm of eukaryotic cells

39. _____ involves RNA polymerase

40. _____ involves amino acids

41. _____ involves ribosomes

42. _____ involves codon-anticodon interactions

43. _____ involves copying the genetic code

44. _____ involves deciphering the genetic code

Multiple Choice: Pick the most correct choice for each question.

45. The one-gene, one-protein hypothesis states that
    a. each gene is made up of a single protein
    b. a gene contains the code for one protein.
    c. a mutation always leads to a new protein.
    d. cells have only one gene
    e. cells contain different genes if they make different proteins

46. Which of the following is coded for by the *shortest* piece of DNA?
    a. a tRNA having 75 nucleotides
    b. an mRNA having 50 codons
    c. a protein having 40 amino acids
    d. a protein with 2 polypeptides, each having 35 amino acids
    e. an mRNA having 100 bases

47. If a bacterial protein has 30 amino acids, how many nucleotides are needed to code for it?
    a. 30
    b. 60
    c. 90
    d. 120
    e. 600

48. Blood cells and muscle cells make different enzymes because
    a. blood cells contain only genes for blood cell proteins and muscle cells contain only muscle protein genes
    b. all cells of an organism have all genes
    c. not every gene acts in every type of cell
    d. blood cells have hemoglobin while muscle cells have microtubules
    e. adult red blood cells lack nuclei in mammals

49. Because of random X chromosome inactivation, one of the X chromosomes of a mammalian female
    a. is functionally inactive
    b. is present in each cell in three doses
    c. does not divide during meiosis
    d. disappears from each cell early during development
    e. is genetically identical to the other X chromosome

Fill-In: Refer to the figure to the right, to answer questions 50 through 53.

50. The step indicated by (1) in the figure is commonly known as

    _____.

51. The step indicated by (1) in the figure is carried out by the enzyme

    _____.

52. The step indicated by (2) in the figure is commonly known as

    _____.

53. The step indicated by (2) in the figure occurs on

    _____

    in the cytoplasm.

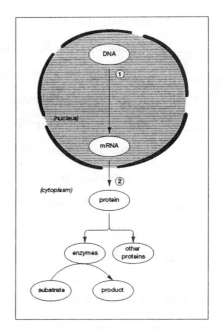

Fill In. Complete the following table.

Type of molecule	Sequences of bases or amino acids See text Table 9-2 for genetic code.					
54. DNA template strand	_____	TAG	_____	AGC	_____	TCA
55. DNA non-template strand	GAA	_____	TTA	_____	CCG	_____
56. messenger RNA codons	_____	_____	_____	_____	_____	_____
57. transfer RNA anticodons	_____	_____	_____	_____	_____	_____
58. protein amino acid sequence	_____	_____	_____	_____	_____	_____

Fill-In: Fill in the blanks below.

Suppose a section of DNA from a normal gene has the following sequences of bases in one of its polynucleotide strands:

normal base sequence:　　　TACTTTACGTCGTGAAAACGGTAT

If this strand is used to make a mRNA molecule:

• the base sequence in the mRNA is (59)_____

• the normal amino acid sequence in the polypeptide is (use text Table 9-2)

(60)_____

Now, suppose a point mutation occurs and a single base (C*) is added (an insertion mutation) to the gene sequence, causing a new, altered sequence to occur:

mutant base sequence:　　　TACC*TTTACGTCGTGAAAACGGTAT

If this mutant strand is used to make a mRNA molecule:

• the base sequence in the mRNA is (61)_____

• the abnormal amino acid sequence in the polypeptide is (use text Table 9-2)

(62)_____

CLUES TO APPLYING THE CONCEPTS

This practice question is intended to sharpen your ability to apply critical thinking and analysis to biological concepts covered in this chapter.

63. Briefly explain why in questions 59 through 62 the addition of a single base in the DNA caused so many amino acids to change in the polypeptide.

_____

_____

_____

_____

_____

_____

_____

_____

_____

ANSWERS TO EXERCISES

1. genetic code
2. RNA polymerase
3. one-gene, one-protein hypothesis
4. anticodon
5. translation
6. start codon
7. stop codons
8. messenger RNA (mRNA)
9. transcription
10. mutation
11. transfer RNA (tRNA)
12. point mutation
13. insertion mutations
14. deletion mutations
15. codon
16. ribosome
17. false, DNA
18. true

19. true
20. false, single
21. false, nucleus
22. false, codons
23. false, translation
24. false, amino acid
25. true
26. false, inactive
27. b
28. b
29. a
30. b
31. c
32. a
33. b
34. b
35. transcription
36. translation

37. transcription
38. translation
39. transcription
40. translation
41. translation
42. translation
43. transcription
44. translation
45. b
46. a
47. c
48. c
49. a
50. transcription
51. RNA polymerase
52. translation
53. ribosomes

Type of molecule	Sequences of bases or amino acids See text Table 9-2 for genetic code.					
54. DNA template strand	CTT	TAG	AAT	AGC	GGC	TCA
55. DNA non-template strand	GAA	ATC	TTA	TCG	CCG	AGT
56. messenger RNA codons	GAA	AUC	UUA	UCG	CCG	AGU
57. transfer RNA anticodons	CUU	UAG	AAU	AGC	GGC	UCA
58. protein amino acid sequence	glutamic acid	isoleucine	leucine	serine	proline	serine

59. AUG-AAA-UGC-AGC-ACU-UUU-GCC-AUA

60. methionine-lysine-cysteine-serine-threonine-phenylalanine-alanine-isoleucine

61. AUG-GAA-AUG-CAG-CAC-UUU-UGC-CAU-A

62. methionine-glutamic acid-methionine-glutamine-histidine-phenylalanine-cysteine-histidine-

63. The reason so many amino acids are changed is that the addition of one base causes all the codons to become different because they are read by ribosomes as three consecutive mRNA bases and the addition of one base results in a shift in the "reading frame" the ribosome uses to determine the codons.

Chapter 10: The Continuity of Life: Cellular Reproduction

OVERVIEW

This chapter focuses on mitosis and meiosis. After briefly discussing the cell cycle in prokaryotes, the authors cover mitosis, a basic type of eukaryotic cell division. They describe the structure of eukaryotic chromosomes and review the typical chromosome numbers in body cells and sex cells. The eukaryotic cell cycle is discussed, as well as the stages it includes: interphase, mitosis, and cytokinesis. Then, the authors focus on meiosis. They describe the stages of meiosis I and meiosis II as they relate to the production of sex cells. Meiosis I and II are compared, as are mitosis and meiosis.

1) What Are the Essential Features of Cell Division?

The DNA of all cells is packaged in **chromosomes** (darkly staining nuclear rods of condensed DNA and protein). In nondividing cells, chromosomal material is called **chromatin** (thin, uncondensed DNA and protein). When a cell divides, it passes on (1) a complete set of hereditary information (the chromosomes) and (2) cytoplasmic materials essential for survival. The **cell cycle** includes cell activities from one cell division to the next.

2) What Are the Events of the Prokaryotic Cell Cycle?

The DNA of prokaryotic cells is found in a single, circular chromosome within the cytoplasm. Cell division in prokaryotes is called **binary fission**, and their cell cycle can occur in 30 minutes or less. The cell absorbs nutrients, grows, replicates its DNA, and divides. Steps in the prokaryotic cell cycle are as follows: (1) one point on the chromosome attaches to the plasma membrane; (2) binary fission begins when the chromosome replicates, each identical chromosome attaching at a separate point of the plasma membrane; (3) the cell elongates, pushing the chromosomes apart; (4) the plasma membrane, around the middle of the cell, grows inward; and (5) two new daughter cells form, each receiving one of the replicated chromosomes and about half the cytoplasm.

3) What Is the Structure of the Eukaryotic Chromosome?

Each human cell has a total of 200 centimeters (6.5 feet) of DNA in its chromosomes. Most chromosomes consist of two arms extending from a **centromere**. Before cells divide, each chromosome replicates to form a duplicated chromosome, with its two copies (identical sister **chromatids**) attached at their centromeres. During cell division, the two sister chromatids separate, and each chromatid becomes an independent daughter chromosome.

Eukaryotic chromosomes usually occur in pairs (called **homologues**) with similar size, staining pattern, and genetic information. Cells with pairs of homologous chromosomes are called **diploid** ($2n$). Nonreproductive cells (such as human body cells) have 46 chromosomes that can be organized into 23 homologous pairs. At some point in the life cycle of sexually reproducing organisms, **meiosis** produces **haploid** cells (n) called **gametes** (sperm and egg), with one copy of each type of chromosome.

4) What Are the Events of the Eukaryotic Cell Cycle?

Growth, replication of chromosomes, and most cell functions occur during **interphase**, the period between cell divisions. During the first part of interphase, the cell acquires nutrients, performs specialized functions, and grows. Cells then either enter a nondividing state or begin to prepare to divide by duplicating each chromosome. For the remainder of interphase, cells make molecules required for cell division.

   Mitotic cell division consists of nuclear division (**mitosis**) and cytoplasmic division (**cytokinesis**). The two cells produced by mitotic cell division are essentially identical to each other cytoplasmically and genetically identical to the parent cell. Different types of body cells (brain and liver, for example) are genetically identical but undergo **differentiation**, the process by which cells assume specialized functions because they use different genes as they develop.

5) What Are the Phases of Mitosis?

Mitosis has four phases within a continuous process: (1) **prophase** (chromosomes condense and microtubular **spindle fibers** form from the **centrioles** and attach to the chromosomes); (2) **metaphase** (chromosomes become aligned along the equator of the cell); (3) **anaphase** (sister chromatids separate and are pulled to opposite poles of the cell); and (4) **telophase** (nuclear envelopes form around both groups of chromosomes). Each sister chromatid has a **kinetochore** (attachment point for spindle fibers) located at the centromere.

6) What Are the Events of Cytokinesis?

In most cells, cytokinesis occurs during telophase, enclosing each daughter nucleus into a separate cell. In animal cells, microfilaments attached to the plasma membrane around the equator contract and constrict the equator region, pinching the cell in two. In plant cells, the Golgi complex buds off carbohydrate-filled vesicles along the equator. The vesicles fuse, forming the **cell plate**, which expands to fuse with the plasma membrane. Cytokinesis is followed by interphase.

7) What Are the Functions of Mitotic Cell Division?

Mitotic cell division has two primary functions : (1) growth (from zygote to adult), maintenance, and repair of body tissues; and (2) **asexual reproduction** (the formation of genetically identical offspring, **clones**, without fusion of eggs and sperm) in simple organisms and plants.

8) What Are the Events of Meiosis?

Meiosis separates homologous chromosomes in a diploid nucleus, producing haploid daughter nuclei. In **meiotic cell division** (meiosis followed by cytokinesis), each new cell receives one member from each pair of homologous chromosomes. Meiosis involves two nuclear divisions (meiosis I and II), and the following events occur: (1) Chromosomes replicate before meiosis begins; (2) during meiosis I, duplicated homologous chromosomes separate, one duplicated chromosome moving into each of the two daughter cells ($2n$ becomes a pair of n cells); (3) in meiosis II, the sister chromatids in each daughter cell separate, and cytokinesis may occur to produce four haploid cells, each with one set of unduplicated chromosomes (each haploid cell with duplicated chromosomes becomes a pair of n cells with unduplicated chromosomes).

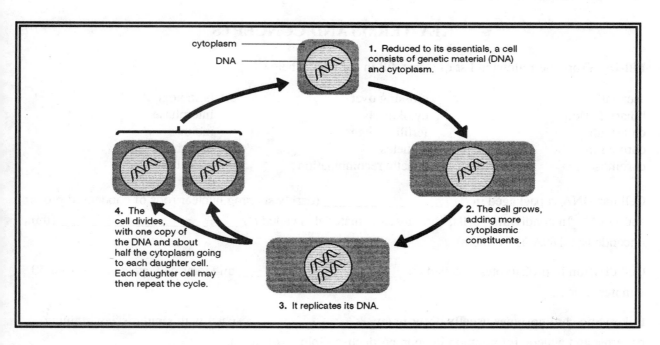

cytoplasm

DNA

1. Reduced to its essentials, a cell consists of genetic material (DNA) and cytoplasm.

2. The cell grows, adding more cytoplasmic constituents.

3. It replicates its DNA.

4. The cell divides, with one copy of the DNA and about half the cytoplasm going to each daughter cell. Each daughter cell may then repeat the cycle.

Meiosis I separates homologous chromosomes into two daughter nuclei. During prophase I, homologous chromosomes pair up and exchange DNA through **crossing over** and the formation of **chiasmata** (regions of exchange), resulting in genetic **recombination** (the formation of new combinations of different alleles on a chromosome). During metaphase I, paired homologous chromosomes move to the equator of the cell. Different pairs of chromosomes align themselves randomly at the equator, allowing independent assortment to occur. During anaphase I, homologous chromosomes separate. During telophase I, two haploid clusters of chromosomes form. Meiosis II (very similar to mitosis) separates sister chromatids. During anaphase II, the centromeres holding sister chromatids together split, and spindle fibers pull each chromatid (daughter chromosome) to opposite poles.

9) What Are the Roles of Meiosis and Sexual Reproduction in Producing Genetic Variability?

During metaphase I, random alignment of homologous chromosomes at the equator creates new combinations of chromosomes. Crossing over creates chromosomes with new combinations of genes. Fusion of gametes adds further genetic variability to the offspring. In humans there are 2^{23}, or about 8 million, different types of gametes based on random alignment of homologous chromosomes during metaphase I. The fusion of gametes from just two people makes 8 million x 8 million (or 64 trillion) possible genetically different children. Crossing over increases this number substantially.

KEY TERMS AND CONCEPTS

Fill-In: From the following list of terms, fill in the blanks below.

asexual	crossing over	homologous
binary fission	cytokinesis	interphase
chiasmata	fertilized egg	meiosis
chromatin	gametes	mitosis
chromosomes	genetic recombination	variation

Cellular DNA is packaged in (1)_____ (darkly staining nuclear rods of condensed protein and DNA). In nondividing cells, chromosomal material is called (2)_____ (thin, uncondensed DNA and protein).

Cell division in prokaryotes is called (3)_____, and their cell cycle an occur in 30 minutes or less.

Eukaryotic chromosomes usually occur in (4)_____ pairs with similar sizes, staining patterns, and genetic information in nonreproductive diploid cells ($2n$).

At some point in the life cycle of sexually reproducing organisms, (5)_____ produces haploid cells (n) called (6)_____ (sperm and egg), with one copy of each type of chromosome.

Growth, replication of chromosomes, and most cell functions occur during (7)_____, the period between cell divisions.

Mitotic cell division consists of nuclear division or (8)_____and cytoplasmic division called (9)_____.

(10)_____ reproduction (formation of genetically identical offspring without fusion of eggs and sperm) occurs in simple organisms and plants.

The reshuffling of genes among individuals to create genetically unique offspring results in increased genetic (11)_____.

Sperm and egg fuse to yield a $2n$ cell, the (12)_____ (zygote) that divides mitotically to form the adult body.

(13)_____ separates homologous chromosomes in a diploid nucleus, producing haploid daughter nuclei.

Meiosis I separates homologous chromosomes into two daughter nuclei. During prophase I, homologous chromosomes pair up and exchange DNA through (14)_____ and the formation of (15)_____ (regions of exchange), resulting in (16)_____ (the formation of new combinations of different alleles on a chromosome).

Key Terms and Definitions

anaphase (an´-a-fāz): in mitosis, the stage in which the sister chromatids of each chromosome separate from one another and are moved to opposite poles of the cell; in meiosis I, the stage in which homologous chromosomes, consisting of two sister chromatids, are separated; in meiosis II, the stage in which the sister chromatids of each chromosome separate from one another and are moved to opposite poles of the cell.

asexual reproduction: reproduction that does not involve the fusion of haploid sex cells. The parent body may divide and new parts regenerate, or a new, smaller individual may form as an attachment to the parent, to drop off when complete.

binary fission: the process by which a single bacterium divides in half, producing two identical offspring.

cell cycle: the sequence of events in the life of a cell, from one division to the next.

cell plate: in plant cell division, a series of vesicles that fuse to form the new plasma membranes and cell wall separating the daughter cells.

centriole (sen´-trē-ōl): in animal cells, a short, barrel-shaped ring consisting of nine microtubule triplets; a microtubule-containing structure at the base of each cilium and flagellum; gives rise to the microtubules of cilia and flagella and is involved in spindle formation during cell division.

centromere (sen´-trō-mēr): the region of a replicated chromosome at which the sister chromatids are held together until they separate during cell division.

chiasma (kī-as´-muh; pl., **chiasmata**): a point at which a chromatid of one chromosome crosses with a chromatid of the homologous chromosome during prophase I of meiosis; the site of exchange of chromosomal material between chromosomes.

chromatid (krō´-ma-tid): one of the two identical strands of DNA and protein that forms a replicated chromosome. The two sister chromatids are joined at the centromere.

chromatin (krō´-ma-tin): the complex of DNA and proteins that makes up eukaryotic chromosomes.

chromosome (krō´-mō-sōm): in eukaryotes, a linear strand composed of DNA and protein, located in the nucleus of a cell, that contains the genes; in prokaryotes, a circular strand composed solely of DNA.

clone: offspring that are produced by mitosis and are therefore genetically identical to each other.

cloning: the process of producing many identical copies of a gene; also the production of many genetically identical copies of an organism.

crossing over: the exchange of corresponding segments of the chromatids of two homologous chromosomes during meiosis.

cytokinesis (sī-tō-ki-nē´-sis): the division of the cytoplasm and organelles into two daughter cells during cell division; normally occurs during telophase of mitosis.

differentiation: the process whereby relatively unspecialized cells, especially of embryos, become specialized into particular tissue types.

diploid (dip´-loid): referring to a cell with pairs of homologous chromosomes.

gamete (gam´-ēt): a haploid sex cell formed in sexually reproducing organisms.

haploid (hap´-loid): referring to a cell that has only one member of each pair of homologous chromosomes.

homologue (hō-mō-log): a chromosome that is similar in appearance and genetic information to another chromosome with which it pairs during meiosis; also called *homologous chromosome*.

interphase: the stage of the cell cycle between cell divisions; the stage in which chromosomes are replicated and other cell functions occur, such as growth, movement, and acquisition of nutrients.

kinetochore (ki-net´-ō-kor): a protein structure that forms at the centromere regions of chromosomes; attaches the chromosomes to the spindle.

meiosis (mī-ō´-sis): a type of cell division, used by eukaryotic organisms, in which a diploid cell divides twice to produce four haploid cells.

meiotic cell division: meiosis followed by cytokinesis.

metaphase (met´-a-fāz): the stage of mitosis in which the chromosomes, attached to spindle fibers at kinetochores, are lined up along the equator of the cell.

mitosis (mī-tō´-sis): a type of nuclear division, used by eukaryotic cells, in which one copy of each chromosome (already duplicated during interphase before mitosis) moves into each of two daughter nuclei; the daughter nuclei are therefore genetically identical to each other.

mitotic cell division: mitosis followed by cytokinesis.

prophase (prō´-fāz): the first stage of mitosis, in which the chromosomes first become visible in the light microscope as thickened, condensed threads and the spindle begins to form; as the spindle is completed, the nuclear envelope breaks apart, and the spindle fibers invade the nuclear region and attach to the kinetochores of the chromosomes. Also, the first stage of meiosis: In meiosis I, the homologous chromosomes pair up and exchange parts at chiasmata; in meiosis II, the spindle re-forms and chromosomes attach to the microtubules.

recombination: the formation of new combinations of the different alleles of each gene on a chromosome; the result of crossing over.

spindle fiber: a football-shaped array of microtubules that moves the chromosomes to opposite poles of a cell during anaphase of meiosis and mitosis.

telophase (tēl´-ō-fāz): in mitosis, the final stage, in which a nuclear envelope re-forms around each new daughter nucleus, the spindle fibers disappear, and the chromosomes relax from their condensed form; in meiosis I, the stage during which the spindle fibers disappear and the chromosomes normally relax from their condensed form; in meiosis II, the stage during which chromosomes relax into their extended state, nuclear envelopes re-form, and cytokinesis occurs.

THINKING THROUGH THE CONCEPTS

True or False: Determine if the statement given is true or false. If it is false, change the underlined word(s) so that the statement reads true.

17. _____   Asexually produced organisms are <u>similar but not identical</u> to their parents.

18. _____   Prokaryotes have <u>many</u> chromosomes per cell.

19. _____   The somatic, or body cells, of a human are <u>haploid</u>.

20. _____   A fertilized egg is <u>diploid</u>.

21. _____   Diploid organisms contain <u>two copies</u> of each chromosome type.

22. _____   DNA replication occurs during <u>mitosis</u>.

23. _____   Cell plates form during <u>metaphase</u> of the cell cycle.

24. _____   Diploid cells produce haploid cells by the process of <u>meiosis</u>.

25. _____   Crossing over occurs during <u>meiosis II</u>.

26. _____   In plants, a <u>cell plate</u> forms dur cytokinesis, producing two daughter cells.

27. _____   Reduction of chromosome number occurs during <u>meiosis I</u>.

28. _____   DNA <u>replicates</u> between meiosis I and meiosis II.

29. _____   <u>Meiosis II</u> resembles mitosis.

30. _____   Sister chromatids become daughter chromosomes during <u>anaphase I</u> of meiosis.

Identification: Determine whether the following statements refer to **mitosis**, **meiosis**, **both**, or **neither**.

31. _____   production of haploid cells from haploid cells

32. _____   the mechanism by which unicellular organisms reproduce

33. _____   produces genetically variable cells

34. _____   produces sperm and egg cells in animals

35. _____   allows multicellular organisms to grow

36. _____   produces genetically identical prokaryotic cells

37. _____   ensures that each body cell gets a complete set of genes

38. _____   can produce haploid cells

39. _____   cell division used by bacteria

40. _____   produces genetically identical cells

41. _____   produces haploid cells from diploid cells

42. _____   occurs in the human body

43. _____   maintains the same number of chromosomes

44. _____   doubles the number of chromosomes

45. _____   reduces the number of chromosomes by half

46. _____   chromosomes replicate once

47. _____   cells divide twice

Identification: Determine whether the following statements refer to the **prophase, metaphase, anaphase,** or **telophase** stage of mitosis.

48. _____ chromosomes have reached the opposite ends of the spindle

49. _____ chromosomes migrate to the cell's equator

50. _____ replicated chromosomes coil up and condense

51. _____ the centromeres divide

52. _____ daughter chromosomes move to the poles

53. _____ the spindle breaks down

54. _____ the nuclear envelope disintegrates

55. _____ sister chromatids become daughter chromosomes

56. _____ the spindle forms

57. _____ cytokinesis begins

Matching: Meiosis.

58. _____ individual chromosomes migrate to the equator

59. _____ chiasmata form

60. _____ chromosomes, each with 2 chromatids, move toward the poles

61. _____ centromeres divide

62. _____ homologous chromosomes pair up

63. _____ daughter chromosomes migrate toward opposite poles

64. _____ homologous pairs of chromosomes move together to the equator

65. _____ crossing over occurs

66. _____ homologous chromosomes move toward opposite poles

Choices:

a.   prophase I

b.   metaphase I

c.   anaphase I

d.   telophase I

e.   prophase II

f.   metaphase II

g.   anaphase II

h.   telophase II

Multiple Choice: Pick the most correct choice for each question.

67. The genetic material in bacteria consists of
    a. several circular DNA molecules
    b. one circular RNA molecule
    c. many rodlike DNA molecules
        with protein
    d. one circular DNA molecule
    e. DNA in mitochondria

68. The daughter cells of binary fission are
    a. structurally identical
    b. chromosomally different
    c. genetically identical
    d. structurally similar and genetically identical
    e. not genetically the same as the parent cell

69. Cell reproduction in prokaryotic cells differs
    from that in eukaryotic cells in that
    a. prokaryotic cells reproduce asexually, but
        eukaryotic cells do not
    b. each prokaryotic cell has a circular
        chromosome, but the chromosomes of
        eukaryotic cells are linear
    c. prokaryotic cells lack nuclei and do not
        replicate their DNA before dividing, but
        eukaryotic cells have nuclei and replicate
        their DNA before dividing
    d. prokaryotic chromosomes have DNA and
        protein, but eukaryotic chromosomes are
        made of only DNA
    e. they do not differ significantly

70. A diploid cell contains six chromosomes.
    After meiosis I, each of the cells contains
    a. three maternal and three paternal
        chromosomes each time
    b. a mixture of maternal and paternal
        chromosomes totaling three
    c. six maternal or six paternal chromosomes
        each time
    d. a mixture of maternal and paternal
        chromosomes totaling six
    e. three pairs of chromosomes

71. Which of the following does not occur during
    prophase?
    a. the nuclear membrane disintegrates
    b. nucleoli break up
    c. the spindle apparatus forms
    d. the chromosomes condense
    e. DNA replicates

72. In sexually reproducing organisms, the source
    of chromosomes in the offspring is
    a. almost all from one parent, usually the
        father
    b. almost all from one parent, usually the
        mother
    c. half from the father and half from the
        mother
    d. a random mixing of chromosomes from
        both parents

73. Meiosis results in the production of
    a. diploid cells with unpaired chromosomes
    b. diploid cells with paired chromosomes
    c. haploid cells with unpaired chromosomes
    d. haploid cells with paired chromosomes
    e. none of the above

74. A region of attachment for two sister
    chromatids is the
    a. centriole
    b. centromere
    c. equator
    d. microtubule
    e. spindle fiber

75. Which of the following occurs in meiosis I but
    not in meiosis II?
    a. diploid daughter cells are produced
    b. chromosomes without chromatids line up
        at the equator
    c. centromeres divide
    d. homologous chromosomes pair
    e. the spindle apparatus forms

CLUES TO APPLYING THE CONCEPTS

These practice questions are intended to sharpen your ability to apply critical thinking and analysis to biological concepts covered in this chapter.

76. Suppose you are working in a lab that grows various types of human body cells in petri dishes, a technique known as "cell culturing." While you are looking at one particular cell culture under the microscope, you decide to count up the numbers of cells you see in the various phases of the mitotic cell cycle. You count 45 cells in anaphase, 34 cells in prophase, 23 cells in telophase, 11 cells in metaphase, and 1008 cells in interphase – a total of 1121 cells. Could you use these numbers to determine the relative amounts of time this cell type spends in each phase of the mitotic cell cycle? Explain.

_____

_____

_____

_____

_____

_____

_____

_____

_____

_____

_____

_____

77. Suppose that the cloning process used to make the ewe named Dolly becomes widely used to clone human beings. What might be the effect of widespread cloning on human populations?

_____

_____

_____

_____

_____

_____

_____

ANSWERS TO EXERCISES

1. chromosomes	20. true	39. neither	58. f
2. chromatin	21. true	40. mitosis	59. a
3. binary fission	22. false, interphase	41. meiosis	60. c
4. homologous	23. false, cytokinesis	42. both	61. g
5. meiosis	24. true	43. mitosis	62. a
6. gametes	25. false, meiosis I	44. neither	63. g
7. interphase	26. true	45. meiosis	64. b
8. mitosis	27. true	46. both	65. a
9. cytokinesis	28. false, does not replicate	47. meiosis	66. c
10. asexual	29. true	48. telophase	67. d
11. sexual	30. false, anaphase II	49. metaphase	68. d
12. zygote	31. mitosis	50. prophase	69. b
13. meiosis	32. mitosis	51. anaphase	70. b
14. crossing over	33. meiosis	52. anaphase	71. e
15. chiasmata	34. meiosis	53. telophase	72. d
16. genetic recombination	35. mitosis	54. prophase	73. c
17. false, identical	36. neither	55. anaphase	74. b
18. false, one	37. mitosis	56. prophase	75. d
19. false, diploid	38. both	57. telophase	

76. If the cells are dividing randomly in the culture dish, you can relate the percentage of time the cells spend in each phase of the cell cycle with the percentage of cells observed at each stage of the cell cycle. For instance, if cells spend 50% of the time in interphase, you would expect to find about half of the actively dividing cells in interphase at any particular time. So, if you saw 1121 cells and 34 (34/1121 = 3.0%) were in prophase, 11 (1.0%) were in metaphase, 45 (4.0%) were in anaphase, 23 (2.1%) were in telophase, and 1008 (89.9%) were in interphase, the percentages would indicate the relative amounts of time the cells spend in each phase of the cell cycle. If the average time for a complete mitotic division is known for the cells growing in the culture, these percentages could be used to determine the amounts of time cells spend in each phase. For instance, if it takes 24 hours (1140 minutes) for a complete cell cycle, these cells spend about 34 minutes (3% of 1140) in prophase, 11 minutes in metaphase, 46 minutes in anaphase, 24 minutes in telophase, and 1025 minutes in interphase.

77. One effect might be a reduction in genetic variation in human populations as fewer types of people produce more and more copies of themselves. There is a danger of eugenic manipulation of human traits, since those with "superior" traits might be cloned and those with "inferior" traits might be prohibited from being cloned (or even from reproducing at all). Another effect might be a skewing of sex ratios as more males and fewer females may be cloned, especially in countries where males are considered more "valuable" to society than females. A much higher male sex ratio could, in turn, lead to other societal changes, such as legalized prostitution.

Chapter 11: Patterns of Inheritance

OVERVIEW

This chapter presents Mendel's concepts of inheritance: the segregation and independent assortment of genes, the dominance and recessiveness of different alleles, and the randomness of fertilization. The authors cover the relationship of genes to chromosomes, especially sex-linkage, sex determination, linkage, and crossing over. They also present variations on the Mendelian theme, including mutation, incomplete dominance, multiple alleles, polygenic inheritance, gene interactions, and environmental influences. Chromosomal nondisjunction as a cause of humans with abnormal numbers of chromosomes is discussed, and the more common results of nondisjunction (Turner syndrome, Trisomy X, Klinefelter syndrome, XYY males, and Down syndrome) are presented.

1) How Did Gregor Mendel Lay the Foundation for Modern Genetics?

A gene's specific location on a chromosome is its **locus**. Homologous chromosomes carry similar genes at similar loci. Slightly different DNA nucleotide sequences at the same gene locus on two homologous chromosomes produce alternate forms of the gene, called **alleles**. If both homologous chromosomes in an organism have identical alleles, the organism is **homozygous** at that locus; if the alleles are different, the organism is **heterozygous** at that locus and is called a **hybrid**.

Mendel was successful in his genetics experiments because he: (1) chose the right organism to work with (garden peas which reproduce by **self-fertilization** and are thus **true-breeding**, or homozygous, and not by **cross-fertilization**); (2) designed and performed the experiment correctly, choosing easy-to-distinguish traits and counting up all the offspring from each mating; and (3) analyzed the data properly, using simple statistics such as determining the ratios of offspring with differing traits.

2) How Are Single Traits Inherited?

The inheritance of dominant and recessive alleles on homologous chromosomes can explain the results of Mendel's crosses. For example, purple flowers (*PP*) x white flowers (*pp*) $\rightarrow$ purple flowers (*Pp*); purple flowers (*Pp*) x purple flowers (*Pp*) $\rightarrow$ 75% purple flowers (*PP*) and (*Pp*) and 25% white flowers (*pp*), a 3:1 ratio. Mendel's hypothesis in modern terms is that (1) each trait is determined by a pair of genes, found at corresponding loci in homologous chromosomes; (2) the members of a gene pair separate from each other during meiosis, so each gamete receives only one copy (**law of segregation**); (3) which member of a pair of genes becomes included in a gamete is a matter of chance (**law of independent assortment**); (4) in heterozygous individuals, the **dominant** allele may mask the expression of the **recessive** allele without changing its structure; and (5) true-breeding organisms are homozygous, and. hybrids are heterozygous. The actual combination of alleles carried by an organism is its **genotype** (*PP*, *Pp*, and *pp*, for example), whereas the organism's traits (things that can be seen or measured) are its **phenotype** (for example, purple or white flower color).

Mendel's hypothesis can be used to predict the outcome of new types of single-gene crosses. For instance, cross-fertilization of an individual with the dominant phenotype but unknown genotype (purple flower with either *PP* or *Pp* genotype) with a homozygous recessive individual (white flower = *pp*) is called a **test cross**, and can be used to determine the exact genotype of the dominant parent (*Pp* if recessive offspring occur, *PP* if no recessive offspring occur).

3) How Are Multiple Traits on Different Chromosomes Inherited?

Multiple traits may be controlled by genes on different chromosomes,. Such traits are inherited independently of each other (law of independent assortment). For example, smooth yellow seeds (*SSYY*) x wrinkled green seeds (*ssyy*) → smooth yellow seeds (*Ss Yy*); smooth yellow seeds (*Ss Yy*) x smooth yellow seeds (*Ss Yy*) → 9/16 smooth yellow seeds (*S-Y-*) + 3/16 smooth green seeds (*S-yy*) + 3/16 wrinkled yellow seeds (*ssY-*) + 1/16 wrinkled green seeds (*ssyy*), a 9:3:3:1 ratio. Genes for seed color and seed shape are inherited independently of each other (move independently of each other during meiosis) since they are located in different (non-homologous) chromosomes, which align themselves randomly during meiotic metaphase I.

4) How Are Genes Located on the Same Chromosome Inherited?

Chromosomes contain many hundreds of gene loci. Genes on the same chromosome tend to be inherited together, a situation called **linkage**. However, **crossing over** may separate linked genes, and the exchange of corresponding segments of DNA forms new gene combinations on both homologous chromosomes. This **genetic recombination** is one way that genetic variability occurs in gametes.

5) How Is Sex Determined, and How Are Sex-Linked Genes Inherited?

Females have two identical **sex chromosomes**, called X chromosomes, whereas males have one X chromosome and one Y chromosome. All other chromosomes are called **autosomes**. The sex chromosomes carried by males determine the sex of offspring (X from egg + X from sperm = daughter, X from egg + Y from sperm = son). **Sex-linked** genes are found on one sex chromosome (X or Y) but not on the other. Males express any genes found on the X chromosome, and each male inherits his X chromosome from his mother. So, the sons of a mother heterozygous for a sex-linked recessive condition (like hemophilia or color blindness) could be affected.

6) What Are Some Variations on the Mendelian Theme?

Inheritance is not usually as simple as what has been presented above. An allele is not always completely dominant over another allele, many genes exist in a population that have **multiple alleles**, and there are situations when several genes interact to produce one trait. The environment can influence the expression of a gene as well.

When **incomplete dominance** occurs, heterozygotes have a phenotype that is intermediate between the homozygotes. In snapdragons, for example, red flowers (*RR*) crossed with white flowers (*R´R´*) yield pink heterozygotes (*RR´*), which yield, when self-fertilized, 1/4 red + 2/4 pink + 1/4 white. Incomplete dominance occurs when both copies of a functional allele are needed to produce enough protein to give rise to the dominant phenotype. For example, in snapdragons, the degree of color depends on the number of active genes present. Imagine that the *R* allele is responsible for 50 units of red pigment and the *R´* allele is responsible for 0 units of red pigment. An *RR* plant would produce 100 units of red pigment in the homozygote and would have red flowers, an *RR´* plant would produce 50 units of red pigment in the heterozygote and would have pink flowers, and an *R´R´* plant would produce 0 units of red pigment in the homozygote and would produce white flowers.

Many traits (like height, skin color, and eye color) are influenced by interactions among several genes. Some traits show a continuous variation of phenotypes in a population and cannot be split up into convenient, easily defined categories. These traits show **polygenic inheritance**: The effects of two or more pairs of functionally similar genes add up to produce the phenotype. For instance, as the amount of melanin pigment increases in irises, eye color darkens from blue to green to brown to black. The more genes that contribute to a trait, the greater the number of phenotypes and the finer the distinctions between them.

Single genes typically have multiple effects on phenotype, a phenomenon called **pleiotropy**. For example, the SRY (sex-determining region of the Y chromosome) gene produces the many anatomical and hormonal differences between males and females.

The environment may influence the expression of genes. The phenotype of an organism is influenced by both its genotype and its environment. For example, the cooler body areas of a Himalayan rabbit produce hair pigment, and the warmer regions do not; human height and weight are products of genes and nutrition; human skin color is a product of genes and degree of sun exposure; and human IQ is a product of genes and educational environment.

7) How Are Human Genetic Disorders Investigated?

Because experimental crosses with humans are unethical, human geneticists search medical, historical, and family records to study past crosses, often arranged as **pedigrees** (diagrams that show the genetic relationships among a set of individuals). Since the mid-1960s, great strides have been made in understanding gene function on the molecular level.

8) How Are Human Disorders Caused by Single Genes Inherited?

Most human genetic disorders are caused by homozygous recessive alleles, since the conditions occur because the recessive genes do not generate enough enzymes. Albinism, for example, results from a defect in melanin production due to homozygosity for recessive alleles. **Sickle-cell anemia** is caused by homozygosity for a defective hemoglobin synthesis allele. A few human genetic disorders, like **Huntington's disease**, are caused by dominant alleles. Some human disorders, like red-green color blindness and **hemophilia**, are sex-linked.

9) How Do Errors in Chromosome Number Affect Humans?

Nondisjunction, defined as errors involving chromosome distribution during meiosis, produces gametes with one (or a few) extra or missing sex chromosomes or autosomes. Most embryos formed from such gametes miscarry, but some survive. Some genetic disorders are caused by abnormal numbers of sex chromosomes. These include: (1) **Turner syndrome** (XO females); (2) **Trisomy X** (XXX females); (3) **Klinefelter syndrome** (XXY males); and (4) **XYY males**. Some genetic disorders are caused by abnormal numbers of autosomes, the most common of which is **trisomy 21 (Down syndrome)**.

KEY TERMS AND CONCEPTS

Fill-In: From the following list of key terms, fill in the blanks in the following statements.

allele	Down syndrome	heterozygote	nondisjunction
carrier	gene	homozygote	phenotype
crossing over	genotype	locus	recessive
dominant			

One of several alternative forms of a particular gene is an (1)_____.

(2)_____ is a genetic disorder caused by the presence of three copies of chromosome 21.

An organism carrying two copies of the same allele of a gene is a(n) (3)_____, whereas an organism carrying two different alleles of a gene is a(n) (4)_____.

A unit of heredity containing the information for a particular characteristic is called a(n) (5)_____.

(6)_____ is an error in meiosis in which chromosomes fail to segregate properly into the daughter cells.

The genetic composition of an organism is its (7)_____, and the physical properties of an organism are called its (8)_____.

A(n) (9)_____ is an individual that is heterozygous for a recessive condition.

The physical location of a gene on a chromosome is its (10)_____.

The exchange of corresponding segments of the chromatids of two homologous chromosomes during meiosis is called (11)_____.

A(n) (12)_____ allele determines the phenotype of heterozygotes completely, whereas a(n) (13)_____ allele is expressed only in homozygotes.

Key Terms and Definitions

allele (al-ēl´): one of several alternative forms of a particular gene.

autosome (aw´-tō-sōm): a chromosome that occurs in homologous pairs in both males and females and that does not bear the genes determining sex.

carrier: an individual who is heterozygous for a recessive condition; displays the dominant phenotype but can pass on the recessive allele to offspring.

cross-fertilization: the union of sperm and egg from two individuals of the same species.

crossing over: the exchange of corresponding segments of the chromatids of two homologous chromosomes during meiosis.

dominant: an allele that can determine the phenotype of heterozygotes completely, such that they are indistinguishable from individuals homozygous for the allele; in the heterozygotes, the expression of the other (recessive) allele is completely masked.

Down syndrome: a genetic disorder caused by the presence of three copies of chromosome 21; common characteristics include mental retardation, distinctively shaped eyelids, a small mouth with protruding tongue, heart defects, and low resistance to infectious diseases; also called *trisomy 21*.

genetic recombination: the generation of new combinations of alleles on homologous chromosomes due to the exchange of DNA during crossing over.

genotype (jĕn´-ō-tīp): the genetic composition of an organism; the actual alleles of each gene carried by the organism.

hemophilia: a recessive, sex-linked disease in which the blood fails to clot normally.

heterozygous (het-er-ō-zī´-gus): carrying two different alleles of a given gene; also **hybrid**.

homozygous (hō-mō-zī´-gus): carrying two copies of the same allele of a given gene; also called **true-breeding**.

Huntington's disease: an incurable genetic disorder, caused by a dominant allele, that produces progressive brain deterioration, resulting in the loss of motor coordination, flailing movements, personality disturbances, and eventual death.

hybrid: an organism that is the offspring of parents differing in at least one genetically determined characteristic; also used to refer to the offspring of parents of different species.

incomplete dominance: a pattern of inheritance in which the heterozygous phenotype is intermediate between the two homozygous phenotypes.

independent assortment: see *law of independent assortment*.

Klinefelter syndrome: a set of characteristics typically found in individuals who have two X chromosomes and one Y chromosome; these individuals are phenotypically males but are sterile and have several femalelike traits, including broad hips and partial breast development.

law of independent assortment: the independent inheritance of two or more distinct traits; states that the alleles for one trait may be distributed to the gametes independently of the alleles for other traits.

law of segregation: Gregor Mendel's conclusion that each gamete receives only one of each parent's pair of genes for each trait.

linkage: the inheritance of certain genes as a group because they are parts of the same chromosome. Linked genes do not show independent assortment.

locus: the physical location of a gene on a chromosome.

multiple alleles: as many as dozens of alleles produced for every gene as a result of different mutations.

nondisjunction: an error in meiosis in which chromosomes fail to segregate properly into the daughter cells.

pedigree: a diagram showing genetic relationships among a set of individuals, normally with respect to a specific genetic trait.

phenotype (fēn'-ō-tīp): the physical characteristics of an organism; can be defined as outward appearance (such as flower color), as behavior, or in molecular terms (such as glycoproteins on red blood cells).

pleiotropy (plē'-ō-trō-pē): a situation in which a single gene influences more than one phenotypic characteristic.

polygenic inheritance: a pattern of inheritance in which the interactions of two or more functionally similar genes determine phenotype.

Punnett square method: an intuitive way to predict the genotypes and phenotypes of offspring in specific crosses.

recessive: an allele that is expressed only in homozygotes and is completely masked in heterozygotes.

self-fertilization: the union of sperm and egg from the same individual.

segregation: see *law of segregation*.

sex chromosome: one of the pair of chromosomes that differ between sexes and normally determine the sex of an individual; in humans, females have similar sex chromosomes (XX) whereas males have dissimilar ones (XY).

sex-linked: referring to a pattern of inheritance characteristic of genes located on one type of sex chromosome (for example, X) and not found on the other type (for example, Y); also called X-linked. In sex-linked inheritance, traits are controlled by genes carried on the X chromosome; females show the dominant trait unless they are homozygous recessive, whereas males express whichever allele is on their single X chromosome.

sickle-cell anemia: a recessive disease caused by a single amino acid substitution in the hemoglobin molecule. Sickle-cell hemoglobin molecules tend to cluster together, distorting the shape of red blood cells and causing them to break and clog capillaries.

test cross: a breeding experiment in which an individual showing the dominant phenotype is mated with an individual that is homozygous recessive for the same gene. The ratio of offspring with dominant versus recessive phenotypes can be used to determine the genotype of the phenotypically dominant individual.

trisomy 21: see *Down syndrome*.

trisomy X: a condition of females who have three X chromosomes instead of the normal two; most such women are phenotypically normal and are fertile.

true-breeding: pertaining to an individual all of whose offspring produced through self-fertilization are identical to the parental type. True-breeding individuals are homozygous for a given trait.

Turner syndrome: a set of characteristics typical of a woman with only one X chromosome: sterile, with a tendency to be very short and to lack normal female secondary sexual characteristics.

THINKING THROUGH THE CONCEPTS

True or False: Determine if the statement given is true or false. If it is false, change the underlined word(s) so that the statement reads true.

14. _____   Each trait is determined by a pair of discrete units called <u>chromosomes</u>.

15. _____   Alternate forms of a gene are called <u>chromatids</u>.

16. _____   In a heterozygote, the gene that is not expressed is <u>recessive</u>.

17. _____   An *AabbDdEeGg* individual will produce <u>16</u> different types of gametes.

18. _____ Linkage modifies Mendel's law of <u>segregation</u>.

19. _____ New combinations of traits controlled by linked genes occur because of <u>crossing over</u>.

20. _____ The crossing of red snapdragons with white snapdragons to produce pink snapdragons is an example of <u>polygenic inheritance</u>.

21. _____ Human <u>females</u> determine the sex of their children.

22. _____ Males are <u>haploid</u> for sex-linked genes.

23. _____ A son inherits sex-linked traits from his <u>father</u>.

24. _____ A person with Turner syndrome is <u>XXY</u>.

25. _____ A person with Klinefelter syndrome is a <u>male</u>.

26. _____ People who have Turner syndrome have <u>two</u> Barr bodies.

Matching: Chromosome anomalies in humans.

27. _____ an abnormal number of autosomes

28. _____ sterile males with some breast development

29. _____ females with three X chromosomes per nucleus

30. _____ may be male or female

31. _____ fertile females with normal phenotypes

32. _____ short, sterile females

33. _____ a normal number of sex chromosomes

34. _____ much more common among the babies of older mothers

35. _____ males with more than one X chromosome

36. _____ sterile females with fewer than two X chromosomes

37. _____ may have a possible predisposition toward violence

38. _____ the most common chromosome anomaly among newborns

39. _____ body cells have 45 chromosomes

40. _____ trisomy 21

41. _____ body cells have 46 chromosomes

Choices:

a. Turner syndrome

b. Klinefelter syndrome

c. trisomy X syndrome

d. XYY syndrome

e. Down syndrome

f. all of the above

g. none of the above

Multiple Choice: Pick the most correct choice for each question.

42. Which of the following could be detected by a count of the number of chromosomes in a cell of the affected person?
    a.   hemophilia
    b.   albinism
    c.   Huntington's disease
    d.   color-blindness
    e.   trisomy 21

43. Each normal human possesses in his or her body cells
    a.   2 pairs of sex chromosomes and 46 pairs of autosomes
    b.   2 pairs of sex chromosomes and 23 pairs of autosomes
    c.   1 pair of sex chromosomes and 46 pairs of autosomes
    d.   1 pair of sex chromosomes and 23 pairs of autosomes
    e.   1 pair of sex chromosomes and 22 pairs of autosomes

44. A color-blind woman marries a non color-blind man. Which of the following is true of their children?
    a.   all will be color-blind
    b.   all daughters will be normal and all sons will be carriers
    c.   all daughters will be color-blind and all sons will be normal
    d.   all daughters will be heterozygous and all sons will be color-blind
    e.   it is impossible to predict with any reasonable degree of certainty

45. A recessive allele on the X chromosome causes color-blindness. A non color-blind woman (whose father is color-blind) marries a color-blind man. What is the chance their son will be color-blind?
    a.   0
    b.   25%
    c.   50%
    d.   75%
    e.   100%

46. Hemophilia is a blood disorder caused by an X-linked recessive gene. What are the chances that the daughter of a normal man and a heterozygous woman will have hemophilia?
    a.   0
    b.   25%
    c.   50%
    d.   75%
    e.   100%

47. A color-blind boy has a non color-blind mother and a color-blind father. From which parent did he get the gene for color-blindness?
    a.   father
    b.   mother
    c.   either parent could have given him the gene

48. A man who carries a harmful X-linked gene will pass the gene on to
    a.   all of his daughters
    b.   half of his daughters
    c.   half of his sons
    d.   all of his sons
    e.   all of his children

49. Which of the following is not a genetic disorder?
    a.   sickle-cell anemia
    b.   hemophilia
    c.   albinism
    d.   Huntington's disease
    e.   malaria

50. Traits controlled by sex-linked recessive genes are expressed more often in males because
    a.   males inherit these genes from their fathers
    b.   males are always homozygous
    c.   all male offspring of a female carrier get the gene
    d.   the male has only one gene for the trait

Short Answer: Genetics Problems; Crosses Involving a Single Trait.

51. When two plants with red flowers are mated together, the offspring always are red, but if two purple-flowered plants are mated together, sometimes some of the offspring have red flowers. Which flower color is dominant?

   _____

52. In sheep, white (B) is dominant to black (b). Give the F_2 phenotypic and genotypic ratios resulting from the cross of a pure-breeding white ram with a pure-breeding black ewe.

   _____

53. If you found a white sheep and wanted to determine its genotype, what color animal would you cross it with and why?

   _____

54. Squash may be either white or yellow. However, for a squash to be white, at least one of its parents must also be white. Which color is dominant?

   _____

55. In peas, yellow seed color is dominant to green. Give the expected proportion of each color in the offspring of the following crosses.

   a) a heterozygous yellow with a heterozygous yellow _____

   b) a heterozygous yellow with a green _____

   c) a green with a green _____

56. If tall (D) is dominant to dwarf (d), give the genotypes of the parents that produce 3/4 tall plants and 1/4 dwarf plants among their progeny.

   _____

Short Answer: Genetics Problems; Crosses Involving Two Traits.

57. In pigs, mule hoof (fused hoof) is dominant (C), and cloven hoof is recessive (c). Belted coat pattern (S) is dominant to solid color (s). Give the F_2 genotype and phenotype ratios expected from the cross $CCSS$ x $ccss$.

   _____

   _____

   _____

58. In the F_2 generation of the previous question, what proportion of the cloven-hoof, belted pigs would be homozygous?

_____

_____

59. Flat tail (F) is dominant to fuzzy tail (f), and toothed (T) is dominant to toothless (t). Give the results of a cross between two completely heterozygous parents.

_____

_____

60. In rabbits, black (B) is dominant to brown (b), and spotted coat (S) is dominant to solid coat (s). Give the genotypes of the parents if a black, spotted male is crossed with a brown, solid female and all the offspring are black and spotted.

_____

61. In the preceding problem, give the genotypes of the parents if some of the offspring were brown and spotted.

_____

62. In cattle, horned (p) is recessive to hornless, or polled (P). Coat color is controlled by incompletely dominant genes, RR for red, rr for white, and Rr for roan. If two heterozygous polled, roan cattle are mated, what kinds of offspring are expected?

_____

_____

_____

63. In a cross between a yellow guinea pig and a white one, the offspring are cream-colored.

a) What is the simplest explanation for this result? _____

_____

b) What kinds of offspring are expected if two cream-colored guinea pigs mate? _____

_____

64. In carnations, red or white phenotypes are dependent on homozygous genotypes, and the heterozygotes are pink. Give the F_1 and F_2 genotypic and phenotypic ratios expected from a cross: red x white.

_____

Short Answer: Genetics Problems; Crosses Involving Sex-Linked Traits.

65. A normal woman whose father was a hemophiliac marries a normal man. What are the chances of hemophilia occurring in their children?

_____

_____

66. A woman with no history of hemophilia in her family marries a normal man whose father was a hemophiliac. What are the chances of hemophilia occurring in their children?

_____

67. Color-blindness (c) is a sex-linked recessive trait, and normal color vision (C) is dominant.

a) If two normal-visioned parents have a color-blind son, what are the parents' genotypes? _____

_____

b) What are the chances that their daughter will be color-blind?_____

_____

68. In cats, yellow is due to gene B, and black to its allele, b. These genes are sex-linked. The heterozygous condition results in tortoiseshell. What kinds of offspring (sex and color) are expected from a cross of a black male with tortoiseshell female?

_____

_____

69. In fruit flies, normal long wings are dominant (V), and vestigial (shortened) wings are recessive (v). These genes are autosomal. The sex-linked gene controlling red eye color (W) is dominant to white eyes (w). A male with red eyes and normal wings mates with a white-eyed vestigial-winged female. Give the expected ratio of phenotypes in the F_2 generation.

_____

_____

Short Answer: Genetics Problems; Crosses Involving Gene Interactions.

70. In poultry, there are two independently assorting gene loci, each with two alleles that affect the shape of a chicken's comb. One locus has a dominant allele (*R*) for rose comb and a recessive allele (*r*) for single comb. The other locus has a dominant allele (*P*) for pea comb, and its recessive allele (*p*) also produces single combs. When the two dominant genes occur together (*R-P-*), a walnut comb is produced. So, *R-P-* = walnut, *R-pp* = rose, *rrP-* = pea, and *rrpp* = single. Give the expected phenotypic ratios of offspring from the following matings:

a) *RRPP* x *rrpp* _____

b) *RrPp* x *rrpp* _____

c) *Rrpp* x *rrPp* _____

d) *RrPP* x *RrPp* _____

e) *rrPp* x *RrPP* _____

71. In humans, deafness can be the result of a recessive allele affecting the middle ear (*dd* = deaf), or another recessive allele that affects the inner ear (*ee* = deaf). Suppose two deaf parents have a child that can hear. Give the genotypes of all three individuals.

_____

72. If two hearing people, heterozygous at both loci (*DdEe*) for deafness marry, what are the chances that their first child will hear normally? What is the chance of deafness in this child?

_____

_____

CLUES TO APPLYING THE CONCEPTS

This practice question is intended to sharpen your ability to apply critical thinking and analysis to biological concepts covered in this chapter.

73. Occasionally, a family occurs in which both parents have recessive albinism but all of their children have normal amounts of skin pigmentation. Propose a genetic explanation for the inheritance of albinism in these families.

_____

_____

_____

_____

_____

_____

_____

ANSWERS TO EXERCISES

1. allele
2. Down syndrome
3. homozygote
4. heterozygote
5. gene
6. nondisjunction
7. genotype
8. phenotype
9. carrier
10. locus
11. crossing over
12. dominant
13. recessive
14. false, genes
15. false, alleles
16. true
17. true

18. false, independent assortment
19. true
20. false, incomplete dominance
21. false, males
22. true
23. false, mother
24. false, XO
25. true
26. false, no
27. e
28. b
29. c
30. e
31. c
32. a
33. e
34. f

35. b
36. a
37. d
38. e
39. a
40. e
41. g
42. e
43. e
44. d
45. c
46. a
47. b
48. a
49. e
50. d

51. Purple is dominant.

52. Genotypic ratio: 1 *BB* : 2 *Bb* : 1 *bb*; Phenotypic ratio: 3 white : 1 black

53. You would cross the white sheep with a black (*bb*) sheep. Since black is the recessive phenotype, you know that its genotype is *bb*. With this known, you use it to determine the unknown phenotype of the white sheep.

54. White is dominant.

55. a) 3/4 yellow : 1/4 green
    b) 1/2 yellow : 1/2 green
    c) all green

56. *Dd* x *Dd*

57. 9 *C-S-* mule-hoof, belted pigs : 3 *C-ss* mule-hoof, solid pigs : 3 *ccS-* cloven-hoof, belted pigs : 1 *ccss* cloven-hoof, solid pig.

58. There are 3 cloven-hoof, belted pigs, but only one is homozygous (*ccSS*); the other two are heterozygous (*ccSs*).

59. 9 *F-T-*, flat and toothed : 3 *F-tt*, flat and toothless : 3 *ffT-*, fuzzy and toothed : 1 *fftt*, fuzzy and toothless

60. Black spotted male (*BBSS*) and brown solid female (*bbss*).

61. *BbSS* male and *bbss* female

62. 3 *P-RR* polled red : 6 *P-Rr* polled roan : 3 *P-rr* polled white : 1 *ppRR* horned red: 2 *ppRr* horned roan : 1 *pprr* horned white.

63. a) Incomplete dominance in which cream is heterozygous
    b) 1 yellow : 2 cream : 1 white.

64. F$_1$: all *Rr* pink;
    F$_2$: 1/4 *rr* red : 2/4 *Rr* pink : 1/4 *rr* white.

65. Half of the sons could inherit the defective gene from the mother and get Y from the father. Half of the daughters could also inherit the defective gene from the mother but they would be heterozygous because they would also inherit a normal gene from the father.

66. None is expected to have hemophilia or to inherit the gene.

67. a) *Cc* (normal but carrier woman) and *CY* (normal man).
    b) No chance; she inherits a normal *C* gene from the father as well as either *C* or *c* from the mother.

68. Black female, tortoiseshell female, black male, yellow male

69. F$_2$ for both sexes: 3/8 red normal long, 3/8 white normal long, 1/8 red vestigial, 1/8 white vestigial

70. a) all walnut
    b) 1/4 walnut : 1/4 rose: 1/4 pea : 1/4 single
    c) 1/4 walnut : 1/4 rose: 1/4 pea : 1/4 single
    d) 3/4 walnut : 1/4 pea
    e) 1/2 walnut : 1/2 pea

71. *DDee* x *ddEE* → *DdEe*

72. 9/16 *D-E-* normal : 3/16 *D-ee* deaf : 3/16 *ddE-* deaf : 1/16 *ddee* deaf;
    so, 9/16 normal : 7/16 deaf

73. As with recessive deafness, several different genetic situations lead to albinism. In one type of albinism, the gene necessary for making an enzyme needed to convert a substrate into melanin pigment is missing (genotype *aa*); in another type of albinism, the gene necessary for transporting the substrate for melanin into the pigment-producing cells is lacking (genotype *bb*). So, both *aaBB* and *AAbb* people would have albinism. However, if *aaBB* married *AAbb*, all their children would be *AaBb* and would have normal pigmentation because the children would make the enzyme necessary to produce melanin and the enzyme necessary to transport the substrate for melanin into the pigment cells.

Chapter 12: Biotechnology

OVERVIEW

This chapter begins by describing natural examples of genetic recombination and then discusses several techniques used in recombinant DNA technology, including building DNA libraries, identifying and making copies of genes, and using the genes to modify living organisms. The methods used to locate and sequence genes also are covered. The authors discuss the medical uses of biotechnology and the ethical issues that arise.

1) What Is Biotechnology?

Biotechnology is any industrial or commercial use or alteration of organisms, cells, or biological molecules for practical purposes. Common examples are the domestication of plants and animals. Modern biotechnology uses **genetic engineering** (modification of DNA to achieve specific goals) to: (1) understand more about inheritance and gene expression; (2) better understand and treat various diseases, espcially genetic disorders; and (3) generate economic benefits, including better agricultural organisms and valuable biological molecules. One important tool is **recombinant DNA** (DNA altered by the incorporation of genes from other organisms) transferred into animals or plants by **vectors** (carriers such as bacteria or viruses) to make **transgenic** organisms.

2) How Does DNA Recombination Occur in Nature?

DNA recombination occurs naturally through processes such as sexual reproduction, bacterial **transformation**, and viral infection. Bacteria are transformed when genes are transfered between different bacteria as they pick up either free DNA from the environment or tiny circular DNA **plasmids** that often carry genes for antibiotic resistance. DNA recombination may also occur through viral infections, which may transfer DNA between bacteria (via viruses called **bacteriophages**) or between eukaryotic species.

3) What Are Some of the Methods of Biotechnology?

A **DNA library** is produced by inserting the DNA from the entire **genome** of a selected organism into bacterial plasmids, making the DNA readily accessible and easy to duplicate. Researchers use **restriction enzymes**, produced by bacteria, to cut DNA at specific nucleotide sequences that often are palindromes (mirror-image sequences like "madam"), producing small pieces of DNA with "sticky ends" that can hydrogen-bond with other pieces of DNA (from different species) with complementary sticky ends. Restriction enzymes are used to insert DNA into plasmids to build a DNA library. For example, using a restriction enzyme, bacterial plasmids and DNA from white blood cells (wbc) can be cut open to produce fragments with sticky ends, the molecules can be mixed together so that plasmids and wbc DNA hydrogen-bond at their sticky ends. Each recombinant plasmid can then be inserted into a separate bacterium; the resulting population of bacteria with recombinant plasmids constitutes a human DNA library.

Researchers can find genes of interest in a library by using **DNA probes** (sequences of nucleotides complementary to those genes) to identify bacteria in the library that carry plasmids with the gene of interest. Once the gene of interest has been located, it must be amplified. Amplification can be done either by culturing the bacteria containing the gene to create multiple copies or by using the **polymerase chain reaction (PCR)** which makes billions of copies of the gene using heat-stable DNA polymerase enzymes. The steps in PCR are: (1) separating double-stranded DNA into single strands by heating the DNA to 90°C; (2) using specific primers to start the reaction at appropriate places; (3) using heat-resistant DNA polymerase to construct new DNA copies; and (4) cooling the mixture to stop the reaction. The cycle is then repeated. Each cycle takes a few minutes, so billions of genes can be made in a single afternoon starting with a single copy.

4) What Are Some Applications of Biotechnology?

Amplified genes provide enough DNA to determine the exact base sequence of the gene. From the nucleotide sequence of the gene, the amino acid sequence of the protein it makes can be determined, which can lead to the determination of the protein's normal function in cells. This process was undertaken for the gene for **cystic fibrosis**. Information about a gene's base sequence can lead to rapid tests to determine the presence or absence of defective genes in fetuses (prenatal diagnosis), newborns, and adults.

    DNA fingerprinting facilitates genetic detection. If DNA is cut into **restriction fragments** of different sizes, these can be separated by size by **gel electrophoresis** because smaller fragments move faster through a gel through which an electrical current is flowing. If the restriction fragments from a defective gene and a normal gene differ in size (that is, they exhibit **restriction fragment length polymorphisms** or **RFLPs**), comparing the fragments on a gel can determine which genes are present. RFLPs can be used to locate mutated genes that cause genetic disorders. Researchers collect DNA from a number of genetically related people. They look for a uniquely sized DNA fragment whose presence correlates with the presence of a particular disease. RFLP analysis was used to identify the genes causing cystic fibrosis and Huntington's disease. It can then be used for the prenatal diagnosis of individuals carrying the gene.

    Genetic engineering is rapidly replacing traditional breeding techniques to produce improved varieties of crops. Recombinant plants can be made using the bacterial Ti plasmid to insert genes for desirable traits, such as cold tolerance or the ability to make insecticides against insect pests. Genetically identical organisms are then produced from clumps of cultured cells through **cloning**. Each cell will carry the inserted genes. "Gene guns" also are used to insert foreign DNA directly into plant seedlings that don't grow well in culture, although the success rates are low. The largest agricultural application of genetic engineering lies in using genes to improve resistance to various pests such as insects and weeds and to the chemicals used to kill pests. Genetic engineering may also improve other qualities of food plants and animals. For example, the Flavr-Savr® tomato ripens on the vine but remains firm longer than typical tomatoes so that they can be harvested later (to taste better) and shipped without damage.

5) What Are Some Medical Uses of Biotechnology?

Genetic engineering allows the production of therapeutic proteins like insulin and human growth hormone (both grown in *E. coli* bacteria). Using transgenic "pharm" animals (into which human genes have been introduced using viral vectors or DNA injected into fertilized eggs), products such as alpha-1-antitrypsin (to treat emphysema) can be harvested from milk. The two potential types of human gene therapy are (1) replacing defective genes in body cells (currently being tested for cystic fibrosis, using liposomes as vectors); and (2) altering genes in fertilized eggs, thus permanently repairing the genetic defect in that individual. The Human Genome Project aims to sequence the entire human genome by the year 2003.

6) What Are Some Ethical Implications of Human Biotechnology?

Since approximately 850 babies are born each year in the United States with cystic fibrosis (CF), scientists have recommended that all couples be tested to find carriers of CF. Will unbiased and affordable genetic counseling be available for all couples in which both are heterozygous for CF? Should society bear the expenses of treating a child born with CF to parents who knew they were carriers? Should insurance companies be allowed to deny coverage to such couples? The increasing availability and use of tests for genetic diseases raise concerns about genetic discrimination by employers and insurance companies as was the case after widespread screening for **sickle cell anemia** in the early 1970's. With appropriate education and counseling, genetic testing can reduce the incidence of sickle cell anemia as well as other fatal diseases such as **Tay-Sachs disease**.

The potential of cloning humans raises additional ethical issues. Are there valid reasons to clone or not to clone humans? Would a clone of you, *really* be you?

Key Terms and Definitions

amniocentesis (am-nē-ō-sen-tē´-sis): a procedure for sampling the amniotic fluid surrounding a fetus: A sterile needle is inserted through the abdominal wall, uterus, and amniotic sac of a pregnant woman; 10 to 20 milliliters of amniotic fluid is withdrawn. Various tests may be performed on the fluid and the fetal cells suspended in it to provide information on the developmental and genetic state of the fetus.

bacteriophage: a virus specialized to infect bacteria; also called a phage.

biotechnology: any industrial or commercial use or alteration of organisms, cells, or biological molecules to achieve specific practical goals.

chorionic villus sampling (kor-ē-on-ik; **CVS**): a procedure for sampling cells from the chorionic villi produced by a fetus: A tube is inserted into the uterus of a pregnant woman, and a small sample of villi are suctioned off for genetic and biochemical analyses.

cloning: the process of producing many identical copies of a gene; also the production of many genetically identical copies of an organism.

cystic fibrosis: an inherited disorder characterized by the buildup of salt in the lungs and the production of thick, sticky mucus that clogs the airways, restricts air exchange, and promotes infection.

DNA fingerprinting: the use of restriction enzymes to cut DNA segments into a unique set of restriction fragments from one individual that can be distinguished from the restriction fragments of other individuals by gel electrophoresis.

DNA library: a readily accessible, easily duplicable complete set of all the DNA of a particular organism, normally cloned into bacterial plasmids.

DNA probe: a sequence of nucleotides that is complementary to the nucleotide sequence in a gene under study; used to locate a given gene within a DNA library.

gel electrophoresis: a technique in which molecules (such as DNA fragments) are placed on restricted tracks in a thin sheet of gelatinous material and exposed to an electric field; the molecules then migrate at a rate determined by certain characteristics, such as length.

genetic engineering: the modification of genetic material to achieve specific goals.

genome (jē´-nōm): the entire set of genes carried by a member of any given species.

plasmid (plaz´-mid): a small, circular piece of DNA located in the cytoplasm of many bacteria; normally does not carry genes required for the normal functioning of the bacterium but may carry genes that assist bacterial survival in certain environments, such as a gene for antibiotic resistance.

polymerase chain reaction (**PCR**): a method of producing virtually unlimited numbers of copies of a specific piece of DNA, starting with as little as one copy of the desired DNA.

recombinant DNA: DNA that has been altered by the recombination of genes from a different organism, typically from a different species.

restriction enzyme: an enzyme, normally isolated from bacteria, that cuts double-stranded DNA at a specific nucleotide sequence; the nucleotide sequence that is cut differs for different restriction enzymes.

restriction fragment: a piece of DNA that has been isolated by cleaving a larger piece of DNA with restriction enzymes.

restriction fragment length polymorphism (RFLP): a difference in the length of restriction fragments, produced by cutting samples of DNA from different individuals of the same species with the same set of restriction enzymes; the result of differences in nucleotide sequences among individuals of the same species.

sickle-cell anemia: a recessive disease caused by a single amino acid substitution in the hemoglobin molecule. Sickle-cell hemoglobin molecules tend to cluster together, distorting the shape of red blood cells and causing them to break and clog capillaries.

Tay-Sachs disease: a recessive disease caused by a deficiency in enzymes that regulate lipid breakdown in the brain.

transformation: a method of acquiring new genes, whereby DNA from one bacterium (normally released after the death of the bacterium) becomes incorporated into the DNA of another, living, bacterium.

transgenic: referring to an animal or a plant that expresses DNA derived from another species.

vector: a carrier that introduces foreign genes into cells.

KEY TERMS AND CONCEPTS

From the information in this chapter and previous chapters, fill in the crossword puzzle on the basis of the clues provided.

Across

6. A procedure for sampling the fluid surrounding a fetus.
8. A method of producing large numbers of copies of a specific piece of DNA.
9. Type of nucleic acid containing uracil.
10. A procedure for sampling cells from the fetal chorionic villi.
11. A sequence of complementary nucleotides that can be used to identify a DNA segment that carries a gene.
12. A technique that separates DNA fragments on the basis of size.
14. The process of producing a new organism that is genetically identical to an existing organism.
16. Transgenic "_____" animals are used to produce human gene products.
17. A virus specialized to infect bacteria.

Down

1. A bacterium, plasmid, or virus that carries DNA between different organisms.
2. A palindrome with the letters *A*, *D*, and *M*.
3. The use of DNA to identify an individual on the basis of a unique set of restriction fragment length polymorphisms.
4. A protein, normally isolated from bacteria, that cuts double-stranded DNA at a specific nucleotide sequence.
5. A readily accessible, easily duplicable assemblage of all the DNA of a particular organism, normally cloned into bacterial plasmids.
7. Genetic material altered by the incorporation of genes from a different organism.
13. A small, circular piece of DNA found in the cytoplasm of many bacteria.
15. A difference in the lengths of fragments produced by cutting DNA from different individuals of the same species with the same restriction enzymes.

THINKING THROUGH THE CONCEPTS

True or False: Determine if the statement given is true or false. If it is false, change the underlined word(s) so that the statement reads true.

18. _____ DNA recombination <u>does not</u> occur in nature.

19. _____ Sexual reproduction between humans <u>is</u> an example of DNA recombination in nature.

20. _____ Bacteria pick up free DNA and incorporate it into their chromosomes during <u>sexual reproduction</u>.

21. _____ A recessive condition caused by an inability to break down fatty materials in nerve cells is called <u>sickle cell anemia</u>.

22. _____ A readily accessible, easy-to-duplicate collection of all the DNA of a particular organism is a <u>DNA library</u>.

23. _____ An example of a palindrome is the word <u>*madman*</u>.

24. _____ An enzyme that cuts palindromic DNA open to form sticky ends is called <u>ligase enzyme</u>.

25. _____ Bacterial DNA is protected from the action of restriction enzymes by <u>methylation</u>.

26. _____ A method for making many copies of a small amount of DNA is the <u>restriction fragment length polymorphism reaction</u>.

27. _____ RFLPs are helpful in <u>gene mapping</u>.

Fill-In: Refer to the figure to the right to answer questions 28 through 31.

28. Describe what is happening in step 1.

29. Describe what is happening in step 2.

30. Describe what is happening in step 3.

31. Describe what is happening in step 4.

Matching: Recombinant DNA.

32. _____ accessory chromosomes in bacteria

33. _____ defend bacteria against viral infection by cutting apart the viral DNA

34. _____ self-replicating, tiny loops of DNA

35. _____ used to identify marker genes in chromosomes

36. _____ readily accessible, easy-to-duplicate collection of all the DNA of a particular organism

37. _____ bacteria protect themselves from these by methylating their DNA

38. _____ a bacterium may contain dozens or hundreds of copies of these

39. _____ can cut apart DNA to create single-stranded ends

40. _____ restriction fragment length polymorphisms

41. _____ cut at palindromic DNA sequences

42. _____ often contain genes for antibiotic-digesting enzymes

43. _____ cut up DNA into fragments of various sizes that can be separated by gel electrophoresis

Choices:

a. DNA library

b. restriction enzymes

c. plasmids

d. RFLPs

Multiple Choice: Pick the most correct choice for each question.

44. Small accessory chromosomes found in bacteria and useful in recombinant DNA procedures are called
    a. plasmids
    b. palindromes
    c. centrioles

45. Which of the following is <u>not</u> a goal of biotechnology?
    a. generating economic benefits
    b. efficiently producing biologically important molecules
    c. improving agriculturally important food plants
    d. more effectively treating disease
    e. creating humans with higher intelligence levels

46. In biotechnology research, DNA fragments created by restriction enzyme action are separated from one another by
    a. crossing over
    b. gel electrophoresis
    c. centrifugation
    d. filtering
    e. the polymerase chain reaction

47. The enzymes used to cut genes in recombinant DNA research are called
    a. DNA polymerases
    b. RNA polymerases
    c. spliceosomes
    d. replicases
    e. restriction enzymes

48. DNA recombinations controlled by scientists in the laboratory
    a. are random and undirected
    b. involve specific pieces of DNA moved between deliberately chosen organisms
    c. use natural selection to determine their usefulness
    d. are of little practical use to humans
    e. usually cause harmful mutations

49. The polymerase chain reaction (PCR) is useful in
    a. analyzing a person's fingerprints
    b. cutting DNA into many small pieces
    c. allowing restriction enzymes to cut DNA at palindromes
    d. creating recombinant plasmids
    e. making many copies of a small amount of DNA

50. Which of the following is a palindrome?
    a. CCGTA
       GGCAT
    b. GAATTC
       CTTAAG
    c. CATTG
       GTAAC
    d. GGAATC
       CCTTAG
    e. AAAAA
       TTTTT

CLUES TO APPLYING THE CONCEPTS

This practice question is intended to sharpen your ability to apply critical thinking and analysis to biological concepts covered in this chapter.

51. What are some of the potential risks of releasing genetically engineered organisms into the environment, and what are some of the ethical issues raised by recombinant DNA technology?

_____

_____

_____

_____

_____

_____

_____

_____

_____

_____

_____

_____

ANSWERS TO EXERCISES

18. false, does
19. true
20. false, transformation
21. false, Tay-Sachs disease
22. true
23. false, *madam*
24. false, restriction enzyme
25. true
26. false, polymerase chain reaction
27. true

28. A plasmid vector is removed from a bacterial cell and cut open with a restriction enzyme.

29. DNA from another organism is cut with the same restriction enzyme.

30. The plasmid DNA and a piece of DNA from the other organism are joined by complementary base pairing to form a recombinant molecule.

31. The recombinant plasmid is taken up by a host cell.

32. c	37. b	42. c	47. e
33. b	38. c	43. b	48. b
34. c	39. b	44. a	49. e
35. d	40. d	45. e	50. b
36. a	41. b	46. b	

51. Recombinant organisms could compete with existing organisms and possibly replace them in nature, leading to undesirable consequences. Genetic engineering could produce organisms that act as hazardous pathogens, infecting plants, animals, and/or humans to cause hard-to-treat diseases. Newly engineered organisms also could transfer genes to other species, harming them or causing them to become harmful. Some ethical questions that should be considered: Are the potential benefits worth the potential risks? Who decides what kinds of alterations in a species are acceptable? Should ecosystems be altered by introducing altered species? Do scientists or governments have the right to stop or forbid recombinant DNA research if there is a potential for it to solve medical or environmental problems? Who has the right to decide whether human genes should be altered, and who should decide whose genes and which genes should be changed? What uses should be made of genetic information, and who should decide what these uses are?

Chapter 13: Principles of Evolution

OVERVIEW

This chapter introduces the concept of evolution. The authors present an historical account of pre-Darwinian thought, followed by the Darwin-Wallace theory of evolution by natural selection. Finally, supporting evidence of evolution is given.

1) How Did Evolutionary Thought Evolve?

Pre-Darwinian science, heavily influenced by theology, held that all organisms were created simultaneously by God and that each distinct life-form remained unchanged from the moment of creation. Plato said that each object on Earth is a temporary reflection of an "ideal form," and Aristotle categorized all organisms into a linear hierarchy (the "ladder of Nature"). These ideas went unchallenged for nearly 2000 years. However, as European explorers noted in the 1700s, the numbers of **species** (different kinds of organisms) in newly discovered lands was greater than expected and led to thoughts that similar species might have developed from a common ancestor.

   Fossils (preserved remains of organisms that lived long ago) found in rocks resemble parts of living organisms. The organization of fossils is consistent: (1) older fossils are found in rock layers beneath younger fossils; (2) the resemblance to modern forms of life gradually increases as increasingly younger fossils are examined, as if they are indeed a ladder of Nature stretching back in time; and (3) many of the fossils are of species now extinct. Scientists have concluded that different types of organisms have lived at various times in the past.

   Geology has provided evidence that Earth is exceedingly old. Biblical calculations suggest Earth is 4000 to 6000 years old. The theory of **catastrophism** claimed that successive catastrophes on Earth (like the biblical Great Flood) produced layers of rock and caused many species to become extinct in short time periods, perhaps with more species being created after each event. Actually, Earth is very old, having been formed from the forces of wind, water, earthquakes, and volcanoes in much the same way then as now (the theory of **uniformitarianism**). Modern geologists estimate Earth to be about 4.5 billion years old.

   The French biologist Lamarck proposed in 1801 that organisms evolved through the **inheritance of acquired characteristics**: Through an innate drive for perfection (never scientifically demonstrated), living organisms modify their bodies through the use or disuse of parts (actually true) and these modifications can be inherited by their offspring (actually false). Though Lamarck's theory was abandoned, by the mid-1800s biologists began to realize that the fossil record suggested that present-day species had evolved from preexisting ones. But how?

SUMMARY OF THE DARWIN-WALLACE THEORY OF EVOLUTION

Observation 1: All natural **populations** have the potential to increase rapidly because of reproductive abilities.

Observation 2: Most natural populations maintain a relatively constant size.

Conclusion 1: Thus, many organisms must die young, producing few or no offspring in each generation.

Observation 3: Individuals in a population differ from one another in many abilities that affect survival and reproduction (some are "better adapted").

Conclusion 2: The most well-adapted organisms probably reproduce the most, since they survive the best. This differential reproduction is due to **natural selection**.

Observation 4: Some of the variation in adaptiveness among individuals is genetic and is passed on to the offspring.

Conclusion 3: Over many generations, differential reproduction among individuals with different genotypes changes the overall frequencies of genes in populations, resulting in **evolution**.

***Note:

Darwin did not know the mechanism of heredity (to explain observation 4) and could not prove conclusion 3, a weakness to his theory.

---

2) How Do We Know That Evolution Has Occurred?

The fossil record provides evidence of evolutionary change over time. Giraffes, elephants, horses, and other types of organisms show a progressive series of fossils leading from ancient primitive organisms, through several intermediary stages, to the modern forms.

Comparative anatomy provides structural evidence of evolution. Through **convergent evolution**, unrelated species in similar environments have evolved similar body functions from internally dissimilar structures, called **analogous structures** (for example, wings of birds and flies). In addition, closely related species in dissimilar environments have evolved dissimilar body functions from internally similar structures, called **homologous structures** (for example, among mammals, the forelimbs of apes, seals, dogs, and bats). Some species of organisms have **vestigial structures** (structures with no apparent purpose), which are homologous to functional structures in other species (for example, molar teeth in vampire bats, and pelvic bones in snakes).

Embryological stages of animals can provide evidence of common ancestry. All vertebrate embryos look similar to one another early in their development (all have gill slits and tails, even humans), indicating that all vertebrate species have similar genes.

Modern biochemical and genetic analyses reveal relatedness among diverse organisms. For example, all cells have DNA, RNA, ribosomes, similar genetic codes, similar amino acids in proteins, and similar chromosome structures.

3) What Is the Evidence That Populations Evolve by Natural Selection?

Artificial selection (breeding domestic organisms, such as dogs, to produce specific desired features) demonstrates that organisms may be modified by controlled breeding. Additionally, evolution by natural selection occurs today, as illustrated by the selection for dark-colored moths in industrially polluted areas and the evolution of populations of roaches in Florida for which the poison roach bait called Combat® is ineffective.

When considering evolutionary mechanisms, is important to keep in mind: (1) the variations on which natural selection works are produced by chance mutations; (2) selection does not necessarily produce well-adapted species (if the right mutant does not exist, natural selection may drive a species to extinction; and (3) evolution by natural selection selects for organisms that are best adapted to a particular environment.

KEY TERMS AND CONCEPTS

Fill-In: From the following list of terms, fill in the blanks below. A term may be used more than once.

analogous	homologous
artificial	inheritance of acquired characteristics
catastrophism	uniformitarianism
convergent	vestigial
fossils	

(1)_____, the preserved remains of organisms that lived long ago, are often found in rocks and typically resemble parts of living organisms.

The theory of (2)_____ claims that successive worldwide events, like the biblical Great Flood, produced layers of rock and caused many species to become extinct in short periods of time.

According to the theory of (3)_____, Earth is very old, having been formed by the forces of wind, water, earthquakes, and volcanoes in much the same way then as now.

In 1801, the French biologist Lamarck proposed that organisms evolved through the (4)_____.

Through (5)_____ evolution, unrelated species in similar environments evolve similar body functions from internally dissimilar structures, called (6)_____ structures.

Closely related species living in dissimilar environments, evolve dissimilar body functions from internally similar structures, called (7)_____ structures.

Some species of organisms have (8)_____ structures with no apparent purpose, which are homologous to functional structures in other species.

The wing of a butterfly and the wing of a bird are (9)_____ structures while the forelimb of a human and the forelimb of a whale are (10)_____ structures.

(11)_____ selection, the breeding of domestic organisms such as dogs to produce specific desired features, demonstrates that organisms may be modified by controlled breeding.

Key Terms and Definitions

analogous structures: structures that have similar functions and superficially similar appearance but very different anatomies, such as the wings of insects and birds. The similarities are due to similar environmental pressures rather than to common ancestry.

artificial selection: a selective breeding procedure in which only those individuals with particular traits are chosen as breeders; used mainly to enhance desirable traits in domestic plants and animals; may also be used in evolutionary biology experiments.

catastrophism: the hypothesis that Earth has experienced a series of geological catastrophes, probably imposed by a supernatural being that accounts for the multitude of species, both extinct and modern, and preserves creationism.

convergent evolution: the independent evolution of similar structures among unrelated organisms as a result of similar environmental pressures; see *analogous structures*.

evolution: the descent of modern organisms with modification from preexisting life-forms; strictly speaking, any change in the proportions of different genotypes in a population from one generation to the next.

fossil: the remains of a dead organism, normally preserved in rock; may be petrified bones or wood; shells; impressions of body forms, such as feathers, skin, or leaves; or markings made by organisms, such as footprints.

homologous structures: structures that may differ in function but that have similar anatomy, presumably because the organisms that possess them have descended from common ancestors.

inheritance of acquired characteristics: the hypothesis that organisms' bodies change during their lifetimes by use and disuse and that these changes are inherited by their offspring.

natural selection: the unequal survival and reproduction of organisms due to environmental forces, resulting in the preservation of favorable adaptations. Usually, natural selection refers specifically to differential survival and reproduction on the basis of genetic differences among individuals.

population: all the members of a particular species within an ecosystem, found in the same time and place and actually or potentially interbreeding.

species (spē´-sēs): all of the organisms that are potentially capable of interbreeding under natural conditions or, if asexually reproducing, are more closely related to one another than to other organisms within a given genus; the smallest major taxonomic category.

uniformitarianism: the hypothesis that Earth developed gradually through natural processes, similar to those at work today, that occur over long periods of time.

vestigial structure (ves-tij´-ē-ul): a structure that serves no apparent purpose but is homologous to functional structures in related organisms and provides evidence of evolution.

THINKING THROUGH THE CONCEPTS

True or False: Determine if the statement given is true or false. If it is false, change the underlined word(s) so that the statement reads true.

12. _____ Before Darwin, most people thought species were capable of change.

13. _____ The idea that God created some new species after every catastrophe was proposed by Agassiz.

14. _____ The remains of organisms preserved in rock are called vestigial structures.

15. _____ Lamarck proposed that an internal drive toward complexity within cells is the driving force in evolution.

16. _____ The similarity in the bones making up a bird's wing and a horse's foot are due to convergent evolution.

17. _____ Amino acid sequences in proteins of different animals tend to support evolution.

18. _____ Aristotle's "ladder of Nature" was considered immutable.

19. _____ In convergent evolution, the two forms being modified are closely related.

20. _____   The many different varieties of dogs are the result of <u>natural</u> selection.

21. _____   Analogous structures arise as a result of <u>convergent</u> evolution.

Matching: Theories about life. Some questions may have more than one answer and some choices may be used more than once.

22. _____   uniformitarianism

23. _____   ladder of Nature

24. _____   "ideal forms"

25. _____   inheritance of acquired characteristics

26. _____   catastrophism

27. _____   multiple creations

28. _____   natural selection

29. _____   *Essay on Population*

30. _____   Earth is "millions of years old"

Choices:

a.   Lamarck

b.   Aristotle

c.   Wallace

d.   Plato

e.   Malthus

f.   Agassiz

g.   Cuvier

h.   Hutton and Lyell

i.   Darwin

Multiple Choice: Pick the most correct choice for each question.

31. Which of the following proposes that living organisms inherited body parts modified through use or disuse?
   a.   natural selection
   b.   catastrophism
   c.   inheritance of acquired characteristics
   d.   evolution

32. Fossils resulted from a successive series of geological upheavals according to the theory of
   a.   natural selection
   b.   catastrophism
   c.   uniformitarianism
   d.   independent assortment

33. The evolution of superficially similar structures by unrelated species is termed
   a.   analogous evolution
   b.   divergent evolution
   c.   convergent evolution
   d.   coevolution

34. Which of the following is homologous to the human arm?
   a.   wing of insect
   b.   wing of bird
   c.   body of snake
   d.   fin of fish
   e.   tail of salamander

35. Supportive evidence for evolution is found in studies of
   a.   biochemistry
   b.   embryos
   c.   comparative anatomy
   d.   domestication of plants and animals
   e.   all of the above

36. Fossils provide direct evidence for
   a.   behavioral adaptations
   b.   physiological characteristics
   c.   habitat preference
   d.   structural similarities and differences
   e.   catastrophism

CLUES TO APPLYING THE CONCEPTS

This practice question is intended to sharpen your ability to apply critical thinking and analysis to biological concepts covered in this chapter.

37. A species of moth has a very long proboscis (tubular mouthpart) that is used to suck nectar from the inner base of a particular type of long, trumpet-shaped flower. Closely related moth species, however, have much shorter mouthparts and feed off nectar from plants with shorter tubular flowers. How would Lamarck and Darwin each explain the evolution of the species of moth with the exceptionally long proboscis?

_____

_____

_____

_____

_____

_____

_____

_____

ANSWERS TO EXERCISES

1. fossils
2. catastrophism
3. uniformitarianism
4. inheritance of acquired characteristics
5. convergent
6. analogous
7. homologous
8. vestigial
9. analogous
10. homologous
11. artificial
12. false, incapable of change
13. true
14. false, fossils
15. true
16. false, common ancestry
17. true
18. true
19. false, unrelated
20. false, artificial
21. true
22. h
23. b
24. d
25. a
26. g
27. f
28. c, i
29. e
30. h
31. c
32. b
33. c
34. b
35. e
36. d

37. Lamarck would explain the long proboscis by the "inheritance of acquired characteristics." The ancestral species was uniform for a short proboscis, but the moths began to habitually stretch their probosci deep into the long trumpet flowers to get nectar, stretching their probosci in the process. These slightly stretched probosci were in turn passed down to the next generation, which repeated the process of stretching their probosci into the flowers and passing the longer proboscis on. After many generations of this, all the moths of this species were born with very long probosci.

Darwin would explain the long probosci by natural selection. Individuals in the ancestral species displayed genetic variation in proboscis length and those with longer probosci could get more nectar from the flowers, allowing them to live longer and out reproduce those with shorter probosci. The next generation thus had with a higher percentage of moths with longer probosci. After many generations of natural selection favoring moths with longer probosci, the entire species showed this trait.

Chapter 14: How Organisms Evolve

OVERVIEW

This chapter covers the basic principles of population genetics, including how to calculate gene and genotype frequencies and the Hardy-Weinberg principle. The authors examine the major forces causing evolution (mutation, small population size, and natural selection), and discuss the ultimate fate for most species (extinction). This chapter also covers speciation. After defining biological species, the authors discuss how they form by describing premating and postmating mechanisms for maintaining reproductive isolation. The rate at which speciation occurs is also presented

1) How Are Populations, Genes, and Evolution Related?

Evolutionary changes occur from generation to generation and cause descendants to be different from their ancestors. Evolution is a property not of individuals but of **populations** (all individuals of a species living in a given area). Inheritance provides the link between the lives of individuals and the evolution of populations. **Population genetics** is the study of the frequency, distribution, and inheritance of alleles in populations. The **gene pool** is the sum of all the genes in a population. The relative frequencies of various alleles in a population are the **allele frequencies**. Evolution, then, is the result of changes in gene frequencies that occur in a gene pool over time.

An **equilibrium population** is a hypothetical population in which evolution does not occur. The **Hardy-Weinberg principle** states that under certain conditions, allele and genotype frequencies in a population will remain constant over time (evolution will not occur). Such an evolution-free population is an equilibrium population that will remain in **genetic equilibrium** as long as (1) there is no mutation; (2) there is no **gene flow** (migration) between populations; (3) the population is extremely large; (4) all mating is random; and (5) there is no **natural selection** (all genotypes reproduce equally well). Few, if any, natural populations are in genetic equilibrium.

2) What Causes Evolution?

There are three major causes of evolutionary change: mutation, small population size, and natural selection. Mutations (changes in DNA sequence) are the ultimate source of genetic variability.

Mutations occur at rates between 1 in 10,000 and 1 in 100,000 genes per individual per generation. Although mutation by itself is not a major evolutionary force, without mutations there would be no evolution and no diversity among life-forms. Mutation is not goal-directed; it is random.

Small populations are subject to random changes in allele frequencies (**genetic drift**). In large populations, chance events are unlikely to significantly alter the overall gene frequencies, but in small populations chance events could reduce or eliminate alleles, greatly altering, in a random way, the population's genetic makeup. Genetic drift tends to reduce genetic variability within small populations, as illustrated by the example of the two ladybug populations in the text (page 248-49). Two special cases of genetic drift illustrate the enormous consequences that small population size may have on allele frequencies. When a **population bottleneck** occurs, a population is drastically reduced in size (as a result of a natural catastrophe or overhunting, for example). One cause of population bottlenecks is the **founder effect**, which occurs when isolated colonies are founded by a small number of organisms. In both bottleneck and founder effect events, only a small group of individuals, which may have allele frequencies very different from the those of the parent population, are available to contribute genes to the entire future population.

Not all genotypes are equally adaptive. Anytime an allele confers a slight advantage to some individuals, natural selection will favor the enhanced reproduction of those individuals. Four important points about natural selection and evolution are (1) natural selection does not cause genetic changes in individuals; (2) natural selection acts on individuals (unequal reproduction), but evolution occurs in populations; (3) the **fitness** of an organism is a measure of its reproductive success; and (4) evolutionary changes are not progressive in an absolute sense, but are relative to the environmental circumstances present at any particular time and place.

3) How Does Natural Selection Work?

Natural selection is primarily an issue of **differential reproduction**: Individuals with favorable alleles leave more offspring (who inherit those alleles) than do individuals with less favorable alleles. Natural selection acts on the phenotype, which reflects the underlying genotype.

A variety of processes can cause natural selection. Organisms with reproductively successful phenotypes have the best **adaptations** to their particular environments. These characteristics help an individual survive and reproduce. **Competition** for scarce resources favors the best-adapted individuals. Competition may occur among individuals of the same species or between members of different species. When two species interact extensively, as seen with predators and their prey, each exerts strong selection pressure on the other. If one species evolves a new feature or modifies an old one, the other species typically evolves new adaptations in response. This constant mutual feedback situation is called **coevolution**. **Predation** includes any situation in which one organism (the predator) eats another (the prey). **Sexual selection** favors traits that help an organism mate. The competition between males for access to matings with females may involve specific behaviors or physical features that females find attractive.

4) What Causes Extinction?

Natural selection may lead to **extinction** (death of all members of a species). The actual cause of extinction is probably always environmental change. Three major environmental changes that drive a species to extinction are (1) competition among species, (2) the introduction of new predators or parasites, and (3) habitat destruction. Interactions with other organisms may drive a species to extinction, as happened when the Panama land bridge allowed North American species to migrate into South America, causing the extinction of most native South American species as a result of competition. Habitat change and destruction are the leading causes of extinction. **Mass extinctions**, disappearances of many varied species in a short time over a large area, may be caused by traumatic environmental events such as the impact of a large meteorite.

5) What Is a Species?

Biologists define **species** as groups of actually or potentially interbreeding natural populations, which are reproductively isolated from other such groups. So, two organisms are the same species if they interbreed in nature and have normal, vigorous, fertile offspring. However, this definition does not apply to species that reproduce asexually.

6) How Do New Species Form?

Speciation is the process by which new species form. Speciation depends on two factors: (1) isolation of two populations (interbreeding and thus gene flow, between diverging populations must be small or nonexistent); and (2) genetic divergence of two populations (the two populations must evolve large genetic differences so that they can no longer interbreed or produce vigorous, fertile offspring).

Speciation can occur in populations that are physically separated. There is some debate as to whether genetic drift or natural selection normally plays the major role in speciation, but geographical isolation is involved in most cases of speciation, especially in animals. Circumstances dictate whether anatomical change and speciation are linked. Anatomical change (for example, change in butterfly coloration; see text Figure 14-14b) can occur without speciation.

7) How Is Reproductive Isolation Between Species Maintained?

Speciation occurs through the evolution of mechanisms that prevent interbreeding. Genetic divergence during the period of isolation is necessary for new species to arise, but speciation will occur only if mechanisms that ensure **reproductive isolation** also develop. **Isolating mechanisms** are structural and/or behavioral modifications that prevent interbreeding.

Premating isolating mechanisms prevent mating between species. They include geographical isolation, ecological isolation, temporal isolation, behavioral isolation, and mechanical incompatibility. **Geographical isolation** prevents members of different species from meeting each other and usually is considered to be a mechanism that allows new species to form. **Ecological isolation** occurs when populations with different resource requirements use different local habitats within the same general area; thus, they seldom meet during the mating season. **Temporal isolation** occurs between species that breed at different times of the year. Even if two species occupy similar habitats, they cannot mate if they have different breeding seasons. **Behavioral isolation** involves species with different courtship rituals. Courtship rituals involve recognition and evaluation signals between males and females and also aid in distinguishing among species. Colors and songs of birds, frog croaks, cricket chirping patterns, and firefly flashing colors and frequencies are examples of signals used in courtship rituals. **Mechanical incompatibility** occurs when physical barriers between species prevent fertilization. For example, male and female sex organs of different species may not fit together properly for sperm transfer in animals, or different flower sizes or structures of different species may prevent pollen transfer in plants.

Postmating isolating mechanisms prevent the production of vigorous, fertile offspring, They include gametic incompatibility, hybrid inviability, and hybrid infertility. **Gametic incompatibility** occurs when sperm from one species are unable to fertilize eggs of another. **Hybrid inviability** occurs if hybrid offspring survive poorly. Hybrids may die during development or may display behaviors that are mixtures of the two parental types and be unable to attract mates. **Hybrid infertility** occurs if hybrid offspring are unable to produce normal sperm or eggs. Most animal hybrids such as mules (a horse mating with a donkey) or ligers (a male lion mating with a female tiger) are sterile because their chromosomes do not pair properly during meiosis. Crosses between tetraploid ($4n$) and diploid ($2n$) plant species usually result in sterile triploid ($3n$) offspring.

8) At What Rate Does Speciation Occur?

The rate of speciation varies considerably over evolutionary time, and bursts of speciation are seen in both the fossil record and in the distribution of modern organisms. In animals, instantaneous speciation is unlikely, although it can happen in plants because of polyploidy. During periods of **adaptive radiation**, in which populations of a single species invade a variety of new habitats and evolve in response to the differing environmental pressures in these habitats, one species gives rise to many in a relatively short time.

KEY TERMS AND CONCEPTS

Fill-In: From the following list of terms, fill in the blanks below.

adaptive radiation
behavioral
ecological
geographical

hybrid infertility
mechanical
postmating
premating

reproductive
speciation
species
temporal

Michael took his son Zachary to the zoo. Zachary is taking a high school biology class and was loaded with questions for his dad. "How do we know that African lions and Asian tigers are different (1)_____?" he asked. Mike replied, "Zach, they have different physical characteristics, but more importantly, they show (2)_____ isolation, since they don't try to interbreed in nature or even in zoos." This answer led to another question: "Dad, since both lions and tigers are mammals and cats, how could (3)_____ have occurred in such closely related organisms?" "Well, son, when a single group of organisms, like mammals, give rise to many closely related species, we call this (4)_____. In the case of lions and tigers, first there was (5)_____ isolation, since they evolved in different parts of the world. And even if they lived for a time in the same general area, there may have been (6)_____ isolation, since they would occupy different habitats there. These are examples of (7)_____ isolating mechanisms, son, since they prevent lions and tigers from mating."

They then entered the amphibian and reptile house, where many different species of frogs were living. "Dad, the wood frogs and green frogs breed in the same areas each year, but are different species. How can this be?" "Son, the reason they don't interbreed is that wood frogs mate during early spring and green frogs mate during late spring, a situation called (8)_____ isolation. Also, the males of the two species have different-sounding croaks, and the females are attracted only to males of their own kind. This is an example of (9)_____ isolation because they have different courtship rituals." When they looked at the lizards, Zach said, "Dad, I just thought of something weird. Suppose a large lizard of one species tried to mate with a small lizard of another species. Could they succeed?" "Probably not, son," replied Mike as he chuckled at the thought of such an unlikely liaison, "since their sex organs couldn't fit together properly. This is a type of isolation due to (10)_____ incompatibility."

Moving to the building housing hoofed animals, Zach noticed the horses, donkeys, and mules. "Dad, since horses and donkeys produce mules when farmers force them to mate, aren't they all members of the same species?" "Son, horses and donkeys would never interbreed under natural conditions, and besides, the mules they produce are sterile, an example of (11)_____. This is an example of a (12)_____ isolating mechanism, since it acts after mating between different species takes place."

"Dad, this is all way cool, but now I have a really important question. When do we eat?" "Soon, son, but just eat your banana right now. By the way, Zach, bananas don't have seeds and are sterile because they have three copies of each chromosome. "Banana, smanana!" exclaimed Zach. "I want a burger with fries!"

Key Terms and Definitions

adaptation: a characteristic of an organism that helps it survive and reproduce in a particular environment; also, the process of acquiring such characteristics.

adaptive radiation: the rise of many new species in a relatively short time as a result of a single species that invades different habitats and evolves under different environmental pressures in those habitats.

allele frequency: for any given gene, the relative proportion of each allele of that gene in a population.

behavioral isolation: the lack of mating between species of animals that differ substantially in courtship and mating rituals.

coevolution: the evolution of adaptations in two species due to their extensive interactions with one another, such that each species acts as a major force of natural selection on the other.

competition: interaction among individuals who attempt to utilize a resource (for example, food or space) that is limited relative to the demand for it.

differential reproduction: differences in reproductive output among individuals of a population, normally as a result of genetic differences.

ecological isolation: the lack of mating between organisms belonging to different populations that occupy distinct habitats within the same general area.

equilibrium population: a population in which allele frequencies and the distribution of genotypes do not change from generation to generation.

extinction: the death of all members of a species.

fitness: the reproductive success of an organism, usually expressed in relation to the average reproductive success of all individuals in the same population.

founder effect: a type of genetic drift in which an isolated population founded by a small number of individuals may develop allele frequencies that are very different from those of the parent population as a result of chance inclusion of disproportionate numbers of certain alleles in the founders.

gametic incompatibility: the inability of sperm from one species to fertilize eggs of another species.

gene flow: the movement of alleles from one population to another owing to the migration of individual organisms.

gene pool: the total of all alleles of all genes in a population; for a single gene, the total of all the alleles of that gene that occur in a population.

genetic drift: a change in the allele frequencies of a small population purely by chance.

genetic equilibrium: a state in which the allele frequencies and the distribution of genotypes of a population do not change from generation to generation.

geographical isolation: the separation of two populations by a physical barrier.

Hardy-Weinberg principle: a mathematical model proposing that, under certain conditions, the allele frequencies and genotype frequencies in a sexually reproducing population will remain constant over generations.

hybrid infertility: reduced fertility (typically, complete sterility) in the hybrid offspring of two species.

hybrid inviability: the failure of a hybrid offspring of two species to survive to maturity.

isolating mechanism: a morphological, physiological, behavioral, or ecological difference that prevents members of two species from interbreeding.

mass extinction: the extinction of an extraordinarily large number of species in a short period of geologic time. Mass extinctions have recurred periodically throughout the history of life.

mechanical incompatibility: the inability of male and female organisms to exchange gametes, normally because their reproductive structures are incompatible.

natural selection: the unequal survival and reproduction of organisms due to environmental forces, resulting in the preservation of favorable adaptations. Usually, natural selection refers specifically to differential survival and reproduction on the basis of genetic differences among individuals.

population: all the members of a particular species within an ecosystem, found in the same time and place and actually or potentially interbreeding.

population bottleneck: a form of genetic drift in which a population becomes extremely small; may lead to differences in allele frequencies as compared with other populations of the species and to a loss in genetic variability.

population genetics: the study of the frequency, distribution, and inheritance of alleles in a population.

postmating isolating mechanism: any structure, physiological function, or developmental abnormality that prevents organisms of two different populations, once mating has occurred, from producing vigorous, fertile offspring.

predation (pre-dā′-shun): the act of killing and eating another living organism.

premating isolating mechanism: any structure, physiological function, or behavior that prevents organisms of two different populations from exchanging gametes.

reproductive isolation: the failure of organisms of one population to breed successfully with members of another; may be due to premating or postmating isolating mechanisms.

sexual selection: a type of natural selection in which the choice of mates by one sex is the selective agent.

speciation: the process whereby two populations achieve reproductive isolation.

species (spē′-sēs): all of the organisms that are potentially capable of interbreeding under natural conditions or, if asexually reproducing, are more closely related to one another than to other organisms within a given genus; the smallest major taxonomic category.

temporal isolation: the inability of organisms to mate if they have significantly different breeding seasons.

THINKING THROUGH THE CONCEPTS

True or False: Determine if the statement given is true or false. If it is false, change the underlined word(s) so that the statement reads true.

13. _____ Individual plants or animals change in response to selection.

14. _____ For a population to remain at equilibrium, it must be large.

15. _____ Mutation is the factor that controls the direction of evolution.

16. _____ Genetic drift is a characteristic of large populations.

17. _____ Natural selection acts on genotypes directly.

18. _____ Population bottlenecks result in reduced variability in the future population.

19. _____ Most species eventually give rise to new species.

20. _____ Temporal isolation is isolation by distance.

21. _____ Mechanical incompatibility is a postmating isolating mechanism.

22. _____ The most valid way to determine whether two organisms belong to different species is to look at mating behavior.

23. _____ Speciation depends on lack of isolation between populations.

24. _____ Geographic isolation is a premating isolating mechanism.

25. _____ Hybrid infertility is a postmating isolating mechanism.

26. _____ Habitat distruction forces speciation.

Short Answer.

A population of 600 plants contains 294 *AA*, 252 *Aa*, and 54 *aa* individuals. The *AA* and *Aa* plants produce purple flowers while the *aa* plants produce white flowers. What are the frequencies of the following?

27. _____ allele *A*

28. _____ allele *a*

29. _____ genotype *AA*

30. _____ genotype *Aa*

31 _____ genotype *aa*

32. _____ purple-flowered plants

33. _____ white-flowered plants

34. Explain why mutation by itself is not a major force in evolution but that mutation is necessary for evolution to occur.

_____

_____

_____

_____

_____

_____

_____

_____

35. Explain why population size greatly influences the potential for chance events to change allele frequencies.

_____

_____

_____

_____

_____

_____

_____

_____

_____

Matching: Maintaining reproductive isolation.

36. _____ interbreeding does not occur in nature between British peppered moths and Canadian peppered moths

37. _____ interbreeding does not occur between closely related species of fruit flies with slightly different courtship rituals

38. _____ when horses and donkeys are forced to interbreed, sterile mules are produced

39. _____ leopard frogs and pickerel frogs that live in the same area with similar mating seasons do not interbreed because one species breeds in swamps and the other breeds in clear lakes

40. _____ closely related species of katydid insects do not interbreed because the male and female sex organs cannot fit together properly to allow sperm transfer

41. _____ wood frogs and green frogs breed in the same lakes but do not interbreed because one species breeds in April while the other species breeds in May

42. _____ two closely related species of fruit flies sometimes mate, but the female's immune system kills the male's sperm as though it were a foreign, invading microbe

Choices:

a. geographical isolation

b. ecological isolation

c. temporal isolation

d. behavioral isolation

e. mechanical incompatibility

f. gametic incompatibility

g. hybrid inviability

h. hybrid infertility

Multiple Choice: Pick the most correct choice for each question.

43. Which of the following is <u>not</u> true?
    a. differential reproduction leads to a change in allele frequency
    b. evolution occurs in populations
    c. evolution is a change in allele frequency
    d. natural selection causes genetic changes in individuals

44. Which of the following is <u>not</u> one of the Hardy-Weinberg requirements for equilibrium in a population?
    a. no random mating may occur
    b. no mutations may occur
    c. no migrations may occur
    d. no natural selection may occur
    e. populations must be very large

45. A population that meets the Hardy-Weinberg requirements
    a. evolves
    b. is small and usually isolated
    c. has allele frequency in equilibrium
    d. changes genotypic distribution from generation to generation
    e. always has 75% *A* and 25% *a* allele frequencies

46. In a hypothetical population, the frequency of the dominant *A* allele is 80% and the frequency of the recessive allele *a* is 20%. What percentage of the population would you expect to be heterozygous (*Aa*) in genotype?
    a. 4%
    b. 16%
    c. 32%
    d. 50%
    e. 25%

47. Which of the following is more likely to occur in a small population than in a large population?
    a. gene flow
    b. immigration
    c. genetic drift
    d. nonrandom mating
    e. natural selection

48. A characteristic that better enables an organism to survive and reproduce is
    a. a mutation
    b. an adaptation
    c. a bottleneck gene
    d. a stabilizing factor

49. Among animals in particular, which of the following must occur for speciation to happen?
    a. geographical isolation
    b. adaptive radiation
    c. reproductive isolation
    d. ecological isolation
    e. migration

50. Two species of pines releasing pollen at separate times in the same habitat is an example of
    a. geographical isolation
    b. ecological isolation
    c. temporal isolation
    d. behavioral isolation
    e. mechanical incompatibility

CLUES TO APPLYING THE CONCEPTS

These practice questions are intended to sharpen your ability to apply critical thinking and analysis to biological concepts covered in this chapter.

51. In certain parts of Africa, the frequency of sickle-cell anemia among newborn African infants is about 2% and holding steady. In the United States, the frequency of sickle-cell anemia among newborn African-Americans is about 0.2% and slowly declining. Why are these populations behaving differently in evolutionary terms regarding sickle-cell anemia?

_____

_____

_____

_____

_____

_____

_____

_____

_____

_____

_____

52. Dogs (*Canis familiaris*) and coyotes (*Canis latrans*) are given different species names by biologists. Interestingly, dogs and coyotes eagerly mate with each other in captivity and produce healthy, fertile offspring. What criteria do you think biologists have used to determine that dogs and coyotes are different species? Do you personally think that dogs and coyotes should be considered different species? Do you think that dogs and coyotes are closely related types of animals?

_____

_____

_____

_____

_____

_____

_____

_____

ANSWERS TO EXERCISES

1. species
2. reproductive
3. speciation
4. adaptive radiation
5. geographical
6. ecological
7. premating
8. temporal
9. behavioral

10. mechanical
11. hybrid infertility
12. postmating
13. false, do not change
14. true
15. false, selection
16. false, small
17. false, phenotypes
18. true

19. false, become extinct
20. false, time
21. false, premating
22. true
23. false, isolation
24. true
25. true
26. false, leads to species extinction

27. 588 (294 *AA* x 2) + 252 (252 *Aa* x 1) = 840/1200 (600 plants x 2 alleles each) = 0.70 = 70%.

28. 108 (54*aa* x 2) + 252 (252 *Aa* x 1) = 360/1200 = 0.30 = 30%.

29. 294 *AA* /600 total plants = 0.49 = 49%.

30. 252/600 = 0.42 = 42%.

31. 54/600 = 0.09 = 9%.

32. 294 *AA* + 252 *Aa* /600 total plants = 546/600 = 0.91 = 91%.

33. 54 *aa* /600 = 0.09 = 9%.

34. Because the rate of mutation is very low (less than 1 in 100,000 for most genes), mutation alone will not change gene frequencies quickly enough to account for observed evolutionary changes. However, mutation is important in the process of evolution by natural selection because mutation is the ultimate source of the genetic variation upon which natural selection acts in natural populations.

35. Small populations are subject to relatively large random changes in allele frequencies (genetic drift). In large populations, chance events are unlikely to significantly alter the overall gene frequencies, but in small populations chance events could reduce or eliminate alleles, greatly altering in a random way its genetic makeup. Genetic drift tends to reduce genetic variability within small populations.

36. a	39. b	42. f	45. c	48. b
37. d	40. e	43. d	46. c	49. a
38. h	41. c	44. a	47. c	50. c

53. In Africa, normal individuals (*AA*) are at a disadvantage due to susceptibility to malaria, and those with sickle-cell anemia (*aa*) are at a disadvantage as well. Heterozygotes (*Aa*) have the highest fitness since they are somewhat resistant to malaria and do not suffer from sickle-cell disease. Thus, both alleles are maintained at relatively high frequencies in malarial areas of Africa. In the United States, normal individuals (*AA*) have the highest fitness, since there is no malaria and their children will not have sickle-cell disease. Heterozygotes (*Aa*) are healthy but can produce offspring with sickle-cell disease (*aa*) if two heterozygotes mate; hence, their fitness is slightly reduced. Thus, in the United States, the *A* allele is slowly rising and the *a* allele is slowly declining due to selection favoring "normal" homozygotes.

54. Since dogs and coyotes successfully interbreed in captivity, they must be closely related, having diverged from common ancestors in the not-too-distant past. Biologists consider them different species because they hardly ever interbreed under natural conditions in the wild. Additionally recent molecular genetics studies have shown that dogs are much more closely related to wolves than they are to coyotes.

Chapter 15: The History of Life on Earth

OVERVIEW

This chapter traces the evolution of life from the beginning of the universe through prebiotic evolution, spontaneous generation of the first living prokaryotic cells, metabolic evolution, the rise of eukaryotes and multicellularity, the invasion of land, and finally human evolution.

1) How Did Life Begin?

In the 1600s, biologists thought life arose through **spontaneous generation** from nonliving matter and unrelated life-forms (like trees giving rise to fish and birds). This idea was not substantially refuted until the mid-1800s, by Louis Pasteur. In the 1930s, Oparin and Haldane proposed **prebiotic** (or chemical) **evolution**: evolution before life, when the atmosphere of Earth contained hydrogen, methane, carbon dioxide, nitrogen, hydrogen sulfide, hydrochloric acid, water vapor, and ammonia gases but no free oxygen gas. In 1953, Miller and Urey conducted lab experiments to show that under prebiotic atmospheric conditions, organic molecules like amino acids, nucleotides, and ATP could be produced. Since no organisms or oxygen gas existed in prebiotic times, organic molecules could accumulate in shaded, shallow pools not subjected to ultraviolet solar radiation, forming a "primordial soup."

In the 1980s, Cech and Altman discovered that certain small RNA molecules called **ribozymes** act as enzymes to make more RNA. Possibly, molecular evolution began in the primordial soup when ribozymes began to copy themselves and make other molecules. Cellular life requires self-replicating molecules enclosed within membranes. If water containing proteins and lipids is agitated, hollow membranelike balls called **microspheres** form. If microspheres formed around ribozymes, nonliving **protocells** would have formed, possibly evolving into living cells.

2) What Were the Earliest Organisms Like?

Life began about 3.5 to 3.9 billion years ago, according to fossil and chemical data. The first cells were prokaryotic and obtained nutrients and energy by absorbing organic molecules from the environment and breaking down these molecules anaerobically (no oxygen gas was present) to gain a small amount of energy. These cells were primitive anaerobic bacteria. Eventually, some cells evolved photosynthesis, the ability to use solar energy to make their own complex, energy-rich molecules from water and carbon dioxide. The cyanobacteria evolved and, through photosynthesis, released oxygen gas into the atmosphere. About 2.2 billion years ago, free oxygen gas began to accumulate in the atmosphere. This increased oxygen level, in turn, allowed the evolution of microbes capable of aerobic respiration, using oxygen gas to completely break down organic molecules and release a significant amount of chemical energy.

Predation soon evolved, with larger prokaryotic cells engulfing bacteria. About 1.7 billion years ago, eukaryotic cells having membrane-bound nuclei and cytoplasmic organelles evolved from predatory bacteria. According to Lynn Margulis's **endosymbiont hypothesis**, primitive cells acquired the precursors of mitochondria and chloroplasts by engulfing certain types of bacteria and forming a symbiotic (mutually supportive) relationship with them. The fact that these organelles retain their own bacteria-like DNA supports the hypothesis. Cilia, flagella, centrioles, and microtubules may all have evolved from a symbiosis between spiral-shaped bacteria and a primitive eukaryotic cell. The origin of the nucleus is obscure.

3) How Did Multicellularity Arise?

Once predation had evolved, increased size was an advantage, but large unicellular organisms could not survive due to the slowness of diffusion. Multicellular organisms evolved about 1 billion years ago, mostlikely in the oceans. Fossil evidence, however, tells little about the origins of multicellularity. Researchers do know that multicellular plants developed specialized structures (roots and leaves) that helped them invade diverse habitats, and multicellular animals developed specializations to help them capture prey, feed, and escape their enemies.

4) How Did Life Invade the Land?

Terrestrial organisms must find adequate water, protect their gametes from drying out, and resist the effects of gravity without a buoyant watery environment. The plants that first colonized the land, however, had ample sunlight, rich nutrient sources in the soil, and no predators. Some plants developed specialized structures that adapted them to dry land. Waterproof coatings on the aboveground parts reduced water loss, rootlike structures were anchored in the soil, extracting water and nutrients, and extra-thick cell walls enabled stems to stand erect.

Primitive land plants (mosses and ferns) retained swimming sperm and required water to reproduce, but the **conifers** (cone-bearing plants) retained their eggs internally and encased sperm within pollen grains blown around by the wind, allowing the conifers to flourish in dry habitats. Landing on a female cone near the egg, the pollen released sperm cells directly into living tissue, eliminating the need for a surface film of water. As the moist climate dried up, conifers flourished. Flowering plants enticed animals (mainly insects) to carry pollen from flower to flower, thus wasting much less pollen than conifers do. Flowering plants also reproduce more rapidly and grow more quickly than do conifers.

Some animals evolved specialized structures that adapted them to life on dry land. Some animals were **preadapted** for land-life (they already had structures suitable for life on land, such as **exoskeletons** in the arthropods).   Amphibians evolved from lobefin fishes which had two preadaptations for land: (1) stout, fleshy fins for crawling; and (2) a pouch off the digestive tract that could act as a primitive lung. With improvements in lungs and legs, lobefins evolved into amphibians. But amphibians still depended on water to keep the skin moist (for gas exchange) and for egg laying.

Reptiles, which evolved from amphibians, developed several adaptations to dry land: (1) internal fertilization; (2) shelled, waterproof eggs containing a supply of water and food; (3) scaly, waterproof skin; and (4) improved lungs. Two groups of small reptiles developed insulation (feathers or hair) to retain body heat. Reptiles gave rise to both birds (feathers) and mammals (hair). Unlike birds, which lay eggs, mammals evolved live birth and mammary (milk-producing) glands to feed their young. When the reptilian dinosaurs became extinct (65 million years ago), the mammals adaptively radiated out into the vast array of modern forms.

5) How Did Humans Evolve?

Early **primates** lived in trees. Dryopithecine primates evolved into the **hominids** (humans and their fossil relatives) and pongids (great apes) some 5 to 8 million years ago. The earliest hominids, called the *australopithecines* (southern apes of Africa) could stand and walk upright. Upright posture freed the hands to carry weapons and manipulate tools. The genus *Homo* diverged from the *australopithecines* about 2.5 million years ago. The evolution of *Homo* was accompanied by advances in tool technology.

The Neanderthals (*Homo neanderthalensis*) appeared about 150,000 years ago and had large brains and ritualistic behaviors but, according to DNA analysis, did not give rise to modern humans. Modern humans (*Homo sapiens*) evolved about 150,000 years ago in Africa and spread into the Near East, Europe, and Asia, supplanting all other hominids. Humans and Neanderthals coexisted in Europe, perhaps until humans overran and displaced the Neanderthals.

KEY TERMS AND CONCEPTS

Fill-In: From the following list of terms, fill in the blanks below.

aquatic	ferns	preadapted
conifers	hominids	ribozymes
Cro-Magnon	microspheres	spontaneous generation
endosymbiont hypothesis	Neanderthals	terrestrial

In the 1600s, biologists thought life arose through (1)_____ from nonliving matter.

Certain small RNA molecules called (2)_____ act as enzymes to make more RNA. Possibly, molecular evolution began in the primordial soup when these molecules began to copy themselves and make other molecules.

If water containing proteins and lipids is agitated, hollow membranelike balls called (3)_____ form.

According to Lynn Margulis's (4)_____, primitive cells acquired the precursors of mitochondria and chloroplasts by engulfing certain types of bacteria and forming a symbiotic (mutually supportive) relationship with them.

(5)_____ organisms must find adequate water, protect their gametes from drying out, and resist the effects of gravity without a buoyant watery environment.

Primitive land plants (mosses and ferns) retained swimming sperm and required water to reproduce, but the (6)_____ retained their eggs internally within cones and encased sperm within pollen grains blown around by the wind, allowing them to flourish in dry habitats.

Some animals were (7)_____ for land-life, since they already had structures suitable for life on land, such as exoskeletons in the arthropods.

Dryopithecine primates evolved into the (8)_____ (humans and their fossil relatives) and the pongids (great apes) about 5 to 8 million years ago.

(9)_____ appeared about 150,000 years ago and had large brains and ritualistic behaviors but, according to DNA analysis, did not give rise to modern humans.

Key Terms and Definitions

conifer (kon´-eh-fer): a member of a class of tracheophytes (Coniferophyta) that reproduces by means of seeds formed inside cones and that retains its leaves throughout the year.

endosymbiont hypothesis: the hypothesis that certain organelles, especially chloroplasts and mitochondria, arose as mutually beneficial associations between the ancestors of eukaryotic cells and captured bacteria that lived within the cytoplasm of the pre-eukaryotic cell.

exoskeleton (ex´-ō-skel´-uh-tun): a rigid external skeleton that supports the body, protects the internal organs, and has flexible joints that allow for movement.

hominid: a human or a prehistoric relative of humans, beginning with the Australopithecines, whose fossils date back at least 4.4 million years.

microsphere: a small, hollow sphere formed from proteins or proteins complexed with other compounds.

preadaptation: a feature evolved under one set of environmental conditions that, purely by chance, helps an organism adapt to new environmental conditions.

prebiotic evolution: evolution before life existed; especially, the abiotic synthesis of organic molecules.

primate: a mammal characterized by the presence of an opposable thumb, forward-facing eyes, and a well-developed cerebral cortex; includes lemurs, monkeys, apes, and humans.

protocell: the hypothetical evolutionary precursor of living cells, consisting of a mixture of organic molecules within a membrane.

ribozyme: an RNA molecule that can catalyze certain chemical reactions, especially those involved in the synthesis and processing of RNA itself.

spontaneous generation: the proposal that living organisms can arise from nonliving matter.

THINKING THROUGH THE CONCEPTS

True or False: Determine if the statement given is true or false. If it is false, change the <u>underlined word(s)</u> so that the statement reads true.

10. _____   Primitive Earth was characterized by an <u>abundance</u> of free oxygen.

11. _____   The first living organisms were most likely <u>prokaryotic</u>.

12. _____   The first living organisms were <u>autotrophic</u>.

13. _____   Photosynthesis arose first in the <u>green algae</u>.

14. _____   The evolution of plants to land requiredthe development of <u>no specialized structures</u>.

15. _____   Conifers, as a rule, produce <u>more</u> pollen than flowering plants.

16. _____   Feathers probably evolved first for <u>insulation</u>.

17. _____   Arthropods were preadapted for life on land because of their <u>exoskeletons</u>.

Short Answer.

18. Define spontaneous generation. Explain why scientists assert that it cannot happen today. Explain why scientists say that it probably happened many years ago.

_____

_____

_____

_____

_____

_____

_____

_____

_____

_____

_____

_____

_____

_____

_____

_____

_____

19. Arrange the following events into the sequence that scientists assert occurred during the history of Earth.

   a.   evolution of terrestrial organisms

   b.   oxygen gas begins to accumulate in the atmosphere

   c.   spontaneous formation of simple organic molecules, which, in the absence of O_2, accumulated in the seas

   d.   evolution of anaerobic prokaryotic cells

   e.   evolution of mitochondria and chloroplasts (the endosymbiont hypothesis)

   f.   chance formation of ribozymes with the ability to make accurate and inaccurate copies of itself

   g.   evolution of aerobic prokaryotic cells

   h.   evolution of multicellular eukaryotic organisms

   i.   evolution of primitive photosynthetic anaerobic cells

   j.   by chance, primitive microspheres surround the proper mix of organic molecules and form primitive living cells

_____   _____   _____   _____   _____   _____   _____   _____   _____   _____

20. List four reptilian adaptations that help them cope successfully with a fully terrestrial lifestyle.

_____   _____

_____   _____

Identification: Determine whether the following statements refer to **flowering plants, ferns and mosses,** or **conifers**.

21. _____ first plants to adapt to drier climates

22. _____ use insects to transport pollen

23. _____ need water for sexual reproduction, since sperm must swim to the eggs

24. _____ use wind to transport pollen

25. _____ evolved from conifer-like ancestors

26. _____ dominant plants today

27. _____ dominant plants 250 million years ago

28_____ dominant plants 325 million years ago

Matching: Terrestrial animals. Some questions may have more than one answer.

29. _____ evolved from reptilian ancestors

30. _____ evolved from lobefins whose fins evolved into limbs for crawling

31. _____ dinosaurs

32. _____ use their lungs and moist skin to exchange gases with the air

33. _____ first land animals to evolve waterproof eggs

34. _____ humans

35. _____ first land animals

36. _____ land animals that shed their eggs and sperm into the water

37. _____ were preadapted to life on land because of their exoskeletons

38. _____ evolved directly from amphibian-like ancestors

Choices:

a. reptiles

b. amphibians

c. mammals

d. arthropods

e. birds

Multiple Choice: Pick the most correct choice for each question.

39. It is proposed that the primitive atmosphere contained all of the following *except*
    a. CO_2
    b. O_2
    c. NH_2
    d. H_2O

40. The first living "cells" probably were hollow, ball-shaped structures called
    a. microspheres
    b. protenoids
    c. polypeptides
    d. ribozymes
    e. bacteria

41. The first organisms probably were primitive
    a. photosynthetic bacteria
    b. cyanobacteria
    c. anaerobic bacteria
    d. aerobic microbes
    e. viruses

42. The first cells probably
    a. produced their own food
    b. absorbed food from the environment
    c. engulfed food from the environment
    d. did not require food
    e. underwent sexual reproduction

43. Reptiles are more advanced than amphibians because of
    a. internal fertilization
    b. eggs with shells
    c. scaly skin
    d. improved lungs
    e. all of the above

Short Answer. Refer to the figure on page 136 answer questions 44 through 46.

44. Using the scientific name, identify member "a" of the human family tree:

    _____

45. Using the scientific name, identify member "b" of the human family tree:

    _____

46. Using the scientific name, identify member "c" of the human family tree:

    _____

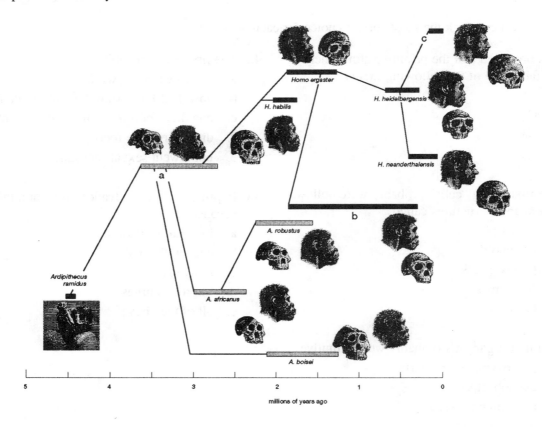

CLUES TO APPLYING THE CONCEPTS

This practice question is intended to sharpen your ability to apply critical thinking and analysis to biological concepts covered in this chapter.

47. Which of the following discoveries, if true, would force scientists to revise drastically their thinking about the origin of life on Earth? (1) Earth is 5 billion years old, not 4.6 billion years old; (2) lipids can spontaneously form selectively permeable membranes without the presence of proteins; or (3) the atmosphere of Earth 4.5 billion years ago contained about the same amount of oxygen gas as it does today. Explain your choice.

_____

_____

_____

_____

_____

_____

_____

_____

_____

ANSWERS TO EXERCISES

1. spontaneous generation
2. ribozymes
3. microspheres
4. endosymbiont hypothesis
5. terrestrial
6. conifers
7. preadapted

8. hominids
9. Neanderthals
10. false, absence
11. true
12. false, heterotrophic
13. false, cyanobacteria

14. false, water proof covering, vascular tissues, extra thick cell walls
15. true
16. true
17. true

18. Spontaneous generation is the generation of living cells from nonliving matter and unrelated life forms. This idea was not substantially refuted until the mid-1800s, by Louis Pasteur. In the 1930s, Oparin and Haldane proposed prebiotic (or chemical) evolution: evolution before life, when the atmosphere of Earth contained hydrogen, methane, carbon dioxide, nitrogen, hydrogen sulfide, hydrochloric acid, water vapor, and ammonia gases but no free oxygen gas. In 1953, Miller and Urey conducted lab experiments to show that under prebiotic atmospheric conditions, organic molecules like amino acids, nucleotides, and ATP could be produced. Since no organisms or oxygen gas existed in prebiotic times, organic molecules could accumulate in shaded shallow pools not subjected to ultraviolet solar radiation, forming a "primordial soup" and making spontaneous generation of the first living cells possible. Once living organisms and oxygen gas existed on Earth, spontaneous generation was no longer possible.

19. c, f, j, d, i, b, g, e, h, a

20. Reptiles, which evolved from amphibians, developed several adaptations to dry land: (1) internal fertilization; (2) shelled, waterproof eggs containing a supply of water and food; (3) scaly, waterproof skin; and (4) improved lungs.

21. conifers
22. flowering plants
23. ferns and mosses
24. conifers
25. flowering plants

26. flowering plants
27. conifers
28. ferns and mosses
29. c, e
30. b

31. a
32. b
33. a
34. c
35. d

36. b
37. d
38. a
39. b

40. a
41. c
42. b
43. e

44. *Australopithecus afarensis*

45. *Home erectus*

46. *Homo sapiens*

47. The atmosphere of Earth 4.5 billion years ago contained about the same amount of oxygen gas as it does today. If this were true, the thinking of scientists regarding the possibility of spontaneous generation in prebiotic times would be erroneous, since large molecules would have been broken down by free oxygen gas, not allowing large quantities of such molecules to accumulate and serve as the raw materials for the chance development of living cells from nonliving materials.

Chapter 16: The Diversity of Life

OVERVIEW

This chapter presents the basic principles used to classify organisms into discrete groups for the purpose of systematic study. The authors describe the various Kingdoms of living organisms, including the prokaryotic bacteria and archaea, the protists, and the fungi, as well as the plants and animals.

1) How Are Organisms Named and Classified?

Systematics is the science of reconstructing **phylogeny** (evolutionary history). **Taxonomy** is the science of naming organisms and placing them into categories based on their evolutionary relationships. The more characteristics two organisms share, the closer is their evolutionary relationship. The seven major taxonomic categories are (1) **kingdom**, (2) **division** (plants) or **phylum** (animals), (3) **class**, (4) **order**, (5) **family**, (6) **genus**, and (7) **species**. These categories form a nested hierarchy in which each level includes all the levels below it. As we move down the hierarchy, smaller and smaller groups are included. Each category is increasingly narrow and specifies a group whose common ancestor is increasingly recent. The **scientific name** (always underlined or italicized) of an organism is formed from its genus (closely related species that do not interbreed) and species (populations of organisms that can interbreed under natural conditions). These names are recognized by biologists worldwide.

Numerous criteria are used for classification. Past evolutionary relationships are inferred on the basis of features shared by living organisms that inherited them from common ancestors. Historically, the most important distinguishing characteristics have been anatomical (bones and teeth, for instance). Developmental stages also provide clues to common ancestry. Ultimately, evolutionary relationships among species must reflect genetic similarities (DNA nucleotide sequences and chromosome structures).

2) What Are the Kingdoms of Life?

Before 1970, taxonomists classified all life into two kingdoms (plants and animals), an oversimplification. In 1969, Whittaker proposed five kingdoms: (1) Monera (unicellular prokaryotes); (2) Protista (unicellular eukaryotes); (3) Plantae (multicellular eukaryotes that obtain nutrients by photosynthesis); (4) Fungi (multicellular eukaryotes that absorb externally digested nutrients); and (5) Animalia (multicellular eukaryotes that ingest food and digest it internally). Recent evidence based on rRNA sequences indicates the Monera are two distinct groups. Woese has proposed classifying life into three broad categories or **domains**: (1) **Bacteria** (or eubacteria), (2) **Archaea** (or archaebacteria), and (3) Eukarya (eukaryotic organisms). Each domain could contain a number of kingdoms (see text Table 16-2).

3) Which Organisms Make Up the Prokaryotic Domains—Bacteria and Archaea?

Prokaryotes lack nuclei, chloroplasts, and mitochondria and are 10 times smaller than eukaryotic cells. Lack of sexual reproduction and sparse fossil evidence make bacteria hard to classify. Taxonomists use criteria such as shape, means of movement, pigments, staining properties, nutrient requirements, DNA and RNA sequences, and the appearance of colonies to classify them. Bacterial cell walls afford protection from osmotic rupture in watery environments and give bacteria their various shapes (rodlike

bacilli, corkscrew-shaped **spirilla**, and spherical **cocci**). Cell walls contain **peptidoglycan** (sugar chains attached by short peptides of amino acids). Some bacteria use **flagella** to move rapidly through a liquid environment.

Bacteria reproduce rapidly by cell division called **binary fission**. Bacteria inhabit almost every habitat including such extreme habitats as 110°C ocean vents and Antarctic sea ice. Bacteria that are **pathogenic** cause disease and pose a threat to human health.

Archaea are fundamentally different from bacteria, especially in their membrane lipids, cell walls, and rRNA nucleotide sequences. The domain Archaea includes (1) **methanogens**, which convert carbon dioxide to methane; (2) **halophiles**, which live in very salty environments; and (3) **thermoacidophiles**, which live in hot, acidic environments. Eukaryotes probably evolved from archaeal ancestors.

4) Which Organisms Make Up the Kingdom Protista?

Protists are a diverse group. They include funguslike slime molds, plantlike unicellular algae, and animal-like protozoa, among others.

Funguslike protists absorb nutrients from the environment and typically decompose dead organisms. Slime molds have a mobile feeding stage and a stationary reproductive stage (**fruiting body**) that produces spores. The **acellular (plasmodial) slime molds** consist of a mass of cytoplasm (a **plasmodium**) containing thousands of nuclei.

Plantlike unicellular algae, or **phytoplankton**, gain energy by photosynthesis. **Dinoflagellates** have two flagella for movement and have a red pigment, sometimes causing "red tides" when the water is warm and rich in nutrients.

Animal-like protists (**protozoa**) ingest food and digest it internally. **Sarcodines** include the freshwater **amoebae** (shell-less; one form causes amoebic dysentery), and the marine **foraminiferans** (chalky limestone shells) and **radiolarians** (glassy shells). Sarcodines move and capture food by forming pseudopodia. **Ciliates**, which move by **cilia**, are the most complex unicellular organisms; they behave as if they have well-developed nervous systems and may have prey-capturing explosive darts, as well as mouth openings, anal openings, and contractile vacuoles to excrete water.

5) What Are the Main Adaptations of Fungi?

Most fungi have a body called a **mycelium**, which is an interwoven mass of threadlike filaments called **hyphae**. The hyphae are made either of one cell with many nuclei, or of many cells separated by porous partitions called **septa**. Fungal cell walls contain chitin. Fungi do not move about, but hyphae can grow rapidly in any direction within suitable environments.

Fungi obtain nutrients from other organisms. Some are **saprobes**, digesting the bodies of dead organisms, secreting enzymes outside their bodies to digest complex molecules, and then absorbing the smaller subunits. Others are parasites, feeding on living organisms and causing disease. Still others live in mutually beneficial relationships with other organisms. A few are predatory.

Most fungi can reproduce both sexually and asexually. In simple asexual reproduction, a mycelium breaks into pieces, each of which grows into a new mycelium. Some fungi produce sexual and asexual **spores** (small, spherical, thick-walled single cells that are dispersed by wind or water and develop into new mycelia).

Some fungi, such as mushrooms and truffles, serve as food for humans. Some are decomposers of other organisms, releasing nutrients such as carbon, nitrogen, and phosphorus and minerals used by plants. Cycling of nutrients within ecosystems would cease without fungal and bacterial decomposers. Parasitic fungi can cause skin diseases such as ringworm and athlete's foot, lung diseases such as valley fever and histoplasmosis, and vaginal yeast infections. Fungi cause plant diseases such as chestnut blight, Dutch elm disease, and corn smut. Farmers use parasitic fungi to their advantage in "fungal pesticides" to kill crop predators (termites, tent caterpillars, aphids, citrus mites, rice weevils). Fungi are used to make bread rise, produce wine from grapes, flavor cheeses, and make beer.

6) What Are the Key Features and Evolutionary Origin of Plants?

Most plants are multicellular and use photosynthesis to convert carbon dioxide and water into sugar and oxygen gas. They have an **alternation of generation** life cycle consisting of both a diploid **sporophyte** generation and a haploid **gametophyte** generation. The separate diploid and haploid generations alternate with each other. Generally, a diploid **zygote** develops (by mitosis) into a diploid sporophyte, which then produces haploid spores by meiosis. A haploid spore develops (by mitosis) into a haploid gametophyte, then produces haploid gametes by mitosis. The fusion of sperm and egg make a diploid zygote. Increasing prominence of the sporophyte generation, accompanied by decreasing size and duration of the gametophyte generation, is the general trend in plant evolution.

Plant ancestors were most likely aquatic, photosynthetic protists, similar to present-day **algae**. Algae (1) lack true roots, stems, leaves, and complex reproductive structures like flowers and cones; (2) shed gametes directly into the water; (3) have varied and complex life cycles – some with dominant haploid gametophyte stages, some with dominant diploid sporophyte stages, and others with nearly identical sporophyte and gametophyte stages; and (4) are colored by pigments that capture light energy for photosynthesis.

The plant body increased in complexity as plants invaded the land. Plants adapted to dry land by (1) anchoring roots to absorb water and nutrients; (2) developing conducting vessels to transport water and minerals upwards from roots to leaves and move sugars from leaves to other body parts; (3) producing a stiffening polymer **lignin** in the conducting vessels to support the plant body; (4) developing a waxy waterproof **cuticle** on leaf and stem surfaces to limit water evaporation; and (5) developing **stomata** (pores) in leaves and stems that open for gas exchange and close when water is scarce to reduce evaporation. Instead of flagellated gametes and spores (**zoospores**) that algae release into the water, plants evolved pollen, seeds, and later flowers and fruits to protect spores, gametes, and young embryos from desiccation, to attract pollinators, and to aid in dispersion of offspring.

The **bryophytes** (16,000 species of mosses and liverworts) are nonvascular plants that lack true roots, stems, and leaves. Anchoring structures (**rhizoids**) bring water and nutrients into the plant body, which then diffuse throughout the body, which must remain small (less than 1 inch tall).

Adaptations that allowed plants to grow taller included (1) support structures for the body and (2) vessels to conduct water and nutrients. Evolution of rigid conducting cells (**vessels**) in the **vascular** plants (**tracheophytes**) allowed plants to live on dry land.

Seedless vascular plants include the small divisions of club mosses and horsetails, and a large division of ferns (12,000 species). Ferns are the only seedless vascular plants that have broad leaves.

The seed plants dominate the land because of the evolution of **pollen** grains (to allow for sperm to find eggs without swimming through water) and **seeds** (to allow embryos to develop without being immersed in water). The pollen grain, containing sperm-producing cells, is all that remains of the male gametophyte generation in seed plants. The female gametophyte is a small group of haploid cells that produces the egg. Pollen grains are dispersed by wind or by animal pollinators like bees. Analogous to the eggs of birds and reptiles, seeds consist of (1) an embryonic plant, (2) a supply of food for the embryo, and (3) a protective outer coat.

Gymnosperms (nonflowering seed plants) evolved earlier than the flowering plants and include the conifers (500 species) and two smaller groups (cycads, and gingkos). **Conifers** (pines, firs, spruces, hemlocks, and cypresses) are most abundant in the far north and at high elevations. They are adapted to dry, cold conditions by (1) retaining green leaves throughout the year (**evergreens**), allowing them to photosynthesize and grow all year long; (2) producing leaves that are thin needles covered with a thick waterproof cuticle to minimize evaporation; and (3) producing an "antifreeze" in their sap to allow transport of nutrients in subfreezing temperatures.

The 230,000 species of **angiosperms** (flowering plants) evolved from gymnosperm ancestors that formed an association with animals who carried pollen from plant to plant. Pollen transfer by animals was more accurate and less wasteful than pollen transfer by wind. Angiosperms are successful due to: (1) **flowers** (sporophyte structures containing the male and female gametophytes) where fertilizations occur within the flower ovary (where the eggs are and the seeds develop); (2) **fruits** (ripened flower ovaries containing seeds) that attract animals and entice them to disperse seeds; and (3) broad leaves that increase the amount of sunlight trapped for photosynthesis in warm, moist climates.

Most temperate climate angiosperms drop their leaves annually, during fall and winter, and become dormant to reduce water loss. To discourage animals from eating tender leaves, angiosperms have evolved many defenses, including thorns, spines, resins, and chemical defenses now harvested by humans (used in such substances as Taxol®, aspirin, nicotine, caffeine, mustard, and peppermint).

7) What Characteristics Define an Animal?

All animals (1) have multicellular bodies; (2) obtain energy by eating the bodies of other organisms; (3) reproduce sexually; (4) have cells that lack cell walls; (5) are motile during some life stage; and (6) respond rapidly to external stimulation.

8) What Are the Major Animal Phyla?

There are two major categories of animals. **Invertebrates**, animals without backbones, are the earliest animals, comprising 97% of animals today. **Vertebrates**, animals with backbones (fish, amphibians, reptiles, birds, and mammals), all are in the phylum Chordata.

Sponges (more than 5,000 species) lack true tissues and organs. An internal skeleton composed of spines called **spicules** supports the body. All adult sponges are **sessile**. Sponges may reproduce asexually by **budding** or sexually through fusion of sperm and egg.

Annelid worms (about 9,000 species) have bodies made up of repeating segments (**segmentation**), each with nerve ganglia, excretory structures, and muscles. Segmented worms include terrestrial earthworms (oligochaetes with few bristles), marine polychaetes with many bristles, and the carnivorous or parasitic leeches.

The insects, arachnids, and crustaceans are arthropods. Arthropods (more than 1 million species) are the most successful group of animals on Earth because of the following adaptations: (1) an external skeleton (**exoskeleton**) made of **chitin** and having jointed appendages; (2) segmentation into **head** (sensory and feeding structures), **thorax** (locomotion structures), and **abdomen** (digestive structures); and (3) a well-developed sensory and nervous systems, including **compound eyes** and a brain composed of fused **ganglia**. The exoskeleton periodically must be shed (**molted**) and replaced with a larger one. Insects are the most diverse and abundant arthropods (about 850,000 species), with three pairs of legs and two pairs of wings. Some insects undergo complete **metamorphosis**: from the egg to the **larva**, which is adapted for feeding, to the **pupa**, a nonfeeding form in which physical changes occur, to the adult, which is adapted for reproduction.

Snails, clams, and squid are mollusks. Mollusks (about 50,000 species) have (1) a moist, muscular body supported by a **hydrostatic skeleton** and (2) a **mantle** (body wall extension that forms a gill chamber). Some have a calcium carbonate shell secreted by the mantle. Snails are gastropod mollusks (about 35,000 species) that have a muscular foot and a rasping **radula** used to scrape algae from rock for food. Scallops, clams, and oysters are bivalve mollusks. They have two shells connected by a flexible hinge. Bivalves are filter feeders, using gills for both respiration and feeding. Octopuses, squid, and their relatives are cephalopod mollusks, mostly marine predators. The foot has evolved into tentacles with suction disks, and they move by jet propulsion caused by forceful expulsion of water from the mantle cavity.

Chordates (tunicates, lancelets, and vertebrates) share certain characteristics: (1) a **notochord**, a stiff but flexible anterior-posterior rod made of cartilage, for muscle attachment, which is replaced by the bony backbone (vertebral column) in vertebrates; (2) a **dorsal, hollow nerve cord** with an anterior brain; (3) **pharyngeal gill slits** (may occur only early in development); and (4) a **post-anal tail** (may occur only early in development). The invertebrate chordates include lancelets and tunicates (sea squirts). Vertebrates have an **endoskeleton** of **cartilage** (sharks) or bone including the backbone (**vertebral column**), paired appendages (fins, limbs, wings), and large complex brains.

There are several classes of vertebrates. Bony fish (about 17,000 species) have invaded nearly every aquatic habitat. Adaptations that allowed animals to make the transition to life on land included (1) skeletal structure that provided better support, (2) coverings for skin and eggs that reduced water loss, (3) control of body temperature, and (4) more efficient circulation.

Amphibians (about 2,500 species of frogs, toads, and salamanders) have limbs, lungs, three-chambered hearts. Reptiles (about 7,000 species of lizards, snakes, turtles, alligators, and crocodiles) have three particularly useful adaptaions to life on dry land: (1) tough, scaly, skin that resists water loss; (2) internal fertilization; (3) a shelled **amniote egg** with an internal **amnion** membrane that encloses the embryo in a watery environment.

Birds (about 9,000 species) are adapted to the demands of flight. They are exceptionally light for their size (with hollow bones), and they have feathers for lift and control in flight and for insulation of the body, extraordinary coordination and balance combined with acute eyesight, and are warm-blooded (which enables them to fly regardless of the outside temperature).

Mammals (about 4,500 species) are warm-blooded and have fur or hair to protect and insulate the body, four-chambered hearts, highly developed brains, internal fertilization, and limbs that are modified for running, swimming, flying, or grasping. **Mammary glands** produce milk for feeding young offspring

KEY TERMS AND CONCEPTS

Fill-In: Using the key terms from this chapter and previous chapters fill in the crossword puzzle based on the following clues.

Across

3. Taxonomic category contained within a kingdom and consisting of related classes of plants.
5. Multicellular, eukaryotic organisms that absorb externally digested nutrients.
6. Taxonomic category composed of related orders.
8. Taxonomic category contained within an order and consisting of related genera.
12. The science of reconstructing the evolutionary histories of life forms on Earth.
13. Multicellular, eukaryotic, photosynthetic organisms.
14. Unicellular eukaryotic organisms.

Down

1. Broadest taxonomic category, consisting of phyla.
2. New taxonomic category based on molecular analysis indicating that two groups of bacteria exist.
4. Domain containing all eukaryotic organisms.
7. A group of organisms within a genus that interbreed under natural conditions.
9. Taxonomic category of animals contained within a kingdom and consisting of related classes.
10. Multicellular, eukaryotic organisms that ingest food and digest it internally.
11. Taxonomic group containing closely related species.

Fill-In: From the following list of terms, fill in the blanks below.

algae	ferns	seeds
alternation of generations	gametophyte	sporophyte
angiosperms	gymnosperms	stomata
bryophytes	lignin	vessels
cuticle	roots	

Most plants have an (15)_____ life cycle consisting of both a diploid

(16)_____ generation (that develops from a zygote and produces haploid spores

by meiosis) and a haploid (17)_____ generation (that develops from a spore and

produces, by mitosis, gametes that fuse to produce a diploid zygote).

Plant ancestors were most likely aquatic, photosynthetic protists, similar to present-day

(18)_____.

Plant adaptations to dry land include (19)_____ to absorb water and nutrients;

(20)_____ to transport water and minerals upward from roots to leaves, and to move

sugars from leaves to other body parts; (21)_____ in the conducting vessels to

support the plant body; a waterproof (22)_____ on leaf and stem surfaces to limit

water evaporation; (23)_____ in leaves and stems that open for gas exchange and

close when water is scarce to reduce evaporation; and (24)_____ to protect young

embryos from dessication.

The (25)_____ (mosses and liverworts) are nonvascular plants lacking true roots,

stems, and leaves. (26)_____ are seedless vascular plants with broad leaves.

(27)_____ include the conifers. (28)_____ produce seeds,

flowers, and fruits.

Key Terms and Definitions

abdomen: the body segment at the posterior end of an animal with segmentation; contains most of the digestive structures.

acellular slime mold: a type of funguslike protist that forms a multinucleate structure that crawls in amoeboid fashion and ingests decaying organic matter; also called *plasmodial slime mold*.

alga (al´-ga; pl., algae, al´-jē): simple aquatic plants that lack vascular tissue.

alternation of generations: a life cycle, typical of plants, in which a diploid sporophyte (spore-producing) generation alternates with a haploid gametophyte (gamete-producing) generation.

amnion (am´-nē-on): one of the embryonic membranes of reptiles, birds, and mammals; encloses a fluid-filled cavity that envelops the embryo.

amniote egg (am-nē-ōt´): the egg of reptiles and birds; contains an amnion that encloses the embryo in a watery environment, allowing the egg to be laid on dry land.

amoeba: a type of animal-like protist that uses a characteristic streaming mode of locomotion by extending a cellular projection called a *pseudopod*.

angiosperm (an´-jē-ō-sperm): a flowering vascular plant.

Archaea: one of life's three domains; consists of prokaryotes that are only distantly related to members of the domain Bacteria.

bacillus (buh-sil´-us; pl., bacilli): a rod-shaped bacterium.

Bacteria: one of life's three domains; consists of prokaryotes that are only distantly related to members of the domain Archaea.

binary fission: the process by which a single bacterium divides in half, producing two identical offspring.

bryophyte (brī´-ō-fīt): a simple nonvascular plant of the division Bryophyta, including mosses and liverworts.

budding: asexual reproduction by the growth of a miniature copy, or bud, of the adult animal on the body of the parent. The bud breaks off to begin independent existence.

cartilage (kar´-teh-lij): a form of connective tissue that forms portions of the skeleton; consists of chondrocytes and their extracellular secretion of collagen; resembles flexible bone.

chitin (kī´-tin): a compound found in the cell walls of fungi and the exoskeletons of insects and some other arthropods; composed of chains of nitrogen-containing, modified glucose molecules.

ciliate (sil´-ē-et): a protozoan characterized by cilia and by a complex unicellular structure, including harpoonlike organelles called *trichocysts*. Members of the genus *Paramecium* are well-known ciliates.

cilium (sil´-ē-um; pl., **cilia**): a short, hairlike projection from the surface of certain eukaryotic cells that contains microtubules in a 9 + 2 arrangement. The movement of cilia may propel cells through a fluid medium or move fluids over a stationary surface layer of cells.

class: the taxonomic category composed of related genera. Closely related classes form a division or phylum.

coccus (kah´-kus; pl., cocci): a spherical bacterium.

compound eye: an image-forming eye consisting of numerous similar light-gathering and light-detecting elements.

conifer (kon´-eh-fer): a member of a class of tracheophytes (Coniferophyta) that reproduces by means of seeds formed inside cones and that retains its leaves throughout the year.

cuticle (kū´-ti-kul): a waxy or fatty coating on the exposed surfaces of epidermal cells of many land plants, which aids in the retention of water.

dinoflagellate (dī-nō-fla´-jel-et): a protist that includes photosynthetic forms in which two flagella project through armorlike plates; abundant in oceans; can reproduce rapidly, causing "red tides."

division: the taxonomic category contained within a kingdom and consisting of related classes of plants, fungi, bacteria, or plantlike protists.

domain: the broadest category for classifying organisms; organisms are classified into three domains: Bacteria, Archaea, and Eukarya.

dorsal, hollow nerve cord: a hollow neural structure characteristic of chordates, that lies dorsal to the digestive tract and develops an anterior thickening that becomes a brain.

endoskeleton (en´-dō-skel´-uh-tun): a rigid internal skeleton with flexible joints to allow for movement.

evergreen: a plant that retains green leaves throughout the year.

exoskeleton (ex´-ō-skel´-uh-tun): a rigid external skeleton that supports the body, protects the internal organs, and has flexible joints that allow for movement.

family: the taxonomic category contained within an order and consisting of related genera.

flagellum (fla-jel´-um; pl., flagella): a long, hairlike extension of the plasma membrane; in eukaryotic cells, it contains microtubules arranged in a 9 + 2 pattern. The movement of flagella propel some cells through fluids.

flower: the reproductive structure of an angiosperm plant.

foraminiferan (for-am-i-nif´-er-un): an aquatic (largely marine) protist characterized by a typically elaborate calcium carbonate shell.

fruit: in flowering plants, the ripened ovary (plus, in some cases, other parts of the flower), which contains the seeds.

fruiting body: a spore-forming reproductive structure of certain protists, bacteria, and fungi.

gametophyte (ga-mēt´-ō-fīt): the multicellular haploid stage in the life cycle of plants.

ganglion (gang´-lē-un): a cluster of neurons.

genus (jē-nus): the taxonomic category contained within a family and consisting of very closely related species.

gymnosperm (jim´-nō-sperm): a nonflowering seed plant, such as a conifer, cycad, or gingko.

halophile (hā´-lō-fīl): literally, "salt-loving"; a type of archaen that thrives in concentrated salt solutions.

head: the anterior-most segment of an animal with segmentation.

hydrostatic skeleton: fluid contained in body compartments that provides support for the body and mass against which muscles can contract.

hypha (hī´-fuh; pl., **hyphae**): a threadlike structure that consists of elongated cells, typically with many haploid nuclei; many hyphae make up the fungal body.

invertebrate (in-vert´-uh-bret): an animal that never possesses a vertebral column.

kingdom: the second broadest taxonomic category, contained within a domain and consisting of related phyla or divisions. This textbook recognizes four kingdoms within the domain Eukarya: Protista, Fungi, Plantae, and Animalia.

larva (lar´-vuh): an immature form of an organism with indirect development prior to metamorphosis into its adult form; includes the caterpillars of moths and butterflies and the maggots of flies.

lignin: a hard material that is embedded in the cell walls of vascular plants; provides support in terrestrial species; an early and important adaptation to terrestrial life.

mammary gland (mam´-uh-rē): a milk-producing gland used by female mammals to nourish their young.

mantle (man´-tul): an extension of the body wall in certain invertebrates, such as mollusks; may secrete a shell, protect the gills, and, as in cephalopods, aid in locomotion.

metamorphosis (met-a-mor´-fō-sis): in animals with indirect development, a radical change in body form from larva to sexually mature adult, as seen in amphibians (tadpole to frog) and insects (caterpillar to butterfly).

methanogen (me-than´-ō-jen): a type of anaerobic archaean capable of converting carbon dioxide to methane.

molt: to shed an external body covering, such as an exoskeleton, skin, feathers, or fur.

mycelium (mī-sēl´-ē-um): the body of a fungus, consisting of a mass of hyphae.

nerve cord: see *dorsal, hollow nerve cord*

notochord (nōt´-ō-kord): a stiff but somewhat flexible, supportive rod found in all members of the phylum Chordata at some stage of development.

order: the taxonomic category contained within a class and consisting of related families.

pathogenic (path´-ō-jen-ik): capable of producing disease; refers to an organism with such a capability (a pathogen).

peptidoglycan (pep-tid-ō-glī´-kan): a component of prokaryotic cell walls that consists of chains of sugars cross-linked by short chains of amino acids called **peptides**.

pharyngeal gill slit (far-in´-jē-ul): an opening, located just posterior to the mouth, that connects the digestive tube to the outside environment; present (as some stage of life) in all chordates.

phylum (fī-lum): the taxonomic category of animals and animal-like protists that is contained within a kingdom and consists of related classes.

phytoplankton (fī´-tō-plank-ten): photosynthetic protists that are abundant in marine and freshwater environments.

plasmodial slime mold: see *acellular slime mold*.

plasmodium (plaz-mō´-dē-um): a sluglike mass of cytoplasm containing thousands of nuclei that are not confined within individual cells.

pollen: see *pollen grain*.

pollen grain: the male gametophyte of a seed plant; also called *pollen*.

post-anal tail: a tail that extends beyond the anus; exhibited by all chordates at some stage of development.

Protista (prō-tis´-tuh): a taxonomic kingdom including unicellular, eukaryotic organisms.

protozoan (prō-tuh-zō´-an; pl., **protozoa**): a nonphotosynthetic or animal-like protist.

pupa: a developmental stage in some insect species in which the organism stops moving and feeding and may be encased in a cocoon; occurs between the larval and adult phases.

radiolarian (rā-dē-ō-lar´-ē-un): an aquatic protist (largely marine) characterized by typically elaborate silica shells.

radula (ra´-dū-luh): a ribbon of tissue in the mouth of gastropod mollusks; bears numerous teeth on its outer surface and is used to scrape and drag food into the mouth.

rhizoid (rī´-zoid): a rootlike structure found in bryophytes that anchors the plant and absorbs water and nutrients from the soil.

saprobe (sap´-rōb): an organism that derives its nutrients from the bodies of dead organisms.

sarcodine (sar-kō´-dīn): a nonphotosynthetic protist (protozoan) characterized by the ability to form pseudopodia; some sarcodines, such as amoebae, are naked, whereas others have elaborate shells.

scientific name: the name of an organism formed from the two smallest major taxonomic categories—the genus and the species.

seed: the reproductive structure of a seed plant; protected by a seed coat; contains an embryonic plant and a supply of food for it.

segmentation: division of the body into repeated, often similar units.

septum (pl., **septa**): a partition that separates the fungal hypha into individual cells; pores in septa allow the transfer of materials between cells.

sessile (ses´-ul): not free to move about, usually permanently attached to a surface.

species (spē´-sēs): all of the organisms that are potentially capable of interbreeding under natural conditions or, if asexually reproducing, are more closely related to one another than to other organisms within a given genus; the smallest major taxonomic category.

spicule (spik´-ūl): a subunit of the endoskeleton of sponges that is made of protein, silica, or calcium carbonate.

spirillum (spi´-ril-um; pl., spirilla): a spiral-shaped bacterium.

spore: a haploid reproductive cell capable of developing into an adult without fusing with another cell; in the alternation-of-generation life cycle of plants, a haploid cell that is produced by meiosis and then undergoes repeated mitotic divisions and differentiation of daughter cells to produce the gametophyte, a multicellular, haploid organism.

sporophyte (spor´-ō-fīt): the diploid form of a plant that produces haploid, asexual spores through meiosis.

stoma (stō´-muh; pl., **stomata**): an adjustable opening in the epidermis of a leaf, surrounded by a pair of guard cells, that regulates the diffusion of carbon dioxide and water into and out of the leaf.

systematics: the branch of biology concerned with reconstructing phylogenies and with naming and classifying species.

taxonomy (tax-on-uh-mē): the science by which organisms are classified into hierarchically arranged categories that reflect their evolutionary relationships.

thermoacidophile (ther-mō-a-sid´-eh-fīl): an archaean that thrives in hot, acidic environments.

thorax: the segment between the head and abdomen in animals with segmentation; the segment to which structures used in locomotion are attached.

tracheophyte (trā´-kē-ō-fīt): a plant that has conducting vessels; a vascular plant.

vascular: describing tissues that contain vessels for transporting liquids.

vertebral column (ver-tē´-brul): a column of serially arranged skeletal units (the vertebrae) that enclose the nerve cord in vertebrates; the backbone.

vertebrate: an animal that possesses a vertebral column.

vessel: a tube of xylem composed of vertically stacked vessel elements with heavily perforated or missing end walls, leaving a continuous, uninterrupted hollow cylinder.

zoospore: a nonsexual reproductive cell that swims using flagella, such as is formed by some fungi.

zygote (zī´-gōt): in sexual reproduction, a diploid cell (the fertilized egg) formed by the fusion of two haploid gametes.

THINKING THROUGH THE CONCEPTS

True or False: Determine if the statement given is true or false. If it is false, change the <u>underlined</u> word so that the statement reads true.

29. _____   The science that places organisms into categories based on their evolutionary relationships is <u>evolution</u>.

30. _____   A genus contains several <u>classes</u>.

31. _____   A kingdom is a more <u>general</u> category than a phylum.

32. _____   The two-part name for a type of organism uses its <u>genus and species</u>.

33. _____   Organisms within the same <u>genus</u> interbreed in nature.

34. _____   All bacterial and protistan organisms are <u>prokaryotic</u>.

35. _____   Plants are, but fungi are not, <u>multicellular</u>.

36. _____   Protistan organisms are <u>eukaryotic</u>.

37. _____   Bacilli bacteria are <u>rod-shaped</u>.

38. _____   Bacteria reproduce asexually by <u>mitosis</u>.

39. _____   Unicellular algae are often called <u>phytoplankton</u>.

40. _____   <u>Dinoflagellates</u> are unicellular, eukaryotic, heterotrophic protists.

41. _____   The single threadlike filaments that make up the body of a fungus are called <u>mycelia</u>.

42. _____   Fungi digest food particles <u>outside</u> their bodies.

43. _____   Fungi and <u>protozoa</u> are decomposers.

44. _____   The gametophyte generation is <u>diploid</u>.

45. _____   Spores develop into the <u>gametophyte</u> generation.

46. _____   The gametophyte produces <u>gametes</u>.

47. _____   The dominant generation of the ferns is the <u>sporophyte</u>.

48. _____   A liverwort is an example of a <u>vascular</u> plant.

49. _____   The <u>angiosperms</u> are the flowering plants.

50. _____   All adult sponges are <u>motile</u>.

51. _____   Birds have <u>three-chambered</u> hearts.

52. _____   Mammals evolved from <u>birds</u>.

Multiple Choice: Pick the most correct choice for each question.

53. Which hierarchical order goes from more specific to more general?
    a. kingdom → division → class
    b. genus → family → order
    c. order → family → genus
    d. order → kingdom → species
    e. family → order → species

54. With few exceptions, the fungal body is composed of
    a. hyphae
    b. chitin
    c. chlorophyll
    d. vascular tissue
    e. cellulose

55. The classification of organisms is called
    a. taxonomy
    b. morphology
    c. ecology
    d. nomenclature
    e. phylogeny

56. Segmentation first appeared in the
    a. annelid worms
    b. insects
    c. roundworms
    d. mollusks
    e. chordates

57. In the alternation of generations life cycle, the haploid stage is called the
    a. zygote
    b. gametophyte
    c. sporophyte
    d. fruit
    e. seed

58. Which of the following is seen as a basic trend in plant evolution?
    a. gametophyte generation increases in size
    b. gametophyte generation decreases in size
    c. sporophyte generation produces gametes
    d. sporophyte generation decreases in size
    e. water becomes more necessary for reproduction

59. The haploid stage of an alternation of generations life cycle produces
    a. seeds
    b. spores
    c. reproductive cells
    d. zygotes
    e. cones

60. During alternation of generations, meiosis results in the production of
    a. egg cells
    b. sperm cells
    c. spores
    d. a and b
    e. a, b, and c

61. Gymnosperms are characterized by all of the following except
    a. cones
    b. seeds
    c. needle-shaped leaves
    d. evergreen
    e. fruit

Identification: Determine whether the following statements refer to the kingdom **protista, fungi, planta**, or **animalia**, or to the domains **Bacteria and Archaea**.

62. _____ unicellular, eukaryotic organisms

63. _____ multicellular, nonphotosynthetic organisms with extracellular digestion

64. _____ prokaryotic organisms

65. _____ unicellular organisms that lack nuclei

66. _____ all organisms are photosynthetic

67. _____ bacteria

68. _____ multicellular, non-photosynthetic organisms with digestion within the body

69. _____ unicellular organisms that have nuclei

Matching: Land plants. Some questions may have more than one answer.

70. _____ do not produce seeds

71. _____ make pollen grains

72. _____ lack true vascular tissues

73. _____ some rely on insect pollinators

74. _____ straddles the aquatic/terrestrial life boundry

75. _____ produce fruits

76. _____ seedless vascular plants

77. _____ produce rootlike rhizoids

78. _____ flowering plants

79. _____ make cones

80. _____ most successful land plants today

81. _____ vascular plants

82. _____ mosses

83. _____ seed plants

Choices:
a. angiosperms
b. gymnosperms
c. ferns
d. bryophytes

Identification: Determine whether the following statements refer to **arthropods, mollusks, both,** or **neither**.

84. _____ octopuses

85. _____ have internal skeletons composed of spicules

86. _____ largest phylum of animals

87. _____ some have calcium carbonate shells

88. _____ have exoskeletons

89. _____ clams

90. _____ have a boney skeleton

91. _____ evolved from annelid worms

92. _____ metamorphosis during development

93. _____ snails

Matching: Chordates. Some questions may have more than one answer.

94. _____ produce amniote eggs

95. _____ have a notochord

96. _____ produce placentas

97. _____ frogs

98. _____ have two-chambered hearts

99. _____ dinosaurs

100. _____ have four-chambered hearts

101. _____ on the boundary between aquatic and terrestrial existence

102. _____ most diverse vertebrates

103. _____ feed milk to their young

104. _____ have three-chambered hearts

105. _____ have backbones

106. _____ are warm blooded

107. _____ evolved into amphibians

108. _____ have hollow bones and air sacs

109. _____ whales

Choices:

a.   none of these choices

b.   bony fishes

c.   amphibians

d.   reptiles

e.   birds

f.   mammals

g.   all choices b-f

Identification: Determine whether the following statements refer to the **sporophyte** generation, **gametophyte** generation, **both** or **neither**.

110. _____   haploid

111. _____   begins as a zygote

112. _____   multicellular

113. _____   produces sex cells by meiosis

114. _____   begins as a spore

115. _____   produces spores by meiosis

116. _____   grows by mitosis

117. _____   dominant form in flowering plants

CLUES TO APPLYING THE CONCEPTS

These practice questions are intended to sharpen your ability to apply critical thinking and analysis to biological concepts covered in this chapter.

118. The common intestinal bacterium, *E. coli*, is a typical bacterium in that it can reproduce rapidly under favorable growth conditions. Suppose you placed 10 bacteria in a very large flask containing the ideal culture medium for bacterial growth and reproduction. Under these conditions, the bacteria will divide every 20 minutes. How long would it take until the flask contained about 1 billion bacteria? How many bacteria would be present after 12 hours? If bacteria reproduce so rapidly, why aren't we neck-deep in bacteria all over the world?

_____

_____

_____

_____

_____

_____

_____

_____

_____

_____

_____

_____

119. In recent years, bees domestic to the United States have decreased in numbers for several reasons: the rise in bee parasites, unfavorable changes in climate, and the spread of so-called killer bees from South America. The decline of domestic bees has worried many farmers, especially those who own orchards. Why should farmers be concerned with bees when they grow apples and peaches?

_____

_____

_____

_____

_____

120. Which groups of land vertebrate animals are found in the Arctic and Antarctic regions, the coldest parts of Earth? Why are they able to live in these regions while other types of animals, especially the arthropods, which are tremendously successful elsewhere, are unable to survive there very well?

_____

_____

_____

_____

_____

_____

_____

_____

ANSWERS TO EXERCISES

15. alternation of generations
16. sporophyte
17. gametophyte
18. algae
19. roots
20. vessels
21. lignin

22. cuticle
23. stomata
24. seeds
25. bryophytes
26. ferns
27. gymnosperms
28. angiosperms

29. false, taxonomy	52. false, reptiles	72. d	95. g
30. false, species	53. b	73. a	96. f
31. true	54. a	74. c, d	97. c
32. true	55. a	75. a	98. b
33. false, species	56. a	76. c	99. d
34. false, unicellular	57. b	77. d	100. e, f
35. false, photosynthetic	58. b	78. a	101. c
36. true	59. c	79. b	102. b
37. true	60. c	80. a	103. f
38. false, binary fission	61. e	81. a, b, c	104. c, d
39. true	62. protista	82. d	105. g
40. false, protozoa	63. fungi	83. a, b	106. e, f
41. false, hyphae	64. Bacteria and	84. mollusks	107. b
42. true	Archaea	85. neither	108. e
43. false, bacteria	65. Bacteria and	86. arthropods	109. f
44. false, haploid	Archaea	87. mollusks	110. gametophyte
45. true	66. planta	88. arthropods	111. sporopyte
46. true	67. Bacteria and	89. mollusks	112. both
47. true	Archaea	90. neither	113. neither
48. false, nonvascular	68. animalia	91. both	114. gametophyte
49. true	69. protista	92. arthropods	115. sporopyte
50. false, sessile	70. c, d	93. mollusks	116. both
51. false, four-chambered	71. a, b	94. d, e, f	117. sporopyte

118. Since the bacteria double in number every 20 minutes, after 1 hour there would be 10 x 2 x 2 x 2 = 80 bacteria (an eight-fold increase every hour). At that rate of increase, it would take about 9 hours to accumulate 1.342 billion bacteria.   After 12 hours, there would be approximately 700 billion bacteria in the flask (about 1.342 billion after 9 hours x 8 = about 10.74 billion after 10 hours x 8 = about 85.92 billion after 11 hours x 8 = about 687.36 billion after 12 hours).   There are estimates that the total weight of all bacteria on Earth is much higher than the total weight of all other organisms combined. But we are not swamped with bacteria because seldom do they find the ideal conditions necessary to reproduce as rapidly as they can.

119. Orchard owners are concerned about the decline in native bee populations because bees are the major organisms responsible for cross-pollination of the flowering trees in their orchards, carrying pollen from one tree's flowers to those of another tree. Without adequate numbers of bees, maximum pollination will not occur, leading to reductions in the amount of fruit produced.

120. Just about all the land vertebrates in the Arctic and Antarctic regions are birds (penguins, for instance) and mammals (polar bears, for instance). What sets these vertebrate groups apart from the rest is that they are warm blooded animals. They maintain a high constant body temperature, which enables them to function well even in the constant coldness of the polar regions. Reptiles and amphibians, the other types of land vertebrates, cannot remain active in the Arctic or Antarctic environments since, their body temperature would be as cold as their surroundings. The same is true for all types of terrestrial invertebrates.

Chapter 17: Plant Form and Function

OVERVIEW

This chapter introduces the structure of plants and how the individual structures function so that the plant survives. Important interactions between the plant and other organisms, such as bacteria, are discussed. Additionally, this chapter presents an overview of how flowering plants reproduce. The organization of the flower and the importance of each part are discussed. The methods of pollination, including some of the animals involved, are identified. These animals have coevolved with plants to develop pollinator-nutrient resource relationships. Once pollination has occurred, fertilization may take place, leading to the development of the embryo plant within a dormant seed. The chapter ends by examining the importance of seed development, dormancy, and germination.

1) How Are Plant Bodies Organized?

Plant bodies are organized into the **root system**, typically the belowground portion, and the **shoot system**, typically the aboveground portion. The root system functions to (1) anchor the plant to a substrate (i.e.: soil), (2) absorb water and minerals from the soil, (3) store excess sugars (usually as starch), (4) transport water, minerals, and other substances to the shoot, (5) produce certain hormones, and (6) interact with soil microorganisms. The shoot system is composed of **stems** with **leaves** and buds and, when appropriate, **flowers** and **fruits**. The aboveground portion functions to absorb sunlight energy and conduct photosynthesis, to transport nutrients and other substances between structures, and to produce certain hormones. Flowers and fruits are stuctures that are specialized for reproduction.

The way in which plant structures are organized depends, in part, on their relationship to one of two evolutionary groups. **Monocots** (such as grasses, lilies, palms, and orchids) and **dicots** (including deciduous trees and bushes and many garden plants) differ in the structure of their flowers, leaves, vascular tissue, root systems, and seeds.

2) How Do Plants Grow?

Most plants grow throughout their lives. Growth occurs from undifferentiated **meristem cells**, which divide by mitosis. Some of the daughter cells produced mature into cells specialized in form and function; these are **differentiated cells**. Plants grow taller or longer from the tips of shoots and roots through division of **apical meristems**. Thus, apical meristems are responsible for **primary growth**. Growth that results in increased diameter occurs due to divisions of **lateral meristems**, also called the **cambium**. Growth due to lateral meristems is **secondary growth**.

3) What Are the Tissues and Cell Types of Plants?

The tissue systems of plant structures include the **dermal tissue system**, which covers the outer surfaces of the plant body; the **ground tissue system**, which consists of all tissues that are nondermal or nonvascular; and the **vascular tissue system**, which transports water, nutrients, minerals, sugars,and hormones throughout the plant.

Dermal tissue may be either **epidermal tissue** (the **epidermis**) or the **periderm**. The epidermis is the cell layer covering leaves, stems, roots, flowers, seeds, and fruit. The epidermis of aboveground organs, in turn, is covered by a waxy coating, the **cuticle**, which protects the plant from disease microbes and reduces water loss from the plant. Some epidermal cells elongate, forming hairs. Hairs located on the root system are called **root hairs** and they serve to greatly increase the absorptive surface area of the roots. As woody stems and roots age, the periderm replaces the epidermis. It is made up of specialized waterproof **cork cells**.

Cells that form ground tissue may be specialized for photosynthesis, storage, or hormone production. Ground tissue also provides support.

Vascular tissue is composed of the transport tissues **xylem** and **phloem**. Xylem transports water and minerals from the roots to the shoot. The conducting cells found in xylem are either **tracheids** or **vessel elements**. Tracheids lie end to end, allowing water and minerals to flow through **pits** in the ends of the cells. Vessel elements are larger in diameter than tracheids but also lie end to end. The ends may have open pores or they may be completely open, forming long tubes (**vessels**). Neither tracheids nor vessel elements are alive when they are mature. The phloem, which transports metabolic substances, is made up of **sieve-tube elements** connected end to end forming long, continuous **sieve tubes**. Between each sieve-tube element are **sieve plates**, the ends of the sieve-tube elements with pores in them allowing substances to flow through the sieve tube. Although sieve-tube elements are alive when they are mature, they do not contain nuclei. The functions of sieve-tube elements are directed instead by **companion cells**.

4) Roots: Anchorage, Absorption, and Storage

Often the first visible sign of seed germination is the appearance of the **primary root**. The primary root of a dicot will grow deep into the soil and mature into a **taproot system**, in which the taproot is maintained while smaller, much less developed roots grow out from its sides. The primary root of a monocot will grow down into the soil but soon dies; new roots are produced from the base of the stem, forming a **fibrous root system**.

Growth and development of individual roots is similar between taproot and fibrous root systems. A **root cap** is produced at the tip of a root by the apical meristem. The root cap protects the root apical meristem as the root grows downward. The root apical meristem also produces the water-permeable epidermis, a **cortex**, and a **vascular cylinder**. Epidermal cells grow root hairs into the soil, greatly increasing their ability to absorb water and minerals. The cells of the cortex surround the vascular cylinder, storing excess sugar as starch. The vascular cylinder consists of the root xylem and phloem. The outer cells of the vascular cylindar can divide and function as the apical meristem of a **branch root**.

5) Stems: Reaching for the Light

As the stem grows, it may differentiate into buds, leaves, or flowers. Clusters of meristem cells within the **terminal bud** of the stem form **leaf primordia**, the beginnings of new leaves. **Lateral buds** are also produced by the meristem cells and will later develop into branches. Leaves and lateral buds are located at **nodes** on the stem. The areas of the stem between the nodes are called **internodes**.

Stems are formed from dermal tissue, vascular tissue, and two types of ground tissue, cortex and **pith**. A waxy cuticle covers the epidermis of stems (and leaves) and retards water loss. However, the cuticle also slows gas exchange between the cells and the atmosphere. To overcome this problem, specialized cells form pores, or **stomata**, in the epidermis that allow CO_2 and O_2 to pass through. As in roots, the cortex is located between the epidermis and the vascular tissue. The pith is located inside the vascular tissue. Cortex and pith provide support to stems, store starch, and may conduct photosynthesis.

Vascular tissue in stems is similar to that of roots and is continuous from the root system, through the stem structures, to the leaves. The apical meristem produces vascular tissue in young stems. The xylem that is produced is **primary xylem** and the phloem that is produced is **primary phloem**. In woody plants, meristematic tissue called the **vascular cambium** produces **secondary xylem** and **secondary phloem**, giving rise to lateral growth. The young, newly formed secondary xylem is called **sapwood**, while the older xylem is called **heartwood**. In the spring, xylem that is produced tends to contain large cells because water is plentiful; as the season progresses and summer droughts occur, smaller xylem cells are produced. This creates the typical **annual rings** seen in tree trunks. To the outside of the secondary phloem, epidermal cells are stimulated by hormones to produce the **cork cambium**. This meristematic tissue gives rise to cork cells which protect the trunk and prevent it from drying out. The **bark** of a tree consists of phloem, cork cambium, and cork cells.

6) Leaves: Nature's Solar Collectors

Leaves are the major photosythetic structures of most plants. Most leaves consist of a broad, flat **blade** specialized to capture sunlight and a **petiole** that attaches the blade to the stem. Vascular tissue runs through the petiole, branching out in the blade, forming **vascular bundles**, or **veins**. As in the stem, the cuticle covers the leaf, retarding water loss and compromising gas exchange. Specialized epidermal cells, **guard cells**, form openings called stomata allowing the exchange of CO_2 and O_2. Beneath the epidermis, cells specialized for photosynthesis constitute the **mesophyll**, which is often organized into two layers of cells: **palisade cells** and **spongy cells**.

7) How Do Plants Acquire Nutrients and Water?

Plants require **nutrients** to function normally. Plants require large amounts of carbon, hydrogen, oxygen, phosphorus, nitrogen, magnesium, calcium, and potassium. Additional nutrients are needed in much smaller amounts. Oxygen and carbon dioxide diffuse into the plant from the air. Water and the other nutrients (**minerals**) are absorbed by the roots.

Symbiotic relationships between plants and soil bacteria increase a plant's ability to acquire nitrogen in nutrient-poor soils. Nitrogen is often limited for many plants. **Legumes** have overcome this by forming a relationship with **nitrogen-fixing bacteria**. These bacteria possess the enzymes needed to convert N_2 from the atmosphere into ammonium or nitrate (the forms plants can use), a process called **nitrogen fixation**. The bacteria enter the root hairs of a legume and travel to the cortex of the root. The bacteria multiply and stimulate the cortex cells to multiply as well. A root **nodule** is produced. Within the nodule nitrogen fixation occurs, supplying the plant with a steady supply of usable nitrogen. In return, the bacteria receive carbohydrates for their energy needs.

Water flows into root cells by osmosis. It then flows through the root tissue until it reaches the xylem. Water in the xylem is pulled up the plant by **transpiration** (the evaporation of water from leaves and stems). Transpiration is able to pull water up the plant (to the tips of the tallest trees) because of the strong cohesive attraction between water molecules.

8) What Are the Features of Plant Life Cycles?

The plant life cycle is represented by two distinct generations, the diploid **sporophyte** and the haploid **gametophyte**. For this reason, the plant life cycle is referred to as the **alternation of generations**. Ferns are most commonly used as an example of the alternation of generations. The fern sporophyte produces haploid **spores** through meiosis. The spores are dispersed to the soil by wind. When conditions are favorable, a spore **germinates** and develops into a mature, haploid gametophyte. The gametophyte produces **eggs** and sperm without another meiotic event. When egg and sperm fuse, a diploid zygote is formed that will mature into the sporophyte. A similar life cycle occurs in all plants. In primitive land plants, such as mosses and ferns, the gametophyte is an independent plant that requires free water to complete reproduction. More evolved land plants have microscopic gametophytes that are dependent on the sporophyte. In flowering plants the sporophyte produces the flower. Within the flower, meiosis produces the spores that develop into gametophytes, still within the flower. One type of spore divides by mitosis to produce the female gametophyte, and a second type divides by mitosis to produce the male gametophyte, the **pollen grain**. The female gametophyte produces the egg while the male gametophyte produces the sperm.

When pollen is distributed from one flower to another by wind or an animal, the pollen grain germinates, producing a long tube that will deliver the sperm to the egg for fertilization. The zygote that is formed develops into an embryo sporophyteand lies dormant within a **seed** until favorable conditions exist.

9) How Are Flowers Structured?

Flowers developed as plants acquired characteristics to attract pollinators. Plants that carried genetic mutations resulting in the production of energy-rich nectar or pollen and a way to display its availability to pollinators passed those traits on to their offspring. The evolution of flowers has allowed the flowering plants to become the dominant plants on land. Through changes in leaves, **sepals, petals, stamens**, and **carpels** developed. If the flower is a **complete flower**, then sepals, petals, stamens, and carpels are all present. If one or more of the flower parts are not present, the flower is an **incomplete flower**. The sepals, the outermost whorl of flower parts, protect the bud. The petals are located just inside the sepals and are often brightly colored as a display. If the stamens are present, they are located just inside the petals. The stamens include a **filament** that supports an **anther**, which produces pollen. If the carpel is present, it is the innermost structure. The carpel is composed of the ovary with a rather long **style** ending in a sticky **stigma**. Within the ovary is one or more **ovules** containing the female gametophytes. After fertilization of the egg, the ovule will mature into the seed and the ovary will develop into the fruit.

10) How Have Flowers and Pollinators Adapted to One Another?

As mutations occurred in plants that resulted in the attraction of pollinators, mutations also occurred in pollinators that resulted in traits that helped them pollinate certain plants. Plants and pollinators have acted as a significant force of natural selection in the evolution of each other. Thus, the two have **coevolved**. For example, bee-pollinated flowers attract the bees by emitting a sweet smell. At the same time, the flowers often have ultraviolet markings that direct the bee to the nectar it desires. When the bee feeds, pollen is brushed onto her back. When she visits another flower, the bee deposits some of the pollen from the first flower on the stigma of the second flower. In contrast, flowers that have evolved without a sweet smell and that are red, attract hummingbirds. The long bill and tongue of the bird are perfect for reaching the rich nectar at the base of the long, tubular flower. Still other flowers are adapted to pollination by bats, moths, butterflies, or beetles. Some species have so perfectly coevolved that they rely solely on one another for survival.

11) Where Are the Gametophytes of Flowering Plants Found?

The familiar form of most plants is the diploid sporophyte. The pollen grain (male) and the **embryo sac** (female) are the haploid gametophytes that develop within the flowers produced by the sporophytes. The embryo sac develops within the ovule and contains seven cells, including the **primary endosperm cell** and the egg. Both the pollen grain and the egg are very small and cannot live independently of the sporophyte.

12) How Does Pollination Lead to Fertilization?

When a compatible pollen grain lands on the stigma of a flower, it absorbs water from the stigma, causing it to germinate. When it germinates, a long tube grows down through the style to the ovary. The pollen tube carries two sperm with it. As the tip of the tube reaches the ovule, it penetrates the embryo sac and releases both of the sperm. One sperm fertilizes the egg to form the diploid zygote. The second sperm enters the primary endosperm cell, fusing with both nuclei. This triploid cell divides mitotically, forming the nutritional **endosperm**. Since there are two fertilization events, this process is called **double fertilization**. It is important to distinguish between **pollination**, the pollen grain landing on the stigma, and **fertilization**, the fusion of sperm and egg, as two separate events.

13) How Do Seeds and Fruits Develop?

Once fertilization has occurred, the embryo sac and the surrounding ovule develop into the seed. The ovule develops into the **seed coat**. Fertilization of the primary endosperm cell produces the endosperm, which will provide nutrients for the developing embryo. As the embryo forms from the zygote, it develops the primary root, the shoot, and the **cotyledons**, or seed leaves. The wall of the ovary will devlop into the fruit. The fruit may be soft and fleshy, firm and rigid, or otherwise modified for a specific type of dispersal.

The mature embryo within the seed enters a state of lowered metabolic activity; it becomes **dormant**. In this dormant state, the embryo can endure adverse environmental conditions, such as a harsh, cold winter, or a period of drought. Often, the dormant state will not cease, and the seed will not germinate until an adaptive set of requirements has been met. This avoids germination during warm, moist autumn days that will be followed by winter temperatures.

14) How Do Seeds Germinate and Grow?

When a seed breaks dormancy and begins to germinate, it absorbs a great deal of water, causing it to swell. The seed coat breaks open and the primary root emerges. As the shoot grows, it pushes upward, out of the soil. To protect the fragile apical meristem, monocot shoots are protected by the **coleoptile**. Dicots do not have a coleoptiles. Instead, they protect their shoot apical meristem by forming a hook. In other words, the shoot remains bent as it pushes upward. While the young plant is becoming established, it receives nourishment from its cotyledons until newly formed leaves develop and begin photosynthesizing.

KEY TERMS AND CONCEPTS

Fill-In I: From the following list of terms fill in the blanks below.

annual rings
apical meristems
bark
blade
cambium
cork cambium
cortex
cuticle
dermal tissue system
differentiated
epidermis
fibrous root system
ground tissue system
heartwood

internode
lateral buds
lateral meristem
leaf primordia
leaves
minerals
node
periderm
petiole
primary growth
primary phloem
primary root
primary xylem

root cap
root system
sapwood
secondary growth
secondary phloem
secondary xylem
shoot system
stems
stomata
taproot system
transpiration
vascular cambium
vascular tissue system

The above ground portion of a plant is called the (1)_____ and is composed of
(2)_____, (3)_____, buds, flowers, and fruits. The belowground portion of a plant is the (4)_____, which absorbs water and
(5)_____ from the soil.

The area of the stem where leaves attach is called a(n) (6)_____, and the area
of the stem between leaves is a(n) (7)_____. A leaf is composed of the
(8)_____, which absorbs sunlight, and the (9)_____,
which attaches to the stem.

Shoots grow taller and roots grow longer by cell division of the (10)_____, which
are responsible for (11)_____. Cells that specialize in form and function have
(12)_____. Shoots grow in diameter by division of cells of the
(13)_____, also called the (14)_____. The growth in diameter
leads to (15)_____.

The three tissue systems of a plant include the (16)_____,
(17)_____, and the (18)_____.

Epidermal tissue is also referred to as the (19)_____, or, in older tissue, it is
called the (20)_____, made up of cork cells. A waxy layer, the
(21)_____ covers the shoot system.

The first plant structure to emerge from a seed is the (22)_____. In dicots,
this root matures into a(n) (23)_____, and in monocots, it matures into a
(24)_____. The tip of a growing root is protected by the

(25)_____, and water can permeate the cells of the root epidermis, the

(26)_____.

New leaves are formed by growth of (27)_____, and branches mature from

(28)_____.

In young, developing stems, the vascular tissue is formed by the apical meristem. The xylem that is

formed is (29)_____, and the phloem that is formed is

(30)_____. As woody plants mature, the (31)_____

produces (32)_____ and (33)_____.

Young, newly formed secondary xylem is called (34)_____, while the older

xylem is called (35)_____. Variations in rainfall during the growing season

produce alternating spring wood and summer wood, the recognizable (36)_____ of

tree trunks.

Outside the secondary phloem, hormones stimulate epidermal cells to produce the

(37)_____, which in turn produces cork cells. The secondary phloem, cork

cambium, and cork cells constitute the (38)_____ of a tree.

Water leaves the plant through (39)_____. The loss of water from the plant is

regulated by the opening and closing of (40)_____.

Fill-In II: From the following list of terms fill in the blanks below.

alternation of generations	fertilize	pollination
anthers	filament	seed
carpel	flowers	seed coat
coevolution	fruit	sepals
coleoptile	gametophyte	spores
complete flower	germination	sporophyte
cotyledons	incomplete flower	stamens
dormant	ovary	stigma
double fertilization	ovules	style
embryo sac	petals	
endosperm	pollen grain	

The plant life cycle includes a haploid generation and a diploid generation. The cycling between the two

is referred to as (41)_____. During the plant life cycle, the diploid

(42)_____ produces (43)_____, and the haploid

(44)_____ produces gametes.

In flowering plants the male gametophyte is actually the (45)_____. The zygote that is

formed after fertilization is protected in a drought-resistant (46)_____.

(47)_____ are composed of modified leaves. The (48)_____ protect the bud, and the (49)_____ attract pollinators.

The male reproductive structures are called the (50)_____ and are composed of a long stalk, the (51)_____, with the pollen-producing (52)_____ at its tip. The female reproductive structures are called the (53)_____ and are composed of a sticky (54)_____ that is at the tip of an elongated (55)_____. At the base is a bulbous (56)_____, which contains (57)_____. It is the ovary that will develop into the (58)_____, which may be edible.

The female gametophyte is the (59)_____. It develops within an ovule.

If a flower contains all flower parts, it is considered to be a(n) (60)_____. If, however, a flower is missing one or more of the structures, it is a(n) (61)_____.

When the pollen has matured, it will be distributed to the stigma of another flower. This is referred to as (62)_____. Flowering plants and their animal pollinators have adapted to one another; this is an example of (63)_____.

Once pollination has occurred, the pollen grain germinates, producing the pollen tube with two sperm inside. One sperm will (64)_____ the egg, while the second sperm will fuse with the two nuclei, producing the triploid (65)_____. The use of two sperm in the fertilization process is termed (66)_____.

After fertilization, the outside of the ovule develops into the (67)_____, and the endosperm nourishes the developing embryo. Most of the endosperm is absorbed into the seed leaves, or (68)_____. The seed will remain (69)_____ until conditions are favorable for (70)_____.

Once germination is initiated, the primary root will emerge from the seed, followed by the young shoot. In monocots, the emerging shoot is protected by the (71)_____.

Key Terms and Definitions

alternation of generations: a life cycle, typical of plants, in which a diploid sporophyte (spore-producing) generation alternates with a haploid gametophyte (gamete-producing) generation.

annual ring: a pattern of alternating light (early) and dark (late) xylem of woody stems and roots, formed as a result of the unequal availability of water in different seasons of the year, normally spring and summer.

anther (an´-ther): the uppermost part of the stamen, in which pollen develops.

apical meristem (āp´-i-kul mer´-i-stem): the cluster of meristematic cells at the tip of a shoot or root (or one of their branches).

bark: the outer layer of a woody stem, consisting of phloem, cork cambium, and cork cells.

blade: the flat part of a leaf.

branch root: a root that arises as a branch of a preexisting root, through divisions of pericycle cells and subsequent differentiation of the daughter cells.

cambium (kam´-bē-um; pl., **cambia**): a lateral meristem, parallel to the long axis of roots and stems, that causes secondary growth of woody plant stems and roots. See *cork cambium*; *vascular cambium*.

carpel (kar´pel): the female reproductive structure of a flower, composed of stigma, style, and ovary.

coevolution: the evolution of adaptations in two species due to their extensive interactions with one another, such that each species acts as a major force of natural selection on the other.

coleoptile (kō-lē-op´-tīl): a protective sheath surrounding the shoot in monocot seeds, allowing the shoot to push aside soil particles as it grows.

companion cell: a cell adjacent to a sieve-tube element in phloem, involved in the control and nutrition of the sieve-tube element.

complete flower: a flower that has all four floral parts (sepals, petals, stamens, and carpels).

cork cambium: a lateral meristem in woody roots and stems that gives rise to cork cells.

cork cell: a protective cell of the bark of woody stems and roots; at maturity, cork cells are dead, with thick, water-proofed cell walls.

cortex: the part of a primary root or stem located between the epidermis and the vascular cylinder.

cotyledon (kot-ul-ē´don): a leaflike structure within a seed that absorbs food molecules from the endosperm and transfers them to the growing embryo; also called *seed leaf*.

cuticle (kū´-ti-kul): a waxy or fatty coating on the exposed surfaces of epidermal cells of many land plants, which aids in the retention of water.

dermal tissue system: a plant tissue system that makes up the outer covering of the plant body.

dicot (dī-kaht): short for dicotyledon; a type of flowering plant characterized by embryos with two cotyledons, or seed leaves, modified for food storage.

differentiated cell: a mature cell specialized for a specific function; in plants, differentiated cells normally do not divide.

dormancy: a state in which an organism does not grow or develop; usually marked by lowered metabolic activity and resistance to adverse environmental conditions.

double fertilization: in flowering plants, the fusion of two sperm nuclei with the nuclei of two cells of the female gametophyte. One sperm nucleus fuses with the egg to form the zygote; the second sperm nucleus fuses with the two haploid nuclei of the primary endosperm cell, forming a triploid endosperm cell.

egg: the haploid female gamete, normally large and non-motile, containing food reserves for the developing embryo.

embryo sac: the haploid female gametophyte of flowering plants.

endosperm: a triploid food storage tissue in the seeds of flowering plants that nourishes the developing plant embryo.

epidermal tissue: dermal tissue in plants that forms the epidermis, the outermost cell layer that covers young plants.

epidermis (ep-uh-der´-mis): in plants, the outermost layer of cells of a leaf, young root, or young stem.

fertilization: the fusion of male and female haploid gametes, forming a zygote.

fibrous root system: a root system, commonly found in monocots, characterized by many roots of approximately the same size arising from the base of the stem.

filament: in flowers, the stalk of a stamen, which bears an anther at its tip.

flower: the reproductive structure of an angiosperm plant.

fruit: in flowering plants, the ripened ovary (plus, in some cases, other parts of the flower), which contains the seeds.

gametophyte (ga-mēt´-ō-fīt): the multicellular haploid stage in the life cycle of plants.

germination: the growth and development of a seed, spore, or pollen grain.

ground tissue system: a plant tissue system consisting of parenchyma, collenchyma, and sclerenchyma cells that makes up the bulk of a leaf or young stem, excluding vascular or dermal tissues. Most ground tissue cells function in photosynthesis, support, or carbohydrate storage.

guard cell: one of a pair of specialized epidermal cells surrounding the central opening of a stoma of a leaf, which regulates the size of the opening.

heartwood: older xylem that contributes to the strength of a tree trunk.

incomplete flower: a flower that is missing one of the four floral parts (sepals, petals, stamens, or carpels).

internode: the part of a stem between two nodes.

lateral bud: a cluster of meristematic cells at the node of a stem; under appropriate conditions, it grows into a branch.

lateral meristem: a meristematic tissue that forms cylinders parallel to the long axis of roots and stems; normally located between the primary xylem and primary phloem (vascular cambium) and just outside the phloem (cork cambium); also called *cambium*.

leaf: an outgrowth of a stem, normally flattened and photosynthetic.

leaf primordium (pri-mor´-dē-um; pl., **primordia**): a cluster of meristem cells, located at the node of a stem, that develops into a leaf.

legume (leg´-ūm): a member of a family of plants characterized by root swellings in which nitrogen-fixing bacteria are housed; includes soybeans, lupines, alfalfa, and clover.

meristem cell (mer´-i-stem): an undifferentiated cell that remains capable of cell division throughout the life of a plant.

mesophyll (mez´-ō-fil): loosely packed parenchyma cells beneath the epidermis of a leaf.

mineral: an inorganic substance, especially one in rocks or soil.

monocot: short for monocotyledon; a type of flowering plant characterized by embryos with one seed leaf, or cotyledon.

nitrogen fixation: the process that combines atmospheric nitrogen with hydrogen to form ammonium (NH_4^+).

nitrogen-fixing bacterium: a bacterium that possesses the ability to remove nitrogen (N_2) from the atmosphere and combine it with hydrogen to produce ammonium (NH_4^+).

node: in plants, a region of a stem at which leaves and lateral buds are located.

nodule: a swelling on the root of a legume or other plant that consists of cortex cells inhabited by nitrogen-fixing bacteria.

nutrient: a substance acquired from the environment and needed for the survival, growth, and development of an organism.

ovary: in flowering plants, a structure at the base of the carpel that contains one or more ovules and develops into the fruit.

ovule: a structure within the ovary of a flower, inside which the female gametophyte develops; after fertilization, develops into the seed.

palisade cell: a columnar mesophyll cell, containing chloroplasts, just beneath the upper epidermis of a leaf.

periderm: the outer cell layers of roots and a stem that have undergone secondary growth, consisting primarily of cork cambium and cork cells.

petal: part of a flower, typically brightly colored and fragrant, that attracts potential animal pollinators.

petiole (pet´-ē-ōl): the stalk that connects the blade of a leaf to the stem.

phloem (flō´-um): a conducting tissue of vascular plants that transports a concentrated sugar solution up and down the plant.

pit: an area in the cell walls between two plant cells in which secondary walls did not form, such that the two cells are separated only by a relatively thin and porous primary cell wall.

pith: cells forming the center of a root or stem.

pollen grain: the male gametophyte of a seed plant; also called *pollen*.

pollination: in flowering plants, when pollen grains land on the stigma of a flower of the same species; in conifers, when pollen grains land within the pollen chamber of a female cone of the same species.

primary endosperm cell: the central cell of the female gametophyte of a flowering plant, containing the polar nuclei (usually two), after fertilization, undergoes repeated mitotic divisions to produce the endosperm of the seed.

primary growth: growth in length and development of the initial structures of plant roots and shoots, due to the cell division of apical meristems and differentiation of the daughter cells.

primary phloem: phloem in young stems produced from an apical meristem.

primary root: the first root that develops from a seed.

primary xylem: xylem in young stems produced from an apical meristem.

root: the part of the plant body, normally underground, that provides anchorage, absorbs water and dissolved nutrients and transports them to the stem, produces some hormones, and in some plants serves as a storage site for carbohydrates.

root cap: a cluster of cells at the tip of a growing root, derived from the apical meristem; protects the growing tip from damage as it burrows through the soil.

root hair: a fine projection from an epidermal cell of a young root that increases the absorptive surface area of the root.

root system: the part of a plant, normally below ground, that anchors the plant in the soil, absorbs water and minerals, stores food, transports water, minerals, sugars, and hormones, and produces certain hormones.

sapwood: young xylem that transports water and minerals in a tree trunk.

secondary growth: growth in the diameter of a stem or root due to cell division in lateral meristems and differentiation of their daughter cells.

secondary phloem: phloem produced from the cells that arise toward the outside of the vascular cambium.

secondary xylem: xylem produced from cells that arise at the inside of the vascular cambium.

seed: the reproductive structure of a seed plant; protected by a seed coat; contains an embryonic plant and a supply of food for it.

seed coat: the thin, tough, and waterproof outermost covering of a seed, formed from the integuments of the ovule.

sepal (sē´-pul): the set of modified leaves that surround and protect a flower bud, typically opening into green, leaflike structures when the flower blooms.

shoot system: all the parts of a vascular plant exclusive of the root; normally above ground, consisting of stem, leaves, buds, and (in season) flowers and fruits; functions include photosynthesis, transport of materials, reproduction, and hormone synthesis.

sieve plate: in plants, a structure between two adjacent sieve-tube elements in phloem, where holes formed in the primary cell walls interconnect the cytoplasm of the elements.

sieve tube: in phloem, a single strand of sieve-tube elements that transports sugar solutions.

sieve-tube element: one of the cells of a sieve tube, which form the phloem.

spongy cell: an irregularly shaped mesophyll cell, containing chloroplasts, located just above the lower epidermis of a leaf.

spore: in the alternation-of-generation life cycle of plants, a haploid cell that is produced by meiosis and then undergoes repeated mitotic divisions and differentiation of daughter cells to produce the gametophyte, a multicellular, haploid organism.

sporophyte (spor´-ō-fīt): the diploid form of a plant that produces haploid, asexual spores through meiosis.

stamen (stā´-men): the male reproductive structure of a flower, consisting of a filament and an anther, in which pollen grains develop.

stem: the portion of the plant body, normally located above ground, that bears leaves and reproductive structures such as flowers and fruit.

stigma (stig´-muh): the pollen-capturing tip of a carpel.

stoma (stō´-muh; pl., **stomata**): an adjustable opening in the epidermis of a leaf, surrounded by a pair of guard cells, that regulates the diffusion of carbon dioxide and water into and out of the leaf.

style: a stalk connecting the stigma of a carpel with the ovary at its base.

taproot system: a root system, commonly found in dicots, that consists of a long, thick main root and many smaller lateral roots, all of which grow from the primary root.

terminal bud: meristem tissue and surrounding leaf primordia that are located at the tip of the plant shoot.

tracheid (trā´-kē-id): an elongated xylem cell with tapering ends that contains pits in the cell wall; forms tubes that transport water.

transpiration: the evaporation of water through the stomata of a leaf.

vascular bundle (vas´-kū-lar): a strand of xylem and phloem in leaves and stems; in leaves, commonly called a *vein*.

vascular cambium: a lateral meristem that is located between the xylem and phloem of a woody root or stem and that gives rise to secondary xylem and phloem.

vascular cylinder: the centrally located conducting tissue of a young root, consisting of primary xylem and phloem.

vascular tissue system: a plant tissue system consisting of xylem (which transports water and minerals from root to shoot) and phloem (which transports water and sugars throughout the plant).

vein: in vascular plants, a vascular bundle, or a strand of xylem and phloem in leaves.

vessel: a tube of xylem composed of vertically stacked vessel elements with heavily perforated or missing end walls, leaving a continuous, uninterrupted hollow cylinder.

vessel element: one of the cells of a xylem vessel; elongated, dead at maturity, with thick, lignified lateral cell walls for support but with end walls that are either heavily perforated or missing.

xylem (zī-lum): a conducting tissue of vascular plants that transports water and minerals from root to shoot.

THINKING THROUGH THE CONCEPTS

True or False: Determine if the statement given is true or false. If it is false, change the <u>underlined</u> word so that the statement reads true.

72. _____ The epidermis of the <u>root system</u> is covered by the cuticle.

73. _____ The function of root systems is greatly enhanced by the presence of <u>root hairs</u>.

74. _____ Tracheids and vessel elements transport water and minerals through <u>phloem</u> tissue.

75. _____ Sieve-tube elements <u>function independently</u> even though they have no nucleus.

76. _____ A <u>monocot</u> such as a dandelion produces a taproot.

77. _____ The root cap must be <u>continuously replaced</u> as the root pushes its way through the soil.

78. _____ When regulating stomatal openings, plants must <u>balance</u> the need for CO_2 with the need to conserve water.

79. _____ Some <u>stems</u> are the primary site of photosynthesis.

80. _____ <u>Leaves</u> grow from lateral buds.

81. _____ Removing a ring of <u>bark</u> will ultimately kill a tree.

82. _____ The <u>ovule</u> develops into the seed after fertilization occurs.

83. _____ During <u>pollination</u>, pollen is attached to the stigma.

84. _____ Spores are produced by the <u>gametophyte</u>.

85. _____ The <u>pollen grain</u> is the male gametophyte.

86. _____ Conifers are wind pollinated, a <u>very efficient</u> process.

87. _____ A complete flower has <u>only stamens</u>.

88. _____ Flower evolution occurred <u>separately</u> from the evolution of insects.

89. _____ Pollination and fertilization are <u>the same event</u>.

90. _____ <u>Double fertilization</u> occurs only in flowering plants.

91. _____ The <u>embryo</u> is uniquely triploid.

92. _____ The <u>flesh</u> of a peach develops from the ovary.

93. _____ After germination, the <u>cotyledons</u> of monocots stay undergound.

94. _____ The purpose of the fruit is to aid in <u>pollen</u> distribution.

95. _____ Newly developed seeds often <u>germinate immediately</u>.

Fill-In:

96. Complete the following table comparing features of monocots and dicots.

	Monocots	Dicots
flowers		
leaves		
vascular tissue		
root pattern		
embryo in seed		

Matching: Plant structures and their functions.

97. _____ leaf   Choices:

98. _____ stem   a. absorbs water and minerals

99. _____ root system   b. covers and protects leaves, stems, and roots

100. _____ petiole   c. waxy layer; prevents water loss

101. _____ epidermis   d. transports water and minerals

102. _____ internode   e. regulate diffusion of O_2 and CO_2 and water loss

103. _____ node   f. increase absorptive surface area

104. _____ root hairs   g. transports sugars, amino acids, and hormones

105. _____ phloem   h. absorbs sunlight

106. _____ lateral bud   i. develops into branches

107. _____ cuticle   j. stem area between leaves

108. _____ stomata   k. attachment point of leaf to stem

109. _____ xylem   l. stalk of leaf; attaches blade to stem

                                   m. supports plant

Matching: Cell types and their functions or characteristics.

110. _____ increases absorption surface area   Choices:

111. _____ waterproof cells of stems and roots   a. guard cell

112. _____ transports water and minerals   b. mesophyll cell

113. _____ transports carbohydrates   c. companion cell

114. _____ lie end to end; connect through pits   d. xylem

115. _____ conducts photosynthesis   e. cork cells

116. _____ controls functions of sieve-tube element f. meristem cell

117. _____ lie end to end; open ends   g. root hair

118. _____ controls stomatal openings   h. tracheids

119. _____ active cellular division; allows plant growth   i. phloem

120. _____ make up phloem; open tubes   j. vessel elements

                                                     k. sieve-tube elements

Identification: Determine whether the following statements refer to dispersal: by **animal**, by **wind**, by **water**, by "**shotgun**", or because they are **edible**.

121. _____ seeds with hairy tufts

122. _____ explosive fruits

123. _____ featherweight fruits

124. _____ round and buoyant fruits

125. _____ fruits with hooked spines

126. _____ juicy and tasty fruits

127. _____ winged fruits

128. _____ seeds have supply of fertilizer

Identification: Name the numbered flower parts on the diagram below.

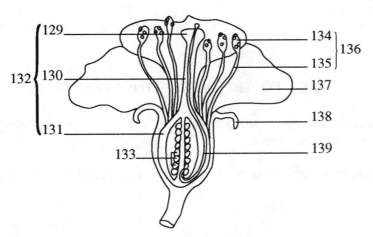

129._____   135._____

130._____   136._____

131._____   137._____

132._____   138._____

133._____   139._____

134._____

140. Provide two examples of legumes:

   a. _____   b. _____

Identification: Name the numbered seedling structures on the diagram below.

141. _____   142. _____

143. _____   144. _____

CLUES TO APPLYING THE CONCEPTS

These practice questions are intended to sharpen your ability to apply critical thinking and analysis to the biological concepts covered in this chapter.

146. Using the following terms, discuss how bacteria aid roots in acquiring nutrients.

ammonium	nitrate	nodule
carbohydrate	nitrogen	root hairs
legume	nitrogen fixation	roots
N_2	nitrogen-fixing bacteria	

_____

_____

_____

_____

_____

_____

_____

_____

_____

_____

145. Compare a taproot system and a fibrous root system.

_____

_____

_____

_____

_____

147. What is meant by the term *double fertilization*?

_____

_____

_____

_____

_____

ANSWERS TO EXERCISES

1. shoot system
2. leaves
3. stems
4. root system
5. minerals
6. node
7. internode
8. blade
9. petiole
10. apical meristems
11. primary growth
12. differentiated
13. lateral meristem
14. cambium
15. secondary growth
16. dermal tissue system
17. ground tissue system
18. vascular tissue system
19. epidermis
20. periderm
21. cuticle
22. primary root
23. taproot system
24. fibrous root system
25. root cap
26. cortex

27. leaf primordia
28. lateral buds
29. primary xylem
30. primary phloem
31. vascular cambium
32. secondary xylem
33. secondary phloem
34. sapwood
35. heartwood
36. annual rings
37. cork cambium
38. bark
39. transpiration
40. stomata
41. alternation of generations
42. sporophyte
43. spores
44. gametophyte
45. pollen grain
46. seed
47. flowers
48. sepals
49. petals
50. stamens
51. filament
52. anthers

53. carpels
54. stigma
55. style
56. ovary
57. ovules
58. fruit
59. embryo sac
60. complete flower
61. incomplete flower
62. pollination
63. coevolution
64. fertilize
65. endosperm
66. double fertilization
67. seed coat
68. cotyledons
69. dormant
70. germination
71. coleoptile
72. false, shoot system
73. true
74. false, xylem
75. false, are dependent on companion cells
76. false, dicot
77. true

78. true
79. true
80. false, branches
81. true
82. true
83. true

84. false, sporophyte
85. true
86. false, very inefficient
87. false, all flower parts
88. false, along with
89. false, separate events

90. true
91. true
92. true
93. true
94. false, seed
95. false, are dormant

96.

	Monocots	Dicots
flowers	multiples of 3	multiples of 4 or 5
leaves	smooth, narrow, parallel veins	oval or palmate, net-like veins
vascular tissue	vascular bundles scattered	vascular bundles in ring
root pattern	fibrous root system	taproot system
embryo in seed	one cotyledon	two cotyledons

97. h
98. m
99. a
100. l
101. b
102. j
103. k
104. f
105. g
106. i
107. c

108. e
109. d
110. g
111. e
112. d
113. i
114. h
115. b
116. c
117. j
118. a

119. f
120. k
121. wind
122. "shotgun"
123. wind
124. water
125. animal
126. edible
127. wind
128. edible
129. stigma

130. style
131. ovary
132. carpel
133. ovules
134. anther
135. filament
136. stamen
137. petal
138. sepal
139. pollen tube

140. Peas, clover, soybeans, alfalfa.

141. seed   142. primary root   143. seed coat   144. cotyledons

145. Taproot systems are composed of a persistent primary root with many smaller roots growing out from the sides of the taproot. In fibrous root systems, the primary root does not persist. New roots are produced from the base of the stem. These new roots are approximately equal in size.

146. Symbiotic relationships between plants and soil bacteria increase nutrient acquisition in nutrient-poor soils. Nitrogen is also often in limiting quantities to many plants. Legumes have overcome this problem by forming an association with nitrogen-fixing bacteria. These bacteria possess the enzymes needed to convert N_2 from the atmosphere into ammonium or nitrate – the process of nitrogen fixation. The bacteria enter the root hairs of a legume and travel to the cortex of the root. The bacteria multiply and stimulate the cortex cells to multiply as well. A root nodule is produced. It is within the nodule that nitrogen fixation occurs, supplying the plant with a steady supply of usable nitrogen. In return, the bacteria receive carbohydrates for their energy needs

147. The term *double fertilization* is used to describe the fertilization events in flowering plants. One sperm fertilizes the egg, producing the zygote. A second sperm enters the primary endosperm cell and fuses with the two polar nuclei, producing the triploid endosperm.

Chapter 18: Plant Responses to the Environment

OVERVIEW

This chapter presents information on how chemicals produced by plants act as hormones and induce a response to an environmental signal such as gravity or the direction of the sun's rays (both induce a growth response) or the length of a day (induces flowering). Thus, how a plant will grow, flower, or initiate dormancy is due to stimuli from the environment that results in hormone production.

1) How Were Plant Hormones Discovered?

Observations about how plants grow and respond to their environment provided the first clues to the presence of hormones in plants. On the basis of such observations, Darwin conducted experiments using grass coleoptiles and studied their **phototropism** response. It was later determined that the phototropic response is due to a chemical produced by the coleoptile. That chemical was identified as auxin.

2) What Are Plant Hormones, and How Do They Act?

Hormones are chemicals that are produced by cells in one area of an organism (the plant) and are transported to another area where they cause a response. Five classes of **plant hormones** have been identified to date. **Auxins** promote elongation of cells in the shoot. They affect roots differently: In low concentrations they stimulate elongation, however slightly higher concentrations inhibit root growth. The distribution of auxin within the plant body is affected by light and gravity. Therefore, the hormone influencing phototropism and **gravitropism** is auxin. **Gibberellins** also stimulate stem elongation, but in addition, they stimulate flowering, fruit development, seed germination, and bud sprouting. **Cytokinins** tend to stimulate cell division; thus they influence events relating to cell division, including bud sprouting, fruit development, endosperm production, and embryo growth. Cytokinins also influence plant metabolism. **Ethylene** is a unique hormone because it is a gas at room temperature. Ethylene stimulates fruit ripening and induces leaf, flower, and fruit drop. **Abscisic acid** controls stomatal opening and closing and inhibits the effects of gibberellins so that seeds and buds remain dormant until conditions are favorable.

3) How Do Hormones Regulate the Plant Life Cycle?

Abscisic acid reduces the metabolic rate of the embryo within the seed so that its growth is suspended. The high concentration of abscisic acid must be reduced before germination can occur. Heavy rains may rinse the abscisic acid out of the seed or freezing temperatures may cause its breakdown. As abscisic acid levels decrease, gibberellin levels increase. Gibberellin triggers the production of enzymes that will digest the endosperm, providing energy and nutrients for the growing embryo. As the embryo grows out of the seed, it must determine which way to grow its shoot system and root system. Organelles in the cells of the stem detect gravity and cause auxin to accumulate on the lower side of the stem. This accumulation of auxin causes the lower cells to elongate, curving the stem upward. In roots auxin may induce opposite results: Again, organelles in the cells of the root detect gravity and cause auxin to accumulate on the lower side of the root. As auxin accumulates on the lower side of a horizontal root, the cells are inhibited from elongating, while the cells on the upper side grow more quickly, causing the root to curve downward.

The size and shape of a plant's shoot and root systems are determined by the interactions between auxin and cytokinin. For instance, in some plants the shoot tip produces auxin, inhibiting lateral bud growth. As the auxin concentration decreases down the stem, lateral buds become less inhibited and will grow to produce branches. At the same time, cytokinins produced in the roots move up the stem, stimulating lateral bud growth. The interactions between the two hormones give the plant a characteristic shape. The interactions between auxin and cytokinin also influence the size of the shoot system relative to the size of the root system.

Most plants use daylength to regulate their production of flowers. However, some, such as snapdragons and tomatoes, flower as soon as the plant has matured. These plants are **day-neutral plants**. If daylength is important, then a critical length of daylight must be reached or not exceeded. If a species is a **long-day plant**, then it must receive daylight for periods longer than a species-specific critical value. For example, spinach must experience days longer than 13 hours or it will not flower. If a species is a **short-day plant**, then it must not receive daylight for periods longer than a species-specific critical value. For example, cockleburs will not flower if the daylength exceeds 15.5 hours. Daylength stimulates the production of hormones called **florigens** to induce flowering. Florigens, however, have yet to be identified.

Once a flower is mature, pollination followed by fertilization is likely and will lead to fruit and seed development. Hormones are also involved in regulating fruit and seed development. The pollen that lands on the stigma releases auxin or gibberellin, which causes the ovary to begin developing into a fruit. Fertilization further stimulates fruit development as the seeds mature. The ripening of the fruit is caused by the production of ethylene by the fruit cells after they have been exposed to a high concentration of auxin from the mature seeds.

As the plant reaches the end of a growing season, the leaves, flowers, and fruits undergo **senescence**, forming an **abscission layer** at the point of stem attachment. The formation of the abscision layer allows the plant to drop its leaves and ripened fruit when stimulated by ethylene. Senescence and the abscission layer are induced by a decrease in the production of cytokinin by the roots and of auxin by the leaves and fruits. Furthermore, lateral buds become dormant in response to the presence of abscisic acid. The plant has ended its growing season and will remain dormant until environmental stimuli activate hormones again in the spring.

4) Do Plants Communicate by Means of Chemicals?

Plants are capable of communicating with one another and with other organisms by releasing chemicals into the air. Plants do this when under attack to protect themselves and plants nearby. Some virus-infected plants have been found to release salicylic acid and methyl salicylate. Salicylic acid enhances the immune response by the plant to fight off the virus. Methyl salicylate diffuses through the air to nearby plants, which convert it to salicylic acid, enhancing their immune defenses to resist the virus. The chemical volicitin is produced by maize plants in response to herbivory by a caterpillar. The release of volicitin induces a response in a parasitic wasp that lays its eggs in the caterpillar, eventually killing it.

KEY TERMS AND CONCEPTS

Fill-In: From the following list of key terms fill in the blanks in the following statements.

abscisic acid	day-neutral plants	gravitropism	plant hormones
abscission layer	ethylene	hormone	senescence
auxin	florigen	long-day plants	short-day plants
cytokinin	gibberellin	phototropism	

(1)_____ can be observed as a plant grows toward the light. This response to an environmental stimulus is induced by the action of a(n) (2)_____ called (3)_____.

To date, five classes of (4)_____ have been classified. Auxins are involved in stem elongation. Auxins also influence root growth downward in response to gravity. This response is called (5)_____.

Fruit development and seed germination are influenced by the hormone (6)_____. Meanwhile, growth responses involving cell division, such as bud sprouting, are controlled by (7)_____. One of the more economically important hormones is the gas (8)_____, since it regulates fruit ripening. Plants growing under drought conditions are able to regulate water loss by closing their stomata, which are controlled by (9)_____.

Although a flowering hormone has not been identified, the term (10)_____ is used to refer to its presence. Flowering in most plants is regulated by daylength. Plants that need short days (with long nights) are called (11)_____. In turn, plants that need long days are called (12)_____. Some species, however, flower independently of daylength if the plant is mature; these plants are (13)_____.

At the close of the growing season for a plant, a rapid aging process occurs in leaves and fruits. This event is known as (14)_____ and is followed by leaf or fruit drop. Leaf or fruit drop can occur only after the formation of the (15)_____ at the point of stem attachment.

KEY TERMS AND DEFINITIONS

abscisic acid (ab-sis´-ik): a plant hormone that generally inhibits the action of other hormones, enforcing dormancy in seeds and buds and causing the closing of stomata.

abscission layer: a layer of thin-walled cells, located at the base of the petiole of a leaf, that produces an enzyme that digests the cell wall holding leaf to stem, allowing the leaf to fall off.

auxin (awk´-sin): a plant hormone that influences many plant functions, including phototropism, apical dominance, and root branching; generally stimulates cell elongation and, in some cases, cell division and differentiation.

cytokinin (sī-tō-kī´-nin): a plant hormone that promotes cell division, fruit growth, and the sprouting of lateral buds and prevents the aging of plant parts, especially leaves.

day-neutral plant: a plant in which flowering occurs as soon as the plant has grown and developed, regardless of daylength.

ethylene: a plant hormone that promotes the ripening of fruits and the dropping of leaves and fruit.

florigen: one of a group of plant hormones that can both trigger and inhibit flowering; daylength is a stimulus.

gibberellin (jib-er-el´-in): a plant hormone that stimulates seed germination, fruit development, and cell division and elongation.

gravitropism: growth with respect to the direction of gravity.

hormone: a chemical that is synthesized by one group of cells and then transported to other cells, whose activity is influenced by reception of the hormone.

long-day plant: a plant that will flower only if the length of daylight is greater than some species-specific duration.

phototropism: growth with respect to the direction of light.

plant hormone: the plant-regulating chemicals auxin, gibberellins, cytokinins, ethylene, and abscisic acid; somewhat resemble animal hormones in that they are chemicals produced by cells in one location that influence the growth or metabolic activity of other cells, typically some distance away in the plant body.

senescence: in plants, a specific aging process, typically including deterioration and the dropping of leaves and flowers.

short-day plant: a plant that will flower only if the length of daylight is shorter than some species-specific duration.

THINKING THROUGH THE CONCEPTS

True or False: Determine if the statement given is true or false. If it is false, change the <u>underlined</u> word so that the statement reads true.

16. _____ <u>Charles Darwin</u> conducted hormone experiments using grass seedlings.

17. _____ The high concentration of auxin produced in stems would <u>inhibit</u> the growth of roots.

18. _____ Abscisic acid maintains dormancy in seeds by <u>reducing</u> the metabolic rate of the embryo.

19. _____ The branching pattern of a plant is determined by the interaction of <u>ethylene and water</u>.

20. _____ Pinching off the tip of a *Coleus* plant will create a <u>bushier plant</u> since the source of auxin has been removed and lateral buds will sprout.

21. _____ The environmental cue that induces flowering is <u>temperature</u>.

22. _____ Day-neutral plants flower only <u>under long-day conditions</u>.

23. _____ When fruits are ripe, they are often <u>green</u> in color.

24. _____ Increased ethylene production by aging leaves causes <u>loosening</u> of cell walls of the abscission layer.

25. _____ Methyl salicylate production <u>decreases</u> the immune defenses of a plant under a virus attack.

26. _____ The chemical <u>volicitin</u> in caterpillar saliva causes maize plants to "signal" a parasitic wasp by releasing a mixture of chemicals.

Identification: Determine whether the following statements refer to **phototropism**, **gravitropism**, or **both**?

27. _____   growth toward light

28. _____   movement induced by gravity sensing organs

29. _____   regulated by auxin

30. _____   coleoptile bending

31. _____   root growth into soil

32. _____   bending due to cell elongation

33. _____   growth in response to gravity

34. _____   bending due to stem inhibition

Matching: Responses to inducing hormones.

35. _____   seed germination

36. _____   phototropism

37. _____   maintains seed dormancy

38. _____   shoot elongation

39. _____   leaf drop

40. _____   stimulates lateral bud sprout

41. _____   influences flowering

42. _____   gravitropism

43. _____   closes stomata

44. _____   prevents lateral bud sprout

45. _____   fruit development

46. _____   fruit ripening

47. _____   is a gas

48. _____   has not yet been found

Choices:

a.   auxin

b.   gibberellin

c.   cytokinin

d.   abscisic acid

e.   ethylene

f.   florigen

CLUES TO APPLYING THE CONCEPTS

These practice questions are intended to sharpen your ability to apply critical thinking and analysis to the biological concepts covered in this chapter.

49. Give a general definition of a hormone.

_____

_____

50. "One bad apple spoils the bunch . . ." is a common phrase often referring to society's ills. It is, however, a true statement. Explain the phenomenon from which this phrase is derived.

_____

_____

_____

_____

_____

_____

51. Briefly explain how the hormones auxin and cytokinin interact to regulate root and stem branching.

_____

_____

_____

_____

_____

_____

_____

_____

52. How does a Venus flytrap catch a fly? Briefly explain how the leaves close, trapping the insect inside, and how they open again.

_____

_____

_____

_____

_____

ANSWERS TO EXERCISES

1. phototropism	17. true	33. gravitropism
2. hormone	18. true	34. gravitropism
3. auxin	19. false, auxin and cytokinin	35. b
4. plant hormones	20. true	36. a
5. gravitropism	21. false, daylength	37. d
6. gibberellin	22. false, when mature	38. a
7. cytokinin	23. false, red	39. e
8. ethylene	24. true	40. c
9. abscisic acid	25. false, increases	41. f
10. florigen	26. true	42. a
11. short-day plants	27. phototropism	43. d
12. long-day plants	28. gravitropism	44. a
13. day-neutral plants	29. both	45. b
14. senescence	30. phototropism	46. e
15. abscision layer	31. gravitropism	47. e
16. true	32. phototropism	48. f

49. Hormones are chemicals that are produced by cells in one area and are transported to another area, where they exert specific effects.

50. The phrase "one bad apple spoils the bunch." is derived from the fact that ripe fruit gives off ethylene gas. Since ethylene influences fruit ripening, any fruit nearby will be affected by the gas being released. If an overripe apple is in a barrel, surrounded by less-ripe apples, the ethylene released from the overripe apple will cause the surrounding apples to ripen quickly. These apples will, in turn, release more ethylene, affecting the apples around them. In a relatively short time, the entire barrel will be overripe and spoiled.

51. High concentrations of auxin at the apical meristem suppress lateral bud growth at the top of the plant. As the concentration of auxin decreases down the stem, the inhibitory effects are lessened. Low concentrations of auxin stimulate root growth and branching. At the same time, cytokinin produced by roots moves up the stem, stimulating lateral bud growth. The two balance the growth of the plant. Large shoot systems will produce auxin in sufficient amounts to stimulate root-system expansion. If the shoot system becomes too large for the root system to support nutritionally, cytokinin levels will decrease, reducing the rate of expansion of the shoot system until the root system can catch up.

52. Simply, the triggering of the sensory hairs on the leaves causes extremely rapid growth of an outer layer of cells. This growth causes the leaves to shut, much like the growth of outer stem cells stimulated by auxin causes the stem to bend toward light. Over time, the cells of the second layer of the leaf grow, balancing the size of the cells of the two layers and slowly opening the trap.

Chapter 19: Homeostasis and the Organization of the Animal Body

OVERVIEW

This chapter presents an overview of the mechanisms that enable animals to regulate and control their bodily functions, even when they inhabit harsh environments or are under harsh conditions. These mechanisms include ways to maintain a stable internal environment, as well as organs and organ systems that have specialized functions within that internal environment.

1) How Do Animals Maintain Internal Constancy?

Animals maintain internal consistency (**homeostasis**) in part through **negative feedback**. Negative feedback systems counteract the effects of the external environment so that the body system is returned to its original condition. An example of a negative feedback response is your body regulating its internal temperature. When specific nerve endings sense a change in body temperature, the message is sent to your hypothalamus. The hypothalamus then activates the mechanisms needed to bring your body temperature back to its set point (98.6° F). When your body temperature has reached its set point, your hypothalamus deactivates the mechanisms used to restore your body temperature to normal.

Homeostasis is also maintained through **positive feedback**. Positive feedback systems reinforce changes, thus the change continues in a controlled but self-limiting chain reaction. The initiation of childbirth is controlled by such a mechanism. The initial uterine contractions begin a sequence of events that result in stronger and stronger contractions. This self-limiting event ends with the birth of the child and the placenta.

Numerous negative and positive feedback systems act together to maintain internal consistency. In order to achieve homeostasis, the body has evolved complex mechanisms to coordinate the systems and exchange signals.

2) How Is the Animal Body Organized?

The animal body is composed of cells organized into **tissues**. The tissues combine to make up **organs**, each with specific functions. The organs in turn combine to form **organ systems**.

Epithelial tissues form the **membranes** that cover the body and line its cavities. They provide a barrier that controls what substances cross them. Epithelial tissues withstand a great deal of wear and tear; thus, they must constantly be replaced through mitotic cell divisions. A second function of epithelial tissue is to form **glands**. **Exocrine glands** are connected to the epithelium by a duct. **Endocrine glands** are no longer attached to the epithelium. Most commonly, these glands produce and secrete hormones.

Connective tissues tend to be surrounded by an extracellular substance produced by the tissue and are often complexed with fibers of **collagen**. Immediately beneath the epidermis of the skin is a layer of connective tissue, the **dermis**. **Tendons** function to connect muscles to bones, and **ligaments** attach bones to other bones. **Cartilage** covers the ends of bones at joints, forms pads between vertebrae, and structures the respiratory passages, ears, and nose. **Bone**, itself, is a connective tissue that is complexed with deposits of calcium phosphate. **Fat** cells make up the connective tissue called **adipose tissue** that specializes in long-term, high energy storage. Also included in connective tissue are **blood** and **lymph** since they are primarily composed of extracellular fluid.

Muscle tissue cells are specialized to contract and relax. **Skeletal muscle** typically contracts in response to a conscious decision to move a portion of the skeleton. **Cardiac muscle**, found only in the heart, contracts and relaxes spontaneously as the heart beats. **Smooth muscle** contractions are slow, rhythmic, and involuntary.

Nerve tissue is composed of two types of cells: neurons and glial cells. **Neurons** are specialized to generate and conduct electrical signals. The **dendrites** of a neuron receive a stimulus from the external environment or from other neurons. The **cell body** controls the functions of the cell. **Axons** of the neuron conduct the signal to the target cell, and **synaptic terminals** transmit the signal to the target cell, (which may be another neuron, a muscle cell, or a gland cell). **Glial cells** allow neurons to function properly by surrounding and protecting them.

When two or more tissue types function together, an organ is formed. The skin, for example, is a typical organ. The **epidermis** is covered and protected by a layer of dead cells containing the protein **keratin**. Beneath the epidermis is the connective tissue layer, the dermis. The dermis is densely imbedded with arterioles and capillaries, lymph vessels, and nerve endings. **Hair follicles** are glands within the dermis that produce hair. Sweat glands cool the skin and remove waste products. **Sebaceous glands** produce oil to moisturize and lubricate the epithelium.

KEY TERMS AND CONCEPTS

Fill-In: From the following list of terms, fill in the blanks below.

adipose tissue	dendrites	hair follicles	organs
axon	dermis	homeostasis	organ system
blood	endocrine glands	keratin	positive feedback
bones	epidermis	ligaments	sebaceous glands
cardiac muscle	epithelial tissue	lymph	skeletal muscle
cartilage	exocrine glands	membrane	smooth muscle
cell body	fat	negative feedback	synaptic terminals
collagen	glands	nerve tissue	tendons
connective tissue	glial cells	neurons	tissues

(1)_____ refers to the body's ability to maintain a relatively constant internal environment. This consistency is maintained through (2)_____, which counteracts change, and (3)_____, which responds to enhance change.

The cells of multicellular organisms, such as animals, are organized into (4)_____ that have a specific function. These organized cells then form (5)_____, such as the lungs, heart, or stomach. Several different organs involved in a similar process form a(n) (6)_____.

The body's cavities are lined with (7)_____, creating a(n) (8)_____, which restricts substances moving from inside an organ to the outside as well as the reverse. Epithelial tissue also forms (9)_____ that secrete substances. (10)_____ remain connected to the epithelial tissue by way of a duct. (11)_____ separate from the epithelium and tend to secrete hormones into surrounding extracellular fluid.

The most diverse tissue in structure and function is (12)_____. Most of this tissue is complexed with fibrous strands of the protein (13)_____. The connective tissue located under the skin's epidermis is the (14)_____.

The human body shape is maintained, in part, by the internal skeleton. Connective tissue plays a part in that (15)_____ connect muscle to bones, and (16)_____ connect bones to bones. (17)_____ themselves are connective tissue made rigid by calcium phosphate deposits. Adipose tissue is composed of (18)_____ cells, which specifically store energy. The most unusual connective tissues are the fluids (19)_____ and (20)_____.

Muscle tissue is specialized for contraction and exists as three types. (21)_____ contracts when told to do so by a conscious thought. (22)_____ is found only in the heart and contracts spontaneously. (23)_____ also contracts involuntarily and is found in the gastrointestinal (digestive) tract.

The brain and spinal cord are composed of (24)_____. Nerve cells, or (25)_____, generate and conduct electrical impulses. The (26)_____ receive signals, the (27)_____ maintains and repairs the neuron, and the (28)_____ conducts the impulse to a target cell. The signal is actually transmitted through (29)_____ , while (30)_____ allow the neuron to function optimally.

The skin as an organ has an outer layer, the (31)_____, that is protected with dead cells containing the protein (32)_____. The connective tissue of the skin, the dermis, contains glands that produce hair. These glands are the (33)_____. Additionally, the (34)_____ secrete oil to keep the skin lubricated.

Key Terms and Definitions

adipose tissue (a´-di-pōs): tissue composed of fat cells.

axon: a long extension of a nerve cell, extending from the cell body to synaptic endings on other nerve cells or on muscles.

blood: a fluid consisting of plasma in which blood cells are suspended; carried within the circulatory system.

bone: a hard, mineralized connective tissue that is a major component of the vertebrate endoskeleton; provides support and sites for muscle attachment.

cardiac muscle (kar´-dē-ak): the specialized muscle of the heart, able to initiate its own contraction, independent of the nervous system.

cartilage (kar´-teh-lij): a form of connective tissue that forms portions of the skeleton; consists of chondrocytes and their extracellular secretion of collagen; resembles flexible bone.

cell body: the part of a nerve cell in which most of the common cellular organelles are located; typically a site of integration of inputs to the nerve cell.

collagen: a fibrous protein found in connective tissue such as bone and cartilage.

connective tissue: a tissue type consisting of diverse tissues, including bone, fat, and blood, that generally contain large amounts of extracellular material.

dendrite (den´-drīt): a branched tendril that extends outward from the cell body of a neuron; specialized to respond to signals from the external environment or from other neurons.

dermis (dur´-mis): the layer of skin beneath the epidermis; composed of connective tissue and containing blood vessels, muscles, nerve endings, and glands.

endocrine gland: a ductless, hormone-producing gland consisting of cells that release their secretions into the extracellular fluid from which the secretions diffuse into nearby capillaries.

epidermis (ep-uh-der´-mis): in animals, specialized epithelial tissue that forms the outer layer of skin.

epithelial tissue (eh-puh-the̅´-le̅-ul): a tissue type that forms membranes that cover the body surface and line body cavities, and that also gives rise to glands.

exocrine gland: a gland that releases its secretions into ducts that lead to the outside of the body or into the digestive tract.

fat (tissue): adipose tissue; connective tissue that stores the lipid fat; composed of cells packed with triglycerides.

gland: a cluster of cells that are specialized to secrete (release) substances such as sweat or hormones.

glial cell: a cell of the nervous system that provides support and insulation for neurons.

hair follicle: a gland in the dermis of mammalian skin, formed from epithelial tissue, that produces a hair.

homeostasis (ho̅m-e̅-o̅-sta̅´-sis): the maintenance of a relatively constant environment required for the optimal functioning of cells, maintained by the coordinated activity of numerous regulatory mechanisms, including the respiratory, endocrine, circulatory, and excretory systems.

keratin (ker´-uh-tin): a fibrous protein in hair, nails, and the epidermis of skin.

ligament: a tough connective tissue band connecting two bones.

lymph (limf): a pale fluid, within the lymphatic system, that is composed primarily of interstitial fluid and lymphocytes.

membrane: in multicellular organism, a continuous sheet of epithelial cells that covers the body and lines body cavities; in a cell, a thin sheet of lipids and proteins that surrounds the cell or its organelles, separating them from their surroundings.

negative feedback: a situation in which a change initiates a series of events that tend to counteract the change and restore the original state. Negative feedback in physiological systems maintains homeostasis.

nerve tissue: the tissue that makes up the brain, spinal cord, and nerves; consists of neurons and glial cells.

neuron (noor´-on): a single nerve cell.

organ: a structure (such as the liver, kidney, or skin) composed of two or more distinct tissue types that function together.

organ system: two or more organs that work together to perform a specific function; for example, the digestive system.

positive feedback: a situation in which a change initiates events that tend to amplify the original change.

sebaceous gland (se-ba̅´-shus): a gland in the dermis of skin, formed from epithelial tissue, that produces the oily substance sebum, which lubricates the epidermis.

skeletal muscle: the type of muscle that is attached to and moves the skeleton and is under the direct, normally voluntary, control of the nervous system; also called *striated muscle*.

smooth muscle: the type of muscle that surrounds hollow organs, such as the digestive tract, bladder, and blood vessels; normally not under voluntary control.

striated muscle: see *skeletal muscle*.

synaptic terminal: a swelling at the branched ending of an axon; where the axon forms a synapse.

tendon: a tough connective tissue band connecting a muscle to a bone.

tissue: a group of (normally similar) cells that together carry out a specific function; for example, muscle; may include extracellular material produced by its cells.

THINKING THROUGH THE CONCEPTS

True or False: Determine if the statement given is true or false. If it is false, change the underlined words so that the statement reads true.

35. _____   Cells are the building blocks of organs.

36. _____   The kidney is an example of an organ system.

37. _____   Skin is composed of epithelial tissue.

38. _____   The eidermis is replaced about two times a year.

39. _____   Salivary glands are an example of <u>exocrine</u> glands.

40. _____   <u>Endocrine glands</u> are connected to the epithelium by ducts.

41. _____   <u>Blood</u> is a connective tissue.

42. _____   <u>Cartilage</u> forms the internal structure of the ear.

43. _____   <u>Smooth</u> muscle is found only in the heart.

44. _____   Skeletal muscle contractions are <u>voluntary</u>.

45. _____   Blood vessels contain <u>muscle tissue</u>.

46. _____   <u>Dendrites</u> conduct an electrical signal to a target cell.

47. _____   An animal's bladder contracts using <u>smooth</u> muscle.

48. _____   Hair follicles are <u>glands</u> found in the dermis.

Identification: Determine whether the following statements refer to **negative** feedback or **positive** feedback.

49. _____   body temperature

50. _____   childbirth

51. _____   water balance

52. _____   blood sugar level

53. _____   oxygen content of blood

54. _____   occurs infrequently

55. _____   is self-limiting

56. _____   reverses the initial change

57. _____   common in physiological systems

Short Answer.

58. Identify the four major categories of animal tissues.

   a. _____   c. _____

   b. _____   d. _____

59. Identify the three types of muscle found in the animal body.

   a. _____   c. _____

   b. _____

Fill-In: Complete the following table relating the major vertebrate organ systems.

Organ system	Major structures	Physiological role
respiratory system	(60)	(61)
(62)	lymph, lymph nodes and vessels, white blood cells	(63)
excretory system	(64)	(65)
(66)	(67)	supplies body with nutrients for growth and maintenance
(68)	smooth muscle, cardiac muscle, skeletal muscle	(69)
endocrine system	(70)	(71)
(72)	(73)	provides support, protects organs, muscle attachment sites
reproductive system	(74)	(75)
circulatory system	(76)	(77)
(78)	brain, spinal cord, peripheral nerves	(79)

Short answer.

80. Provide an example of an organ system. listing the organs within the system.

_____

_____

_____

_____

_____

_____

_____

_____

CLUES TO APPLYING THE CONCEPTS

These practice questions are intended to sharpen your ability to apply critical thinking and analysis to the biological concepts covered in this chapter.

81. The term _homeostasis_ means "unchanging". Is this an accurate description of the state of the body's internal environment? Why or why not?

_____

_____

_____

_____

_____

_____

_____

82. Explain why the example of your home thermostat represents a type of negative feedback mechanism.

_____

_____

_____

_____

_____

ANSWERS TO EXERCISES

1. homeostasis
2. negative feedback
3. positive feedback
4. tissues
5. organs
6. organ system
7. epithelial tissue
8. membrane
9. glands
10. Exocrine glands
11. Endocrine glands
12. connective tissue
13. collagen
14. dermis
15. Tendons
16. ligaments
17. Bones
18. fat
19. blood

20. lymph
21. Skeletal muscle
22. Cardiac muscle
23. Smooth muscle
24. nerve tissue
25. neurons
26. dendrites
27. cell body
28. axon
29. synaptic terminals
30. glial cells
31. epidermis
32. keratin
33. hair follicles
34. sebaceous glands
35. false, tissues
36. false, organ
37. true
38. false, two times per month

39. true
40. false, Exocrine
41. true
42. true
43. false, Cardiac
44. true
45. true
46. false, axons
47. true
48. true
49. negative
50. positive
51. negative
52. negative
53. negative
54. positive
55. positive
56. negative
57. negative

58. a. epithelial tissue
    b. connective tissue
    c. muscle tissue
    d. nerve tissue

59. a. skeletal muscle
    b. cardiac muscle
    c. smooth muscle

Organ system	Major structures	Physiological role
respiratory system	(60) nose, trachea, lungs, or gills	(61) gas exchange between blood and environment
(62) lymphatic/immune system	lymph, lymph nodes and vessels, white blood cells	(63) carries fat, excess fluids to blood, destroys invading microbes
excretory system	(64) kidneys, ureters, bladder, urethra	(65) filters cellular waste, toxins, and excess water and nutrients; stabilizes bloodstream
(66) digestive system	(67) mouth, esophagus, stomach, small & large intestines, digestive glands	supplies body with nutrients for growth and maintenance
(68) muscular system	smooth muscle, cardiac muscle, skeletal muscle	(69) movement through digestive tract, large blood vessels; begins and carries out heart contractions; moves skeleton
endocrine system	(70) hormone secreting glands: hypothalamus, pituitary, thyroid, pancreas, adrenals	(71) regulates physiological processes along with nervous system
(72) skeletal system	(73) bones, cartilage, tendons, ligaments	provides support, protects organs, muscle attachment sites
reproductive system	(74) testes, seminal vesicles, penis Ovaries, oviducts, uterus, vagina, mammary glands	(75) produces sperm, inseminates female Produces egg cells, nurtures developing offspring
circulatory system	(76) heart, vessels, blood	(77) transports nutrients, gases, hormones, wastes; temperature control
(78) nervous system	brain, spinal cord, peripheral nerves	(79) senses environment, directs behavior, controls physiological processes along with endocrine system

80. **Respiratory system**: nose, trachea, lungs, or gills; **lymphatic/immune system**: lymph, lymph nodes and vessels, white blood cells; **excretory system**: kidneys, ureters, bladder, urethra; **digestive system**: mouth, esophagus, stomach, small and large intestines, digestive glands; **muscular system**: smooth muscle, cardiac muscle, skeletal muscle; **endocrine system**: hormone-secreting glands: hypothalamus, pituitary, thyroid, pancreas, adrenals; **skeletal system**: bones, cartilage, tendons, ligaments; **reproductive system**: testes, seminal vesicles, penis, ovaries, oviducts, uterus, vagina, mammary glands; **circulatory system**: heart, vessels, blood; **nervous system**: brain, spinal cord, peripheral nerves.

81. The term *homeostasis* is used to describe the body's ability to maintain an internal constancy even though the animal's body is exposed to an external environment that is continually changing. However, the term suggests a static (unchanging) state. In fact, this is not an accurate description. The body's internal environment is dynamic (always changing). Chemical and physical changes are constantly occurring. At the same time, the changes occur within certain parameters, enabling cells to function. Thus, *dynamic equilibrium* is a more appropriate term.

82. Negative feedback mechanisms respond to counteract a change. If the temperature in your home cools beyond a certain set point, the sensor on the thermometer will detect the change and signal the heating device to turn on. Once the set-point temperature has been reached, the thermometer again detects the change, and signals the heating device to turn off. This system turns on to counteract a drop in temperature. When the temperature has been restored, it turns off.

Chapter 20: Circulation and Respiration

OVERVIEW

This chapter explores the circulatory system, its components and their functions. The focus of the chapter is the human system; however, parallels to other vertebrate systems can be made. Since the lymphatic system functions so closely with the circulatory system, it is included here. This chapter also covers the structures of the respiratory system and their specialized functions. Not all organisms use lungs for gas exchange; these adaptations are reviewed. The focus of the chapter, however, is vertebrate respiratory systems, specifically of humans.

1) What Are the Major Features and Functions of Circulatory Systems?

The circulatory system includes **blood**, a fluid that transports nutrients and oxygen to cells and wastes away from cells; **blood vessels**, which carry the fluid to and away from the cells; and the **heart**, which serves as the pump to circulate the fluid. A circulatory system may be an **open circulatory system** (found in many invertebrates), or a **closed circulatory system** (found in humans and most other vertebrates). In open systems, the organs and tissues are bathed in blood in a **hemocoel**; in a closed system, the blood is maintained within vessels and the heart – a more efficient way of transporting nutrients and wastes.

   The functions of a circulatory system include the transport of oxygen from the respiratory system to cells and the removal of carbon dioxide from cells, the transport of nutrients to cells and wastes from cells to the liver or kidney, and the distribution of hormones. The circulatory system also helps regulate body temperature as blood flow is adjusted, and prevents blood loss. Finally, the circulatory system enhances the immune system by circulating antibodies and white blood cells.

2) What Are the Features and Functions of the Vertebrate Heart?

The heart is the pump behind the circulation of blood through the body. Within the heart, the blood collects in **atria** (or one **atrium**). The muscular atria contract, pushing the blood into the **ventricles**. When the ventricles contract, blood is pumped through the body.

   In the four-chambered vertebrate heart, blood flows from the body through a **vein** into the right atrium. The atrium pumps the blood to the right ventricle. When the right ventricle contracts, it pumps blood through the pulmonary **arteries** to the lungs. This constitutes **pulmonary circulation**. The deoxygenated blood picks up oxygen in the lungs and flows back to the heart through pulmonary veins into the left atrium. The left atrium pumps the oxygen-rich blood into the left ventricle. The left ventricle contracts and pumps the oxygen-rich blood out the aorta and to the rest of the body. This constitutes **systemic circulation**. The alternating contractions of the atria and the ventricles generate the **cardiac cycle**.

   Once blood is pumped from an atrium to a ventricle, it must be kept from flowing back into the atrium. The **atrioventricular valves** open as blood is pumped through to the ventricles and then are kept shut by pressure of the blood in the ventricle. In turn, backflow of blood leaving the heart is governed by **semilunar valves** between the right atrium and the pulmonary artery and the left atrium and the aorta. The contractions of the chambers are regulated by a cluster of cardiac muscle cells that specialize as a

pacemaker. The principal pacemaker is found in the wall of the right atrium and is called the **sinoatrial (SA) node**. In order to coordinate atrial and ventricular contractions so that the atria contract before the ventricles, the electrical impulse is delayed at the **atrioventricular (AV) node**. If the pacemaker is unable to regulate contractions, **fibrillation** (irregular contractions) occurs.

3) What Are the Features and Functions of Blood?

Blood is composed of fluid **plasma** and specialized cells within the plasma. Dissolved within plasma are proteins, nutrients, hormones, gases, wastes, and salts. The specialized cells include **erythrocytes**, the red blood cells. The red color is due to an iron-containing pigment, **hemoglobin**. Hemoglobin carries oxygen to cells and carbon dioxide away from cells. Red blood cells are manufactured in bone marrow and have a life span of only 120 days
  Additional specialized cells within blood are the **leukocytes**, the white blood cells. Leukocytes are involved in the body's immune system. **Lymphocytes** are the white blood cells that produce antibodies in response to disease.
  Platelets (membrane-enclosed fragments of **megakaryocytes** that reside in the bone marrow) are involved in **blood clotting**. Clotting is initiated when platelets encounter an irregular surface, such as a wound. The platelets stick to the irregular surface. In the meantime, production of the enzyme **thrombin** is induced, converting the plasma protein fibrinogen to **fibrin**. Fibrin fibers form a mesh that traps red blood cells and platelets. Eventually, a dense scab is formed over the wound.

4) What Are the Structures and Functions of Blood Vessels?

Blood leaves the heart through arteries. The muscular, elastic walls of arteries help maintain a steady flow of blood to smaller vessels. As the diameter of an artery decreases, **arterioles** are formed. Arterioles are capable of responding to electrical and hormonal signals when changes in tissue needs are detected. When the diameter of the arterioles diminishes, **capillaries** are formed. The capillaries exchange gases, nutrients, and wastes between the blood and body cells. Pressure within capillaries causes fluid to leak continuously from them into spaces around the capillaries and tissues forming **interstitial fluid**. Interstitial fluid allows the gas, nutrient, and waste exchange to occur. As blood returns to the heart, the capillaries increase in diameter, becoming **venules** and finally veins. Blood always returns to the heart through veins. The walls of veins are thin and expandable. There is little resistance to blood flow through veins. Contractions of skeletal muscle, squeezing veins, help move blood through them. One-way valves prevent backward flow of blood during the muscle contractions.

5) What Are the Structures and Functions of the Lymphatic System?

Within the **lymphatic system** are lymph capillaries and larger vessels, **lymph nodes**, the **thymus**, and the **spleen**. The lymphatic system removes excess interstitial fluid and molecules that have leaked from capillaries. **Lymph** fluid is the interstitial fluid collected by lymph capillaries. It is carried back to the circulatory system in lymph vessels. The lymphatic system also carries fat globules from the small intestine to the bloodstreamand carries white blood cells throughout the body to fight off bacteria and viruses. Clusters of connective tissue containing large numbers of lymphocytes are found throughout the body. The largest of these are the **tonsils**. Lymphocytes are produced in lymph nodes, the thymus, and the spleen. The spleen also filters the blood. As blood flows through the spleen, macrophages and lymphocytes remove and destroy foreign material and aged red blood cells.

6) What Are Some Evolutionary Adaptations for Gas Exchange?

All respiratory systems use diffusion for gas exchange and may alternate diffusion with **bulk flow**. Bulk flow occurs when fluids or gases move across relatively large spaces from an area of high pressure to an area of low pressure.

The surface across which diffusion will occur must be moist and must have a large surface area that is in contact with the environment. Some aquatic animals do not have specialized respiratory structures. Oxygen and carbon dioxide simply diffuse across their bodies. This works well for extremely small animals, thin flat animals, or for those that do not move quickly. Other aquatic animals circulate water from their environment through their bodies. Most animals, however, have specialized respiratory structures that work closely with the circulatory system to exchange gases between cells and the environment. Many larger aquatic animals utilize **gills** to exchange O_2 and CO_2 with the environment. Gills have a dense network of capillaries just beneath their outer membrane, allowing gas exchange to occur. Most terrestrial vertebrates primarily respire using saclike **lungs**. The larval form of amphibians (tadpoles) however, use gills for gas exchange.

7) What Are the Features and Functions of the Human Respiratory System?

The respiratory system of humans consists of the **conducting portion**, a series of passageways that carry air, and the **gas-exchange portion**, where O_2 and CO_2 are exchanged with the blood in sacs within the lung. Air flowing through the conducting portion first enters the nose or mouth and passes through the **pharynx** to the **larynx**. The **vocal cords** are located within the larynx. When the vocal cords partially block the larynx, exhaled air causes them to vibrate, producing sounds. From the larynx, air passes through the **trachea**. Within the chest, the trachea divides into branches, forming two bronchi, one going into each lung. Within the lungs each **bronchus** branches many times forming smaller tubes called **bronchioles**. The bronchioles terminate in microscopic **alveoli**, where gas exchange will occur. The alveoli increase the gas-exchange surface area of lung tissue and are infused with capillaries. Gases dissolve in the water covering each alveolus and diffuse through alveolar and capillary membranes. Oxygen in inhaled air diffuses into the oxygen-poor blood returning from the body. In turn, carbon dioxide in the blood diffuses into the alveoli. Oxygen-rich blood is then transported to the cells and tissues.

Air enters the respiratory system actively through **inhalation**. During inhalation, the chest cavity is enlarged by the contraction of **diaphragm** muscles drawing the diaphragm downward. Muscles within the rib cage also contract, moving the ribs up and out. Since the lungs are held in a vacuum, the expansion of the chest causes the lungs to expand as well, drawing in air. **Exhalation** of air occurs passively as the muscles relax and the chest cavity decreases in size again. The lungs are protected within the chest cavity by the rib cage, the diaphragm, and the neck muscles and connective tissues. An airtight seal between the chest wall and the lungs is enhanced by the **pleural membranes**. The inhalation-exhalation process occurs without conscious thought through muscle contractions stimulated by the **respiratory center** of the brainstem. The breathing rate is determined by a combination of sensors detecting high CO_2 levels, low O_2 levels, and an increase in activity level.

KEY TERMS AND CONCEPTS

Fill-In I: From the following list of terms, fill in the blanks below.

arteries	fibrin	plasma
arterioles	heart	platelets
atria	hemocoel	pulmonary circulation
atrioventricular (AV) node	hemoglobin	semilunar valves
atrioventricular valves	interstitial fluid	sinoatrial (SA) node
blood	leukocytes	spleen
blood clotting	lymph	systemic circulation
blood vessels	lymph nodes	thrombin
capillaries	lymphatic system	thymus
cardiac cycle	lymphocytes	tonsils
closed circulatory systems	megakaryocytes	veins
erythrocytes	open circulatory systems	ventricles
fibrillations	pacemaker	venules

All circulatory systems consist of (1)_____ to transport, (2)_____
to conduct fluid, and a(,) (3)_____ to pump the fluid throughout the body. A
circulatory system may contain a large open space called the (4)_____, in which
organs and tissues are bathed in circulating blood. This space exists in (5)_____,
found in most invertebrates. (6)_____, found in humans and other vertebrates,
maintains the blood within vessels.

The (7)_____ of the heart collect blood from the body or from the lungs. When
these chambers pump, the blood goes into the (8)_____. Unoxygenated blood
coming back to the heart from the body and then on to the lungs to release CO_2 and receive O_2
constitutes (9)_____. Oxygenated blood being pumped throughout the body
to deliver O_2 to the cells and to receive CO_2 from the cells constitutes (10)_____.

Blood flowing toward the heart is always carried in (11)_____; blood flowing
away from the heart is always carried in (12)_____.

The alternating pumping of the atria and the ventricles is called the (13)_____.

One-way blood flow within and from the heart is controlled by valves. Specifically, one-way blood flow
from the atria into the ventricles is controlled by the (14)_____. Blood flowing to
the pulmonary artery or the aorta must pass through the (15)_____ from the
respective ventricle.

The rhythm of the beating heart is coordinated by a natural (16)_____. The
specialized cluster of cells in the wall of the right atrium that is primarily responsible for the coordination
is the (17)_____. In order for the ventricles to pump a fraction of a second after
the atria, the electrical signal is delayed at the (18)_____. When the pumping
cycle fails to be coordinated, irregular contractions, or (19)_____, occur.

The fluid component of blood is called (20)_____. Within this fluid are specialized cells and (21)_____, the membrane-enclosed fragments of larger cells called (22)_____. The red blood cells of blood are called (23)_____ and are red because of the pigment (24)_____ within them.

White blood cells within blood are called (25)_____, which function in the body's immune response. Platelets are intimately involved with the process of (26)_____, which reduces the chances of bleeding to death. In response to a wound, platelets adhere to the injured surface of a blood vessel, in part triggering production of the enzyme (27)_____. This enzyme catalyzes the conversion of fibrinogen to (28)_____.

Arteries branch into smaller vessels called (29)_____, which help regulate the distribution of blood throughout the body. The tiniest of all vessels are the (30)_____, which are responsible for gas and nutrient exchange with the body's cells. Continuous leakage of fluid from these tiny vessels forms the (31)_____, which bathes nearly all the body's cells. Unoxygenated blood in capillaries drains into larger vessels called (32)_____, which empty into large veins.

Closely associated with the circulatory system is a second system of vessels, the (33)_____. This system of vessels receives interstitial fluid leaked from capillaries. The fluid is now referred to as (34)_____ and is carried back to the circulatory system. The function of the system is to help the body defend against foreign invaders. Patches of connective tissue with large numbers of (35)_____ are found in linings of the respiratory, digestive, and urinary tracts. The largest patch of this tissue makes up the (36)_____ behind the mouth. Lymph fluid is passed through kidney-bean-shaped structures called (37)_____. Organs that function as part of the lymphatic system include the (38)_____, which produces lymphocytes, and the (39)_____, which filters blood.

Fill-In II: From the following list of terms, fill in the blanks below.

alveoli	diaphragm	inhalation	pleural membranes
bronchi	exhalation	larynx	respiratory center
bronchioles	gas-exchange portion	lungs	trachea
bulk flow	gills	pharynx	vocal cords
conducting portion			

Fluids or gases moving through large spaces move by (40)_____ from areas of high pressure to areas of low pressure. Diffusion, in contrast, is the movement of individual molecules.

The respiratory structures of aquatic animals are the (41)_____. The respiratory structures of terrestrial animals are internal. Most terrestrial animals use (42)_____, which are usually moist sacs.

The respiratory system is divided into two parts. The (43)_____ carries air to the (44)_____, where gases are exchanged.

After air enters the nose or mouth, it passes through the (45) _____ behind the mouth. The air then passes through the (46) _____, which is protected by the epiglottis. The (47) _____ are found here, allowing sounds to be made during exhalation. Semicircular bands of cartilage form the (48) _____. Within the chest, this tube splits into two tubes called (49) _____. Inside the lungs, each tube repeatedly splits into smaller (50)_____. Microscopic chambers within the lung, called (51)_____, increase the surface area of lung tissue immensely.

The process of breathing occurs with the help of the muscular (52)_____. As these muscles contract and the rib cage expands, air is drawn into the lungs. This is called (53)_____. Air is passively pushed out during (54) _____ when the muscles relax and the chest decreases in size again. The rhythm of breathing is maintained in an area of the brainstem called the (55) _____.

A double layer of membranes, the (56) _____, help provide an airtight seal between the lungs and the chest wall.

Key Terms and Definitions

alveolus (al-vē´-ō-lus; pl., **alveoli**): a tiny air sac within the lungs, surrounded by capillaries, where gas exchange with the blood occurs.

angina (an-jī´-nuh): chest pain associated with reduced blood flow to the heart muscle, caused by the obstruction of coronary arteries.

arteriole (ar-tēr´-ē-ōl): a small artery that empties into capillaries. Contraction of the arteriole regulates blood flow to various parts of the body.

artery (ar´-tuh-rē): a vessel with muscular, elastic walls that conducts blood away from the heart.

atherosclerosis (ath´-er-ō-skler-ō´-sis): a disease characterized by the obstruction of arteries by cholesterol deposits and thickening of the arterial walls.

atrioventricular (AV) node (ā´-trē-ō-ven-trik´-ū-lar nōd): a specialized mass of muscle at the base of the right atrium through which the electrical activity initiated in the sinoatrial node is transmitted to the ventricles.

atrioventricular valve: a heart valve that separates each atrium from each ventricle, preventing the backflow of blood into the atria during ventricular contraction.

atrium (ā´-trē-um): a chamber of the heart that receives venous blood and passes it to a ventricle.

blood: a fluid consisting of plasma in which blood cells are suspended; carried within the circulatory system.

blood clotting: a complex process by which platelets, the protein fibrin, and red blood cells block an irregular surface in or on the body, such as a damaged blood vessel, sealing the wound.

blood vessel: a channel that conducts blood throughout the body.

bronchiole (bron´-kē-ōl): a narrow tube, formed by repeated branching of the bronchi, that conducts air into the alveoli.

bronchus (bron´-kus): a tube that conducts air from the trachea to each lung.

bulk flow: the movement of many molecules of a gas or fluid in unison from an area of higher pressure to an area of lower pressure.

capillary: the smallest type of blood vessel, connecting arterioles with venules. Capillary walls, through which the exchange of nutri-ents and wastes occurs, are only one cell thick.

cardiac cycle (kar´-dē-ak): the alternation of contraction and relaxation of the heart chambers.

chronic bronchitis: a persistent lung infection character-ized by coughing, swelling of the lining of the respiratory tract, an increase in mucus production, and a decrease in the number and activity of cilia.

closed circulatory system: the type of circulatory system, found in certain worms and vertebrates, in which the blood is always confined within the heart and vessels.

conducting portion: the portion of the respiratory system in lung-breathing vertebrates that carries air to the lungs.

diaphragm (dī´-uh-fram): in the respiratory system, a dome-shaped muscle forming the floor of the chest cavity that, when it contracts, pulls itself downward, enlarging the chest cavity and causing air to be drawn into the lungs.

emphysema (em-fuh-sē´-muh): a condition in which the alveoli of the lungs become brittle and rupture, causing decreased area for gas exchange.

erythrocyte (eh-rith´-rō-sīt): a red blood cell, active in oxygen transport, that contains the red pigment hemoglobin.

exhalation: the act of releasing air from the lungs, which results from a relaxation of the respiratory muscles.

fibrillation: rapid, uncoordinated, and ineffective contractions of heart muscle cells.

fibrin (fī´-brin): a clotting protein formed in the blood in response to a wound; binds with other fibrin molecules and provides a matrix around which a blood clot forms.

gas-exchange portion: the portion of the respiratory system in lung-breathing vertebrates where gas is exchanged in the alveoli of the lungs.

gill: in aquatic animals, a branched tissue richly supplied with capillaries around which water is circulated for gas exchange.

heart: a muscular organ responsible for pumping blood within the circulatory system throughout the body.

heart attack: a severe reduction or blockage of blood flow through a coronary artery, depriving some of the heart muscle of its blood supply.

hemocoel (hē´-mō-sēl): a blood cavity within the bodies of certain invertebrates in which blood bathes tissues directly; part of an open circulatory system.

hemoglobin (hē´mō-glō-bin): the iron-containing protein that gives red blood cells their color; binds to oxygen in the lungs and releases it to the tissues.

hypertension: arterial blood pressure that is chronically elevated above the normal level.

inhalation: the act of drawing air into the lungs by enlarging the chest cavity.

interstitial fluid (in-ter-sti´-shul): fluid, similar in composition to plasma (except lacking large proteins), that leaks from capillaries and acts as a medium of exchange between the body cells and the capillaries.

larynx (lar´-inks): that portion of the air passage between the pharynx and the trachea; contains the vocal cords.

leukocyte (loo´-kō-sīt): any of the white blood cells circulating in the blood.

lung: a paired respiratory organ consisting of inflatable chambers within the chest cavity in which gas exchange occurs.

lymph (limf): a pale fluid, within the lymphatic system, that is composed primarily of interstitial fluid and lymphocytes.

lymph node: a small structure that filters lymph; contains lymphocytes and macrophages, which inactivate foreign particles such as bacteria.

lymphatic system: a system consisting of lymph vessels, lymph capillaries, lymph nodes, and the thymus and spleen; helps protect the body against infection, absorbs fats, and returns excess fluid and small proteins to the blood circulatory system.

lymphocyte (lim´-fō-sīt): a type of white blood cell important in the immune response.

megakaryocyte (meg-a-kar´-ē-ō-sīt): a large cell type that remains in the bone marrow, pinching off pieces of itself that then enter the circulation as platelets.

open circulatory system: a type of circulatory system found in some invertebrates, such as arthropods and mollusks, that includes an open space (the hemocoel) in which blood directly bathes body tissues.

pacemaker: a cluster of specialized muscle cells in the upper right atrium of the heart that produce spontaneous electrical signals at a regular rate; the sinoatrial node.

pharynx (far´-inks): in vertebrates, a chamber that is located at the back of the mouth and is shared by the digestive and respiratory systems.

plaque (plak): a deposit of cholesterol and other fatty substances within the wall of an artery.

plasma: the fluid, noncellular portion of the blood.

platelet (plāt´-let): a cell fragment that is formed from megakaryocytes in bone marrow and lacks a nucleus; circulates in the blood and plays a role in blood clotting.

pleural membrane: a membrane that lines the chest cavity and surrounds the lungs.

pulmonary circulation: the circulation of blood from the body, through the right atrium and right ventricle, and to the lungs.

respiratory center: a cluster of neurons, located in the medulla of the brain, that sends rhythmic bursts of nerve impulses to the respiratory muscles, resulting in breathing.

semilunar valve: a paired valve between the ventricles of the heart and the pulmonary artery and aorta; prevents the backflow of blood into the ventricles when they relax.

sinoatrial (SA) node (sī´-nō-āt´-rē-ul): a small mass of specialized muscle in the wall of the right atrium; generates electrical signals rhythmically and spontaneously and serves as the heart's pacemaker.

spleen: an organ of the lymphatic system in which lymphocytes are produced and blood is filtered past lymphocytes and macrophages, which remove foreign particles and aged red blood cells.

stroke: an interruption of blood flow to part of the brain caused by the rupture of an artery or the blocking of an artery by a blood clot. Loss of blood supply leads to rapid death of the area of the brain affected.

systemic circulation: the circulation of blood from the left ventricle, through the rest of the body (except the lungs), and back to the heart.

thrombin: an enzyme produced in the blood as a result of injury to a blood vessel; catalyzes the production of fibrin, a protein that assists in blood clot formation.

thymus (thī-mus): an organ of the lymphatic system that is located in the upper chest in front of the heart and that secretes thymosin, which stimulates lymphocyte maturation; begins to degenerate at puberty and has little function in the adult.

tonsil: a patch of lymphatic tissue consisting of connective tissue that contains many lymphocytes; located in the pharynx and throat.

trachea (trā-kē-uh): in birds and mammals, a rigid but flexible tube, supported by rings of cartilage, that conducts air between the larynx and the bronchi.

vein: in vertebrates, a large-diameter, thin-walled vessel that carries blood from venules back to the heart.

ventricle (ven-tre-kul): the lower muscular chamber on each side of the heart, which pumps blood out through the arteries. The right ventricle sends blood to the lungs; the left ventricle pumps blood to the rest of the body.

venule (ven-ūl): a narrow vessel with thin walls that carries blood from capillaries to veins.

vocal cord: one of a pair of bands of elastic tissue that extend across the opening of the larynx and produce sound when air is forced between them. Muscles alter the tension on the vocal cords and control the size and shape of the opening, which in turn determines whether sound is produced and what its pitch will be.

THINKING THROUGH THE CONCEPTS

True or False: Determine if the statement given is true or false. If it is false, change the underlined words so that the statement reads true.

57. _____   An open circulatory system is an efficient means of transporting nutrients and wastes.

58. _____   A function of the circulatory system is to distribute hormones from their point of production to their target tissue.

59. _____   When atria contract, blood is sent throughout the body.

60. _____   Blood flows away from the heart in veins.

61. _____   At a resting heart rate, the cardiac cycle is complete in less than 1 second.

62. _____   The delay between the pumping of the atria and the ventricles is maintained by the atrioventricular node.

63. _____   The atrioventricular node serves as the pacemaker of the heart.

64. _____   Fibrillation of the ventricles can be fatal.

65. _____   Heart rate is influenced by the hormone epinephrine.

66. _____   The average human has 5 to 6 liters of blood.

67. _____   The protein fibrinogen in erythrocytes carries oxygen to the body's cells.

68. _____   Red blood cells are capable of mitotic division after living 120 days.

69. _____   Both red and white blood cells are produced by cells from bone marrow.

70. _____   White blood cells are part of the circulatory system and the lymphatic system.

71. _____   Platelets are cells derived from megakaryocytes.

72. _____   Interstitial fluid contains water and dissolved nutrients, gases, wastes, and blood proteins.

73. _____ Red blood cells pass through capillaries in <u>pairs</u>.

74. _____ Veins contain <u>one-way valves</u> to prevent backflow of blood.

75. _____ Gases must be <u>dissolved in water</u> when they diffuse in or out of cells.

76. _____ <u>Diffusion</u> is the movement of gases through relatively large spaces from an area of high pressure to an area of low pressure.

77. _____ Gills are extensively branched or folded to <u>increase</u> surface area.

78. _____ The first lungs may have arisen as extensions of the <u>digestive tract</u> in freshwater fish.

79. _____ As some animals develop, <u>both gills and lungs</u> are produced as they go through their life stages.

80. _____ The <u>tongue</u> guards the opening of the larynx.

81. _____ The respiratory tract is lined with <u>mucus,</u> which traps bacteria and debris from inhaled air.

82. _____ The internal lung surface area equals about 75 square meters due to the structure of <u>alveoli</u>.

83. _____ Inhalation is a <u>passive</u> process.

84. _____ Breathing is controlled by the respiratory center in the <u>cerebellum</u>.

Identification: Determine whether the following statements about the results of smoking refer to **atherosclerosis, emphysema,** or **chronic bronchitis**.

85. _____ causes heart attacks

86. _____ mucus is produced in large quantities

87. _____ breathing is labored

88. _____ action of cilia decreases

89. _____ airflow to alveoli decreases

90. _____ arterial walls are thick with fatty deposits

91. _____ alveoli are destroyed

92. _____ lungs resemble blackened Swiss cheese

93. _____ number of cilia decreases

94. _____ lung tissue becomes brittle

95. _____ respiratory tract lining is swollen

Short Answer.

96. Identify the functions of the three proteins involved in blood clotting.

Clotting protein	Function
thrombin	
fibrinogen	
fibrin	

CLUES TO APPLYING THE CONCEPTS

These practice questions are intended to sharpen your ability to apply critical thinking and analysis to biological concepts covered in this chapter.

97. Trace the flow of blood through the heart, including its path to and from the lungs.

_____

_____

_____

_____

_____

_____

_____

98. Explain how arterioles help regulate body temperature on extremely cold or extremely hot days.

_____

_____

_____

_____

_____

_____

_____

_____

_____

99. Outline differences between capillaries of the circulatory system and those of the lymphatic system.

_____

_____

_____

_____

_____

_____

100. Outline the general path of gas exchange through the body. Identify whether movement occurs through bulk flow or diffusion in each step.

_____

_____

_____

_____

_____

_____

_____

_____

_____

101. Explain how the respiratory center regulates breathing rate.

_____

_____

_____

_____

102. Why is the respiratory center less sensitive to O_2 concentrations than to CO_2 concentrations in the blood?

_____

_____

_____

_____

ANSWERS TO EXERCISES

1. blood
2. blood vessels
3. heart
4. hemocoel
5. open circulatory systems
6. Closed circulatory systems
7. atria
8. ventricles
9. pulmonary circulation
10. systemic circulation
11. veins
12. arteries
13. cardiac cycle
14. atrioventricular valves
15. semilunar valves
16. pacemaker
17. sinoatrial (SA) node
18. atrioventricular (AV) node
19. fibrillations
20. plasma
21. platelets
22. megakaryocytes
23. erythrocytes
24. hemoglobin
25. leukocytes
26. blood clotting
27. thrombin
28. fibrin
29. arterioles
30. capillaries
31. interstitial fluid
32. venules
33. lymphatic system

34. lymph
35. lymphocytes
36. tonsils
37. lymph nodes
38. thymus
39. spleen
40. bulk flow
41. gills
42. lungs
43. conducting portion
44. gas-exchange portion
45. pharynx
46. larynx
47. vocal cords
48. trachea
49. bronchi
50. bronchioles
51. alveoli
52. diaphragm
53. inhalation
54. exhalation
55. respiratory center
56. pleural membranes
57. false, closed
58. true
59. false, ventricles
60. false, arteries
61. true
62. true
63. false, sinoatrial node
64. true
65. true

66. true
67. false, hemoglobin
68. false, are not capable of division
69. true
70. true
71. false, membrane-enclosed cell fragments
72. true
73. false, single file
74. true
75. true
76. false, bulk flow
77. true
78. true
79. true
80. false, epiglottis
81. true
82. true
83. false, active
84. false, brainstem
85. atherosclerosis
86. chronic bronchitis
87. emphysema
88. chronic bronchitis
89. chronic bronchitis
90. atherosclerosis
91. emphysema
92. emphysema
93. chronic bronchitis
94. emphysema
95. chronic bronchitis

96.

Clotting protein	Function
thrombin	an enzyme produced in response to an injury to a blood vessel; converts fibrinogen to fibrin
fibrinogen	the precursor protein to fibrin
fibrin	adheres to other fibrin molecules forming a fibrous network, trapping red blood cells and platelets forming a clot

97.   Blood returns to the heart to the right atrium through its atrioventricular valve and into the right ventricle. Blood leaving the right ventricle passes through the semilunar valve as it enters the pulmonary artery into the lungs. After being reoxygenated, the blood leaves the lungs through the pulmonary vein and enters the left atrium. Blood is pumped from the left atrium through its atrioventricular valve and into the left ventricle. Oxygenated blood is pumped through the semilunar valve into the aorta for distribution to the body.

98. Muscles in the arteriole walls are directly controlled by nerves, hormones, and chemicals produced by nearby tissues. Therefore, as the needs of nearby tissues change, arterioles contract and relax in response. The circulatory system helps regulate body temperature. By relaxing and expanding, the arterioles bring blood flow closer to the surface of the skin; thus, the heat dissipates, cooling the body. During cold weather, arteriole walls constrict, pulling the blood away from the skin's surface to maintain body warmth. Under extreme conditions, the blood is shunted to the body's internal organs, specifically to the heart and brain.

99. The capillaries of the circulatory system are composed of cells that have plasma membranes with pores that allow only water, dissolved nutrients, hormones, wastes, and small blood proteins to leak out. White blood cells ooze through openings between capillary cells. The capillaries of the circulatory system form a continuous network between the arterial system and the venous system. The capillaries of the lymphatic system contain cells with one-way openings between them. Thus, larger molecules can be carried into them. These capillaries dead-end in tissues, collecting extra interstitial fluid and its contents.

100. Air or water containing O_2 is moved past a respiratory surface by <u>bulk flow</u>. The flow may be facilitated by muscular breathing movements. O_2 and CO_2 are exchanged through the respiratory surface by <u>diffusion</u>; O_2 diffuses into the capillaries of the circulatory system and CO_2 diffuses out. The gases are transported in the circulatory system from the respiratory system to the tissues by <u>bulk flow</u> of the blood as it is pumped throughout the body by the heart. The gases are exchanged between the tissues and the circulatory system by <u>diffusion</u>; O_2 diffuses out of the capillaries and CO_2 diffuses in. The gases are transported back to the respiratory system by <u>bulk flow</u> of the blood. At the respiratory surface, O_2 <u>diffuses</u> into the capillaries of the circulatory system and CO_2 <u>diffuses</u> out again.

101. The respiratory center, located in the brainstem, receives signals from CO_2 receptor neurons. The CO_2 receptors are sensitive to CO_2 levels in the bloodstream. If CO_2 levels rise only 0.3% above the body's acceptable level, the receptors signal the center to increase breathing rate and the depth of breaths.

102. The respiratory center is less sensitive to the O_2 concentration in the bloodstream because under normal conditions, there is an overabundance of O_2. A relatively small drop in O_2 levels will not present a problem to tissues in need of O_2. If, however, a sudden drop in O_2 levels occurs, receptors in the aorta and carotid arteries will stimulate the respiratory center.

Chapter 21: Nutrition, Digestion, and Excretion

OVERVIEW

This chapter provides an overview of the nutrients animals need and how they get those nutrients from their food. Digestion is the physical grinding and chemical breakdown of food. Since the energy an animal needs for body maintenance, growth, and reproduction amounts to the energy that remains after eating and digestion is complete, animals that have evolved the most efficient means of digesting their food will survive. Many different mechanisms to accomplish this task have arisen; however, this chapter focuses on the relatively unspecialized, but well-orchestrated, digestive system of humans which allows ingestion and digestion of a wide variety of food items.

This chapter also presents the form and function of the urinary system in vertebrates; focusing on humans in particular. The urinary system of animals plays a very important role in the maintenance of homeostasis. It removes excess water, salts, nutrients, and minerals in a precise and regulated manner.

1) What Nutrients Do Animals Need?

Nutrition is the process of aquiring and processing nutrients. Animals need lipids, carbohydrates, proteins, minerals, and vitamins to provide energy for cellular metabolism, the basic molecules for building complex molecules of body function, and vitamins and minerals for metabolic reactions. Fats, carbohydrates, and proteins are used for energy. The energy available in food is measured in **calories**; 1000 calories make up a **Calorie**. In order for an animal to synthesize the fats it needs, it may need to acquire **essential fatty acids** from its food. Carbohydrates are synthesized from fats, amino acids, or other carbohydrates in the diet and are stored as **glycogen** in the liver and muscles.

The human body also uses a small amount of its own protein for energy. When this protein is broken down, the waste product **urea** is produced. The protein is replaced by protein eaten in the diet. Of the 20 amino acids that the body needs to make proteins, the liver can synthesize 9. The other 11 amino acids, called **essential amino acids**, must be acquired through the diet. **Minerals** (elements and small inorganic molecules) must be obtained from food items or dissolved in drinking water. **Vitamins** are essential organic compounds required in small amounts for the proper functioning of the human body.

Most Americans have access to a nutritious food supply but often make poor choices when eating. To help people make better choices, the U.S. government (1) developed dietary recommendations, (2) designed a food pyramid, and (3) required nutritional labels on commercial food packaging.

2) How Is Digestion Accomplished?

All digestive systems must accomplish five tasks: (1) ingestion (placement of food into the digestive tract, usually through an opening called the **mouth**), (2) mechanical breakdown (physical breakdown of the food into smaller pieces), (3) chemical breakdown (exposure of the food to digestive enzymes that break large molecules into smaller subunits), (4) absorption (transport of the small molecules from the digestive cavity to cells), and (5) elimination (expulsion of indigestible materials from the body). The way in which ingestion, digestion, absorption, and elimination occurs differs, depending on the animal.

Digestion may occur, as in sponges, within cells. **Intracellular digestion** occurs after microscopic food particles have been engulfed by cells. The food particles are enclosed in a **food vacuole**. The vacuole fuses with **lysosomes** containing digestive enzymes, and the food is broken down in the vacuole and transported to the cell cytoplasm. **Extracellular digestion** occurs in larger animals that have evolved specialized digestive chambers, such as a **gastrovascular cavity**. Food is ingested and eliminated through the single opening to the cavity; thus, one meal must be eaten, completely digested, and eliminated before another can begin.

Evolution of a digestive tube allows animals to eat more frequently. In the specialized digestive tube of earthworms, a **pharynx** connects the mouth with the **esophagus**. Beyond the esophagus is the **crop**, which stores food particles. Slowly the food is passed on to the muscular **gizzard**, where the food is ground by sand particles and muscular contractions. The food is passed on to the intestines for chemical digestion and absorbed by the cells of the intestinal lining.

3) How Do Humans Digest Food?

Within the mouth, food is ground by the teeth and mixed with saliva by the tongue. Within saliva is the enzyme **amylase**, which begins the breakdown of starch to sugar. As the food is swallowed, the tongue pushes it into the **pharynx**. The **epiglottis** covers the opening of the trachea as the food is swallowed into the esophagus. The muscles of the esophagus contract, pushing the food toward the **stomach**, in a process called **peristalsis**. Once in the stomach, food is mixed and churned by peristalsis and other muscular contractions before it is slowly released into the small intestine through the **pyloric sphincter**.

While in the stomach, however, the food is mixed with chemicals secreted by cells of the stomach. These chemicals include **gastrin**, a hormone that stimulates the production and secretion of hydrochloric acid by stomach cells, and pepsin, a **protease** enzyme that digests proteins into shorter peptides. The churning and mixing that occurs in the stomach converts the food into **chyme**. Chyme is slowly released into the **small intestine**, where it will be digested into small molecules to be absorbed into the bloodstream.

Digestion in the small intestine is accomplished by secretions from cells of the small intestine, the liver, and the pancreas. The **liver** functions in digestion by producing **bile**, which is stored in the **gallbladder**. Bile is a mixture of **bile salts**, water, cholesterol, and other salts. Bile salts help digest lipids by acting as detergents, breaking fats into microscopic particles. The microscopic lipid particles are then digested by **lipase** enzymes. The **pancreas** secretes **pancreatic juice** into the small intestine, which neutralizes the acid in the chyme and digests carbohydrates, lipids, and proteins. The small intestine is the primary site of chemical digestion and the primary site of nutrient **absorption**. To increase the absorptive surface area of the small intestine, it is extensively folded and is covered internally by **villi**. Each villus, in turn, is covered by **microvilli**. **Segmentation movements** move the chyme around in the small intestine such that nutrients contact the absorptive surface. Peristalsis moves what is left after absorption into the **large intestine**, where water is absorbed to form feces. The large intestine consists of the **colon** and the **rectum**.

Digestion is regulated by both the nervous system and hormones. The nervous system is stimulated by the sight, smell, taste, or even the thought of food, as well as by the process of chewing it. The nervous system readies the mouth and stomach for the arrival of food. The stomach begins to secrete acid, stimulating its cells to produce the hormone gastrin. As chyme enters the small intestine, its acidity stimulates the production of **secretin**. Secretin is released into the bloodstream to stimulate the pancreas to dump sodium bicarbonate into the small intestine, neutralizing the acidity. When chyme enters the small intestine, the hormone **cholestokinin** is produced, stimulating the pancreas to release additional digestive enzymes into the small intestine and stimulating the gallbladder to contract and dump bile into the small intestine. When sugars and fatty acids are detected in chyme, the small intestine secretes **gastric inhibitory peptide** to reduce the rate at which the stomach releases chyme. This results in an increase in the length of time chyme spends in the small intestine for absorption.

4) What Are the Functions of Vertebrate Urinary Systems?

Urinary systems of animals play a very important role in the maintenance of a stable internal environment, or maintaining **homeostasis**. The **kidneys** collect the fluid plasma from blood, and reabsorb nutrients and water while removing toxins, waste products, and excess water, salts, nutrients, and hormones. What is removed is channeled and stored until it is **excreted** from the body. **Urea** is produced when the body digests protein and removes the amino group from an amino acid; the amino group is released as **ammonia**. Since ammonia is highly toxic to mammals, it is converted to urea in the liver. Urea leaves the body as **urine**.

5) How Does the Human Urinary System Function?

Blood to be filtered by the human urinary system enters the pair of kidneys through the **renal artery**. Once filtration is complete, the blood leaves the kidneys through the **renal vein**. Urine is transported from each kidney to the **bladder** through a tube called the **ureter**. The ureter is muscular and uses peristaltic contractions to move the urine to the bladder. Urine leaves the body through the **urethra**.

The kidneys themselves are complex. A hollow inner chamber, the **renal pelvis**, funnels urine to the ureter. Outside the renal pelvis is the **renal medulla**, covered by the **renal cortex**. **Nephrons** fill the cortex and may extend into the medulla. Each nephron is composed of a **glomerulus** (a dense collection of capillaries that filter the blood) surrounded by a **Bowman's capsule**, and a long, twisted **tubule**. The tubule in turn is divided into the **proximal tubule**, the **loop of Henle**, and the **distal tubule**. The distal tubule leads to the **collecting duct**.

Blood flowing through the glomerulus undergoes **filtration**. The fluid **filtrate**, containing water and dissolved substances, is collected in the Bowman's capsule and transported through the tubule. The filtered blood, now very thick and concentrated, moves through highly porous capillaries winding around the tubule. When the capillaries come in contact with the tubule, water and nutrients in the filtrate are reabsorbed by the capillaries. This process, called **tubular reabsorption**, occurs in the proximal tubule using active transport, osmosis, and diffusion. By **tubular secretion**, any wastes still in the blood move into the filtrate in the distal tubule for excretion. The loop of Henle enables the filtrate (urine) to become concentrated. There is a greater osmotic concentration gradient in the interstitial fluid surrounding the loop. As the collecting duct passes through the concentrated interstitial fluid, additional water moves out of the duct by osmosis.

The amount of water that is reabsorbed into the blood is controlled by the level of **antidiuretic hormone (ADH)** in the blood. ADH makes the cells of the distal tubule more permeable to water and is regulated according to the volume of blood in the body.

KEY TERMS AND CONCEPTS

Fill-In I: From the following list of terms, fill in the blanks below.

absorption	food vacuole	pancreas
amylase	gallbladder	pancreatic juice
bile salts	gastrin	peristalsis
calorie	gastrovascular cavity	pharynx
Calorie	gizzard	protease
chyme	glycogen	pyloric sphincter
colon	intracellular digestion	rectum
crop	large intestine	segmentation movements
digestion	lipase	small intestine
epiglottis	liver	stomach
esophagus	lysosome	urea
essential amino acids	microvilli	villi
essential fatty acids	minerals	vitamins
extracellular digestion	mouth	

(1)_____ is the physical grinding and chemical breakdown of food.

A(n) (2)_____ is the amount of energy needed to raise the temperature of 1 gram
of water by 1 degree Celsius. A(n) (3)_____ is 1000 of these units and is
the term most commonly used to express the energy content in foods. Animals store energy as the
carbohydrate (4)_____ in the liver and muscles. A small amount of protein
is metabolized for energy creating the waste product (5)_____.

When digestion occurs within a cell, it is termed (6)_____. This type of
digestion encloses food items in a membrane-bound (7)_____. The food item is
digested when enzymes from a(n) (8)_____ are released into the vacuole.

When digestion occurs by enzymes outside the cell, it is termed (9)_____,
which typically occurs in a digestive sac with a single opening. This sac is referred to as the
(10)_____.

The earthworm's tubular digestive system includes a thin-walled storage organ called a(n)
(11)_____ and a muscular (12)_____, where food is
ground.

The human diet requires (13)_____ to build lipids;
(14)_____ to build proteins. carbohydrates;
(15)_____; and (16)_____.

The enzyme (17)_____ breaks starch into simple sugars, the enzyme
(18)_____ breaks fats into glycerol and fatty acid molecules, and the enzyme
(19)_____ breaks proteins into peptides.

Food enters the digestive tract through an opening called the (20)_____. After the food is chewed, it passes through the (21)_____ on its way to the esophagus. The (22)_____ prevents the food from entering the trachea while it is being swallowed. As food goes down the (23)_____, the smooth muscles contract rhythmically in a process called (24)_____. Food moving from the (25)_____ to the small intestine is called (26)_____, and its entrance into the small intestine is controlled by a ring of muscle, the (27)_____. (28)_____ and the microscopic (29)_____ greatly increase the absorptive surface area of the (30)_____. Once absorption is complete, the contents remaining in the small intestine move into the (31)_____, which is divided into two portions; the first part is the (32)_____, and the last 15 centimeters is called the (33)_____.

Secretion of acid by the stomach is controlled by the hormone (34)_____, and many of the digestive enzymes that are secreted into the small intestine are produced in the (35)_____ and make up the substance called (36)_____. The (37)_____ produces bile, which is stored in the (38)_____. Bile is a complex mixture of (39)_____, water, cholesterol, and other salts.

The primary functions of the small intestine are the chemical breakdown of food and the (40)_____ of small molecules into the bloodstream. (41)_____ increase the amount of nutrients and other molecules absorbed from chyme while it is in the small intestine.

Fill-In II: From the following list of terms, fill in the blanks below.

ammonia	filtration	renal cortex
antidiuretic hormone (ADH)	glomerulus	renal medulla
bladder	hemodialysis	renal pelvis
Bowman's capsule	homeostasis	renal veins
collecting duct	kidneys	tubular reabsorption
dialysis	loop of Henle	tubular secretion
distal tubule	nephridium	urea
excretion	nephrons	ureter
excretory pore	proximal tubule	urethra
filtrate	renal arteries	urine

(42)_____ is defined as the maintenance of a stable environment. The
(43)_____ play a role in maintaining this stability. The wastes that the urinary
system filters from the blood are removed from the body through a process called
(44)_____.

During amino acid digestion, the amine group may be removed, forming the highly toxic chemical
(45)_____. This toxic chemical is taken to the liver, where it is converted to
(46)_____. Eventually, the waste is excreted from the body as
(47)_____.

In human's, a pair of kidneys receive blood to be filtered through the (48)_____.
After it has been filtered, the blood leaves the kidneys through the (49)_____.
Urine leaves each kidney through a long tube called a(n) (50)_____ and is stored in
the (51)_____. Urine leaves the body by way of the (52)_____.

Within the human kidney is a hollow collecting chamber called the (53)_____.
Outside this chamber is the fan-shaped (54)_____, covered by the
(55)_____. Microscopic structures, the (56)_____,
act as filters.

Each nephron contains a mass of capillaries called the (57)_____, which is
surrounded by a cuplike structure, the (58)_____. A long, twisted tubule is
subdivided into the (59)_____, the (60)_____, and
the (61)_____, which leads to the (62)_____.
Within the glomerulus, water and dissolved substances are removed from the blood in a process called
(63)_____. The fluid that is removed is called the (64)_____.

When the proximal tubule reabsorbs water and nutrients from the filtrate, the process of
(65)_____ is occurring. When the distal tubule removes wastes that were not
filtered out initially, the process of (66)_____ is occurring. The amount of
water reabsorbed by the proximal tubule is regulated by the hormone (67)_____.

Individuals with kidney damage are treated with an artificial kidney. The process, called
(68)_____, uses an artificial semipermeable membrane to passively filter
substances from the blood. Since it is blood that is being filtered, the process is specifically called
(69)_____.

Key Terms and Definitions

absorption: the process by which nutrients are taken into cells.

ammonia: NH_3; a highly toxic nitrogen-containing waste product of amino acid breakdown. In the mammalian liver, it is converted to urea.

amylase (am´-i-lās): an enzyme, found in saliva and pancreatic secretions, that catalyzes the breakdown of starch.

antidiuretic hormone (an-tē-dī-ūr-et´-ik; **ADH**): a hormone produced by the hypothalamus and released into the bloodstream by the posterior pituitary when blood volume is low; increases the permeability of the distal tubule and the collecting duct to water, allowing more water to be reabsorbed into the bloodstream.

bile (bīl): a liquid secretion, produced by the liver, that is stored in the gallbladder and released into the small intestine during digestion; a complex mixture of bile salts, water, other salts, and cholesterol.

bile salt: a substance that is synthesized in the liver from cholesterol and amino acids and that assists in the breakdown of lipids by dispersing them into small particles on which enzymes can act.

bladder: a hollow muscular storage organ for storing urine.

Bowman's capsule: the cup-shaped portion of the nephron in which blood filtrate is collected from the glomerulus.

calorie (kal´-ō-rē): the amount of energy required to raise the temperature of 1 gram of water by 1 degree Celsius.

Calorie: a unit of energy, in which the energy content of foods is measured; the amount of energy required to raise the temperature of 1 liter of water 1 degree Celsius; also called a *kilocalorie*, equal to 1000 calories.

cholecystokinin: a digestive hormone, produced by the small intestine, that stimulates the release of pancreatic enzymes.

chyme (kīm): an acidic, souplike mixture of partially digested food, water, and digestive secretions that is released from the stomach into the small intestine.

collecting duct: a conducting tube, within the kidney, that collects urine from many nephrons and conducts it through the renal medulla into the renal pelvis. Urine may become concentrated in the collecting ducts if ADH is present.

colon: the longest part of the large intestine, exclusive of the rectum.

crop: an organ, found in both earthworms and birds, in which ingested food is temporarily stored before being passed to the gizzard, where it is pulverized.

dialysis (dī-āl´-i-sis): the passive diffusion of substances across an artificial semipermeable membrane.

digestion: the process by which food is physically and chemically broken down into molecules that can be absorbed by cells.

distal tubule: in the nephrons of the mammalian kidney, the last segment of the renal tubule through which the filtrate passes just before it empties into the collecting duct; a site of selective secretion and reabsorption as water and ions pass between the blood and the filtrate across the tubule membrane.

epiglottis (ep-eh-glah´-tis): a flap of cartilage in the lower pharynx that covers the opening to the larynx during swallowing; directs food down the esophagus.

esophagus (eh-sof´-eh-gus): a muscular passageway that conducts food from the pharynx to the stomach in humans and other mammals.

essential amino acid: an amino acid that is a required nutrient; the body is unable to manufacture essential amino acids, so they must be supplied in the diet.

essential fatty acid: a fatty acid that is a required nutrient; the body is unable to manufacture essential fatty acids, so they must be supplied in the diet.

excretion: the elimination of waste substances from the body; can occur from the digestive system, skin glands, urinary system, or lungs.

extracellular digestion: the physical and chemical breakdown of food that occurs outside a cell, normally in a digestive cavity.

filtrate: the fluid produced by filtration; in the kidneys, the fluid produced by the filtration of blood through the glomerular capillaries.

filtration: within Bowman's capsule in each nephron of a kidney, the process by which blood is pumped under pressure through permeable capillaries of the glomerulus, forcing out water, dissolved wastes, and nutrients.

food vacuole: a membranous sac, within a single cell, in which food is enclosed. Digestive enzymes are released into the vacuole, where intracellular digestion occurs.

gallbladder: a small sac, next to the liver, in which the bile secreted by the liver is stored and concentrated. Bile is released from the gallbladder to the small intestine through the bile duct.

gastric inhibitory peptide: a hormone, produced by the small intestine, that inhibits the activity of the stomach.

gastrin: a hormone, produced by the stomach, that stimulates the secretion of acid in response to food.

gastrovascular cavity: a chamber with digestive functions, in simple invertebrates. A single opening serves as both mouth and anus, the chamber provides direct access of nutrients to the cells.

gizzard: a muscular organ, found in earthworms and birds, in which food is mechanically broken down prior to chemical digestion.

glomerulus (glō-mer´-ū-lus): a dense network of thin-walled capillaries, located within the Bowman's capsule of each nephron of the kidney, where blood pressure forces water and dissolved nutrients through capillary walls for filtration by the nephron.

glycogen (glī´-kō-jen): a long, branched polymer of glucose stored by animals in the muscles and liver and metabolized as a source of energy.

hemodialysis (hē-mō-dī-al´-luh-sis): a procedure that simulates kidney function in individuals with damaged or ineffective kidneys; blood is diverted from the body, artificially filtered, and returned to the body.

homeostasis (hōm-ē-ō-stā´-sis): the maintenance of a relatively constant environment required for the optimal functioning of cells, maintained by the coordinated activity of numerous regulatory mechanisms, including the respiratory, endocrine, circulatory, and excretory systems.

intracellular digestion: the chemical breakdown of food within single cells.

kidney: one of a pair of organs of the excretory system that is located on either side of the spinal column and filters blood, removing wastes and regulating the composition and water content of the blood.

large intestine: the final section of the digestive tract; consists of the colon and the rectum, where feces are formed and stored.

lipase (lī´-pās): an enzyme that catalyzes the breakdown of lipids such as fats.

liver: an organ with varied functions, including bile production, glycogen storage, and the detoxification of poisons.

loop of Henle (hen´-lē): a specialized portion of the tubule of the nephron in birds and mammals that creates an osmotic concentration gradient in the fluid immediately surrounding it. This gradient in turn makes possible the production of urine more osmotically concentrated than blood plasma.

lysosome (lī´-sō-sōm): a membrane-bound organelle containing intracellular digestive enzymes.

microvillus (mī-krō-vi´-lus; pl., microvilli): a microscopic projection of the plasma membrane of each villus; increases the surface area of the villus.

mineral: an inorganic substance, especially one in rocks or soil.

mouth: the opening of a tubular digestive system into which food is first introduced.

nephron (nef´-ron): the functional unit of the kidney; where blood is filtered and urine formed.

nutrition: the process of acquiring nutrients from the environment and, if necessary, processing them into a form that can be used by the body.

pancreas (pān´-krē-us): a combined exocrine and endocrine gland located in the abdominal cavity next to the stomach. The endocrine portion secretes the hormones insulin and glucagon, which regulate glucose concentrations in the blood. The exocrine portion secretes enzymes for fat, carbohydrate, and protein digestion into the small intestine and neutralizes the acidic chyme.

pancreatic juice: a mixture of water, sodium bicarbonate, and enzymes released by the pancreas into the small intestine.

peristalsis: rhythmic coordinated contractions of the smooth muscles of the digestive tract that move substances through the digestive tract.

pharynx (far´-inks): in vertebrates, a chamber that is located at the back of the mouth and is shared by the digestive and respiratory systems; in some invertebrates, the portion of the digestive tube just posterior to the mouth.

protease (prō´-tē-ās): an enzyme that digests proteins.

proximal tubule: in nephrons of the mammalian kidney, the portion of the renal tubule just after the Bowman's capsule; receives filtrate from the capsule and is the site where selective secretion and reabsorption between the filtrate and the blood begins.

pyloric sphincter (pī-lor´-ik sfink´-ter): a circular muscle, located at the base of the stomach, that regulates the passage of chyme into the small intestine.

rectum: the terminal portion of the vertebrate digestive tube, where feces are stored until they can be eliminated.

renal artery: the artery carrying blood to each kidney.

renal cortex: the outer layer of the kidney; where nephrons are located.

renal medulla: the layer of the kidney just inside the renal cortex; where loops of Henle produce a highly concentrated interstitial fluid, important in the production of concentrated urine.

renal pelvis: the inner chamber of the kidney; where urine from the collecting ducts accumulates before it enters the ureters.

renal vein: the vein carrying cleansed blood away from each kidney.

secretin: a hormone, produced by the small intestine, that stimulates production and release of digestive secretions by the pancreas and liver.

segmentation movement: a contraction of the small intestine that results in the mixing of partially digested food and digestive enzymes. Segmentation movements also bring nutri-ents into contact with the absorptive intestinal wall.

small intestine: the portion of the digestive tract, located between the stomach and large intestine, in which most digestion and absorption of nutrients occur.

stomach: the muscular sac between the esophagus and small intestine where food is stored and mechanically broken down and in which protein digestion begins.

tubular reabsorption: the process by which cells of the tubule of the nephron remove water and nutrients from the filtrate within the tubule and return those substances to the blood.

tubular secretion: the process by which cells of the tubule of the nephron remove additional wastes from the blood, actively secreting those wastes into the tubule.

tubule (toob´-ūl): the tubular portion of the nephron; includes a proximal portion, the loop of Henle, and a distal portion. Urine is formed from the blood filtrate as it passes through the tubule.

urea (ū-rē´-uh): a water-soluble, nitrogen-containing waste product of amino acid breakdown; one of the principal components of mammalian urine.

ureter (ū´-re-ter): a tube that conducts urine from each kidney to the bladder.

urethra (ū-rē´-thruh): the tube leading from the urinary bladder to the outside of the body; in males, the urethra also receives sperm from the vas deferens and conducts both sperm and urine (at different times) to the tip of the penis.

urine: the fluid produced and excreted by the urinary system of vertebrates; contains water and dissolved wastes, such as urea.

villus (vi´-lus; pl., **villi**): a fingerlike projection of the wall of the small intestine that increases the absorptive surface area.

vitamin: one of a group of diverse chemicals that must be present in trace amounts in the diet to maintain health; used by the body in conjunction with enzymes in a variety of metabolic reactions.

THINKING THROUGH THE CONCEPTS

True or False: Determine if the statement given is true or false. If it is false, change the <u>underlined</u> word(s) so that the statement reads true.

70. _____   An advantage of the evolution of a digestive tract is that it enables an organism to eat <u>frequently</u>.

71. _____   The nematode has a <u>complex</u> digestion tube that is unspecialized along its length.

72. _____   Animals with tubular digestive systems use <u>intracellular digestion</u> to break down their food.

73. _____   The primary function of the stomach is <u>water reabsorption</u>.

74. _____   Bacteria in the large intestine <u>serve no purpose in the human body</u>.

75. _____   The <u>secretion of saliva</u>, stimulated by the sight of food, the thought of food, or the presence of food in the mouth, is controlled by the nervous system.

76. _____   Mucus produced by the stomach <u>neutralizes the acid conditions</u>.

77. _____   Within the <u>esophagus</u>, the enzyme pepsin breaks proteins into shorter polypeptides.

78. _____   As food moves into the small intestine, the pancreas is stimulated to produce <u>sodium hydroxide</u> to neutralize the acidic chyme.

79. _____   Bile salts <u>emulsify</u> fats.

80. _____   Nutrients and small food molecules are absorbed in the <u>large intestine</u>.

81. _____   The purpose of villi and microvilli is to increase the surface area of the <u>stomach</u>.

82. _____   The <u>vitamins of the B-complex and vitamin C</u> are used to aid enzymes in chemical reactions.

83. _____   Fat-soluble vitamins may be <u>toxic</u> if taken in high doses.

84. _____   Urea is formed when <u>carbohydrates</u> are digested.

85. _____   Urine is carried to the bladder in the <u>ureter</u>.

86. _____   Urination is under voluntary control of the <u>external sphincter</u>.

87. _____   An adult bladder can hold <u>0.5 liters</u> of urine.

88. _____   Within the kidney, nephrons may extend into the <u>renal medulla</u>.

89. _____   Filtration in the glomerulus occurs because of a <u>difference in diameter</u> between the arterioles bringing blood in and the arterioles taking blood out.

90. _____   Tubular reabsorption occurs in the <u>distal tubule</u>.

91. _____   During tubular secretion, wastes that are actively secreted into the tubule may include <u>drugs</u>.

92. _____   Each drop of blood passes through a kidney <u>10 times</u> a day.

93. _____   ADH is released when receptors in the <u>hypothalamus</u> detect an inappropriate osmotic level in the blood.

94. _____   A long loop of Henle would be found in the kidneys of <u>aquatic</u> animals.

Matching: Digestive enzymes and substrates.

95. _____   disaccharidases   Choices:

96. _____   pepsin   a.   proteins

97. _____   lipase   b.   disaccharides

98. _____   chymotrypsin   c.   individual amino acids

99. _____   amylase   d.   peptides

100. _____ peptidases   e.   lipids

101. _____ trypsin   f.   starches

Fill-In:

102. Complete the table below by identifying the functions of the structures listed.

Area of the digestive tract	Function
mouth	
esophagus	
stomach	
small intestine	
liver	
pancreas	
large intestine	

Identification: Determine whether the following vitamins are soluble in **fat** or **water**.

103. _____   vitamin A

104. _____   vitamin B-complex

105. _____   vitamin C

106. _____   vitamin D

107. _____   vitamin E

108. _____   vitamin K

Refer to the diagram of the nephron below to answer questions 109 through 119.

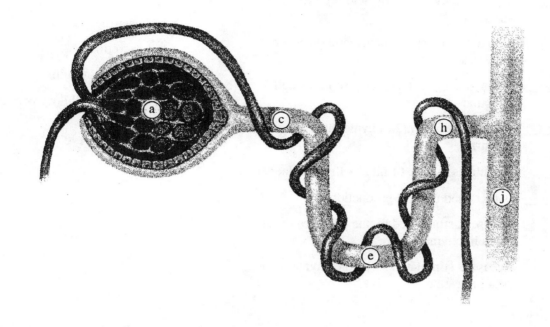

109. _____ identify the structure (a)

110. _____ what is the function of (a)?

111. _____ identify the structure (c)

112. _____ what is the function of (c)?

113. _____ identify the structure (e)

114. _____ if (e) was extremely long, in what sort of habitat would this animal live?

115. _____ if (e) was rather short, in what sort of habitat would this animal live?

116. _____ identify the structure (h)

117. _____ what is the function of (h)?

118. _____ identify the structure (j)

119. _____ what is the function of (j)?

Matching: Hormones and their functions.

120. _____ stimulates hydrochloric acid production by stomach cells

121. _____ stimulates release of pancreatic digestive enzymes

122. _____ stimulates bicarbonate release into small intestine

123. _____ inhibits movement of chyme into the small intestine

124. _____ stimulates release of bile by the gallbladder

125. _____ is regulated by acid production

126. _____ release is stimulated by the presence of fatty acids in chyme

127. _____ release is stimulated by acidic chyme in the small intestine

Choices:

a. gastrin

b. secretin

c. cholecystokinin

d. gastric inhibitory peptide

Short Answer.

128. List the five tasks a digestive system must accomplish, regardless of its level of complexity.

_____

_____

_____

_____

_____

_____

129. What are the two primary functions of a digestive tract?

_____

_____

_____

130. Trace the path of urine from its production in the kidneys to its point of excretion from the body.

Kidneys → _____ → _____ → _____ → excretion

131. Where are trypsin, and chymotrypsin, found? What is the function of each?

_____

_____

_____

_____

_____

_____

CLUES TO APPLYING THE CONCEPTS

These practice questions are intended to sharpen your ability to apply critical thinking and analysis to biological concepts covered in this chapter.

132. Consider the chemicals secreted by the stomach: hydrochloric acid and protein-digesting pepsin. Why does the stomach not digest itself?

_____

_____

_____

_____

_____

_____

133. Some people might react strongly if they knew that their digestive system supported a healthy population of bacteria. How would you convince such a person that the bacteria play a very important role in their health?

_____

_____

_____

_____

_____

_____

_____

134. If you are being treated for a bacterial infection with an antibiotic, a side effect you may experience is diarrhea. Using the information you now have concerning the large intestine, what would you determine to be the reason? How might eating yogurt with live cultures counteract this side effect?

_____

_____

_____

_____

_____

_____

135. Identify the six ways the mammalian urinary system helps maintain homeostasis.

_____

_____

_____

ANSWERS TO EXERCISES

1. digestion
2. calorie
3. Calorie
4. glycogen
5. urea
6. intracellular digestion
7. food vacuole
8. lysosome
9. extracellular digestion
10. gastrovascular cavity
11. crop
12. gizzard
13. essential fatty acids
14. essential amino acids
15. vitamins
16. minerals
17. amylase
18. lipase
19. protease
20. mouth
21. pharynx
22. epiglottis
23. esophagus
24. peristalsis

25. stomach
26. chyme
27. pyloric sphincter
28. Villi
29. microvilli
30. small intestine
31. large intestine
32. colon
33. rectum
34. gastrin
35. pancreas
36. pancreatic juice
37. liver
38. gallbladder
39. bile salts
40. absorption
41. segmentation movements
42. homeostasis
43. kidneys
44. excretion
45. ammonia
46. urea
47. urine
48. renal arteries

49. renal veins
50. ureter
51. bladder
52. urethra
53. renal pelvis
54. renal medulla
55. renal cortex
56. nephrons
57. glomerulus
58. Bowman's capsule
59. proximal tubule
60. loop of Henle
61. distal tubule
62. collecting duct
63. filtration
64. filtrate
65. tubular reabsorption
66. tubular secretion
67. antidiuretic hormone,(ADH)
68. dialysis
69. hemodialysis
70. true
71. false, simple
72. false, extracellular digestion

73. false, food storage
74. false, synthesize vitamins B₁₂, thiamin, riboflavin, K
75. true
76 false, protects stomach cells
77. false, stomach
78. false, sodium bicarbonate
79. true
80. false, small intestine
81. false, small intestine

82. true
83. true
84. false, proteins
85. true
86. true
87. true
88. true
89. true
90. false, proximal tubule
91. true

92. false, about 350 times
93. true
94. false, desert
95. b
96. a
97. e
98. a
99. f
100. d
101. a

102.

Area of the digestive tract	Function
mouth	mechanical (chewing) and chemical (amylase) breakdown of food
esophagus	transfers food from mouth to stomach
stomach	stores food, mechanical breakdown of food, secretes enzymes
small intestine	digests food into small molecules, absorbs food molecules
liver	produces bile to emulsify fats in small intestine
pancreas	produces pancreatic juice to digest carbohydrates, fats, and protein, and to neutralize chyme
large intestine	absorbs water and salts from chyme, absorbs vitamins made by bacteria

103 fat
104. water
105. water
106. fat
107. fat
108. fat
109. glomerulus
110. filtration
111. proximal tubule

112. reabsorption
113. loop of Henle
114. desert
115. aquatic
116. distal tubule
117. tubular secretion
118. collecting duct
119. to concentrate urine

120. a
121. c
122. b
123. d
124. c
125. a
126. d
127. b

128. Ingestion of food item; mechanical breakdown (food is physically broken into smaller pieces); chemical breakdown (food is exposed to digestive enzymes; absorption of small molecules); elimination of wastes.

129. Digestion of food; absorption of nutrients.

130. Kidneys → ureter → bladder → urethra → excretion.

131. These two enzymes are in pancreatic juice secreted by the pancreas into the small intestine. Trypsin and chymotrypsin digest proteins and large peptides into small peptide chains.

132. Thick mucus secreted by cells of the stomach lining protects the stomach cells from the acid environment. The enzyme pepsin is produced in an inactive form, pepsinogen, that is converted to pepsin in the acid environment of the stomach. Again, the mucus lining the stomach would protect the cells from being digested by pepsin. However, cells lining the stomach are damaged or partially digested and must be replaced every few days. In extreme cases, an ulcer forms where the lining and deeper tissues of the stomach have been digested.

133. The bacteria living in the large intestine synthesize the vitamins B_{12}, thiamin, riboflavin, and K, which are absorbed by the large intestine. The normal diet does not provide these vitamins in sufficient amounts. You could include in your argument that without the production of these vitamins a person could be affected by the following vitamin deficiency symptoms:
    B_{12} – pernicious anemia, neurological disorders
    thiamin – muscle weakness, peripheral nerve changes, edema, heart failure
    riboflavin – red, cracked lips, eye lesions
    K – internal hemorrhages, failure of blood to clot

134. An antibiotic that you would be taking for a general bacterial infection would most likely be a broad-spectrum antibiotic. That is, it acts against a wide range of bacteria. This would include the bacteria active in your large intestine. The antibiotic does not distinguish between "good" and "bad" bacteria. With the environment of your large intestine disrupted, diarrhea may result. Eating yogurt containing "active cultures" (live *Acidophilus* bacteria) while taking the antibiotic regimen may help restore the bacterial population in your large intestine, reducing the side effects of the antibiotic.

135. Regulation of blood ion levels; regulation of blood water content;   maintenance of blood pH; retention of important nutrients; secretion of hormones; elimination of cellular waste products.

Chapter 22: Defenses Against Disease:
The Immune Response

OVERVIEW

This chapter presents the ways in which the body defends itself against bacteria, fungi, protists, and environmental toxins. The body is designed so that it is difficult for foreign substances to enter it. But when they do, the body has a well-developed system to detect and destroy invaders. It is able to determine foreign cells from body cells, and it is able to remember invaders that have been present before. Occasionally, however, the system fails. Examples of what occurs when the immune system breaks down are discussed.

1) How Does the Body Defend Against Invasion?

The human body is designed to keep invaders from entering. Its three lines of defense are external barriers, nonspecific internal defenses, and the immune system. The **skin** provides a barrier to microbes. The outer layer of skin is dry and devoid of nutrients, and the dead cells slough off. Sweat and sebaceous glands produce natural antibiotics. Microbes have a difficult time actually getting into the body through the skin. **Mucous membranes** lining the digestive and respiratory tracts trap microbes and contain antibiotic substances. Cilia of cells lining these tracts move the mucous and trapped particles up and out of their respective areas. The mucous is then either coughed or sneezed out, or swallowed.
    When microbes do gain entry, the body has a nonspecific line of defense to remove them. **Phagocytic cells** such as the white blood cells called **macrophages**, ingest microbes by phagocytosis. **Natural killer cells** destroy the body's cells that have been attacked by viruses. When viruses enter a cell, they usually leave viral proteins on the outside of the cell. Natural killer cells respond to those proteins by killing the cell. When the skin is cut, an **inflammatory response** is elicited. The damaged cells release **histamine**, relaxing the smooth muscle of arterioles and making capillaries leak thus increasing blood flow to the area, causing it to become red, swollen, and warm. Phagocytes brought to the wound by the increased blood flow ingest microbes infecting the injury. If the phagocytes cannot remove all of the microbes, the microbes may infect larger areas of the body initiating a **fever**. A fever is part of the body's natural defense against infection. It increases phagocyte activity while reducing microbial reproduction. Fever also induces the production of the virus-fighting protein **interferon**.

2) What Are the Key Characteristics of the Immune Response?

The **immune response** is specifically directed toward a particular invading organism. Lymphocytes called **B cells** and **T cells** recognize foreign organisms, initiate an attack against them, and remember the organisms in order to combat future attacks.

3) How Are Threats Recognized?

B cells produce proteins called **antibodies**. Antibodies may remain attached to the surface of the B cell or they may be secreted into the bloodstream. In the bloodstream, antibodies are called immunoglobulins. T cells produce proteins called **T-cell receptors** that remain attached to them.

Antibodies consist of two heavy peptide chains and two light peptide chains. Both the heavy and the light chains have a **constant region** and a **variable region**. Antibodies that are on the surface of a B cell act as receptors, projecting outward, ready to bind to appropriate **anti**body **gen**erating molecules (**antigens**). Molecules that act as antigens include proteins, glycoproteins, and polysaccharides. When an antigen binds to an antibody receptor, a response is stimulated in that cell. Antibodies also circulate in the bloodstream and neutralize or destroy antigens in the blood. Antibodies are capable of binding to specific antigens because their variable regions are highly specific.

T-cell receptors function only as receptors on the surface of T cells. When they bind to an antigen, they cause a response in the T cell.

The plasma membranes of your body's cells contain proteins and polysaccharides that indicate to your antibodies that these cells belong to your body. These proteins form the **major histocompatability complex (MHC)** and are unique to you (and perhaps to your identical twin). During embryological development, immune cells that do react to "self" cells are destroyed so that cells with the body's own antigens are not attacked.

4) How Are Threats Overcome?

When the body is threatened by an infection, two types of immunity are engaged: humoral immunity and cell mediated immunity. **Humoral immunity** involves B cells and the antibodies they secrete into the bloodstream. When antibodies on B cells bind to antigens from an invading organism, the B cell is induced to divide rapidly, producing genetically identical cells. This is referred to as **clonal selection**. The daughter clones differentiate into either **plasma cells** or **memory cells**. Plasma cells produce large quantities of their specific antibodies and release them into the bloodstream. Memory cells are involved in future immunity if reinfection with the same organism occurs.

Antibodies carry out their effect using four mechanisms. (1) Antibodies may neutralize a toxic antigen preventing damage to the body. (2) They may coat the surface of a microorganism promoting phagocytosis by white blood cells. (3) An antibody may bind to two microbes at a time. Because additional antibodies also bind with more than one organism, these cells clump together, enhancing phagocytosis. (4) Antibodies that circulate in the blood attach to microbe antigens with their variable regions while their stems attach to special proteins. This also enhances phagocytosis.

Cell-mediated immunity involves three types of T cells that attack organisms or viruses within body cells and attack cancerous cells. When receptors on **cytotoxic T cells** bind to antigens on an infected cell, the cytotoxic T cells produce and release proteins that will disrupt the infected cell's plasma membrane. When antigens bind to receptors on the surface of **helper T cells**, the cells produce and release chemicals that act as hormones, stimulating both cytotoxic T cells and B cells to divide and differentiate. Once an infection has been successfully fought, **suppressor T cells** shut off the immune response of both cytotoxic T cells and B cells.

5) How Are Invaders "Remembered"?

When the body is infected with an organism that has antigens to which the immune system has responded before, memory cells specific to that antigen will recognize the organism. The memory cells multiply rapidly and stimulate the production of huge populations of plasma cells and cytotoxic T cells. This second round of defense occurs much more quickly than the first.

6) How Does Medical Care Augment the Immune Response?

The use of antibiotics compromises the ability of microbes to grow and reproduce. With the population growth of these invaders in check, the immune system can fight the infection and stands a better chance of winning. Antibiotics are effective against bacteria, fungi, and protists, but *not* viruses. The overuse or improper use of antibiotics enhances the microbes' already strong qualities of natural selection. Many antibiotic-resistant strains of microbes have developed for this reason.

Injecting dead or weakened disease agents into a healthy individual does not cause the individual to acquire the disease, but it does cause the immune system to mount a vigorous response to the foreign antigens, including production of a large number of memory cells. Thus, **vaccinations** confer immunity against potentially deadly diseases.

7) Can the Immune System Malfunction?

Unfortunately, the immune system can malfunction. **Allergies** are a common example of such a malfunction. When pollen or another foreign substance, such as poison ivy toxin, enters the bloodstream and is identified by a B cell as an antigen, the B cell multiplies. The proliferation of B cells produces plasma cells that generate antibodies against the antigen. When the antigen binds to antibodies in the respiratory or digestive tract, histamine is released. The release of histamine induces the typical "hay fever" symptoms. **Autoimmune diseases** occur when the immune system does not recognize its body's own cells. Thus, a portion of the body is attacked. This is the cause of some forms of anemia and diabetes.

Children born with **severe combined immune deficiency (SCID)** are unable to produce sufficient numbers of immune cells, if any. For the first few months of life, the children are protected from disease by immunity acquired from the mother during pregnancy. During this time, the immune system of an infant typically begins to develop. Once this protection is lost, children with SCID are unable to sustain their own immunity. Bone marrow transplants, to supply the child with healthy marrow that produces white blood cells , is one form of therapy offered to these children.

Some individuals lose the effectiveness of their immune system. Individuals with **acquired immune deficiency syndrome (AIDS)** are infected with the **human immunodeficiency virus (HIV)** either type 1 or 2 (HIV-1 or HIV-2). These viruses attack helper T cells. Thus, both the humoral and cell-mediated responses are severely hindered, and these individuals are susceptible to various otherwise easily combated diseases. Both HIV-1 and HIV-2 are **retroviruses,** that is, they are RNA viruses that transcribe their RNA into DNA using their own enzyme, **reverse transcriptase**. Their DNA is then inserted into the DNA of the helper T cell. When the gene is activated in the helper T cell, HIV particles are manufactured and released into the bloodstream, killing the helper T cell in the process.

HIV cannot survive outside the body for very long. The virus can only be transmitted by direct exchange of body fluids by activities that cause the fluids to come into contact with a break in the skin or mucous membrane. HIV infection thus spreads by sexual activity, by the sharing of needles among intravenous drug users, by the mixing of maternal and fetal blood during prenancy or childbirth, or by blood transfusions if proper precautions have not been taken. Although there is no cure for AIDS, drugs that target retroviruses (reverse transcriptase inhibitors and protease inhibitors) are partially effective in slowing progression of the disease.

AIDS is widespread and lethal. On the worldwide AIDS epidemic, it is estimated that 30 million people are infected with HIV and 16,000 new infections occur each day.

When the immune system is overwhelmed, its effectiveness is severely reduced. This is, in part, what happens when the body develops cancer. A **tumor** develops when a population of cells grows at an abnormal rate. If the tumor is benign, the growth remains local. If the tumor is malignant, the growth is uncontrolled and increasingly uses the body's nutrient and energy supplies. **Cancer** is the disease resulting from uncontrolled growth of a malignant tumor.

When a cell becomes cancerous, one of two types of genes are probably at fault. **Proto-oncogenes and tumor-suppressor genes**, in a normally functioning cell, are involved in controlling cell reproduction. Cancerous cells fail to respond to the control signals. When a mutation occurs in a proto-oncogene, an **oncogene** is formed. Oncogenes constantly produce growth-stimulating proteins. When a mutation occurs in a tumor-suppressor gene, the gene fails to produce the proteins necessary to stop cell division. It actually requires several mutations in the same cell before a cancerous cell is formed.

When cancerous cells are formed, changes occur in their plasma membrane proteins, usually enabling natural killer cells and cytotoxic T cells to destroy them before they can multiply. However, the cancerous cells may multiply faster than the immune system can destroy them, they may suppress the immune system, or they may be resistant to immune attack. Any or all result in a cancerous growth.

Currently, the treatment for cancer includes (1) surgery, (2) radiation, and (3) chemotherapy. Surgical removal of a cancerous growth is the first step in treatment of most cancers, but cannot remove small patches of cells or cells that have spread to other parts of the body. Radiation is used to kill localized cancers and is able to destroy even microscopic clusters of cells. Chemotherapy is the treatment used for cancers that are inoperable, that radiation cannot be used to treat, or that either has spread or has the potential to have spread. The drugs used target the rapidly dividing cancer cells. However, body cells that tend to divide quickly are also often affected resulting in the typical chemotherapy side-effects of nausea and hairloss.

KEY TERMS AND CONCEPTS

Fill-In: From the following list of terms fill in the blanks below.

acquired immune deficiency syndrome (AIDS)	major histocompatibility complex (MHC)
allergy	memory cells
antibodies	mucous membranes
antigens	natural killer cells
autoimmune disease	oncogenes
B cells	phagocytic cells
cancer	plasma cells
cell-mediated immunity	proto-oncogenes
clonal selection	retrovirus
constant region	reverse transcriptase
cytotoxic T cells	severe combined immune deficiency (SCID)
fever	skin
helper T cells	suppressor T cells
histamine	T-cell receptors
human immunodeficiency virus (HIV)	T cells
humoral immunity	tumor
immune response	tumor-suppressor genes
inflammatory response	vaccination
interferon	variable region
macrophages	

The (1)_____ and (2)_____ provide the body barriers to invasion by foreign substances.

The body's nonspecific defenses use (3)_____, specifically

(4)_____ to destroy microbes by phagocytosis and

(5)_____ to destroy virus-infected cells. An injury provokes the
(6)_____. Injured cells release (7)_____,
making capillaries leak and smooth muscles relax. If a major infection becomes established, the body
produces a(n) (8)_____ to slow microbial growth and reproduction and to help
fight viral infections by increasing the production of (9)_____.

When nonspecific defenses fail, the body initiates the highly specific (10)_____.
This response involves two specific lymphocytes. The (11)_____ produce
protein (12)_____ on their plasma membranes or release them into the bloodstream. The (13)_____ produce (14)_____ on their cell
surfaces.

Antibodies consist of a(n) (15)_____ and a(n) (16)_____
that is highly specific. When antibodies are attached to the plasma membrane of a B cell, they serve as
receptors. When they circulate in the bloodstream, they serve as effectors. In both roles, the variable
regions respond and bind to (17)_____ produced by a foreign substance.

The immune system is able to differentiate "self" cells from "nonself" cells because of plasma membrane
proteins making up the (18)_____.

In order to attack microbes before they enter cells, the body uses B cells and antibodies to provide
(19)_____. When antibodies bind to antigens, B cells are stimulated
to divide rapidly. Since the resulting cells are identical, this precess is called
(20)_____. The daughter cells will differentiate into
(21)_____ and (22)_____.

T cells are used in (23)_____ to attack cells infected by an invader. This type
of response involves (24)_____ that disrupt the plasma membrane of
infected cells, (25)_____ that assist other immune cells, and
(26)_____ that shut off the immune system when an infection has been fought.

A(n) (27)_____ is an injection of weakened or killed microbes causing an
immune response, thus decreasing the likelihood of an individual's contracting a severe case of the
disease.

When the immune system recognizes pollen or mold spores as antigens, a(n)
(28)_____ to those substances has developed. When the antigen binds to
antibodies in the respiratory tract, (29)_____ is released.

When the immune system does not recognize cells as belonging to "self," and "anti-self" antibodies are
produced, the result is a(n) (30)_____. If a child is born with little or no
ability to produce immune cells, that child has (31)_____. Because of the
(32)_____, many individuals in the world are now combating the effects of
(33)_____. This virus is a(n) (34)_____,

which uses its RNA and the enzyme (35)_____ to make DNA and insert it into the genome of helper T cells.

A population of cells that is no longer regulated and is growing at an abnormal rate is called a(n) (36)_____. This growth is benign if it is localized or malignant if it grows uncontrollably. (37)_____ is the disease caused by a malignant growth. This disease occurs when two classes of genes mutate. (38)_____ produce proteins used in growth-stimulating pathways. When these genes mutate, forming (39)_____, a continuous supply of growth-stimulating proteins is produced. The second class of genes is the (40)_____. When they mutate, proteins needed to inhibit cell division are not produced.

Key Terms and Definitions

acquired immune deficiency syndrome (AIDS): an infectious disease caused by the human immunodeficiency virus (HIV); attacks and destroys T cells, thus weakening the immune system.

allergy: an inflammatory response produced by the body in response to invasion by foreign materials, such as pollen, that are themselves harmless.

antibody: a protein, produced by cells of the immune system, that combines with a specific antigen and normally facilitates the destruction of the antigen.

antigen: a complex molecule, normally a protein or polysaccharide, that stimulates the production of a specific antibody.

autoimmune disease: a disorder in which the immune system produces antibodies against the body's own cells.

B cell: a type of lymphocyte that participates in humoral immunity; gives rise to plasma cells, which secrete antibodies into the circulatory system, and to memory cells.

cancer: a disease in which some of the body's cells escape from normal regulatory processes and divide without control.

cell-mediated immunity: an immune response in which foreign cells or substances are destroyed by contact with T cells.

clonal selection: the mechanism by which the immune response gains specificity; an invading antigen elicits a response from only a few lymphocytes, which proliferate to form a clone of cells that attack only the specific antigen that stimulated their production.

constant region: the part of an antibody molecule that is similar in all antibodies.

cytotoxic T cell: a type of T cell that, upon contacting foreign cells, directly destroys them.

fever: an elevation in body temperature caused by chemicals (pyrogens) that are released by white blood cells in response to infection.

helper T cell: a type of T cell that helps other immune cells recognize and act against antigens.

histamine: a substance released by certain cells in response to tissue damage and invasion of the body by foreign substances; promotes the dilation of arterioles and the leakiness of capillaries and triggers some of the events of the inflammatory response.

human immunodeficiency virus (HIV): a pathogenic retrovirus that causes acquired immune deficiency syndrome (AIDS) by attacking and destroying the immune system's T cells.

humoral immunity: an immune response in which foreign substances are inactivated or destroyed by antibodies that circulate in the blood.

immune response: a specific response by the immune system to the invasion of the body by a particular foreign substance or microorganism, characterized by the recognition of the foreign substance by immune cells and its subsequent destruction by antibodies or by cellular attack.

inflammatory response: a nonspecific, local response to injury to the body, characterized by the phagocytosis of foreign substances and tissue debris by white blood cells and by the walling off of the injury site by the clotting of fluids that escape from nearby blood vessels.

interferon: a protein released by certain virus-infected cells that increases the resistance of other, uninfected, cells to viral attack.

macrophage (mak´-rō-fāj): a type of white blood cell that engulfs microbes and destroys them by phagocytosis; also presents microbial antigens to T cells, helping stimulate the immune response.

major histocompatibility complex (MHC): proteins, normally located on the surfaces of body cells, that identify the cell as "self"; also important in stimulating and regulating the immune response.

memory cell: a long-lived descendant of a B cell or T cell that has been activated by contact with an antigen; a reservoir of cells that rapidly respond to reexposure to the antigen.

mucous membrane: the lining of the inside of the respiratory and digestive tracts.

natural killer cell: a type of white blood cell that destroys some virus-infected cells and cancerous cells on contact; part of the immune system's nonspecific internal defense against disease.

oncogene: a gene that, when transcribed, causes a cell to become cancerous.

phagocytic cell (fa-gō-sit´-ik): a type of immune system cell that destroys invading microbes by using phagocytosis to engulf and digest the microbes.

plasma cell: an antibody-secreting descendant of a B cell.

proto-oncogene (prō-tō-onk´-ō-jēn): a normal cellular gene that can cause cancer if a mutation transforms it into an oncogene.

retrovirus: a virus that uses RNA as its genetic material. When it invades a eukaryotic cell, a retrovirus "reverse transcribes" its RNA into DNA, which then directs the synthesis of more viruses, using the transcription and translation machinery of the cell.

reverse transcriptase: an enzyme found in retroviruses that catalyzes the synthesis of DNA from an RNA template.

severe combined immune deficiency (SCID): a disorder in which no immune cells, or very few, are formed; the immune system is incapable of responding properly to invading disease organisms, and the individual is very vulnerable to common infections.

skin: the tissue that makes up the outer surface of an animal body.

suppressor T cell: a type of T cell that depresses the response of other immune cells to foreign antigens.

T cell: a type of lymphocyte that recognizes and destroys specific foreign cells or substances or that regulates other cells of the immune system.

T-cell receptor: a protein receptor, located on the surface of a T cell, that binds a specific antigen and triggers the immune response of the T cell.

tumor: a mass that forms in otherwise normal tissue; caused by the uncontrolled growth of cells.

tumor-suppressor gene: a gene that encodes information for a protein that inhibits cancer formation, probably by regulating cell division in some way.

vaccination: an injection into the body that contains antigens characteristic of a particular disease organism and that stimulates an immune response.

variable region: the part of an antibody molecule that differs among antibodies; the ends of the variable regions of the light and heavy chains form the specific binding site for antigens.

THINKING THROUGH THE CONCEPTS

True or False: Determine if the statement given is true or false. If it is false, change the <u>underlined</u> word(s) so that the statement reads true.

41. _____   The skin provides an <u>excellent</u> breeding ground for microbes.

42. _____   Mucous membranes <u>secrete enzymes</u> to destroy microbes.

43. _____   A <u>fever</u> is actually a defense mechanism against disease.

44. _____   <u>Natural killer cells</u> recognize and destroy cancerous cells.

45. _____   Chemicals produced by wounded cells <u>attract</u> phagocytic cells to an injury.

46. _____   <u>Pus formation</u> is an indication that your immune system is working at a wound site.

47. _____   Interferon <u>decreases</u> a cell's resistance to viral attack.

48. _____   <u>Antibodies</u> are formed from a wide array of genes, some of which mutate easily.

49. _____   Antibodies <u>provide no protection against</u> poisons such as snake venom.

50. _____ Antibodies <u>are custom made to fit a specific antigen</u>.

51. _____ B cells, differentiated into <u>plasma cells</u>, release antibodies into the bloodstream.

52. _____ <u>Helper T cells</u> turn the immune system off after an infection has been eradicated from the body.

53. _____ Humans continue to suffer from the common cold because <u>our immune system is unable to produce memory cells for the cold virus</u>.

54. _____ Antibiotics help fight diseases caused by <u>viruses</u>.

55. _____ An anthrax vaccine has been produced using <u>synthetic antigens</u>.

56. _____ <u>Histamine</u> is produced in response to an allergen antigen.

57. _____ Autoimmune diseases can be <u>cured</u> with today's medical technology.

Identification: Do the following statements relate to **B cells**, **T cells**, or **both**.

58. _____ precursor cells produced in bone marrow

59. _____ differentiate in bone marrow

60. _____ differentiate in thymus

61. _____ long lived, can provide future immunity

62. _____ secrete antibodies into the bloodstream

63. _____ destroy cells infected with viruses

64. _____ shut down the immune response when appropriate

65. _____ activate both B and T cells

66. _____ provide humoral immunity

67. _____ provide cell-mediated immunity

Fill-In: Label the numbered structures in the antibody diagram below.

68. _____

69. _____

70. _____

71. _____

72. _____

73. _____

Short Answer:

74. Identify the body's nonspecific defenses against microbial invasion.

_____

_____

75. Explain the three ways antibodies destroy extracellular microbes and molecules.

_____

_____

_____

Short Answer Questions About AIDS.

76. How do HIV-1 and HIV-2 affect the immune system? Once they are in a cell, how are more viruses made?

_____

_____

_____

_____

77. If AIDS does not directly kill its victims, what causes them to die?

_____

_____

_____

_____

_____

78. How do drugs like AZT and protease inhibitors function against HIV? Are they a cure?

_____

_____

_____

_____

_____

_____

79. Why is an effective vaccine against HIV so difficult to produce?

_____

_____

_____

_____

_____

_____

_____

80. Where are the most AIDS cases found in the world, and who is most at risk of being infected with HIV?

_____

_____

_____

_____

_____

_____

Short Answer Questions About Cancer.

81. How are proto-oncogenes and tumor-suppressor genes involved in cancer development?

_____

_____

_____

_____

_____

_____

_____

82. Since humans are constantly exposed to substances that cause mutations in our cells, why does cancer not affect many of us until later in life?

_____

_____

_____

_____

_____

83. How does the immune system combat cells that become cancerous?

_____

_____

_____

_____

_____

CLUES TO APPLYING THE CONCEPTS

These practice questions are intended to sharpen your ability to apply critical thinking and analysis to biological concepts covered in this chapter.

84. Antihistamines are often taken by individuals suffering from allergies. Using what you now know about the role of histamine in the immune response, how would antihistamines decrease your allergy symptoms? Would taking antihistamines lessen your symptoms from a cold virus?

_____

_____

_____

_____

_____

_____

_____

_____

85. Why would your body reject an organ received during a transplant if you did not receive a "close match" followed by immuno-suppressant drugs?

_____

_____

_____

_____

_____

_____

86. Why is it common for cancer patients to experience hair loss, nausea, and severe dry mouth during chemotherapy treatments?

_____

_____

_____

_____

_____

ANSWERS TO EXERCISES

1. skin
2. mucous membranes
3. phagocytic cells
4. macrophages
5. natural killer cells
6. inflammatory response
7. histamine
8. fever
9. interferon
10. immune response
11. B cells
12. antibodies
13. T cells
14. T-cell receptors
15. constant region
16. variable region
17. antigens
18. major histocompatibility complex (MHC)
19. humoral immunity
20. clonal selection
21. plasma cells
22. memory cells
23. cell-mediated immunity
24. cytotoxic T cells
25. helper T cells
26. suppressor T cells
27. vaccination
28. allergy
29. histamine
30. autoimmune disease
31. severe combined immune deficiency (SCID)
32. human immunodeficiency virus (HIV)
33. acquired immune deficiency syndrome (AIDS)
34. retrovirus
35. reverse transcriptase
36. tumor
37. Cancer
38. Proto-oncogenes
39. oncogenes
40. tumor-suppressor genes
41. false, poor
42. true
43. true
44. true
45. true
46. true
47. false, increases
48. true
49. false, neutralize
50. false, fit reasonably well to specific antigens
51. true
52. false, suppressor T cells
53. false, the cold virus mutates frequently
54. false, bacteria, fungi, and protists
55. true
56. true
57. false, suppressed
58. both
59. B cells
60. T cells
61. both
62. B cells
63. T cells
64. T cells
65. T cells
66. B cells
67. T cells
68. light chain
69. heavy chain
70. constant regions
71. variable regions
72. antigen
73. antigen binding site

74. phagocytic cells and natural killer cells, the inflammatory response, and fever

75. Antibodies destroy extracellular microbes and molecules by binding with or covering up the binding site of a toxic antigen; by coating a microbe, thus promoting phagocytosis; or by agglutination of microbes, promoting phagocytosis.

76. HIV-1 and HIV-2 infect and destroy helper T cells. Once in a helper T cell, the RNA uses its reverse transcriptase enzyme to create a DNA fragment molecule. The DNA fragment is inserted into the helper T cell's genome, where it will eventually be used to make more HIV viruses.

77. Because the helper T cell population declines in number as the cells are destroyed, there are fewer and fewer cells to assist other immune cells in their defenses. The hormonelike chemicals that helper T cells release to trigger immune cell division and differentiation, antibody production, and cytotoxic cell development are not circulated. Thus, the person with an active HIV infection becomes increasingly susceptible to other diseases. It is one of these "opportunistic" diseases that will cause the patient's death.

78. AZT inhibits reverse transcriptase, slowing the production of DNA from the viral RNA. The hope is that DNA will never be properly formed from the RNA, thus new virus will not be made. Unfortunately, AZT does not successfully block the reverse transcription. Protease inhibitors inactivate an enzyme responsible for assembling new viral particles. Protease inhibitors are most effective when used in combination with reverse transcriptase inhibitors. Thus the term "cocktail" of drugs has come into common use. No, these drugs are not a cure. That search continues.

79. An effective vaccine against HIV has been difficult to develop for several reasons. One reason is that antibodies naturally produced against HIV seem to offer little protection against infection. This indicates that a vaccine would need to function in a way that produced more effective immune responses than normal HIV does. Another reason is that HIV mutates at a phenomenal rate. Therefore, a vaccine developed for one strain may have absolutely no effect on the person vaccinated. To complicate the situation further, HIV can exist in different forms within the same person.

80. Most individuals infected with HIV live in developing countries. Sub-Saharan Africa has the highest rate of infection (with approximately 20.8 million people infected, while India and Southeast Asia have 6 million people infected). Transmission through heterosexual sex is the most common avenue of infection. Individuals most at risk of being infected are those individuals not practicing "safe sex," regardless of the gender of the individuals involved.

81. Proto-oncogenes contain the genetic codes for many of the proteins that stimulate cell growth. When proto-oncogenes mutate, becoming oncogenes, growth-stimulating proteins are continuously produced. Thus, cell growth continues. Tumor-suppressor genes code for the proteins responsible for inhibiting cell growth. When tumor-suppressor genes mutate, they fail to produce the "stop" signal proteins. Thus cell division continues unabated.

82. Several mutations of proto-oncogenes and/or tumor-suppressor genes must occur in the same cell before the cell becomes cancerous. It may take years for the necessary number of mutations to occur. Individuals who inherit already mutated genes may develop cancer earlier in life.

83. Natural killer cells and cytotoxic T cells detect the protein changes that occur on the plasma membranes of cancerous cells. They destroy nearly all cancerous cells that occur in our bodies before the cells have a chance to proliferate.

84. Histamines are produced when an allergen antigen binds to cells in the respiratory system. The result of histamine circulating in the bloodstream is increased mucus production and the inflammatory response, increasing discomfort. Antihistamines would inhibit the production of histamine or block its effect, thus reducing the production of mucus and inflammation. Since the cold virus does not typically stimulate the appropriate cells to produce histamine, congestion symptoms due to a cold will not be alleviated by taking antihistamines.

85. The cell plasma membranes contain large proteins and polysaccharides that indicate to the immune system that they belong to "self." These proteins make up the major histocompatibility complex. They are unique to each individual (and identical twins). If you receive an organ transplant, a "match" will be made in an attempt to reduce the number of different proteins. Since no match will be perfect (except from an identical twin), the body will naturally mount an immunological attack against the foreign cells, rejecting the transplanted organ. Thus, the patient must take immuno-suppressant drugs to reduce the likelihood of a rejection.

86. Chemotherapy agents target cells that are rapidly growing and frequently dividing. Therefore, any cell in the body that tends to be replaced frequently is affected by the chemotherapy. Hair follicles and cells lining the stomach and the mouth are body cells that divide and grow rapidly. They are, therefore, damaged along with any cancerous cells leading to the hairloss and nausea that accompany treatment.

Chapter 23: Chemical Control of the Animal Body: The Endocrine System

OVERVIEW

This chapter covers how the body's internal chemistry is controlled by hormones. The authors discuss the three classes of animal hormones and the endocrine glands that produce them. Hormone regulation by negative feedback is outlined, and the major mammalian endocrine glands are presented in detail.

1) What Are the Characteristics of Animal Hormones?

A **hormone** is a chemical secreted by cells in one part of the body that is transported in the bloodstream to other parts of the body, where it affects particular **target cells**. Hormones are released by the cells of major endocrine glands and endocrine organs located throughout the body. Hormones can be grouped into three general classes: (1) **peptide hormones**, made of chains of amino acids; (2) amino acid derivatives, formed from single amino acids (such as epinephrine derived from tyrosine); and (3) **steroid hormone** (most of which are derived from cholesterol) secreted by the ovaries, placenta, testes, and adrenal cortex.

Hormones function by binding to specific receptors on target cells that respond to particular hormone molecules. Receptors for hormones are found either on the plasma membrane or inside the cell, normally within the nucleus. Most peptide and amino acid–based hormones cannot penetrate the plasma membrane and must react with protein receptors that protrude from its outer surface. Most hormones binding to a receptor on the outside cell surface trigger the release inside the cell of a chemical, the **second messenger**, that initiates a cascade of biochemical reactions. **Cyclic AMP** (cAMP) is a common second messenger.

Steroid hormones and thyroid-produced hormones are lipid-soluble and pass through the plasma membrane, binding to intracellular receptors, typically to protein receptors in the nucleus. The receptor-hormone complex binds to DNA and stimulates particular genes to become active.

Hormones are regulated by feedback mechanisms. In animals, the secretion of a hormone normally stimulates a response in target cells that inhibits further secretion of the hormone, a mechanism called negative feedback. For example, loss of water through perspiration triggers the pituitary gland to produce *antidiuretic hormone* (ADH), which causes the kidneys to reabsorb water and to produce very concentrated urine. Drinking water replaces what has been lost, triggering negative feedback to turn off ADH secretion when blood water content returns to normal. In a few cases, positive feedback controls hormone release. For example, contractions of the uterus early in childbirth cause the release of the hormone *oxytocin* which stimulates stronger contractions of the uterus.

2) What Are the Structures and Functions of the Mammalian Endocrine System?

Mammals have both **exocrine glands** and **endocrine glands**. Exocrine glands produce secretions released outside the body or into the digestive tract through tubes or openings called **ducts**. Exocrine glands include the sweat and sebaceous glands in the skin, lacrimal glands of the eyes, mammary glands, and glands that produce digestive secretions. Endocrine glands are ductless glands that secrete hormones into capillaries of the bloodstream.

The **hypothalamus** controls the secretions of the **pituitary gland**. The hypothalamus is a part of the brain that contains **neurosecretory cells** that make and store peptide hormones and release them when stimulated. The pituitary gland hangs from the hypothalamus and has two lobes: the **anterior pituitary** and the **posterior pituitary**. The anterior pituitary produces and releases a variety of peptide hormones, four of which regulate hormone release in other endocrine glands. **Follicle-stimulating hormone (FSH)** and **luteinizing hormone (LH)** stimulate production of sperm and testosterone in males, and eggs, estrogen, and progesterone in females. **Thyroid-stimulating hormone (TSH)** stimulates release of **thyroid gland** hormones, and **adrenocorticotropic hormone (ACTH)** stimulates release of hormones from the adrenal cortex. Other hormones of the anterior pituitary do not act on other endocrine glands. **Prolactin** helps stimulate development of the mammary glands during pregnancy. **Endorphins** inhibit the perception of pain by binding to receptors in the brain. **Melanocyte-stimulating hormone (MSH)** stimulates production of the skin pigment melanin. **Growth hormone** regulates body growth (too little causes pituitary *dwarfism*, too much can cause *gigantism*). Growth hormone can be made by genetic engineering.

The posterior pituitary releases two types of peptide hormones produced by cells in the hypothalamus: **antidiuretic hormone (ADH)** and **oxytocin**. ADH helps prevent dehydration by increasing the permeability of the collecting ducts of kidney nephrons, causing water to be reabsorbed from the urine and retained in the body. Alcohol inhibits the release of ADH. Oxytocin causes uterine contractions during childbirth and triggers the "milk letdown reflex" in nursing mothers by causing breast muscle tissue to contract during breast-feeding. Oxytocin also aids in male ejaculation in some animals.

The thyroid gland produces two major hormones: thyroxine and calcitonin. **Thyroxine** (an iodine-containing modified amino acid) raises the metabolic rate of most cells by stimulating the synthesis of enzymes that break down glucose and provide energy. Thyroxine helps regulate body temperature and helps the body respond to stress. In juvenile animals, thyroxine helps regulate growth by stimulating both metabolic rate and development of the nervous system. Too little thyroxine early in life causes *cretinism*. A diet deficient in iodine causes thyroid enlargement, which bulges from the neck producing a condition called **goiter**. Using iodized salt prevents this condition.

Calcitonin, a peptide produced by the thyroid, helps control the concentration of calcium in the blood by regulating calcium release by the bones. If blood calcium levels are too high, calcitonin is released to inhibit release of calcium from bones.

The **pancreas** is both an exocrine gland (digestive secretions released from the pancreatic duct flow into the small intestine) and an endocrine gland (clusters of **islet cells** produce the peptide hormones **insulin** and **glucagon**). Insulin and glucagon work in opposition to regulate carbohydrate and fat metabolism: Insulin reduces blood glucose levels and glucagon increases it by activating a liver enzyme that breaks down glycogen. Glucagon also promotes lipid breakdown, releasing fatty acids for metabolism. Defects in insulin production, release, or reception by target cells result in **diabetes mellitus**, a condition in which blood glucose levels are high and fluctuate wildly with sugar intake. Human insulin can be made by genetic engineering.

The sex organs secrete steroid hormones. The **testes** and **ovaries** are endocrine organs that produce steroid hormones. In males, the testes make a group of hormones collectively called **androgens**, which includes **testosterone**, and in females, the ovaries make **estrogen** and **progesterone**. Sex hormones play key roles in development, pregnancy, the menstrual cycle, and puberty (the physiological changes that lead to reproductive capacity and secondary sexual characteristics). Puberty begins when the testes and ovaries begin to produce higher levels of sex hormones.

The **adrenal glands** have two parts that secrete different hormones. The interior **adrenal medulla** contains secretory cells that originated from and are controlled by the nervous system and produces two amino acid–derived hormones: **epinephrine** (*adrenaline*) and **norepinephrine** (*noradrenaline*). These hormones prepare the body for emergency action; they increase heart and respiratory rates, increase blood glucose levels, and direct blood flow away from digestion and toward muscles and the brain. The outer adrenal layer forms the **adrenal cortex**, which secretes three types of steroid hormones called **glucocorticoids**. These hormones help control glucose metabolism. Stressful stimuli (such as trauma, infection, or hot or cold temperatures) stimulate the hypothalamus to secrete releasing hormones, which then stimulate the anterior pituitary to release ACTH, which in turn stimulates the adrenal cortex to release glucocorticoid hormones. The adrenal cortex also secretes **aldosterone**, which regulates blood sodium content. If blood sodium levels fall, the adrenal cortex releases aldosterone, which causes the kidneys and sweat glands to retain sodium. When blood sodium levels rise to normal, aldosterone secretion ceases. The adrenal cortex also secretes small amounts of testosterone. Adrenal medulla tumors in females can lead to excessive testosterone release, causing masculinization of women.

The **pineal gland** lies between the two hemispheres of the brain and produces the amino acid–derived hormone **melatonin**, which is secreted in a daily rhythm regulated in mammals by the eyes. Melatonin appears to regulate the seasonal reproductive cycles of many mammals. Melatonin may influence sleep-wake cycles in humans.

The **thymus** is located in the chest cavity and produces white blood cells and the hormone **thymosin**. Thymosin stimulates production of T cells, which play a role in the immune system.

Additionally, the kidneys produce a hormone from blood proteins that regulates blood pressure The heart produces a peptide hormone that causes a reduction in blood pressure by decreasing the release of ADH and aldosterone. The stomach and small intestine also produce peptide hormones to help regulate digestion.

KEY TERMS AND CONCEPTS

Fill-In: From the following list of terms, fill in the blanks below.

adrenocorticotropic
amino acid derivatives
antidiuretic
cyclic AMP
endocrine
endorphins
exocrine
follicle-stimulating
glucagon

growth
hormone
insulin
luteinizing
melanocyte-stimulating
melatonin
oxytocin
pancreas
peptide

pineal
prolactin
prostaglandins
second messenger
steroid
target
thymosin
thymus
thyroid-stimulating

A(n) (1)_____ is a chemical secreted by cells in one part of the body that is transported in the bloodstream to other parts of the body, where it affects particular
(2)_____ cells.

Hormones can be grouped into four general classes. (3)_____ hormones are made of chains of amino acids. (4)_____ are formed from single amino acids (for example, epinephrine is derived from tyrosine). Most (5)_____ hormones are derived from cholesterol and are secreted by the ovaries, placenta, testes, and adrenal cortex.

Most hormones binding to a receptor on the outside cell surface trigger the release inside the cell of a chemical called the (6)_____ which initiates a cascade of biochemical reactions.
(7)_____ is a common second messenger.

Mammals have both (8)_____ glands, which produce secretions released outside the body or into the digestive tract through tubes or openings called ducts, and
(9)_____ glands, which are ductless glands that secrete hormones into capillaries of the bloodstream.

The anterior pituitary produces and releases a variety of peptide hormones, four of which regulate hormone release in other endocrine glands. (10)_____ hormone and
(11)_____ hormone stimulate production of sperm and testosterone in males and eggs, estrogen, and progesterone in females. (12)_____ hormone stimulates release of thyroid gland hormones. (13)_____ hormone stimulates release of hormones from the adrenal cortex.

Other hormones of the anterior pituitary do not act on other endocrine glands.
(14)_____ helps stimulate development of the mammary glands during pregnancy.
(15)_____ inhibit the perception of pain by binding to brain receptors.
(16)_____ hormone stimulates production of the skin pigment melanin.
(17)_____ hormone regulates body growth: Too little causes pituitary dwarfism; too much can cause gigantism.

The posterior pituitary releases two types of peptide hormones produced by cells in the hypothalamus: (18)_____ hormone, which helps prevent dehydration by increasing the permeability of the collecting ducts of kidney nephrons (causing water to be reabsorbed from the urine and retained in the body), and (19)_____, which causes uterine contractions and triggers the "milk letdown reflex" in nursing mothers by causing breast muscle tissue to contract during breast-feeding.

In the (20)_____, clusters of islet cells produce the peptide hormones (21)_____, which reduces blood glucose levels, and (22)_____, which increases blood glucose levels by activating a liver enzyme that breaks down glycogen.

The (23)_____ gland lies between the two hemispheres of the brain and produces the amino acid-derived hormone (24)_____, which is secreted in a daily rhythm regulated in mammals by the eyes.

The (25)_____ is in the chest cavity and produces white blood cells and the hormone (26)_____, which stimulates production of T cells which play a role in the immune system.

Key Terms and Definitions

adrenal cortex: the outer part of the adrenal gland, which secretes steroid hormones that regulate metabolism and salt balance.

adrenal gland: a mammalian endocrine gland, adjacent to the kidney; secretes hormones that function in water regulation and in the stress response.

adrenal medulla: the inner part of the adrenal gland, which secretes epinephrine (adrenaline) and norepinephrine (noradrenaline).

adrenocorticotropic hormone (a-drēn-ō-kor-tik-ō-trō′-pik; **ACTH**): a hormone, secreted by the anterior pituitary, that stimulates the release of hormones by the adrenal glands, especially in response to stress.

aldosterone: a hormone, secreted by the adrenal cortex, that helps regulate ion concentration in the blood by stimulating the reabsorption of sodium by the kidneys and sweat glands.

androgen: a male sex hormone.

anterior pituitary: a lobe of the pituitary gland that produces prolactin and growth hormone as well as hormones that regulate hormone production in other glands.

antidiuretic hormone (an-tē-dī-ūr-et′-ik; **ADH**): a hormone produced by the hypothalamus and released into the bloodstream by the posterior pituitary when blood volume is low; increases the permeability of the distal tubule and the collecting duct to water, allowing more water to be reabsorbed into the bloodstream.

calcitonin (kal-si-tōn′-in): a hormone, secreted by the thyroid gland, that inhibits the release of calcium from bone.

cyclic AMP: a cyclic nucleotide, formed within many target cells as a result of the reception of amino acid derivatives or peptide hormones, that causes metabolic changes in the cell; often called a *second messenger*.

diabetes mellitus (dī-uh-bē′-tēs mel-ī′-tus): a disease characterized by defects in the production, release, or reception of insulin; characterized by high blood glucose levels that fluctuate with sugar intake.

duct: a tube or opening through which exocrine secretions are released.

endocrine gland: a ductless, hormone-producing gland consisting of cells that release their secretions into the extracellular fluid from which the secretions diffuse into nearby capillaries.

endocrine system: an animal's organ system for cell-to-cell communication, composed of hormones and the cells that secrete them and receive them.

endorphin: one of a group of peptide neuromodulators in the vertebrate brain that, by reducing the sensation of pain, mimics some of the actions of opiates.

epinephrine (ep-i-nef′-rin): a hormone, secreted by the adrenal medulla, that is released in response to stress and that stimulates a variety of responses, including the release of glucose from skeletal muscle and an increase in heart rate.

estrogen: in vertebrates, a female sex hormone, produced by follicle cells of the ovary, that stimulates follicle development, oogenesis, the development of secondary sex characteristics, and growth of the uterine lining.

exocrine gland: a gland that releases its secretions into ducts that lead to the outside of the body or into the digestive tract.

follicle-stimulating hormone (FSH): a hormone, produced by the anterior pituitary, that stimulates spermatogenesis in males and the development of the follicle in females.

glucagon (gloo´-ka-gon): a hormone, secreted by the pancreas, that increases blood sugar by stimulating the breakdown of glycogen (to glucose) in the liver.

glucocorticoid (gloo-kō-kor´-ti-koid): a class of hormones, released by the adrenal cortex in response to the presence of ACTH, that make additional energy available to the body by stimulating the synthesis of glucose.

goiter: a swelling of the neck caused by iodine deficiency, which affects the functioning of the thyroid gland and its hormones.

growth hormone: a hormone, released by the anterior pituitary, that stimulates growth, especially of the skeleton.

hormone: a chemical that is synthesized by one group of cells, secreted, and then carried in the bloodstream to other cells, whose activity is influenced by reception of the hormone.

hypothalamus (hī-pō-thal´-a-mus): a region of the brain that controls the secretory activity of the pituitary gland; synthesizes, stores, and releases certain peptide hormones; directs autonomic nervous system responses.

insulin: a hormone, secreted by the pancreas, that lowers blood sugar by stimulating the conversion of glucose to glycogen in the liver.

islet cell: a cluster of cells in the endocrine portion of the pancreas that produce insulin and glucagon.

luteinizing hormone (LH): a hormone, produced by the anterior pituitary, that stimulates testosterone production in males and the development of the follicle, ovulation, and the production of the corpus luteum in females.

melanocyte-stimulating hormone (me-lan´-ō-sīt): a hormone, released by the anterior pituitary, that regulates the activity of skin pigments in some vertebrates.

melatonin (mel-uh-tōn´-in): a hormone, secreted by the pineal gland, that is involved in the regulation of circadian cycles.

neurosecretory cell: a specialized nerve cell that synthesizes and releases hormones.

norepinephrine: a neurotransmitter, released by neurons of the parasympathetic nervous system, that prepares the body to respond to stressful situations; also called noradrenaline.

ovary: in animals, the gonad of females; in flowering plants, a structure at the base of the carpel that contains one or more ovules and develops into the fruit.

oxytocin (oks-ē-tō´-sin): a hormone, released by the posterior pituitary, that stimulates the contraction of uterine and mammary gland muscles.

pancreas (pān´-krē-us): a combined exocrine and endocrine gland located in the abdominal cavity next to the stomach. The endocrine portion secretes the hormones insulin and glucagon, which regulate glucose concentrations in the blood. The exocrine portion secretes enzymes for fat, carbohydrate, and protein digestion into the small intestine and neutralizes the acidic chyme.

peptide hormone: a hormone consisting of a chain of amino acids; includes small proteins that function as hormones.

pineal gland (pī-nē´-al): a small gland within the brain that secretes melatonin; controls the seasonal reproductive cycles of some mammals.

pituitary gland: an endocrine gland, located at the base of the brain, that produces several hormones, many of which influence the activity of other glands.

posterior pituitary: a lobe of the pituitary gland that is an outgrowth of the hypothalamus and that releases antidiuretic hormone and oxytocin.

progesterone (prō-ge´-ster-ōn): a hormone, produced by the corpus luteum, that promotes the development of the uterine lining in females.

prolactin: a hormone, released by the anterior pituitary, that stimulates milk production in human females.

second messenger: an intracellular chemical, such as cyclic AMP, that is synthesized or released within a cell in response to the binding of a hormone or neurotransmitter (the first messenger) to receptors on the cell surface; brings about specific changes in the metabolism of the cell.

steroid hormone: a class of hormone whose chemical structure (four fused carbon rings with various functional groups) resembles cholesterol; steroids, which are lipids, are secreted by the ovaries and placenta, the testes, and the adrenal cortex.

target cell: a cell on which a particular hormone exerts its effect.

testis (pl., **testes**): the gonad of male mammals.

testosterone: in vertebrates, a hormone produced by the interstitial cells of the testis; stimulates spermatogenesis and the development of male secondary sex characteristics.

thymosin: a hormone, secreted by the thymus, that stimulates the maturation of cells of the immune system.

thymus (thī´-mus): an organ of the lymphatic system that is located in the upper chest in front of the heart and that secretes thymosin, which stimulates lymphocyte maturation; begins to degenerate at puberty and has little function in the adult.

thyroid gland: an endocrine gland, located in front of the larynx in the neck, that secretes the hormones thyroxine (affecting metabolic rate) and calcitonin (regulating calcium ion concentration in the blood).

thyroid-stimulating hormone (TSH): a hormone, released by the anterior pituitary, that stimulates the thyroid gland to release hormones.

thyroxine (thī-rox´-in): a hormone, secreted by the thyroid gland, that stimulates and regulates metabolism.

THINKING THROUGH THE CONCEPTS

True or False: Determine if the statement given is true or false. If it is false, change the underlined word(s) so that the statement reads true.

27. _____   Endocrine glands usually have ducts.

28. _____   The action of hormones is dependent on gland cells.

29. _____   Endocrine glands produce chemicals that exert their effects outside the body of the animal producing them.

30. _____   Peptide hormones are able to enter cells easily.

31. _____   Animals regulate most hormone release through positive feedback.

32. _____   An increase in antidiuretic hormone will decrease blood pressure.

33. _____   The anterior pituitary is more like part of the brain than an endocrine gland.

34. _____   The posterior pituitary produces most of the body's hormones.

35. _____   The breakdown of glycogen into glucose is favored by the presence of insulin.

36. _____   Insulin increases blood glucose.

37. _____   Epinephrine and norepinephrine prepare the body for emergency action.

38. _____   Adrenaline causes blood to flow toward the stomach.

39. _____   The adrenal medulla secretes a female hormone.

Identification: Determine whether the following statements refer to **endocrine** glands or **exocrine** glands.

40. _____   clusters of hormone-producing cells embedded in capillaries

41. _____   some release hormones into ducts leading to the outside of the body

42. _____   sweat glands

43. _____   release hormones into extracellular spaces surrounded by capillaries

44. _____   mammary glands

Matching: Pituitary hormones. Some questions may have more than one correct answer.

45. _____ affects gamete release in both sexes

46. _____ produced by the posterior pituitary

47. _____ regulates growth of bones

48. _____ reduces dehydration

49. _____ stimulates development of the mammary glands during pregnancy

50. _____ causes uterine contractions during childbirth

51. _____ stimulates release of hormone by the thyroid gland

52. _____ allows milk to flow from the breasts during lactation

53. _____ causes release of hormones from the cortex of the adrenal glands

54. _____ allows ejaculation to occur in males of some animals

Choices:

a. ACTH

b. ADH

c. FSH

d. LH

e. growth hormone

f. oxytocin

g. prolactin

h. TSH

Matching: Adrenal gland hormones. Some questions may have more than one correct answer.

55. _____ produced by the adrenal medulla

56. _____ release is stimulated by ACTH

57. _____ help control glucose metabolism

58. _____ male sex hormone

59. _____ acts like glucagon

60. _____ overproduction, caused by certain tumors, can result in "bearded ladies"

Choices:

a. epinephrine

b. norepinephrine

c. glucocorticoids

d. testosterone

Multiple Choice: Pick the most correct choice for each question.

61. All the following are types of animal hormones *except*
   a. steroids
   b. neurotransmitters
   c. amino acids
   d. proteins

62. An example of a gland with exocrine as well as endocrine function is the
   a. stomach
   b. pituitary
   c. pancreas
   d. thyroid
   e. kidney

63. The pituitary gland is located
    a. in the side of the neck
    b. near the kidneys
    c. in the upper thoracic cavity
    d. at the base of the brain
    e. near the sex organs

64. During childbirth, contraction of the uterus is stimulated by
    a. oxytocin
    b. prolactin
    c. progesterone
    d. estrogen
    e. testosterone

CLUES TO APPLYING THE CONCEPTS

These practice questions are intended to sharpen your ability to apply critical thinking and analysis to biological concepts covered in this chapter.

65. Antidiuretic hormone (ADH) acts on very specific target cells in the kidney, while the hormone insulin affects every cell in the body. Why are some hormones very specific as to which cells they affect and other hormones have a very general effect on many target organs?

_____

_____

_____

_____

_____

_____

66. Explain why diabetes mellitus results in high blood pressure, heart disease, blindness, and kidney failure.

_____

_____

_____

_____

_____

_____

_____

_____

_____

ANSWERS TO EXERCISES

1. hormone
2. target
3. peptide
4. amino-acid derivatives
5. steroid
6. second messenger
7. cyclic AMP
8. exocrine
9. endocrine
10. Follicle-stimulating
11. luteinizing
12. Thyroid-stimulating
13. Adrenocorticotropic
14. Prolactin
15. Endorphins
16. Melanocyte-stimulating
17. Growth
18. antidiuretic
19. oxytocin
20. pancreas
21. insulin
22. glucagon

23. pineal
24. melatonin
25. thymus
26. thymosin
27. false, do not have
28. false, target
29. false, exocrine
30. false, steroid
31. false, negative
32. false, increase
33. false, posterior
34. false, anterior
35. false, glucagon
36. false, decreases
37. true
38. false, away from
39. false, male
40. endocrine
41. exocrine
42. exocrine
43. endocrine

44. exocrine
45. c, d
46. b, f
47. e
48. b
49. g
50. f
51. h
52. f
53. a
54. f
55. a, b
56. c
57. a, b, c
58. d
59. c
60. d
61. b
62. c
63. d
64. a

65. An organ can respond to the presence of a hormone only if it has the proper receptor molecule in its cell membrane or internally. Only kidney cells have the specific receptor for ADH, while most cells have receptors for insulin.

66. Diabetes mellitus causes the body to rely on fat metabolism which results in high levels of lipids circulating in the blood stream. In severe cases, this leads to fat deposits in blood vessels. The presence of the fat deposits results in high blood pressure and heart disease. When the deposits are located in vessels on the eye, the retina may be damaged, causing blindness. When the deposits are located in the small vessels of the kidney, kidney failure may result.

Chapter 24: The Nervous System and the Senses

OVERVIEW

This chapter covers the structure and function of nerve cells, the nature of resting potentials in nerves, and how action potentials (nerve signals) are generated and conducted. The authors discuss the human nervous system, including the central nervous system (brain and spinal cord), the peripheral nervous system, and neurotransmitters. The ways in which animals perceive and respond to nervous stimulation are discussed, and the structures and functions of the major sense organs are covered. Learning, memory, and retrieval are briefly covered.

1) How Do Nervous and Endocrine Communication Differ?

Both hormone-producing cells and nerve cells, called **neurons**, make "messenger" chemicals that they release into extracellular spaces. However, there are four differences in how the nervous and endocrine systems use chemical messages: (1) Endocrine cells release hormones into the bloodstream, while neurons release **neurotransmitters** very close to the cells they influence; (2) blood-borne hormones influence many cells indiscriminately, but a neuron releases its neurotransmitter onto one or a few specific cells; (3) neurons speed information from one place to another by electrical signals that travel within the cell itself and release neurotransmitters only near the target cell, while hormones move slowly and usually are released far away from their target cells; and (4) the effects of messages sent by neurons are of much shorter duration than are the effects of hormones. However, both the endocrine and nervous systems are closely coordinated in their control of bodily functions.

2) What Are the Structures and Functions of Neurons?

An individual neuron has four functions besides normal metabolism: (1) it receives information; (2) it integrates information and produces an appropriate output signal; (3) it conducts the signal to its terminal endings; and (4) it transmits the signal to other nerve cells, glands, or muscles. A typical vertebrate neuron has four structural regions. **Dendrites** receive signals from other neurons or from the environment. Dendrites of *sensory neurons* have specialized membranes to respond to specific stimuli such as pressure, odor, light, or heat. Dendrites of brain and spinal cord neurons respond to chemical neurotransmitters released by other neurons. Electrical signals travel down the dendrites to the neuron's **cell body**. The cell body performs typical metabolic activities and integrates all the signals received from dendrites. A long, thin fiber called an **axon** extends from the cell body. Some axons may be up to three feet long. Axons are normally bundled together into **nerves**, like bundles of wires in an electrical cable. Some axons are wrapped with insulation, called **myelin**, which allows very rapid conduction of the electrical signal.

If the signals received from dendrites are sufficiently positive, the neuron will produce an **action potential**, an electrical output signal. The action potential produced by the cell body begins at the **spike initiation zone** (the site where the axon leaves the cell body is the spike initiation zone). Axons carry action potentials to swellings, the **synaptic terminals**, located at the far ends of each axon. Signals are then conducted to other cells at synaptic terminals. Most synaptic terminals contain a neurotransmitter that is released in response to the passage of an action potential down the axon. The site where synaptic terminals communicate with other cells is called the **synapse**.

3) How Is Neural Activity Generated and Communicated?

Neurons create electrical signals across their membranes. Unstimulated, inactive neurons maintain a constant electrical difference, or potential, across their plasma membranes. This **resting potential** is always negative inside the cell and is measured as –40 to –90 millivolts. If a neuron is stimulated, the inner negative potential can be altered. If it becomes sufficiently less negative, it reaches a **threshold** (usually 15 millivolts less negative than the resting potential). At threshold, an action potential is triggered at the spike initiation zone. This causes the neuron's potential inside to rise rapidly to about +50 millivolts. (This action potential will last a few milliseconds, and then the cell's normal resting potential will be restored.) The positive charge of the action potential flows rapidly down the axon to synaptic terminals where the signal is communicated to another cell at a synapse.

The signals transmitted at synapses are called **postsynaptic potentials** (**PSPs**). The neuron that releases neurotransmitter into the synapse is called the **presynaptic neuron**. If the cell on the other side of the synapse is another neuron, it is called the **postsynaptic neuron**. A tiny gap (the **synaptic cleft**) separates the synaptic terminal of the presynaptic neuron from the postsynaptic neuron. When an action potential reaches a synaptic terminal, the inside of the terminal becomes positively charged, triggering storage vesicles in the synaptic terminal to release a chemical neurotransmitter into the synaptic cleft. These molecules rapidly diffuse across the synaptic cleft and bind briefly to membrane receptors of the postsynaptic neuron.

The binding of the neurotransmitter molecules causes ion-specific channels in the postsynaptic membrane to open, allowing ions to flow across the plasma membrane along their concentration gradients. This causes a small, brief change in electrical charge called the PSP mentioned above. PSPs can be *excitatory* (EPSPs) or *inhibitory* (IPSPs), depending on which channels are opened and which ions flow. EPSPs make the neuron less negative inside and <u>more</u> likely to produce an action potential. IPSPs make the neuron more negative and <u>less</u> likely to produce an action potential. The PSPs travel to the cell body. The cell body determines whether an action potential will be produced. The dendrites and cell body of one neuron may receive both EPSPs and IPSPs from the synaptic terminals of thousands of presynaptic neurons. These are then "added up," or **integrated**, in the cell body of the postsynaptic neuron. An action potential is produced only if the EPSPs and IPSPs collectively raise the electrical potential inside the neuron above threshold.

The nervous system uses over 50 different neurotransmitters. Included in the ever-growing list are **acetylcholine**, **dopamine**, and **serotonin**.

4) How Is the Nervous System Designed?

Information processing requires four basic operations. A nervous system must be able to (1) determine the type of stimulus, (2) signal the intensity of a stimulus, (3) integrate information from many sources, and (4) initiate and direct the response. The type of stimulus is distinguished by wiring patterns in the brain. The nervous system monitors which neurons are firing action potentials. For instance, the brain interprets optic nerve action potentials as light, and olfactory nerve action potentials as odors, etc.

All action potentials are of the same magnitudeand duration; therefore the **intensity**, or strength, of a stimulus is indicated by the number of neurons firing or the frequency of action potentials generated. In response to an intense stimulus, each neuron will produce many action potentials quickly and a large number of neurons will respond. Thus, a loud noise stimulates a larger number of auditory nerves to fire more rapidly than does less intense sound.

The brain must filter all the stimuli it is constantly receiving. Information from many sources is processd through **convergence**. During convergence, many neurons funnel their signals to fewer decision-making neurons in the brain. However, complex responses occur through the **divergence** of signals. During divergence, electrical signals from a relatively small number of decision-making cells in the brain flow to many different neurons that control muscle or glandular activity.

Neuron-to-muscle pathways direct most behaviors and are composed of four elements: (1) **Sensory neurons** respond to a stimulus; (2) **association neurons** receive signals from many sources and activate motor neurons; (3) **motor neurons** receive instructions from association neurons and activate muscles or glands; and (4) **effectors**, usually muscles or glands, perform the response directed by the nervous system.

In animals, the simplest behavior is the **reflex**, a largely involuntary response produced by neurons in the spinal cord that does not require interaction with the brain, for example, the knee–jerk and pain-withdrawal reflexes. However, more complex behaviors rely on neural pathways that are interconnected, integrating the stimuli.

5) How Is the Human Nervous System Organized?

The human nervous system has two parts. The **central nervous system** (CNS) includes the **brain** and the **spinal cord**; the **peripheral nervous system** (PNS) includes **peripheral nerves** that connect the CNS to the rest of the body. Peripheral nerves contain axons of sensory neurons that bring sensory information to the CNS from all the body parts, as well as axons of motor neurons that carry signals from the CNS to the organs and muscles.

The motor portion of the PNS has two parts: the **somatic nervous system** and the **autonomic nervous system**. The somatic nervous system controls skeletal muscles and voluntary muscle movement and its motor neurons are located in the gray matter of the spinal cord, with their axons going directly to the muscles they control. The autonomic nervous system controls involuntary responses, forming synapses on the heart, smooth muscle, and glands. It is controlled by both the *medulla* and the *hypothalamus* of the brain.

The CNS receives and processes information, generates thoughts, and directs responses. The CNS contains up to 100 billion association neurons. The brain and spinal cord are protected in three ways: the *skull* and *vertebral column*; a triple layer of connective tissue (the **meninges**); and the **cerebro-spinal fluid** between the layers of the meninges. The spinal cord is a cable of axons protected by the vertebral column. Nerves carrying axons of sensory neurons and motor neurons come out from between vertebrae and merge to form the peripheral nerves of the spinal cord (part of the PNS). In the center of the spinal cord is the **gray matter**. Gray matter is made up of the cell bodies of neurons that control voluntary muscles and the autonomic nervous system, and neurons that communicate with the brain and other parts of the spinal cord. The gray matter is surrounded by **white matter**, formed of myelin-coated axons of neurons that extend up or down the spinal cord. The spinal cord also contains the neural pathways for simple behaviors such as reflexes.

A reflex response may involve the following scenario: After you touch a hot burner on a stove, the signal travels along the sensory neuron's dendrite to its cell body in a **dorsal root ganglion** on spinal nerves just outside the spinal cord. (A **ganglion** is a cluster of neurons.) An axon from the sensory neuron would synapse with an association neuron whose cell body is located in the gray matter of the spinal cord. The association neuron would send the signal to a motor neuron, resulting in the withdrawal of your finger from the burner. At the same time, the signal would travel along the axon of the association neuron to your brain, alerting it to the pain.

The brain consists of many parts specialized for specific functions. Embryologically, the vertebrate brain begins as a simple tube that develops into three parts: Hindbrain, midbrain, and forebrain. Simplistically, the **hindbrain** controls automatic behaviors such as breathing and heart rate, the **midbrain** controls vision, and the **forebrain** controls smell. However, the brain is much more complex. The human hindbrain includes the **medulla**, which controls automatic functions such as breathing, heart rate, blood pressure, and swallowing; the **pons**, which influences transitions between sleep and wakefulness and between stages of sleep, and the rate and pattern of breathing, and the **cerebellum**, which coordinates movements of the body and is involved in learning and memory storage for behaviors.

The midbrain in humans is small. It contains an auditory relay center, a center that controls reflex movements of the eyes, and another relay center, the **reticular formation**, passes through it. The reticular formation plays a role in sleep and arousal, emotion, muscle tone, and certain movements and reflexes; it filters sensory inputs before they reach the conscious regions of the brain.

The large human forebrain, called the **cerebrum**, includes the **thalamus**, the **limbic system**, and the **cerebral cortex**. The thalamus carries sensory information to and from other forebrain regions. The limbic system produces our most basic and primitive emotions, drives, and behaviors, such as fear, thirst, pleasure, sexual response, and memory formation. The limbic system includes (1) the **hypothalamus**, which contains neurons and neurosecretory cells that release hormones into the blood, control the release of hormones from the pituitary gland, and direct the activities of the autonomic nervous system; (2) the **amygdala**, which contains neurons that produce the sensations of pleasure, sexual arousal, or punishment when stimulated; and (3) the **hippocampus**, which plays a role in emotions and in the formation of long-term memory needed for learning.

The human cerebral cortex forms the outer layer of the forebrain. It is the largest part of the brain. It is divided into the **cerebral hemispheres**, which communicate through axons making up the **corpus callosum**. To accommodate some 100 billion neurons, the cortex forms folds called **convolutions** to increase its area. Cortex neurons receive and process sensory information, store some of it as memory for future use, direct voluntary movements, and are responsible for thinking. The cerebral cortex is divided anatomically into four regions: the frontal, parietal, occipital, and temporal lobes. Damage to the cortex from trauma, stroke, or a tumor results in specific deficits depending on the area(s) damaged.

6) How Does the Brain Produce the Mind?

The "mind-brain" problem has occupied philosophers and neurobiologists. Studies of accident, stroke, or surgery patients have revealed that the "left brain" and the "right brain" are specialized for different functions. The left hemisphere functions in speech, reading, writing, language comprehension, mathematical ability, and logical problem solving, while the right hemisphere functions in musical skills, artistic ability, facial recognition, spatial visualization, and the ability to recognize and express emotions.

The mechanics of learning and memory are poorly understood. Memory may be brief or long lasting. Learning occurs in two phases: an initial **working memory** which may be followed by **long-term memory**. Working memory is temporary electrical or biochemical activity in the brain, and long-term memory involves changes to brain structure, such as the formation of new, long-lasting neural connections or the strengthening of existing ones. Working memory can be converted to long-term memory, perhaps involving the action of the hippocampus. Learning, memory storage, and memory retrieval may be controlled by separate regions of the brain. Learning and memory may be controlled by the hippocampus, while retrieval seems to be controlled by the temporal lobes.

7) How Do Sensory Receptors Work?

Generally, a **receptor** is a structure that changes when acted on by a stimulus. All receptors are **transducers**; they convert signals from one form to another. A **sensory receptor** may be a neuron specialized to produce an electrical response to particular stimuli. Stimulation of a sensory receptor causes a **receptor potential**, an electrical signal whose size is proportional to the strength of the stimulus. However, intensity is still conveyed to the nervous system by the frequency, not the size, of the action potentials generated.

Thermoreceptors are free nerve endings that respond to fluctuations in temperature. **Mechanoreceptors** produce a receptor potential in response to stretching of their plasma membranes.

Hair cells are mechanoreceptors located in the inner ear; these receptors for sound, motion, and gravity produce a receptor potential when their hairs are bent. **Photoreceptors** (receptors for light), **chemoreceptors**, (receptors for chemicals which we perceive as tastes or smells), and **pain receptors** posses specialized membrane receptor proteins.

8) How Is Sound Sensed?

Sound is produced by any vibrating object. The ear structure captures, transmits, and transduces sound. The **outer ear** consists of the **external ear** and the **auditory canal**. The auditory canal conducts sound waves to the **middle ear**, which consists of the **tympanic membrane** (eardrum), three tiny bones (the hammer, the anvil, and the stirrup), and the **Eustachian tube** (which connects to the pharynx and equalizes air pressure between the middle ear and the atmosphere). In the middle ear, sound vibrates the tympanic membrane, which in turn vibrates the hammer, anvil, and stirrup bones. These bones transmit vibrations to the **inner ear**. The fluid-filled hollow bones of the inner ear form a spiral-shaped **cochlea** and other structures that detect head movement and the pull of gravity. Sounds enter the inner ear when the stirrup vibrates the **oval window** membrane that covers a hole in the cochlea.

   The central canal of the cochlea contains the **basilar membrane**, on top of which are receptors, the hair cells. Protruding into the central canal is the gelatinous **tectorial membrane** in which the hairs are embedded. Sound perception occurs when the oval window passes vibrations to the fluid in the cochlea, which in turn vibrates the basilar membrane, causing it to move up and down. This bends the hairs embedded in the tectorial membrane, producing receptor potentials in the hair cells. The hair cells then release transmitter onto neurons of the **auditory nerve**, whose action potentials travel to the brain. The inner ear also allows us to perceive *loudness* (the magnitude of sound vibrations) and *pitch* (the frequency of sound vibrations).

9) How is Light Sensed?

All forms of vision use photoreceptors containing colored receptor molecules called **photopigments**. Photopigments absorb light and are chemically changed in the process. This chemical change alters ion channels in the plasma membrane, producing a receptor potential.

   The mammalian eye collects, focuses, and transduces light waves. Incoming light first encounters the transparent **cornea**, behind which is a chamber filled with a watery nourishing fluid called **aqueous humor**. The **iris** is pigmented muscular tissue with a circular opening, the **pupil**, which controls how much light enters. Light strikes a flattened sphere of transparent protein fibers, the **lens**, which is suspended behind the pupil by ligaments and muscles that regulate its shape. Behind the lens is a chamber filled with clear jellylike **vitreous humor**. After passing through the vitreous humor, light reaches the **retina**, a multilayered sheet of photoreceptors and neurons, where light energy is converted into electrical nerve impulses transmitted to the brain. Behind the retina is the **choroid**, a darkly pigmented tissue. Surrounding the outer portion of the eyeball is the **sclera**, tough connective tissue forming the white of the eye.

   Because the lens is adjustable, it allows focusing of both distant and nearby objects. The visual image is focused most sharply on a small area of the retina called the **fovea**. If your eyeball is too long, you are nearsighted, unable to focus on distant objects; if the eyeball is too short, you are farsighted.

   Light striking the retina is captured by photoreceptors called **rods** and **cones** present in the retina. The signal is then processed by several layers of neurons. The retinal cells closest to the vitreous humor are **ganglion cells**, whose axons make up the **optic nerve**. Ganglion cell axons must pass through the retina to reach the brain. The spot at which the axons pass through the retina is called the **optic disc** or **blind spot**.

Cones and rods differ in distribution and light sensitivity. Although cones are located throughout the retina, they are concentrated in the fovea. Human eyes have three types of cones, each containing a slightly different photopigment that is most strongly stimulated by a particular wavelength of light (red, green, or blue). The brain distinguishes color according to the relative intensity of stimulation of different cones. Rods dominate the peripheral portions of the retina. Rods are more sensitive to light than cones and are largely responsible for our vision in dim light. Rods do not distinguish color.

Binocular vision allows depth perception. Most herbivores have one eye on each side of the head. Predators and omnivores (such as humans) have both eyes facing forward, with slightly different but extensively overlapping visual fields (binocular vision) that allows for depth perception. Herbivores have no depth perception but they have a nearly 360-degree field of view, an advantage when looking out for predators.

10) How Are Chemicals Sensed?

Through chemical senses, animals may find food, avoid poisons, locate homes, and find mates. Terrestrial vertebrates have two chemical senses: **olfaction** (smell) for airborne molecules and **taste** for molecules dissolved in water or saliva. Olfactory receptors are nerve cells with hairlike dendrites in mucus-covered epithelial tissue in the upper portion of each nasal cavity. Taste receptors are located in clusters called **taste buds** on the tongue. Each taste bud has up to 80 taste receptor cells surrounded by supporting cells in a small pit. The four major types of taste receptors are sweet, sour, salty, and bitter. What we call taste is mostly smell.

Pain is actually a specialized chemical sense. Most pain is caused by tissue damage. When cells are damaged, their contents flow into the extracellular fluid. Potassium ions in the cell contents stimulate pain receptors. Damaged cells also release enzymes that produce **bradykinin**, another stimulus that activates pain receptors.

KEY TERMS AND CONCEPTS

Fill-In: From the following list of terms, fill in the blanks below.

action potential	dendrites	olfactory
auditory	fovea	optic disc
axon	inner	oval
blind spot	iris	peripheral nervous system
bradykinin	lens	(PNS)
brain	limbic system	pons
cell body	medulla	resting potential
central nervous system (CNS)	motor	rod
cerebellum	myelin	sensory
cerebral cortex	nerve	spinal cord
cerebrum	neuron	taste buds
cone	neurotransmitters	thalamus
cornea		

A single nerve cell is called a(n) (1)_____. The part of a nerve cell in which most of the common cellular organelles are located is the (2)_____, and the long process that carries impulses away from the cell body to synaptic endings on other nerve cells or on muscles is the (3)_____. Branched tendrils that are specialized to respond to signals from the external environment or from other neurons are (4)_____. A bundle of axons bound together in a sheath makes up a(n) (5)_____.

(6)_____ covers many axons and insulates them.

Chemicals released into synapses by the synaptic terminals of presynaptic neurons are called (7)_____.

The (8)_____ of a neuron is always negative. Once the cell becomes more negative and threshold is reached, a(n) (9)_____ is generated at the spike initiation zone.

(10)_____ neurons respond to a stimulus; and (11)_____ neurons activate muscles or glands.

The human nervous system has two parts: The (12)_____, consisting of the brain and spinal cord; and the (13)_____ which links the brain and spinal cord to the rest of the body.

The (14)_____ is the part of the central nervous system of vertebrates that is enclosed within the skull, and the (15)_____ is protected by the vertebral column.

The hindbrain of humans develops into three parts: The (16)_____ controls automatic activities such as breathing, swallowing, heart rate, and blood pressure; the (17)_____ coordinates movements of the body; and the (18)_____ is just above the medulla and contains neurons that influence sleep and the rate and pattern of breathing.

The human forebrain is called the (19)_____ and includes the (20)_____, which carries sensory information; the (21)_____, which is responsible for our primitive emotions and behaviors, and the (22)_____, which is involved in memory and thinking.

The (23)_____ canal is within the outer ear and conducts sound from the external ear to the eardrum. The (24)_____ ear is composed of the bony, fluid-filled tubes of the cochlea. The membrane-covered entrance to the cochlea is the (25)_____ window, which vibrates in response to vibrations of the stirrup.

The clear outer covering of the eye in front of the pupil and iris is the (26)_____. The (27)_____ is the pigmented muscular tissue of the eye that surrounds and controls the size of the pupil. A flexible or movable (28)_____ is used to focus both close and distant objects.

The photoreceptor cell in the retina that is sensitive to dim light but not involved in color vision is a (29)_____. The central region of the retina, on which images are focused is the (30)_____. The area where ganglion cell axons pass through the retina is the (31)_____, also called the (32)_____.

The sense of smell involves the (33)_____ receptors, and the sense of taste involves clusters of receptors called (34)_____.

(35)_____ is a chemical formed during tissue damage that binds to receptor molecules on pain nerve endings, giving rise to the sensation of pain.

Key Terms and Definitions

acetylcholine (ah-sēt´-il-kō´-lēn): a neurotransmitter in the brain and in synapses of motor neurons that innervate skeletal muscles.

action potential: a rapid change from a negative to a positive electrical potential in a nerve cell. This signal travels along an axon without a change in intensity.

amygdala (am-ig´-da-la): part of the forebrain of vertebrates that is involved in the production of appropriate behavioral responses to environmental stimuli.

aqueous humor (ā´-kwē-us): the clear, watery fluid between the cornea and lens of the eye.

association neuron: in a neural network, a nerve cell that is postsynaptic to a sensory neuron and presynaptic to a motor neuron. In actual circuits, there may be many association neurons between individual sensory and motor neurons.

auditory canal (aw´-di-tor-ē): a canal within the outer ear that conducts sound from the external ear to the tympanic membrane.

auditory nerve: the nerve leading from the mammalian cochlea to the brain, carrying information about sound.

autonomic nervous system: the part of the peripheral nervous system of vertebrates that synapses on glands, internal organs, and smooth muscle and produces largely involuntary responses.

axon: a long extension of a nerve cell, extending from the cell body to synaptic endings on other nerve cells or on muscles.

basilar membrane (bas´-eh-lar): a membrane in the cochlea that bears hair cells that respond to the vibrations produced by sound.

binocular vision: the ability to see objects simultaneously through both eyes, providing greater depth perception and more accurate judgment of the size and distance of an object from the eyes.

blind spot: see optic disc.

bradykinin (brā´-dē-kī´-nin): a chemical, formed during tissue damage, that binds to receptor molecules on pain nerve endings, giving rise to the sensation of pain.

brain: the part of the central nervous system of vertebrates that is enclosed within the skull.

cell body: the part of a nerve cell in which most of the common cellular organelles are located; typically a site of integration of inputs to the nerve cell.

central nervous system: in vertebrates, the brain and spinal cord.

cerebellum (ser-uh-bel´-um): the part of the hindbrain of vertebrates that is concerned with coordinating movements of the body.

cerebral cortex (ser-ē´-brul kor´-tex): a thin layer of neurons on the surface of the vertebrate cerebrum, in which most neural processing and coordination of activity occurs.

cerebral hemisphere: one of two nearly symmetrical halves of the cerebrum, connected by a broad band of axons, the corpus callosum.

cerebrospinal fluid: a clear fluid, produced within the ventricles of the brain, that fills the ventricles and cushions the brain and spinal cord.

cerebrum (ser-ē´-brum): the part of the forebrain of vertebrates that is concerned with sensory processing, the direction of motor output, and the coordination of most bodily activities; consists of two nearly symmetrical halves (the hemispheres) connected by a broad band of axons, the corpus callosum.

chemoreceptor: a sensory receptor that responds to chemicals from the environment; used in the chemical senses of taste and smell.

choroid (kor´-oid): a darkly pigmented layer of tissue, behind the retina, that contains blood vessels and pigment that absorbs stray light.

cochlea (kahk´-lē-uh): a coiled, bony, fluid-filled tube found in the mammalian inner ear; contains receptors (hair cells) that respond to the vibration of sound.

cone: a cone-shaped photoreceptor cell in the vertebrate retina; not as sensitive to light as are the rods. The three types of cones are most sensitive to different colors of light and provide color vision; see also *rod*.

convergence: a condition in which a large number of nerve cells provide input to a smaller number of cells.

convolution: a folding of the cerebral cortex of the vertebrate brain.

cornea (kor´-nē-uh): the clear outer covering of the eye, in front of the pupil and iris.

corpus callosum (kor´pus kal-ō´-sum): the band of axons that connect the two cerebral hemispheres of vertebrates.

dendrite (den´-drīt): a branched tendril that extends outward from the cell body of a neuron; specialized to respond to signals from the external environment or from other neurons.

divergence: a condition in which a small number of nerve cells provide input to a larger number of cells.

dopamine (dōp´-uh-mēn): a transmitter in the brain whose actions are largely inhibitory. The loss of dopamine-containing neurons causes Parkinson's disease.

dorsal root ganglion: a ganglion, located on the dorsal (sensory) branch of each spinal nerve, that contains the cell bodies of sensory neurons.

echolocation: the use of ultrasonic sounds, which bounce back from nearby objects, to produce an auditory "image" of nearby surroundings; used by bats and porpoises.

effector (ē-fek´-tor): a part of the body (normally a muscle or gland) that carries out responses as directed by the nervous system.

electrolocation: the production of high-frequency electrical signals from an electric organ in front of the tail of weak electrical fish; used to detect and locate nearly objects.

Eustachian tube (ū-stā´-shin): a tube connecting the middle ear with the pharynx; allows pressure between the middle ear and the atmosphere to equilibrate.

external ear: the fleshy portion of the ear that extends outside the skull.

forebrain: during development, the anterior portion of the brain. In mammals, the forebrain differentiates into the thalamus, the limbic system, and the cerebrum. In humans, the cerebrum contains about half of all the neurons in the brain.

fovea (fō´-vē-uh): in the vertebrate retina, the central region on which images are focused; contains closely packed cones.

ganglion (gang´-lē-un): a cluster of neurons.

ganglion cell: a type of cell, comprising the innermost layer of the vertebrate retina, whose axons form the optic nerve.

gray matter: the outer portion of the brain and inner region of the spinal cord; composed largely of neuron cell bodies, which give this area a gray color.

hair cell: the type of receptor cell in the inner ear; bears hairlike projections, the bending of which causes the receptor potential between two membranes.

hindbrain: the posterior portion of the brain, containing the medulla, pons, and cerebellum.

hippocampus (hip-ō-kam´-pus): the part of the forebrain of vertebrates that is important in emotion and especially learning.

hypothalamus (hī-pō-thal´-a-mus): a region of the brain that controls the secretory activity of the pituitary gland; synthesizes, stores, and releases certain peptide hormones; directs autonomic nervous system responses.

inner ear: the innermost part of the mammalian ear; composed of the bony, fluid-filled tubes of the cochlea and the vestibular apparatus.

integration: in nerve cells, the process of adding up electrical signals from sensory inputs or other nerve cells to determine the appropriate outputs.

intensity: the strength of stimulation or response.

iris: the pigmented muscular tissue of the vertebrate eye that surrounds and controls the size of the pupil, through which light enters.

lens: a clear object that bends light rays; in eyes, a flexible or movable structure used to focus light on a layer of photoreceptor cells.

limbic system: a diverse group of brain structures, mostly in the lower forebrain, that includes the thalamus, hypothalamus, amygdala, hippocampus, and parts of the cerebrum and is involved in basic emotions, drives, behaviors, and learning.

long-term memory: the second phase of learning; a more-or-less permanent memory formed by a structural change in the brain, brought on by repetition.

mechanoreceptor: a receptor that responds to mechanical deformation, such as that caused by pressure, touch, or vibration.

medulla (med-ū´-luh): the part of the hindbrain of vertebrates that controls automatic activities such as breathing, swallowing, heart rate, and blood pressure.

meninges (men-in´-jēz): three layers of connective tissue that surround the brain and spinal cord.

midbrain: during development, the central portion of the brain; contains an important relay center, the reticular formation.

middle ear: the part of the mammalian ear composed of the tympanic membrane, the Eustachian tube, and three bones (hammer, anvil, and stirrup) that transmit vibrations from the auditory canal to the oval window.

motor neuron: a neuron that receives instructions from the association neurons and activates effector organs, such as muscles or glands.

myelin (mī´-uh-lin): a wrapping of insulating membranes of specialized nonneural cells around the axon of a vertebrate nerve cell; increases the speed of conduction of action potentials.

nerve: a bundle of axons of nerve cells, bound together in a sheath.

neuron (noor´-on): a single nerve cell.

neurotransmitter: a chemical that is released by a nerve cell close to a second nerve cell, a muscle, or a gland cell and that influences the activity of the second cell.

olfaction (ōl-fak´-shun): a chemical sense, the sense of smell; in terrestrial vertebrates, the result of the detection of airborne molecules.

optic disc: the area of the retina at which the axons of the ganglion cell merge to form the optic nerve; the blind spot of the retina.

optic nerve: the nerve leading from the eye to the brain, carrying visual information.

outer ear: the outermost part of the mammalian ear, including the external ear and auditory canal leading to the tympanic membrane.

oval window: the membrane-covered entrance to the inner ear.

pain receptor: a receptor that has extensive areas of membranes studded with special receptor proteins that respond to light or to a chemical.

peripheral nerve: a nerve that links the brain and spinal cord to the rest of the body.

peripheral nervous system: in vertebrates, the part of the nervous system that connects the central nervous system to the rest of the body.

photopigment (fō´-tō-pig-ment): a chemical substance in photoreceptor cells that, when struck by light, changes in molecular conformation.

photoreceptor: a receptor cell that responds to light; in vertebrates, rods and cones.

pons: a portion of the hindbrain, just above the medulla, that contains neurons that influence sleep and the rate and pattern of breathing.

postsynaptic neuron: at a synapse, the nerve cell that changes its electrical potential in response to a chemical (the neurotransmitter) released by another (presynaptic) cell.

postsynaptic potential (PSP): an electrical signal produced in a postsynaptic cell by transmission across the synapse; it may be excitatory (EPSP), making the cell more likely to produce an action potential, or inhibitory (IPSP), tending to inhibit an action potential.

presynaptic neuron: a nerve cell that releases a chemical (the neurotransmitter) at a synapse, causing changes in the electrical activity of another (postsynaptic) cell.

pupil: the adjustable opening in the center of the iris, through which light enters the eye.

receptor: a cell that responds to an environmental stimulus (chemicals, sound, light, pH, and so on) by changing its electrical potential; also, a protein molecule in a plasma membrane that binds to another molecule (hormone, neurotransmitter), triggering metabolic or electrical changes in a cell.

receptor potential: an electrical potential change in a receptor cell, produced in response to the reception of an environmental stimulus (chemicals, sound, light, heat, and so on). The size of the receptor potential is proportional to the intensity of the stimulus.

reflex: a simple, stereotyped movement of part of the body that occurs automatically in response to a stimulus.

resting potential: a negative electrical potential in unstimulated nerve cells.

reticular formation (reh-tik´-ū-lar): a diffuse network of neurons extending from the hindbrain, through the mid-brain, and into the lower reaches of the forebrain; involved in filtering sensory input and regulating what information is relayed to conscious brain centers for further attention.

retina (ret´-in-uh): a multilayered sheet of nerve tissue at the rear of camera-type eyes, composed of photoreceptor cells plus associated nerve cells that refine the photoreceptor information and transmit it to the optic nerve.

rod: a rod-shaped photoreceptor cell in the vertebrate retina, sensitive to dim light but not involved in color vision; see also *cone*.

sclera: a tough, white connective tissue layer that covers the outside of the eyeball and forms the white of the eye.

sensory neuron: a nerve cell that responds to a stimulus from the internal or external environment.

sensory receptor: a cell (typically, a neuron) specialized to respond to particular internal or external environmental stimuli by producing an electrical potential.

serotonin (ser-uh-tō´-nin): in the central nervous system, a neurotransmitter that is involved in mood, sleep, and the inhibition of pain.

somatic nervous system: that portion of the peripheral nervous system that controls voluntary movement by activating skeletal muscles.

spike initiation zone: on a neuron, the site where the action potential begins; where the axon leaves the cell body.

spinal cord: the part of the central nervous system of vertebrates that extends from the base of the brain to the hips and is protected by the bones of the vertebral column; contains the cell bodies of motor neurons that form synapses with skeletal muscles, the circuitry for some simple reflex behaviors, and axons that communicate with the brain.

synapse (sin´-aps): the site of communication between nerve cells. At a synapse, one cell (presynaptic) normally releases a chemical (the neurotransmitter) that changes the electrical potential of the second (postsynaptic) cell.

synaptic cleft: a tiny space that separates the presynaptic and postsynaptic neurons.

taste: a chemical sense for substances dissolved in water or saliva; in mammals, perceptions of sweet, sour, bitter, or salt produced by the stimulation of receptors on the tongue.

taste bud: a cluster of taste receptor cells and supporting cells that is located in a small pit beneath the surface of the tongue and that communicates with the mouth through a small pore. The human tongue has about 10,000 taste buds.

tectorial membrane (tek-tor´-ē-ul): one of the membranes of the cochlea in which the hairs of the hair cells are embedded. In sound reception, movement of the basilar membrane relative to the tectorial membrane bends the cilia.

thalamus: the part of the forebrain that relays sensory information to many parts of the brain.

thermoreceptor: a sensory receptor that responds to changes in temperature.

threshold: the electrical potential (less negative than the resting potential) at which an action potential is triggered.

transducer: a device that converts signals from one form to another. Sensory receptors are transducers that convert environmental stimuli, such as heat, light, or vibration, into electrical signals (such as action potentials) recognized by the nervous system.

tympanic membrane (tim-pan´-ik): the ear-drum; a membrane, stretched across the opening of the ear, that transmits vibration of sound waves to bones of the middle ear.

vitreous humor (vit´-rē-us): a clear, jellylike substance that fills the large chamber of the eye between the lens and the retina.

white matter: the portion of the brain and spinal cord that consists largely of myelin-covered axons and that give these areas a white appearance.

working memory: the first phase of learning; short-term memory that is electrical or biochemical in nature.

THINKING THROUGH THE CONCEPTS

True or False: Determine if the statement given is true or false. If it is false, change the underlined word(s) so that the statement reads true.

36. _____   <u>Dendrites</u> carry an impulse away from the nerve cell body and are the long extensions of a nerve cell.

37. _____   <u>Axons</u> initiate an impulse.

38. _____   Nerves pass on impulses with <u>undiminished</u> intensity.

39. _____   The resting potential inside a nerve cell is always <u>positive</u> within the cell.

40. _____   When the threshold level is reached, an <u>action potential</u> is triggered.

41. _____   The size of the action potential is <u>dependent on</u> the strength of the stimulus.

42. _____   Myelin covers some <u>dendrites</u>.

43. _____   Receptors for neurotransmitters are located on the <u>postsynaptic</u> neuron.

44. _____   The <u>cerebellum</u> controls coordination.

45. _____   The <u>thalamus</u> connects the two sides of the cerebrum.

46. _____   The <u>left</u> side of the brain is associated with creativity.

47. _____ Short-term memory is <u>electrical</u>.

48. _____ Long-term memory is <u>chemical</u>.

49. _____ Structures that change when acted on by stimuli are <u>acceptors</u>.

50. _____ Structures that convert signals from one form to another are <u>reducers</u>.

51. _____ High-frequency vibrations of air or water are <u>sounds</u>.

52. _____ The cochlea is part of the human <u>middle</u> ear.

53. _____ The sense of vision involves <u>chemical</u> changes.

54. _____ The fovea contains virtually no <u>cones</u>.

55. _____ The retinas of nocturnal animals are made up of <u>cones</u>.

56. _____ Pain is a special kind of <u>chemical</u> sense.

57. _____ <u>Rods</u> are responsible for color vision.

Identification: Determine whether the following statements refer to the **cell body, synaptic terminals, dendrites,** or **axons** of neurons.

58. _____ carry action potentials to output terminals

59. _____ the cell's integration center

60. _____ receive information from the environment

61. _____ sites where signals are transmitted to other cells

62. _____ convert environmental information into electrical signals

63. _____ bundled together into nerves

64. _____ initiates action potentials

Matching: Nerve cell function.

65. _____ always negative (−40 to −90 millivolts) within a nerve cell

66. _____ a sudden positive charge within a nerve cell

67. _____ occurs when a nerve cell becomes sufficiently less negative inside

Choices:

a. threshold

b. action potential

c. resting potential

Matching: The human brain. Some questions may have than one correct answer.

68. _____   midbrain

69. _____   like an extension of the spinal cord

70. _____   channels sensory information to other forebrain parts

71. _____   hindbrain

72. _____   controls several automatic functions

73. _____   hypothalamus

74. _____   forebrain

75. _____   receives input from all sense organs and "decides" which require attention

76. _____   controls learning, emotions, and the autonomic nervous system

77. _____   largest part of the brain

78. _____   coordinates body movements and body positions

79. _____   controls speech, reading, math ability, and musical skills

Choices:

a. cerebellum

b. cerebrum

c. limbic system

d. medulla

e. reticular formation

f. thalamus

Identification: Determine whether the following statements refer to **hormones, neurons,** or **both**.

80. _____   indiscriminately affect millions of cells

81. _____   speed transmissions quickly using electrical signals

82. _____   release neurotransmitters very close to the cells they influence

83. _____   are chemicals that travel slowly to the sites of action

84. _____   are chemicals released into the bloodstream and carried great distances

85. _____   precisely affect small numbers of cells

86. _____   some release neurohormones

Multiple Choice: Pick the most correct choice for each question.

87. A rapid change from a negative to a positive electrical potential in a nerve cell is
    a. a reflex
    b. an amygdala
    c. an action potential
    d. a divergence
    e. a synapse

88. The gap between the axon of one neuron and the dendrite of another is called a
    a. synapse
    b. node of Ranvier
    c. cell body
    d. convergence
    e. dendritic junction

89. The resting potential of a neuron becomes less negative when
    a. the spike initiation zone is formed
    b. an IPSP signal is received
    c. it reaches threshold
    d. none of the above, it cannot become less negative

90. The autonomic nervous system innervates all of the following *except*
    a. skeletal muscle
    b. heart
    c. stomach
    d. kidney

91. A mechanoreceptor is a receptor designed for
    a. touch
    b. light
    c. chemicals
    d. pain
    e. pleasure

92. The middle ear contains
    a. the cochlea
    b. three bones (hammer, anvil, and stirrup)
    c. the semicircular canals
    d. receptor cells for hearing

93. The amount of light entering the human eye is regulated by the muscular
    a. iris
    b. pupil
    c. sclera
    d. cornea

94. Completely color-blind animals lack
    a. cones
    b. rods
    c. ommatidia
    d. irises
    e. lenses

CLUES TO APPLYING THE CONCEPTS

These practice questions are intended to sharpen your ability to apply critical thinking and analysis to biological concepts covered in this chapter.

95. The neurotransmitter acetylcholine stimulates postsynaptic neurons to transmit action potentials to skeletal muscles, which then contract. Many chemicals can act on the nervous system and cause problems. Determine the effect each of the following would have on a person subjected to their action. (1) Botulism toxin, from a certain type of bacteria, inhibits the release of acetylcholine. (2) Curare, used by South American Indians to coat the tip of their arrows, binds to the same receptors that normally bind acetylcholine. (3) Diisopropyl fluorophosphate, a chemical that could be used as a nerve gas during war, blocks the enzyme that breaks down acetylcholine after it has crossed the synapse and becomes bound to postsynaptic neurons.

_____

_____

_____

_____

_____

_____

_____

_____

_____

_____

96. Explain how each of the following medical problems could result in deafness. (1) injury to the auditory nerve; (2) arthritis of the middle ear bones; (3) a punctured eardrum; (4) too much earwax in the auditory canal; and (5) damage to the hair cells from being exposed to loud music.

_____

_____

_____

_____

_____

_____

_____

ANSWERS TO EXERCISES

1. neuron	31. optic disc	63. axons
2. cell body	32. blind spot	64. cell body
3. axon	33. olfactory	65. c
4. dendrites	34. taste buds	66. b
5. nerve	35. bradykinin	67. a
6. myelin	36. false, axons	68. e
7. neurotransmitters	37. false, dendrites	69. d
8. resting potential	38. true	70. f
9. action potential	39. false, negative	71. a, d
10. sensory	40. true	72. d
11. motor	41. false, independent of	73. c
12. central nervous system (CNS)	42. false, axons	74. b, c, f
	43. true	75. e
13. peripheral nervous system (PNS)	44. true	76. c
	45. false, corpus callosum	77. b
14. brain	46. false, right	78. a
15. spinal cord	47. true	79. b
16. medulla	48. false, structural	80. hormones
17. cerebellum	49. false, receptors	81. neurons
18. pons	50. false, transducers	82. neurons
19. cerebrum	51. true	83. hormones
20. thalamus	52. false, inner	84. hormones
21. limbic system	53. true	85. neurons
22. cerebral cortex	54. false, rods	86. neurons
23. auditory	55. false, rods	87. c
24. inner	56. true	88. a
25. oval	57. false, cones	89. c
26. cornea	58. axons	90. a
27. iris	59. cell body	91. a
28. lens	60. dendrites	92. b
29. rod	61. synaptic terminals	93. a
30. fovea	62. dendrites	94. a

95. Since acetylcholine stimulates postsynaptic neurons to transmit action potentials to skeletal muscles, which then contract: (1) When botulism toxin inhibits the release of acetylcholine, transmitting cells will not be able to signal receiving cells, and nerve signals will be stopped at the synapse, resulting in paralysis of skeletal muscles. (2) When curare blocks the acetylcholine receptors, skeletal muscles cannot be stimulated to contract, resulting in paralysis. (3) Diisopropyl fluorophosphate prevents acetylcholine from being removed from the receptors where it is bound, so the receiving cells will continue to transmit signals to skeletal muscles, resulting in prolonged contraction of the muscles.

96. (1) If the auditory nerve is injured, the brain will not be able to receive signals that sound is occurring. (2) If the middle ear bones are arthritic, they will be unable to move in response to sound vibrations, preventing them from transmitting vibrations to the cochlea. (3) A punctured eardrum will be unable to pick up vibrations from the air and transmit them to the ear bones. (4) Too much earwax will block sound waves from striking the eardrum and setting it in motion. (5) Damaged hair cells will not produce receptor potentials and thus will not release transmitter onto neurons of the auditory nerve.

Chapter 25: Animal Reproduction and Development

OVERVIEW

This chapter presents the mechanisms by which animals reproduce. These mechanisms are the result of the effects of natural selection on generations of organisms. The chapter, however, focuses on human reproduction. Included is a summary of the reproductive organs and the processes that occur after a zygote has been produced. As the development of an embryo progresses, the cells differentiate so that the specialized body functions can take place. Information concerning embryological development and the changes that occur in the mother's body through pregnancy are also presented. Using the information learned about the human reproductive system, methods to limit or induce fertility are explored.

1) How Do Animals Reproduce?

Reproduction in which gametes are produced through meiosis is considered **sexual reproduction**. The offspring produced will have a genome that combines those of the parents. However, some animals produce offspring through **asexual reproduction** by mitotic divisions of a particular area of the body. These offspring are genetically identical to the parent. Asexual reproduction may involve **budding**. Animals such as hydra and sponges produce a **bud** that is a miniature version of the "parent". The bud eventually breaks off and continues independently. Additionally, some species can produce eggs that will develop into adults without being fertilized.

In sexual reproduction, haploid **eggs**, produced by female,s are **fertilized** by haploid **sperm**, produced by males. The offspring formed are diploid. Individuals of certain species, such as earthworms, produce both eggs and sperm. These individuals are **hermaphrodites**. If the union of egg and sperm happens outside the body of the parents, **external fertilization** has occurred. External fertilization in water is known as **spawning**. Animals that spawn must synchronize their release of egg and sperm. If the union of the egg and sperm happens inside the female's body, **internal fertilization** has occurred. Internal fertilization increases the chances that the sperm will reach the egg and involves **copulation** behavior. Males of some species deposit a packet of sperm, a **spermatophore**, which the female picks up and inserts into her reproductive cavity. Regardless of the method by which sperm enter the female body, fertilization will only occur if the female has released a mature egg. Mature eggs are released during **ovulation**.

2) How Does the Human Reproductive System Work?

The organs that produce the sex cells are called **gonads**. The gonads in the male are the **testes** and are contained outside the body within a sac called the **scrotum**. Within each testis, sperm are produced by the **seminiferous tubules**. **Interstitial cells** between the tubules produce the hormone testosterone. Inside the wall of each seminiferous tubule are **spermatogonia**, the diploid cells from which sperm will be produced. Also within the wall of the tubules are **Sertoli cells**, which regulate **spermatogenesis**, the development of sperm. During spermatogenesis, spermatogonia grow and differentiate into **primary spermatocytes**. The primary spermatocytes divide by meiosis I, producing two **secondary spermatocytes**. Secondary spermatocytes divide by meiosis II, each producing two **spermatids**. The spermatids differentiate into sperm nourished by the Sertoli cells.

The organization of sperm cells is unlike that of any other cell. Within the head of the sperm is the DNA and an **acrosome**. The acrosome contains enzymes that digest protective layers around the egg. Behind the head of the sperm is the midpiece which contains numerous mitochondria to provide energy for the whiplike movement of the sperm's flagellum. Males do not begin producing sperm until puberty, when interstitial cells begin to produce **testosterone**. Testosterone also induces secondary sex character- istics and is needed to maintain an erection of the **penis** for successful intercourse.

Sperm are conducted outside the male body through accessory structures of the reproductive system. The seminiferous tubules merge to form a continuous tube, the **epididymis**, which leads to the **vas deferens**. The vas deferens merges with the **urethra**, forming a path shared with the urinary system to the tip of the penis. Sperm leaving the body (during ejaculation) is mixed in a fluid called **semen**. Semen is formed from three glands, the **seminal vesicles**, the **prostate gland**, and the **bulbourethral glands**.

The gonads in the female are the **ovaries**. Within the ovaries, eggs are formed through **oogenesis**. Oogenesis begins in the ovaries of a developing female fetus when the **oogonia** are formed. By the end of the third month of fetal development, all of the oogonia have matured into **primary oocytes**. The primary oocytes begin meiosis I, but the process is halted at prophase I. It is not until after puberty that development will continue, and then only a few primary oocytes each month will continue oogenesis. Surrounding each primary oocyte are accessory cells that together, form a **follicle**.

After puberty, pituitary hormones stimulate a few follicles at a time to continue development. Within each follicle, the first meiotic division is completed, forming one **secondary oocyte** and one **polar body**. The polar body contains a set of discarded chromosomes. The accessory cells of the follicle secrete **estrogen**. A mature follicle releases its secondary oocyte from the ovary into the **oviduct** (or **fallopian tube**). If fertilization occurs, the secondary oocyte will undergo meiosis II. Meanwhile, accessory cells left behind in the ovary enlarge, forming the **corpus luteum**. The corpus luteum secretes both estrogen and **progesterone**.

The secondary oocyte (now refered to as the egg) is conducted into a fallopian tube by a current created by ciliated **fimbriae**. Fertilization, if it occurs, usually takes place in the fallopian tube, forming a **zygote**. The zygote is carried through the fallopian tube by cilia into the **uterus**. The inner wall of the uterus is well supplied with blood vessels and forms the **endometrium**, the mother's contribution to the **placenta**. The outer wall of the uterus is the muscular **myometrium**, which will contract during delivery.

The development of the endometrium is stimulated by estrogen and progesterone secreted by the corpus luteum. If the egg is not fertilized, the corpus luteum disintegrates causing estrogen and proges- terone levels to decrease. When the hormone levels drop, the endometrium disintegrates and is expelled from the uterus during **menstruation** as part of the **menstrual cycle**. At the outer end of the uterus is a ring of connective tissue forming the **cervix**. On the other side of the cervix is the birth canal, or **vagina**.

Traditionally, in order for a sperm to fertilize an egg, copulation (intercourse, in humans) must occur. Together, the influences of psychological and physical stimulation increase blood flow to tissue spaces of the penis. When the tissues swell, the vessels draining blood from the penis become blocked. As pressure increases, the penis becomes erect, and can be inserted into the vagina. Further stimulation causes the muscles surrounding the epididymis, vas deferens, and urethra to contract, resulting in ejaculation. During an ejaculation, 300 to 400 million sperm are released.

Similarly, psychological and physical stimulation increases blood flow into the vagina and external reproductive tissues. The external reproductive tissues include folds of skin called the **labia** and a rounded projection, the **clitoris**. Since the clitoris develops from the same embryological tissue as the tip of the penis, it becomes erect when blood flow into the area increases. Sperm, released into the vagina following an ejaculation, swim up the female reproductive tract from the vagina, through the cervix, into the uterus, and up into the fallopian tubes. If an egg has been released in the past 24 hours or so, one sperm may succeed in fertilizing it.

The follicle cells that remained around the egg form the **corona radiata**, a barrier between the egg and sperm. Between the corona radiata and the egg is a second barrier, the jellylike **zona pellucida**. The hundreds of sperm reaching the egg release enzymes from their acrosomes, weakening the corona radiata and the zona pellucida, allowing one sperm to wiggle into the egg. The plasma membranes of the sperm and egg fuse, and the head of the sperm is drawn into the egg's cytoplasm. In response, the egg releases chemicals into the zona pellucida that reinforce it so that no other sperm can enter. The egg then begins meiosis II, finally producing a haploid gamete. The two haploid nuclei fuse, forming a diploid cell, the zygote.

3) How Does Animal Development Proceed?

An organism in its early stages of **development** is an **embryo**. A developing embryo is nourished by a protein- and lipid-rich **yolk**. The amount of yolk present in an egg determines the way in which an animal develops. Animal development begins with a series of mitotic divisions called **cleavage**. Although the number of cells increases during cleavage, the size of the overall structure does not increase. As cleavage continues, a ball of cells about the same size as the zygote, called a **morula**, forms. The morula progresses to the development of a hollow ball of cells called a **blastula**. Further divisions of the blastula result in the formation of the **blastopore**.

During the formation of the blastopore, cell movement occurs, called **gastrulation**. Three embryonic tissue layers form during gastrulation. The **endoderm** forms from the cells lining the blastopore. It eventually becomes the digestive tract. The **ectoderm** forms from the cells lining the outside of the **gastrula**. These cells give rise to the epidermis and the nervous system. Cells that move to the area between the endoderm and ectoderm are called the **mesoderm**. Mesoderm cells develop into muscles, the skeleton including the **notochord**, and the circulatory system.

Through a process called induction, chemicals produced by cells influence the development of other cells. **Organogenesis**, the process of organ development, is controlled by induction. Such signals may include "survival" signals or "death" signals. Some cells will die unless they receive a survival signal from surrounding cells; other cells will live unless they receive a death signal from surrounding cells. In this way, motor neurons synapse with muscle cells properly, and separate fingers and toes form in humans.

4) How Do Humans Develop?

Human development reflects our evolutionary ancestry. The fertilized egg undergoes cleavage as it travels through the fallopian tube to the uterus. One week after fertilization a **blastocyst**, rather than a blastula, has formed. The blastocyst has a thick **inner cell mass** on one side of its hollow ball structure. The inner cell mass will develop into the embryo while the cells on the outside are sticky and will adhere to the endometrium of the uterus, a process called **implantation**.

The inner cell mass grows and splits, forming two fluid filled sacs. The sacs are separated by a double layer of cells, the **embryonic disc**. One sac is enclosed by a membrane called the **amnion**. The amnion grows around the embryo so that it is maintained within the watery environment all animal embryos need. The second sac is the yolk sac, but it contains no yolk. As gastrulation begins, the **primitive streak** (which corresponds to the blastopore) forms in the embryonic disc. The mesoderm of the embryo is formed from cells migrating through the primitive streak to the interior of the embryo. The cell layer above the primitive streak forms the ectoderm. The cell layer below the primitive streak forms the endoderm.

As the embryo grows, the endoderm forms a tube that later becomes the digestive tract. The notochord, formed from mesoderm, causes the ectoderm to form a groove. The groove closes over, creating the predecessor to the brain and spinal cord, the **neural tube**. Continued development generates a beating heart and rapid growth of the brain. By the second month, all of the major organs have developed, including the gonads. Sex hormones are secreted by the testes or ovaries, which influence the development of embryonic organs and certain regions of the brain. The embryo is called a **fetus** at the end of the second month.

The placenta begins to develop as the embryo burrows into the endometrium. The outer cells of the embryo form the **chorion**, which sends fingerlike projections called **chorionic villi** into the endometrium, intricately linking the two. The placenta secretes estrogen to stimulate the growth of the uterus and mammary glands, and progesterone to stimulate the mammary glands and prevent premature uterine contractions. The placenta also regulates the exchange of substances between the mother and the fetus. The membranes of the fetal capillaries and the chorionic villi are very selective with respect to the substances that are exchanged; however, some disease-causing organisms and damaging chemicals can pass through.

The next seven months of fetal development involves, for the most part, growth of the already formed structures. The brain and spinal cord grow, and the fetus begins to respond to stimuli. The respiratory, digestive, and urinary tracts enlarge and begin functioning. Meanwhile, changes in the mother's breasts prepare her for nursing the baby. The increased amount of estrogen and progesterone in the blood stimulates the **mammary glands** to grow and develop the capacity to produce milk. **Lactation**, the production of milk, is promoted by the hormone prolactin.

Birth of the fetus is initiated by stretching of the uterus and by hormones from both the fetus and the mother, causing **labor**, a positive feedback reaction. The contractions of the uterine smooth muscle are triggered by the stretching caused by the growing fetus. Toward the end of development, the fetus produces steroid hormones that increase estrogen and prostaglandin production by the uterus and placenta. The increased hormone production, in combination with the stretching, increases the contractions of the uterus. The cervix dilates as the baby's head pushes against it. This stretching signals the hypothalamus to release oxytocin. With oxytocin and prostaglandins circulating in the blood, the uterus contracts even more intensely, pushing the baby from the birth canal (the vagina). Soon after the baby's birth, contractions begin again to expel the placenta, the afterbirth. The umbilical cord produces prostaglandins that cause muscles around fetal umbilical vessels to contract, shutting off blood supply between the mother and the baby. The baby's circulatory system takes over.

5) How Can Fertility Be Limited?

Fertility can be limited by various methods of **contraception**. The most reliable method is, of course, abstinence. **Sterilization** provides a rather permanent means of contraception. Sterilization in men is achieved through a **vasectomy**. This rather minor operation, performed under local anesthetic, cuts the vas deferens. Sperm are still produced, but are not expelled during ejaculation. A vasectomy has no known physical side effects. Sterilization in women is achieved through a **tubal ligation**. This operation, performed under general anesthetic, cuts the fallopian tubes. Ovulation still occurs, but sperm do not reach the eggs, nor can eggs reach the uterus.

More temporary means of contraception prevent ovulation, prevent the sperm from reaching the egg, or prevent a fertilized egg from implanting in the uterus. **Birth control pills** prevent ovulation. The continuous estrogen and progesterone that the pill provides suppress a midcycle hormone surge. Barrier methods prevent sperm from reaching the egg. The **diaphragm** and the **cervical cap** fit securely over the cervix, preventing sperm entry. When used in conjunction with **spermicides**, these devices are very effective and have no known side effects. As an alternative barrier method, a male can wear a **condom** over his penis. Female condoms that completely line the vagina are also available. Less effective methods of contraception include **withdrawal** of the penis from the vagina before ejaculation and

douching in an attempt to wash sperm from the vagina before they reach the uterus. Both of these methods are extremely unreliable. Another method that has a high failure rate is the **rhythm method**: abstinence from intercourse just before, during, and after ovulation. Users of this method often have difficulty determining when ovulation occurs each month or are undisciplined in their habits. An alternative method uses devices, such as the **intrauterine device** (**IUD**), that prevent a fertilized egg from implanting in the uterus. The "morning after" pill, by providing a large dose of estrogen, has essentially the same effect

When contraception fails, and an unplanned and unwanted pregnancy results, the pregnancy can be terminated by **abortion**. Abortion procedures typically involve dilation of the cervix followed by suction to remove the embryo and placenta. An alternative to the surgical procedure can be used within the first month of pregnancy. The drug RU-486, in pill form, is used in some European countries and China. RU-486 blocks the action of progesterone, terminating the pregnancy.

KEY TERMS AND CONCEPTS

Fill-In I: From the following list of terms fill in the blanks below.

acrosome	external fertilization	oogonia	Sertoli cells
asexual reproduction	fallopian tube	ovaries	sexual reproduction
budding	fimbriae	ovulation	sperm
bulbourethral glands	follicle	penis	spermatogenesis
cervix	gonads	placenta	spermatogonia
clitoris	hermaphrodites	polar body	spermatophore
copulation	internal fertilization	primary oocytes	testes
corona radiata	interstitial cells	prostate gland	urethra
corpus luteum	labia	scrotum	uterus
eggs	menstrual cycle	secondary oocyte	vagina
endometrium	menstruation	semen	vas deferens
epididymis	myometrium	seminal vesicles	zona pellucida
estrogen	oogenesis	seminiferous tubules	zygote

During (1)_____, haploid gametes are produced by meiosis. During (2)_____, repeated mitosis of cells of some part of the body produces an exact copy of the parent.

The process of (3)_____ produces a bud off the body of the adult that breaks off as a new individual.

Females produce (4)_____, and males produce (5)_____. Individuals that are (6)_____ produce both gametes.

If the union of the egg and sperm occurs outside the body, (7)_____ has taken place. If sperm are taken into the female's body, (8)_____ occurs. Typically, this process involves (9)_____, in which the male directly deposits the sperm into the female's body. The males of other species may package their sperm as a (10)_____, which the female picks up and places in her reproductive cavity. However sperm reach the egg, fertilization can only occur if a mature egg has been produced and (11)_____ has occurred.

The paired organs that produce sex cells in mammals are called (12)_____. The male structures that produce sperm are the (13)_____, which are enclosed in the (14)_____ outside the body. Coiled within the testes are the (15)_____. The male hormone testosterone is produced by (16)_____. The diploid cells that give rise to sperm are the (17)_____, and the cells that will nourish the sperm are the (18)_____. The process by which sperm are formed is called (19)_____. The human sperm contains enzymes in the specialized lysosome, the (20)_____, and DNA in the head region. Sperm is released from the male body through the (21)_____ during ejaculation.

The seminiferous tubules merge to form the (22)_____, which leads to the (23)_____. This tube finally merges with the (24)_____ of the urinary system. The fluid ejaculated from the penis is called (25)_____ and contains sperm mixed with secretions from the (26)_____, the (27)_____, and the (28)_____.

The female structures that produce eggs are the (29)_____. The process by which eggs are formed is called (30)_____. The diploid cells that give rise to the eggs are the (31)_____. At three months of development, a female fetus has none of these precursor cells left. They have all matured into (32)_____, each of which will begin meiosis I. Surrounding each primary oocyte are accessory cells making up the (33)_____. After puberty, a few primary oocytes at a time will initiate the completion of meiosis I. One oocyte will complete meiosis I, producing one (34)_____ and one (35)_____. The accessory cells of the follicle secrete the hormone

(36)_____. After being released from the ovary, the secondary oocyte may complete meiosis II in the (37)_____. Accessory cells left behind in the ovary form the (38)_____, which produces both estrogen and progesterone.

Each fallopian tube has an open end that almost surrounds the ovary with ciliated "fingers" called (39)_____. After the egg is fertilized, the (40)_____ is swept along the fallopian tube to the (41)_____. This organ has a two-layered wall. The inner layer is dense with blood vessels and forms the (42)_____, the mother's contribution to the (43)_____. If fertilization of the egg does not occur, this layer is shed during (44)_____, as part of the (45)_____. The outer layer of the uterus is muscular. This (46)_____ contracts strongly during birth. The outer end of the uterus is almost closed off by a ring of connective tissue, the (47)_____. On the other side of the ring of connective tissue is the (48)_____, which serves as the birth canal.

Sexual excitement in a female increases blood flow to external reproductive tissues, including external folds of skin, the (49)_____, and a rounded projection, the (50)_____, which becomes erect.

The egg released from the ovary is surrounded by follicle cells that develop into the (51)_____. Between this cell layer and the egg is a clear, jellylike layer called the (52)_____. Both layers protect the egg.

Fill-In II: From the following list of terms fill in the blanks below. A term may be used more than once.

abortion	contraception	gastrulation	neural tube
amnion	development	implantation	notochord
blastocyst	ectoderm	inner cell mass	organogenesis
blastopore	embryo	labor	placenta
blastula	embryonic disc	mammary glands	primitive streak
chorion	endoderm	mesoderm	yolk
chorionic villi	fetus	morula	yolk sac
cleavage	gastrula		

(53)_____ is the process by which an organism progresses from a fertilized egg, through adulthood, to death.

Animal development begins with an egg containing (54)_____, rich in protein and lipids needed by the (55)_____. The (56)_____ surrounds the embryo, maintaining it in a watery environment. The (57)_____ isolates wastes from the embryo. The (58)_____ stores food for the developing embryo.

A series of mitotic divisions initiated after the zygote forms is called (59)_____.
After several division cycles, a solid ball of cells forms, called the (60)_____.
With continued divisions, a cavity develops, and this hollow ball of cells is called a(n)
(61)_____. An indentation forms in the blastula, called the
(62)_____. Three embryonic tissues form as cells migrate through the
enlarging indentation. Cells lining the indentation develop the (63)_____,
eventually becoming the digestive tract. Cells to the outside form the (64)_____,
eventually becoming the epidermis and the nervous system. Cells that migrate between the two layers
form the (65)_____, eventually becoming the muscles and skeleton, including
the (66)_____. The movement of the cells is called (67)_____,
and the structure that forms is the (68)_____. The formation of organs from the
rearrangement of cells is (69)_____.

During human development, about a week after a sperm has broken through the protective layers and fertilized the egg, a hollow ball of cells, called a(n) (70)_____, has developed. The thick (71)_____ will become the (72)_____, and the thin outer wall will become the chorion. The chorion will adhere to and burrow into the endometrium during

(73)_____. The chorion from the embryo penetrates the endometrium of the uterus using (74)_____. The chorion, interacting with the endometrium, generates the (75)_____, which is selective as to which substances pass into the bloodstream of the fetus. Not all harmful substances are blocked, however.

The cells destined to become the embryo grow and split so that two fluid-filled sacs are separated by a double layer of cells, the (76)_____. The double layer of cells splits apart slightly, forming the (77)_____ (or blastopore in other animals). During the third week of development, the (78)_____ (the precursor of the brain and spinal cord) is generated. At the end of the second month, the embryo is referred to as a (79)_____.

When pregnancy occurs, estrogen and progesterone stimulate the (80)_____ to develop the capacity to secrete milk. The growing fetus causes the uterus to stretch. The stretching, in combination with hormones the fetus and mother secrete, triggers contractions of the uterus, and (81)_____ has begun.

The prevention of pregnancy involves various methods of (82)_____. When these methods fail, a pregnancy may be terminated by (83)_____.

Key Terms and Definitions

abortion: the procedure for terminating pregnancy; the cervix is dilated, and the embryo and placenta are removed.

acquired immune deficiency syndrome (AIDS): an infectious disease caused by the human immunodeficiency virus (HIV); attacks and destroys T cells, thus weakening the immune system.

acrosome (ak´-rō-sōm): a vesicle, located at the tip of an animal sperm, that contains enzymes needed to dissolve protective layers around the egg.

amnion (am´-nē-on): one of the embryonic membranes of reptiles, birds, and mammals; encloses a fluid-filled cavity that envelops the embryo.

asexual reproduction: reproduction that does not involve the fusion of haploid sex cells. The parent body may divide and new parts regenerate, or a new, smaller individual may form as an attachment to the parent, to drop off when complete.

birth control pill: a temporary contraceptive method that prevents ovulation by providing a continuing supply of estrogen and progesterone, which in turn suppresses LH release; must be taken daily, normally for 21 days of each menstrual cycle.

blastocyst (blas´-tō-sist): an early stage of human embryonic development, consisting of a hollow ball of cells, enclosing a mass of cells attached to its inner surface, which becomes the embryo.

blastopore: the site at which a blastula indents to form a gastrula.

blastula (blas´-tū-luh): in animals, the embryonic stage attained at the end of cleavage, in which the embryo normally consists of a hollow ball with a wall one or several cell layers thick.

bud: in animals, a small copy of an adult that develops on the body of the parent and eventually breaks off and becomes independent.

budding: asexual reproduction by the growth of a miniature copy, or bud, of the adult animal on the body of the parent. The bud breaks off to begin independent existence.

bulbourethral gland (bul-bō-ū-rē´-thrul): in male mammals, a gland that secretes a basic, mucus-containing fluid that forms part of the semen.

cervical cap: a birth control device consisting of a rubber cap that fits over the cervix, preventing sperm from entering the uterus.

cervix (ser´-viks): a ring of connective tissue at the outer end of the uterus, leading into the vagina.

chlamydia (kla-mid´-ē-uh): a sexually transmitted disease, caused by a bacterium, that causes inflammation of the urethra in males and of the urethra and cervix in females.

chorion: the outermost embryonic membrane in reptiles, birds, and mammals; in birds and reptiles, functions mostly in gas exchange; in mammals, forms most of the embryonic part of the placenta.

chorionic villus (kor-ē-on-ik; pl., **chorionic villi**): in mammalian embryos, a fingerlike projection of the chorion that penetrates the uterine lining and forms the embryonic portion of the placenta.

cleavage: the early cell divisions of embryos, in which little or no growth occurs between divisions; reduces the cell size and distributes gene-regulating substances to the newly formed cell.

clitoris: an external structure of the female reproductive system; composed of erectile tissue; a sensitive point of stimulation during sexual response.

condom: a contraceptive sheath worn over the penis during intercourse to prevent sperm from being deposited in the vagina.

contraception: the prevention of pregnancy.

copulation: reproductive behavior in which the penis of the male is inserted into the body of the female, where it releases sperm.

corona radiata (kuh-rō´-nuh rā-dē-a´-tuh): the layer of cells surrounding an egg after ovulation.

corpus luteum (kor´-pus loo´-tē-um): in the mammalian ovary, a structure that is derived from the follicle after ovulation and that secretes the hormones estrogen and progesterone.

crab lice: an arthropod parasite that can infest humans; can be transmitted by sexual contact.

development: the process by which an organism proceeds from fertilized egg through adulthood to eventual death.

diaphragm (dī´-uh-fram): in a reproductive sense, a contraceptive rubber cap that fits snugly over the cervix, preventing the sperm from entering the uterus and thereby preventing pregnancy.

douching: washing the vagina; after intercourse, an attempt to wash sperm out of the vagina before they enter the uterus; an ineffective contraceptive method.

ectoderm (ek´-tō-derm): the outermost embryonic tissue layer, which gives rise to structures such as hair, the epidermis of the skin, and the nervous system.

egg: the haploid female gamete, normally large and non-motile, containing food reserves for the developing embryo.

embryo: in animals, the stages of development that begin with the fertilization of the egg cell and end with hatching or birth; in mammals in particular, the early stages in which the developing animal does not yet resemble the adult of the species.

embryonic disc: in human embryonic development, the flat, two-layered group of cells that separates the amniotic cavity from the yolk sac.

endoderm (en´-dō-derm): the innermost embryonic tissue layer, which gives rise to structures such as the lining of the digestive and respiratory tracts.

endometrium (en-dō-mē´-trē-um): the nutritive inner lining of the uterus.

epididymis (e-pi-di´-di-mus): a series of tubes that connect with and receive sperm from the seminiferous tubules of the testis.

estrogen: in vertebrates, a female sex hormone, produced by follicle cells of the ovary, that stimulates follicle development, oogenesis, the development of secondary sex characteristics, and growth of the uterine lining.

external fertilization: the union of sperm and egg outside the body of either parent.

fallopian tube: see *oviduct*.

fertilization: the fusion of male and female haploid gametes, forming a zygote.

fetus: the later stages of mammalian embryonic development (after the second month for humans), when the developing animal has come to resemble the adult of the species.

fimbria (fim´-brē-uh; pl., fimbriae): in female mammals, the ciliated, fingerlike projections of the oviduct that sweep the ovulated egg from the ovary into the oviduct.

follicle: in the ovary of female mammals, the oocyte and its surrounding accessory cells.

gastrula (gas´-troo-luh): in animal development, a three-layered embryo with ectoderm, mesoderm, and endoderm cell layers. The endoderm layer normally encloses the primitive gut.

gastrulation (gas-troo-la´-shun): the process whereby a blastula develops into a gastrula, including the formation of endoderm, ectoderm, and mesoderm.

genital herpes: a sexually transmitted disease, caused by a virus, that can cause painful blisters on the genitals and surrounding skin.

gonad: an organ where reproductive cells are formed; in males, the testes, and in females, the ovaries.

gonorrhea (gon-uh-rē´-uh): a sexually transmitted bacterial infection of the reproductive organs; if untreated, can result in sterility.

hermaphrodite (her-maf´-ruh-dīt´): an organism that possesses both male and female sexual organs.

implantation: the process whereby the early embryo embeds itself within the lining of the uterus.

inner cell mass: in human embryonic development, the cluster of cells, on one side of the blastocyst, that will develop into the embryo.

internal fertilization: the union of sperm and egg inside the body of the female.

interstitial cell (in-ter-sti´-shul): in the vertebrate testis, a testosterone-producing cell located between the seminiferous tubules.

intrauterine device (IUD): a small copper or plastic loop, squiggle, or shield that is inserted in the uterus; a contraceptive method that works by irritating the uterine lining so that it cannot receive the embryo.

labium (pl., **labia**): one of a pair of folds of skin of the external structures of the mammalian female reproductive system.

labor: a series of contractions of the uterus that result in birth.

lactation: the secretion of milk from the mammary glands.

mammary gland (mam´-uh-rē): a milk-producing gland used by female mammals to nourish their young.

menstrual cycle: in human females, a complex 28-day cycle during which hormonal interactions among the hypothalamus, pituitary gland, and ovary coordinate ovulation and the preparation of the uterus to receive and nourish the fertilized egg. If pregnancy does not occur, the uterine lining is shed during menstruation.

menstruation: in human females, the monthly discharge of uterine tissue and blood from the uterus.

mesoderm (mēz´-ō-derm): the middle embryonic tissue layer, lying between the endoderm and ectoderm, and normally the last to develop; gives rise to structures such as muscle and skeleton.

morula (mor´-ū-luh): in animals, an embryonic stage during cleavage, when the embryo consists of a solid ball of cells.

myometrium (mī-ō-mē´-trē-um): the muscular outer layer of the uterus.

neural tube: a structure, derived from ectoderm during early embryonic development, that later becomes the brain and spinal cord.

notochord (nōt´-ō-kord): a stiff but somewhat flexible, supportive rod found in all members of the phylum Chordata at some stage of development.

oogenesis: the process by which egg cells are formed.

oogonium (ō-ō-gō´-nē-um; pl., **oogonia**): in female animals, a diploid cell that gives rise to a primary oocyte.

organogenesis (or-gan-ō-jen´-uh-sis): the process by which the layers of the gastrula (endoderm, ectoderm, mesoderm) rearrange into organs.

ovary: in animals, the gonad of females; in flowering plants, a structure at the base of the carpel that contains one or more ovules and develops into the fruit.

oviduct: in mammals, the tube leading from the ovary to the uterus.

ovulation: the release of a secondary oocyte, ready to be fertilized, from the ovary.

penis: an external structure of the male reproductive and urinary systems; serves to deposit sperm into the female reproductive system and delivers urine to the exterior.

placenta (pluh-sen´-tuh): in mammals, a structure formed by a complex interweaving of the uterine lining and the embryonic membranes, especially the chorion; functions in gas, nutrient, and waste exchange between embryonic and maternal circulatory systems and secretes hormones.

polar body: in oogenesis, a small cell, containing a nucleus but virtually no cytoplasm, produced by the first meiotic division of the primary oocyte.

primary oocyte (ō´-ō-sīt): a diploid cell, derived from the oogonium by growth and differentiation that undergoes meiosis, producing the egg.

primary spermatocyte (sper-ma´-tō-sīt): a diploid cell, derived from the spermatogonium by growth and differentiation, that undergoes meiosis, producing four sperm.

primitive streak: in reptiles, birds, and mammals, the region of the ectoderm of the two-layered embryonic disc through which cells migrate, forming mesoderm.

progesterone (prō-ge´-ster-ōn): a hormone, produced by the corpus luteum, that promotes the development of the uterine lining in females.

prostate gland (pros´-tāt): a gland that produces part of the fluid component of semen; prostatic fluid is basic and contains a chemical that activates sperm movement.

rhythm method: a contraceptive method involving abstinence from intercourse during ovulation.

scrotum (skrō´-tum): the pouch of skin containing the testes of male mammals.

secondary oocyte (ō´-o¯-sīt): a large haploid cell derived from the first meiotic division of the diploid primary oocyte.

secondary spermatocyte (sper-ma´-tō-sīt): a large haploid cell derived by meiosis I from the diploid primary spermatocyte.

semen: the sperm-containing fluid produced by the male reproductive tract.

seminal vesicle: in male mammals, a gland that produces a basic, fructose-containing fluid that forms part of the semen.

seminiferous tubule (sem-i-ni´-fer-us): in the vertebrate testis, a series of tubes in which sperm are produced.

Sertoli cell: in the seminiferous tubule, a large cell that regulates spermatogenesis and nourishes the developing sperm.

sexual reproduction: a form of reproduction in which genetic material from two parent organisms is combined in the offspring; normally, two haploid gametes fuse to form a diploid zygote.

sexually transmitted disease (STD): a disease that is passed from person to person by sexual contact.

spawning: a method of external fertilization in which male and female parents shed gametes into the water, and sperm must swim through the water to reach the eggs.

sperm: the haploid male gamete, normally small, motile, and containing little cytoplasm.

spermatid: a haploid cell derived from the secondary spermatocyte by meiosis II; differentiates into the mature sperm.

spermatogenesis: the process by which sperm cells form.

spermatogonium (pl., spermatogonia): a diploid cell, lining the walls of the seminifer-ous tubules, that gives rise to a primary spermatocyte.

spermatophore: in a variation on internal fertilization in some animals, the males package their sperm in a container that can be inserted into the female reproductive tract.

spermicide: a sperm-killing chemical; used for contraceptive purposes.

sterilization: a generally permanent method of contraception in which the pathways through which the sperm (vas deferens) or egg (oviducts) must travel are interrupted; the most common form of contraception.

syphilis (si´-ful-is): a sexually transmitted bacterial infection of the reproductive organs; if untreated, can damage the nervous and circulatory systems.

testis (pl., **testes**): the gonad of male mammals.

testosterone: in vertebrates, a hormone produced by the interstitial cells of the testis; stimulates spermatogenesis and the development of male secondary sex characteristics.

trichomoniasis (trik-ō-mō-nī´-uh-sis): a sexually transmitted disease, caused by the protist *Trichomonas*, that causes inflammation of the mucous membranes than line the urinary tract and genitals.

tubal ligation: a surgical procedure in which a woman's oviducts are cut so that the egg cannot reach the uterus, making her infertile.

urethra: the tube leading from the urinary bladder to the outside of the body; in males, the urethra also receives sperm from the vas deferens and conducts both sperm and urine (at different times) to the tip of the penis.

uterus: in female mammals, the part of the reproductive tract that houses the embryo during pregnancy.

vagina: the passageway leading from the outside of a female mammal's body to the cervix of the uterus.

vas deferens (vaz de´-fer-enz): the tube connecting the epididymis of the testis with the urethra.

vasectomy: a surgical procedure in which a man's vas deferens are cut, preventing sperm from reaching the penis during ejaculation, thereby making him infertile.

withdrawal: the removal of the penis from the vagina just before ejaculation in an attempt to avoid pregnancy; an ineffective contraceptive method.

yolk: protein-rich or lipid-rich substances contained in eggs that provide food for the developing embryo.

zona pellucida (pel-oo´-si-duh): a clear, noncellular layer between the corona radiata and the egg.

zygote (zī´-gōt): in sexual reproduction, a diploid cell (the fertilized egg) formed by the fusion of two haploid gametes.

THINKING THROUGH THE CONCEPTS

True or False: Determine if the statement given is true or false. If it is false, change the underlined word so that the statement reads true.

84. _____   Meiosis occurs in asexual reproduction.

85. _____   Due to the evolution of sexual reproduction, genetic variation occurs, enabling the action of natural selection to take place.

86. _____   In order for external fertilization to be successful, egg and sperm must be released at the same time and in the same area.

87. _____   Copulation occurs during external fertilization.

88. _____ The testes are located in the scrotum, outside the body, which keeps them 4°C <u>warmer</u> than the body's core temperature.

89. _____ Primary spermatocytes are <u>diploid</u>.

90. _____ After <u>meiosis I</u>, spermatids have formed.

91. _____ <u>Oogenesis</u> begins at puberty.

92. _____ In males, the reproductive tract merges with the <u>urinary tract</u>.

93. _____ The egg is, in actuality, a <u>primary</u> oocyte.

94. _____ Human eggs contain <u>a large amount of yolk</u>.

95. _____ Fertilization occurs in the <u>vagina</u>.

96. _____ Every month the uterus prepares for <u>implantation</u>.

97. _____ The presence of a <u>corpus luteum</u> maintains the endometrium.

98. _____ The embryo secretes hormones that <u>maintain the pregnancy</u>.

99. _____ During cleavage, embryonic cells <u>do not grow</u>.

100. _____ <u>Gastrulation</u> involves the migration of cells, forming three layers.

101. _____ Distinct fingers develop because webbing cells receive a "<u>death signal</u>" from other cells.

102. _____ Cell death is <u>preprogrammed</u>.

103. _____ The neural tube is the precursor structure to the <u>digestive tract</u>.

104. _____ The <u>X chromosome</u> determines if the gonads will develop into ovaries or testes.

105. _____ Testosterone and estrogen affect <u>certain areas of the brain</u>.

106. _____ The <u>chorion</u> and the endometrium create the placenta.

107. _____ Many harmful chemicals <u>can pass</u> through the placenta to the fetus.

108. _____ <u>Internal fertilization</u> increases the chances for transmission of disease.

109. _____ The hormone prolactin <u>inhibits</u> milk production by the mammary glands.

110. _____ Contractions resume after the birth of a baby to expel the <u>placenta</u>.

111. _____ Birth control pills prevent <u>sperm from uniting with an egg</u>.

112. _____ Douching after intercourse is an <u>effective</u> method of contraception.

113. _____ Condom use not only prevents pregnancy, but also <u>reduces</u> disease transmission.

114. _____ Successful use of the <u>diaphragm</u> requires diligent observations of changes in body temperature and mucus production from the cervix.

115. _____ <u>Condoms</u> are available for women.

Matching: Birth control methods.

116. _____ IUD

117. _____ condom

118. _____ cervical cap

119. _____ birth control pill

120. _____ tubal ligation

121. _____ spermicide alone

122. _____ douching

123. _____ vasectomy

124. _____ withdrawal

125. _____ rhythm method

Choices:

a. sterilization

b. barrier method

c. prevents ovulation

d. prevents implantation

e. ineffective

Identification: Determine whether the following statements refer to sexually transmitted diseases caused by a **bacterium**, a **virus**, a **protist**, or an **arthropod**?

126. _____ gonorrhea

127. _____ AIDS

128. _____ trichomoniasis

129. _____ genital herpes

130. _____ syphilis

131. _____ crab lice

132. _____ chlamydia

133. _____ genital warts

Matching: Adult tissue types and the embryonic layers from which they developed.

134. _____ epidermis of skin

135. _____ muscle

136. _____ skeleton

137. _____ lining of digestive tract

138. _____ nervous system

139. _____ circulatory system

Choices:

a. endoderm

b. mesoderm

c. ectoderm

Short answer.

140. Trace the path of spermatogenesis from spermatagonium to mature sperm. Include where in the pathway meiosis I and meiosis II occur.

Spermatogonium → _____ → _____ → _____ →

_____ → _____ → _____.

141. What is the purpose of the polar bodies?

_____

_____

_____

_____

142. The cells undergoing cleavage do not increase in size. Why not?

_____

_____

_____

143. Place the following terms in the proper developmental order:
     blastocyst, zygote, fetus, embryo, gastrula, morula

_____ → _____ → _____ →

_____ → _____ → _____

CLUES TO APPLYING THE CONCEPTS

These practice questions are intended to sharpen your ability to apply critical thinking and analysis to the biological concepts covered in this chapter.

144. If a couple is unsuccessful in becoming pregnant, a physician may suggest a sperm count be conducted. Why would the number of sperm produced affect the success of attempts to become pregnant?

_____

_____

_____

_____

_____

_____

_____

145. Explain how the birth process is controlled by a positive feedback mechanism.

_____

_____

_____

_____

_____

_____

_____

_____

_____

_____

ANSWERS TO EXERCISES

1. sexual reproduction
2. asexual reproduction
3. budding
4. eggs
5. sperm
6. hermaphrodites
7. external fertilization
8. internal fertilization
9. copulation
10. spermatophore
11. ovulation
12. gonads
13. testes
14. scrotum
15. seminiferous tubules
16. interstitial cells
17. spermatogonia
18. sertoli cells
19. spermatogenesis
20. acrosome
21. penis
22. epididymis
23. vas deferens
24. urethra
25. semen
26. seminal vesicles

27. prostate gland
28. bulbourethral glands
29. ovaries
30. oogenesis
31. oogonia
32. primary oocytes
33. follicle
34. secondary oocyte
35. polar body
36. estrogen
37. fallopian tube
38. corpus luteum
39. fimbriae
40. zygote
41. uterus
42. endometrium
43. placenta
44. menstruation
45. menstrual cycle
46. myometrium
47. cervix
48. vagina
49. labia
50. clitoris
51. corona radiata
52. zona pellucida

53. Development
54. yolk
55. embryo
56. amnion
57. chorion
58. yolk sac
59. cleavage
60. morula
61. blastula
62. blastopore
63. endoderm
64. ectoderm
65. mesoderm
66. notochord
67. gastrulation
68. gastrula
69. organogenesis
70. blastocyst
71. inner cell mass
72. embryo
73. implantation
74. chorionic villi
75. placenta
76. embryonic disc
77. primitive streak
78. neural tube

79. fetus
80. mammary glands
81. labor
82. contraception
83. abortion
84. false, sexual
85. true
86. true
87. false, internal fertilization
88. false, cooler
89. true
90. false, meiosis II
91. false, spermatogenesis
92. true
93. false, secondary oocyte
94. false, no yolk
95. false, oviduct
    (fallopian tube)
96. true
97. true
98. true

99. true
100. true
101. true
102. true
103. false, brain and
     spinal cord
104. false, Y chromosome
105. true
106. true
107. true
108. true
109. false, stimulates
110. true
111. false, ovulation
112. false, very ineffective
113. true
114. false, rhythm method
115. true
116. d
117. b
118. b

119. c
120. a
121. e
122. e
123. a
124. e
125. e
126. bacterium
127. virus
128. protist
129. virus
130. bacterium
131. arthropod
132. bacterium
133. virus
134. c
135. b
136. b
137. a
138. c
139. b

140. Spermatagonium → primary spermatocyte → meiosis I → secondary spermatocyte → meiosis II → spermatid → sperm

141. Polar bodies serve to hold discarded chromosomes. Meiosis produces haploid cells. Since the egg requires as much of the cytoplasm of the dividing cells as possible and "extra" chromosomes must be discarded to produce the haploid state, polar bodies are the result.

142. The zygote is a relatively large cell, containing a great deal of cytoplasm. In order for body cells to be an appropriate size for efficient functioning, the first divisions during development produce smaller and smaller cells with less cytoplasm.

143. zygote → morula → blastula → gastrula → embryo → fetus

144. The number of sperm produced is important since a large number of sperm are needed to break through the corona radiata and the zona pellucida around the egg. If an insufficient number of sperm is produced to break down the barriers, no sperm can enter the egg to fertilize it.

145. A positive feedback reaction is defined as a situation in which a change initiates events that tend to amplify the original change. Birth of the fetus is initiated by stretching of the uterus and by hormones from both the fetus and the mother, causing labor. The contractions of the uterine smooth muscle are triggered by the stretching caused by the growing fetus. Toward the end of development, the fetus produces steroid hormones that increase estrogen and prostaglandin production by the uterus and placenta. The increased hormone production, in combination with the stretching, increases the contractions of the uterus. The cervix dilates as the baby's head pushes against it. This stretching signals the hypothalamus to release oxytocin. With oxytocin and prostaglandins circulating in the blood, the uterus contracts even more intensely, pushing the baby from the birth canal (the vagina). The changes that occur in the uterus cause further changes to occur until the process reaches a climax, the birth.

Chapter 26: Animal Behavior

OVERVIEW

This chapter considers various aspects of behavior. The authors cover instinctive and learned behaviors, as well as the mechanisms of communication, competitive behaviors within species, cooperative behavior in various animal societies, and the study of human behavior.

1) How Do Innate and Learned Behaviors Differ?

Behavior is any observable muscular response to a stimulus. **Innate** (**instinctive**) behaviors can be performed in reasonably complete form even the first time an animal of the right age and motivational state encounters a particular stimulus. Many simple orientation behaviors are innate. For instance, a newborn human will turn its head toward the side its mouth is touched in order to suckle. Learned behaviors are modified by experience. The capacity to make changes in behavior based on experience is called **learning**. A common form of learning is **habituation** (a decline in response to a repeated stimulus). The ability to habituate prevents an animal from wasting energy and attention on irrelevant stimuli. Humans habituate to many stimuli. In practice, few behaviors are explicitly instinctive or learned but are a mixture. Seemingly innate behavior can be modified by experience. Habituation can fine-tune an organism's innate response to environmental stimuli.

Learning, however, may be governed by innate controls. **Imprinting** is a special form of learning in which learning is rigidly programmed to occur only at a certain critical period of development, the **sensitive period**. For example, mallard ducks learn to follow the animal or object that they most frequently encounter during the period from about 13 to 16 hours after hatching.

Traditionally, innate behaviors were seen as rigidly controlled by genetic factors, and learned behaviors were seen as determined exclusively by an animal's enviroiement. However, all behavior arises out of an interaction between genes and the environment.

2) How Do Animals Communicate?

Communication is the production of a signal by one organism that causes another organism to change its behavior in a way beneficial to one or both. Communication may occur by sound, by movement, or by an emitted chemical. Most communication takes place between members of the same species to resolve conflicts over food, space, or mates with minimal damage.

For animals with well-developed eyes, visual communication is most effective over short distances. Visual signals may be active or passive. When an animal makes a specific movement or posture, it is sending an active visual signal. By contrast, the mere size, shape, or color of an animal serves as a passive visual signal. Active and passive signals can be combined, as is seen in many courtship rituals. Visual signals can be advantageous: They are instantaneous and quiet and therefore unlikely to alert distant predators, and they can be rapidly revised. However, relying on visual signals can also be disadvantageous. Visual signals are ineffective in darkness or dense vegetation and are limited to close distances.

Communication by sound is effective over longer distances. Sound can be transmitted instantaneously through darkness, dense forests, and water. Sound can travel over long distances and can be quickly varied to convey rapidly changing messages.

Chemical messages persist longer but are hard to vary. **Pheromones** are chemical substances produced by an individual that influence the behavior of others of its species. Chemicals may carry messages over long distances for long periods of time, take very little energy to produce, and may not be detected by other species. Fewer messages are communicated with chemicals than with sight or sound, and pheromone signals lack the diversity and gradation of auditory or visual signals. Pheromones act in two ways. Some pheromones cause an immediate, observable behavior in the animal that detects them; others stimulate a physiological change in the animal that detects them. This change is usually a change in its reproductive state. For example, queen bees produce a primer pheromone called **queen substance**, which is eaten by hivemates and prevents other females from becoming sexually mature.

Communication by touch helps establish social bonds among group members. Touch can also influence human well-being.

3) How Do Animals Interact?

Sociality is a widespread feature of animal life. Competition for resources underlies many forms of social interaction. Aggressive behavior helps secure resources such as food, space, or mates. **Aggression** is antagonistic but usually harmless behavior, typically involving symbolic displays or rituals between members of the same species.   During aggressive displays, animals may exhibit weapons such as claws or fangs and often behave in ways that make them appear larger; they may stand upright, fluff their feathers or fur, and extend their ears or fins, and they may emit intimidating sounds. Actual fighting tends to be a last resort.

Dominance hierarchies reduce aggressive interactions. In a dominance hierarchy, each animal establishes a rank that determines its access to resources. Although aggressive encounters occur frequently while the hierarchy is being established, disputes are minimized after each animal learns its place.

Animals may defend territories that contain resources. **Territoriality** is the defense of an area where important resources, such as places to mate and raise young, feed, or store food, are located. Territorial behavior is most commonly seen in adult males. Territories are normally defended against members of the same species who compete most directly for the resources being protected. Once a territory is established through aggressive interaction, relative peace prevails as boundaries are recognized and respected ("good fences make good neighbors"). For males of many species, successful territorial defense has a direct impact on reproductive success. Territories are advertised through sight, sound, and smell.

Sexual reproduction commonly involves social interactions between mates called courtship behavior. Before mating can occur, animals must identify one another as belonging to the same species, as members of the opposite sex, and as being sexually receptive. Vocal and visual signals encode sex, species, and individual quality. The intertwined functions of sex recognition and species recognition, advertisement of individual quality, and synchronization of reproductive behavior commonly require a complex series of signals, both active and passive, by both sexes. Chemical signals (pheromones) bring mates together.

Social behavior within animal societies requires cooperative interactions. Group living has both disadvantages and advantages. Some disadvantages are (1) increased competition for limited resources, (2) increased risk of infection, (3) increased risk that offspring will be killed, and (4) increased risk of being detected by predators. The benefits include (1) increased protection from predators; (2) increased hunting efficiency; (3) advantages from division of labor; (4) conservation of energy; and (5) an increased likelihood of finding mates. If a species has evolved social behavior, the "pros" must outweigh the "cons". Some types of animals cooperate on the basis of changing needs; for instance, coyotes are solitary when food is abundant, but they hunt in packs when food is scarce.

Some cooperative societies are based on behavior that seems to sacrifice the individual for the good of the group; for example, worker ants die in defense of their nest. These behaviors characterize **altruism**, behavior that decreases the reproductive success of one individual to the benefit of another. Although altruism seem inconsistent with the cocept of "survival of the fittest", the individual is actually promoting the survival of some of its own genes by maximizing the survival of its close relatives. This phenomenon is called **kin selection**. Kin selection is exhibited in the extreme by the evolution of the complex societies of honeybees and naked mole rats.

The most difficult of all animal societies to explain are those of the bees, ants, and termites. In these societies, most individuals never breed but labor slavishly to feed and protect the offspring of a different individual. Honeybees form complex insect societies, with one reproductive queen, male drones, and sterile female workers who bring food to other bees, construct and clean the hive, and forage for pollen and nectar, communicating the location of these resources to other workers by means of the **waggle dance**. Pheromones play a major role in regulating the lives of social insects.

With the exception of human society, vertebrate societies are not as complex as insect societies. Bullhead catfish illustrate a simple vertebrate society based almost entirely on pheromones. Naked mole rats form a complex vertebrate society not unlike that of an ant or termite colony.

Many animals have been observed at play which has fascinated and puzzled many researchers. The elements of play are: (1) actions seem to lack any clear immediate function, (2) actions are abandoned in favor of feeding, courtship, or escapeing from danger, (3) actions are seen more frequently in young than in adults, (4) actions typically involve movements borrowed from other behaviors such as stalking, (5) actions use a great deal of energy, and (6) actions are potentially dangerous. Play activities may enable young animals to practice behaviors they will need as adults.

4) Can Biology Explain Human Behavior?

Some scientists hypothesize that because humans are animals whose behaviors have an evolutionary history, the techniques of **ethology** (the study of behavior) can be used to understand human behavior. But human ethologists cannot experiment with people as animal ethologists do with animals. Instead, researchers have tried to determine genetic components of human behavior.

The behavior of newborns is thought to have a large innate component. The rhythmic movement of a baby's head searching for its mother's breast is a fixed action pattern. Sucking, smiling, walking movements when the body is supported, and grasping with the hands and feet, are also innate actions.

Researchers have tried to identify innate behaviors by studying diverse human cultures, including those that are more isolated. Simple behaviors, such as the facial expressions for pleasure and rage and the "eye flash" greeting, are universal and therefore may be innate. In addition, people may respond to pheromones. For example, studies indicate that pheromones may synchronize the menstrual cycles among female roommates and close friends.

Genetic components of behavior have been revealed through comparisons of identical and fraternal twins. When twins are reared together, environmental influences on behavior are very similar for each member of the pair, so behavioral differences between twins must have a large genetic component. If a particular behavior is heavily influenced by genetic factors, we would expect to find similar expression of that behavior in identical twins but not in fraternal twins. In fact, in tests that measure many aspects of personality, identical twins are about twice as similar in personality as are fraternal twins. Such studies have shown significant genetic components for traits such as activity level, alcoholism, anxiety, sociability, intelligence, dominance, and even political attitudes. The field of human behavioral genetics is controversial, because it challenges the long-held belief that environment is the most important determinant of human behavior.

KEY TERMS AND CONCEPTS

Fill-In: From the following list of terms, fill in the blanks below.

altruism   dominance hierarchy   imprinting   pheromone
behavior   ethology   innate   sensitive period
communication   habituation   learning   territoriality

(1)_____ is any observable muscular response to external or internal stimuli.

(2)_____ behaviors can be performed in reasonably complete form even the first time an animal of the right age and motivational state encounters a particular stimulus.

The ability to make changes in behavior based on experience is called (3)_____.

(4)_____ is a decline in response to a repeated stimulus.

(5)_____ is a special form of learning that is rigidly programmed to occur only at a certain critical period of development, called the (6)_____.

(7)_____ is the production of a sound, movement, or chemical by one organism that causes another organism to change its behavior.

A(n) (8)_____ is a chemical substance produced by an individual that influences the behavior of others of its species.

In a(n) (9)_____, each animal establishes a rank that determines its access to resources while reducing aggressive interactions.

(10)_____is the defense of an area where important resources, such as places to mate and raise young, feed, or store food, are located.

(11)_____ is behavior that decreases the reproductive success of one individual to the benefit of another.

(12)_____ is the study of behavior.

Key Terms and Definitions

aggression: antagonistic behavior, normally among members of the same species, often resulting from competition for resources.

altruism: a type of behavior that may decrease the reproductive success of the individual performing it but benefits that of other individuals.

behavior: any observable response to external or internal stimuli.

communication: the act of producing a signal that causes another animal, normally of the same species, to change its behavior in a way that is beneficial to one or both participants.

dominance hierarchy: a social arrangement in which a group of animals, usually through aggressive interactions, establishes a rank for some or all of the group members that determines access to resources.

ethology (ē-thol´-ō-jē): the study of animal behavior in natural or near-natural conditions.

habituation: simple learning characterized by a decline in response to a harmless, repeated stimulus.

imprinting: the process by which an animal forms an association with another animal or object in the environment during a sensitive period of development.

inclusive fitness: the reproductive success of all organisms that bear a given allele, normally expressed in relation to the average reproductive success of all individuals in the same population; compare with *fitness*.

innate (in-āt´): inborn; instinctive; determined by the genetic makeup of the individual.

instinctive: innate; inborn; determined by the genetic makeup of the individual.

kin selection: a type of natural selection that favors a certain allele because it increases the survival or reproductive success of relatives that bear the same allele.

learning: an adaptive change in behavior as a result of experience.

pheromone (fer´-uh-mōn): a chemical produced by an organism that alters the behavior or physiological state of another member of the same species.

queen substance: a chemical, produced by a queen bee, that can act as both a primer and a releaser pheromone.

sensitive period: the particular stage in an animal's life during which it imprints.

territoriality: the defense of an area in which important resources are located.

waggle dance: a symbolic form of communication used by honeybee foragers to communicate the location of a food source to their hivemates.

THINKING THROUGH THE CONCEPTS

True or False: Determine if the statement given is true or false. If it is false, change the <u>underlined</u> word(s) so that the statement reads true.

13. _____   Behavior has some <u>genetic</u> basis.

14. _____   Flexible behaviors are <u>learned</u>.

15. _____   The <u>more complex</u> the animal, the more it relies on instinct.

16. _____   In insect societies, almost all behavior is regulated by <u>pheromones</u>.

17. _____   <u>Habituation</u> is characterized by a crucial time during which it can become part of an animal's behavior.

18. _____   If an animal assumes a particular posture to communicate with another animal, this behavior is considered <u>active</u>.

19. _____   Sound and visual signals <u>cannot</u> be varied.

20. _____   Competition is greatest between members of <u>different</u> species.

21. _____   Most aggressive encounters between members of the same species are <u>real</u>.

22. _____   Territories are more commonly laid out by <u>females</u>.

23. _____   Territories are usually defended against invasion by members of <u>the same</u> species.

24. _____   Established territories promote <u>conflict</u> among members of the same species.

25. _____   The majority of encounters between <u>social</u> animals are competitive and aggressive.

26. _____   Suckling by babies is an <u>instinctive</u> behavior.

27. _____   Menstrual cycles of roommates are usually <u>unsynchronized</u>.

28. _____   Women isolated from men tend to have <u>longer</u> menstrual cycles.

Identification: Determine whether the following statements refer to **habituation**, or **imprinting**.

29. _____ decline in response to a harmless, repeated stimulus

30. _____ a strong association learned during a sensitive period in life

31. _____ primarily instinctive

32. _____ humans ignoring night sounds while asleep

33. _____ the "following response" of young birds

34. _____ not easily altered by later experiences

35. _____ young birds ignoring a goose flying overhead

Matching: Modes of communication. Some questions may have more than one correct answer.

36. _____ dog urine

37. _____ easily alerts predators

38. _____ uses pheromones

39. _____ may be active or passive

40. _____ persists after the animal has departed

41. _____ can establish social bonds among group members

42. _____ limited to close-range communications

43. _____ ignored by other species

44. _____ grooming in primates

Choices:

a. visual

b. sound

c. chemical

d. touch

Matching: Mechanisms of competition.

45. _____ includes behavior that makes the animal appear larger

46. _____ defense of an area where important resources are located

47. _____ alpha members of a wolf pack

48. _____ establishing a rank that determines social status

49. _____ harmless symbolic displays or rituals for resolving conflicts without fighting

50. _____ adult males defend an area against members of the same species

51. _____ scent-marking boundaries with pheromones

Choices:

a. aggression

b. dominance hierarchies

c. territoriality

d. all of these

52. _____ exhibiting fangs, claws, or teeth

53. _____ pecking orders in chickens

54. _____ "good fences make good neighbors"

55. _____ the sheep with the biggest horns gets most access to necessary resources

Multiple Choice: Pick the most correct choice for each question.

56. The basis of all social behavior is
    a. communication
    b. reproduction
    c. obtaining food
    d. competition
    e. aggression

57. Chemicals produced by an individual that influence the behavior of members of the same species are called
    a. hormones
    b. enzymes
    c. stimuli
    d. pheromones

58. The dominance hierarchy within a group of animals functions to
    a. eliminate competition
    b. limit population numbers
    c. minimize aggression
    d. increase competition
    e. ensure reproduction

59. An adaptive change in behavior as a result of experience is called
    a. instinct
    b. learning
    c. an innate behavior
    d. kin selection

Short Answer.

60. List three advantages and three disadvantages of visual communication.

Advantages:

_____

_____

_____

Disadvantages:

_____

_____

_____

61. List two advantages of sound communication over visual communication.

_____

_____

CLUES TO APPLYING THE CONCEPTS

This practice question is intended to sharpen your ability to apply critical thinking and analysis to biological concepts covered in this chapter.

62. How can studies of twins help human ethologists determine the genetic components of human behavior? Specifically, how would instances of identical twins separated at birth aid in the study?

_____

_____

_____

_____

_____

_____

_____

_____

_____

ANSWERS TO EXERCISES

1. behavior	21. false, symbolic	41. d
2. innate	22. false, males	42. a, d
3. learning	23. true	43. c
4. habituation	24. false, peace	44. d
5. imprinting	25. false, solitary	45. a
6. sensitive period	26. true	46. c
7. communication	27. false, synchronized	47. d
8. pheromone	28. true	48. b
9. dominance hierarchy	29. habituation	49. a
10. territoriality	30. imprinting	50. c
11. altruism	31. imprinting	51. c
12. ethology	32. habituation	52. a
13. true	33. imprinting	53. b
14. true	34. imprinting	54. c
15. false, simpler	35. habituation	55. b
16. true	36. c	56. a
17. false, imprinting	37. b	57. d
18. true	38. c	58. c
19. false, can	39. a	59. b
20. false, the same	40. c	

60. Advantages: instantaneous, rapidly revised, quiet, and unlikely to attract predators. Disadvantages: ineffective in darkness, ineffective in dense vegetation, limited to close-range communication, may not be noticed by distracted animals.

61. Sound communication is effective in darkness and through dense forests, in water, and over long distances.

62. Genetic components of behavior have been revealed through comparisons of identical and fraternal twins. When twins are reared together, environmental influences on behavior are very similar for each member of the pair, so behavioral differences between twins must have a large genetic component. If a particular behavior is controlled by genetic factors, we would expect to find that similsr expression of behavior in identical twins but not in fraternal twins. In fact, in tests that measure many aspects of personality, identical twins are about twice as similar in personality as are fraternal twins. Such studies have shown a significant genetic component for traits such as activity level, alcoholism, sociability, intelligence, anxiety, dominance, and even political attitudes. Through anecdotal observations reunited twins separated at birth have been found to be as similar in personality as twins raised together. This finding indicates that environment had little to do with development of their personalities.

Chapter 27: Population Growth and Regulation

OVERVIEW

This chapter examines the factors that control the size and rate of growth of populations. It covers how the environment plays a role in controlling populations and how individual interactions among members of the same species, as well as among members of different species, influence population size. How a population grows may depend on how its members are distributed within a given area. These factors are applied to the human population as well.

Ecology is the study of living things and their interactions with their living (biotic) and non living (abiotic) environment (their **ecosystem**). In turn, ecosystems include **communities** (all the interacting populations).

1) How Do Populations Grow?

The members of a species that live in an area and can interbreeding define a **population**. The size of the population changes depending on the number of births and deaths, the number leaving (**emigration**), and the number coming in (**immigration**). If life in the ecosystem is ideal, the population will increase according to its **biotic potential**, its maximum rate. However, the environment cannot sustain the population at this rate because resources, such as food and space, are limited and organisms interact with one another. Therefore, the population's size is limited according to **environmental resistance**.

The rate at which a population size changes, the **growth rate**, is determined by the following equation: $b - d = r$ (number of births − number of deaths = growth rate). However, if an ecologist wants to know the *number of individuals* that are new to a population within a certain time period, then the rate of growth (r) is multiplied by the number of members in the population at the beginning of the time period (N): rN = population growth within a given time period. If a population is growing at an ever-accelerating rate, the population is experiencing **exponential growth**. Exponential growth is graphed as a **J-curve**.

2) How Is Population Growth Regulated?

Exponetial growth cannot continue indefinately. Populations that grow exponentially may suddenly undergo substantial deaths due to disease, to seasonal changes, or to decreased resource availability. Some populations experience exponential growth and massive die-offs on a cyclical basis; such cycles are referred to as **boom-and-bust cycles**. The size of most populations, however, is controlled by the ecosystem. Any given area can support only a certain population size indefinitely. This size is the **carrying capacity** of the ecosystem. Population numbers that have reached carrying capacity are relatively stable and can be graphed as an **S-curve**.

Population numbers are affected by the course of nature in ways that may or may not be due to the size of the population. Populations that get too crowded or dense may be adversely affected by **density-dependent** factors such as predation, parasitism, disease, or intense competition. On the other hand, **density-independent** factors, such as weather, fire events, or human activities, impact a population regardless of its size.

When an animal kills and eats another organism, **predation** has occurred. The animal doing the killing and eating is the **predator** and the organism eaten is the **prey**. Predation is an important mechanism in natural population control. Predation controls the size not only of prey populations, but also of the predator populations. As predators reduce the number of prey available, they are, in effect, reducing their own food resource. The result is a reduction in the predator population. When predator numbers are reduced, the prey population increases again. Thus, predator populations and prey populations undergo **population cycles**.

When an animal feeds on another organism without killing it, **parasitism** is occurring. The animal feeding is a **parasite**, and the organism on which it is feeding is its **host**.

When population numbers increase, **competition** for the resources on which the organisms depend becomes more intense. Competition among members of different species is **interspecific competition**. Competition among members of the same species is **intraspecific competition** and is more intense than interspecific competition.

3) How Are Populations Distributed?

If members of a population cluster together in herds, packs, or flocks, or around an area of a plentiful resource, these organisms have a **clumped distribution** pattern. Other organisms defend territories that are relatively evenly spaced and thus these organisms have a **uniform distribution** pattern within an area. Rarely, when resources are equally available and plentiful throughout the area, organisms have a **random distribution** throughout the ecosystem.

4) How Is The Human Population Changing?

The human population grew slowly for over a million years. During that time, fire was discovered, tools and weapons were fashioned, shelters were built, and clothing was made to protect individuals. Each of these technological advances led to a cultural revolution as the populations adapted to these innovations. The domestication of crops and animals lead to an agricultural revolution, providing a more dependable food supply. Advances in medicine and health care dramatically reduced the human death rate. This industrial-medical revolution led to an increase in population. In developed countries, the industrial-medical revolution also reduced birth rates, stabilizing their population growth. In developing countries, however, reduced birth rates have not occurred, primarily because of social traditions and a lack of access to education and contraceptives.

The differences in population growth between developing and developed countries can be illustrated using **age-structure** diagrams. These diagrams graph the distribution of males and females in each age group. If a large portion of the population falls below the reproductive years, even if people entering their reproductive years have only the number of children needed to replace themselves [**replacement level fertility (RLF)**], the population will continue to grow *due to the number* of people entering their reproductive years. The United States is experiencing rapid growth because the "baby boom" generation has reached their reproductive years. Continued immigration to the United States also contributes to its population growth.

KEY TERMS AND CONCEPTS

Fill-In: From the following list of terms, fill in the blanks in the blanks below.

age structure	emigration	parasite
agricultural revolution	environmental resistance	parasitism
biotic potential	exponential	population
boom-and-bust cycle	growth rate	population cycle
carrying capacity	host	predation
clumped distribution	immigration	predator
competition	industrial-medical revolution	randomly distributed
cultural revolution	interspecific competition	replacement-level fertility
density-dependent	intraspecific competition	S-curves
density-independent	J-curve	uniformly distributed

All the potentially interbreeding members of a species within an ecosystem is referred to as a
(1)_____.

The size of a population changes as new members are born, move into the area (called
(2)_____), leave the area (called (3)_____), or die.
The actual rate at which a population changes in size depends on the (4)_____,
which is the maximum rate a population could increase with unlimited resources, and the
(5)_____, which includes the limited availability of resources such as food,
water, space, etc. However, to measure the change in population size, the number of deaths per person
is subtracted from the number of births per person that occur in a given time period. This is the
(6)_____ or (*r*).

When a population's size increases at a continuously accelerating rate, the population is experiencing
(7)_____ growth; an increasing number of individuals is added to the
population with each generation. When the population numbers are graphed for this type of growth, a
J-shaped curve. or a(n) (8)_____, is the result.

When resources for a species are temporarily abundant, its population may grow exponentially until it is
limited by an environmental factor (temperature, for example). This pattern of rapid growth followed by
a massive die-off is called a(n) (9)_____.

In populations where birth rates equal death rates, the population stabilizes. Such populations exhibit
S-shaped curves, or (10)_____, when population growth rates are graphed.
Populations often stabilize when their numbers reach the maximum size that the ecosystem can support
indefinitely, the (11)_____ of the ecosystem.

Human activities and environmental factors such as weather events or forest fires may limit population
size regardless of its density. These are examples of (12)_____ factors. In
contrast, parasites, disease, competition for limited resources, and predation are examples of
(13)_____ factors, which affect population size more intensely as
population density increases.

The act of an animal capturing, killing, and eating other organisms is called
(14)_____. This act naturally helps control population size. The animal that
captures, kills, and eats the organism (the prey) is referred to as the (15)_____.
As prey population numbers increase, predator population numbers increase. Then, as more predators
capture and eat more prey, the prey numbers decline, causing the predator population numbers to
decrease as well. This effect, the (16)_____, is always out of phase.

A special type of predation in which an organism feeds within or on a larger organism but does not
kill it outright, is called (17)_____. The organism feeding is the
(18)_____, and the organism that is being fed on is the (19)_____.

When resources in an area are limited, the organisms using the resources are in (20)_____
for the resources. If the organisms vying for the resources belong to different species, then
(21)_____ is occurring. If the organisms vying for the resources belong to
the same species, then (22)_____ is occurring; its effect is more intense.

The populations of species in any given area may be distributed in specific patterns. If the members of a
population live in groups such as herds or flocks or along resource lines, the population has a
(23)_____. If the organisms live a rather consistent distance from each other,
they are (24)_____. Rarely, if the members of the population do not form
social groups or do not use territorial spacing, their dispersal may not have any observable pattern, that is
they are (25)_____.

Humans have developed ways to increase the carrying capacity of the ecosystem of which they are a
part. The use of fire and tools and the development of protective shelter and clothing, resulted in a(n)
(26)_____, allowing previously uninhabitable areas to be habitable. As
farming and animal husbandry evolved, a dependable food supply came about with a(n)
(27)_____. The human population grew slowly until advances were made
that reduced the number of deaths. This (28)_____ began during the
mid-eighteenth century and continues today.

A diagram of a population representing the number of individuals in specific age categories shows the
(29)_____ of the population.

When individuals in a population of reproductive age bear only the number of children needed to replace
themselves, (30)_____ is occurring.

Key Terms and Definitions

age structure: the distribution of males and females in a population according to age groups.

biotic potential: the maximum rate at which a population could increase, assuming ideal conditions that allow a maximum birth rate and minimum death rate.

boom-and-bust cycle: a population cycle characterized by rapid exponential growth followed by a sudden massive die-off, seen in seasonal species and in some populations of small rodents, such as lemmings.

carrying capacity: the maximum population size that an ecosystem can support indefinitely; determined primarily by the availability of space, nutrients, water, and light.

clumped distribution: the distribution characteristic of populations in which individuals are clustered into groups; may be social or based on the need for a localized resource.

community: all the interacting populations within an ecosystem.

competition: interaction among individuals who attempt to utilize a resource (for example, food or space) that is limited relative to the demand for it.

density-dependent: referring to any factor, such as predation, that limits population size more effectively as the population density increases.

density-independent: referring to any factor, such as freezing weather, that limits a population's size and growth regardless of its density.

ecology (ē-kol´-uh-jē): the study of the interrelationships of organisms with each other and with their nonliving environment.

ecosystem (ē´kō-sis-tem): all the organisms and their nonliving environment within a defined area.

emigration (em-uh-grā´shun): migration of individuals out of an area.

environmental resistance: any factor that tends to counteract biotic potential, limiting population size.

exponential growth: a continuously accelerating increase in population size.

growth rate: a measure of the change in population size per individual per unit of time.

host: the prey organism on or in which a parasite lives; is harmed by the relationship.

immigration (im-uh-grā´-shun): migration of individuals into an area.

interspecific competition: competition among individuals of different species.

intraspecific competition: competition among individuals of the same species.

J-curve: the J-shaped growth curve of an exponentially growing population in which increasing numbers of individuals join the population during each succeeding time period.

parasite (par´-uh-sīt): an organism that lives in or on a larger prey organism, called a host, weakening it.

parasitism: a symbiotic relationship in which one organism (commonly smaller and more numerous than its host) benefits by feeding on the other, which is normally harmed but not immediately killed.

population: all the members of a particular species within an ecosystem, found in the same time and place and actually or potentially interbreeding.

population cycle: out-of-phase cyclical patterns of predator and prey populations.

predation (pre-dā´-shun): the act of killing and eating another living organism.

predator: an organism that kills and eats other organisms.

prey: organisms that are killed and eaten by another organism.

random distribution: distribution characteristic of populations in which the probability of finding an individual is equal in all parts of an area.

replacement-level fertility (RLF): the average birth rate at which a reproducing population exactly replaces itself during its lifetime.

S-curve: the S-shaped growth curve that describes a population of long-lived organisms introduced into a new area; consists of an initial period of exponential growth, followed by decreasing growth rate, and, finally, relative stability around a growth rate of zero.

uniform distribution: the distribution characteristic of a population with a relatively regular spacing of individuals, commonly as a result of territorial behavior.

THINKING THROUGH THE CONCEPTS

True or False: Determine if the statement given is true or false. If it is false change the <u>underlined</u> word so that the statement reads true.

31. _____ A <u>population</u> is made up of all the members of a species in a certain area that has the potential to interbreed.

32. _____ The availability of food and space serve to limit the <u>biotic potential</u> of a population.

33. _____ In nature, exponential growth occurs for <u>prolonged</u> periods of time.

34. _____ <u>Carrying capacity</u> of an ecosystem is determined in part by renewable resources.

35. _____   The effect of <u>density-dependent</u> factors is unaffected by population size.

36. _____   As a population increases and becomes more dense, the result is <u>less</u> die-off from disease and parasites.

37. _____   Predators not only exert an influence on the size of their prey populations, but <u>prey populations also affect predator population size</u>.

38. _____   Humans are likely to cause extinctions because impacts such as pollution and habitat alter-ation <u>are not density-dependent</u>.

39. _____   Parasites living in their host <u>quickly</u> weaken and kill their host.

40. _____   Intraspecific competition is <u>less intense</u> then interspecific competition.

41. _____   Populations may exhibit a <u>clumping pattern</u> due to localized resources.

42. _____   Humans have found ways to overcome <u>environmental resistance</u>.

43. _____   In age structure diagrams, if the number of children (ages 0–14) exceeds the number of reproducing individuals (ages 15–45), the population is <u>decreasing</u>.

44. _____   Delayed childbearing <u>slows</u> population growth.

45. _____   The U.S. population is currently growing <u>exponentially</u>.

Matching: Population growth.

46. _____   illustrates exponential growth   Choices:

47. _____   illustrates a stable population   a.   age structure diagram

48. _____ $r = b - d$ b.   population growth

49. _____ rN c.   S-curve

50. _____   illustrates distribution of males and females   d.   growth rate

                                                                      e.   J-curve

Short answer:

51. Population change = (_____ – _____) + (_____ – _____)

52. Identify the 5 factors influencing the biotic potential of a species.

_____

_____

_____

53. Briefly discuss three factors that can lead to boom-and-bust cycles. Include examples of the types of organisms that are susceptible to these cycles.

_____

_____

_____

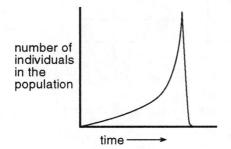

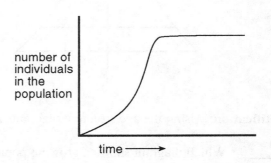

Identification: Using the diagram above determine if the following are characteristics of a **J-shaped population curve**, an **S-shaped population curve**, or **both**. (Write **J**, **S**, or **b** on the line provided)

54. _____   initial population growth is small

55. _____   population growth accelerates with time

56. _____   population growth accelerates with time, then levels off

57. _____   population grows indefinitely, exceeding carrying capacity

58. _____   population is limited at carrying capacity

59. _____   population size is probably limited by environmental factors

60. _____   density-dependent factors influence population size

61. _____   population may suffer a sudden crash

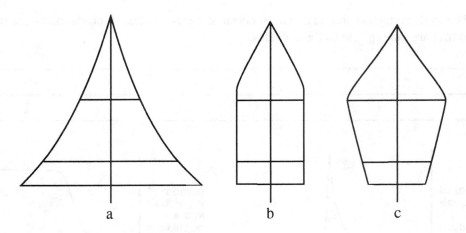

a   b   c

Identification: Using the age structure diagrams **a**, **b**, and **c**, above answer the following.

62. _____   Which diagram shows a growing population?

63. _____   Which diagram shows a shrinking population?

64. _____   Which diagram shows a stable population?

65. _____   Which diagram would represent the population of a developing country?

66. _____   Which diagram would represent the population of a country with replacement level fertility?

67. _____   Which diagram would represent the population of a country with fewer children than reproducing adults?

CLUES TO APPLYING THE CONCEPTS

This practice question is intended to sharpen your ability to apply critical thinking and analysis to the biological concepts covered in this chapter.

68. Explain why introduced species tend to display exponential growth. Discuss the subsequent effects on the ecosystem.

_____

_____

_____

_____

_____

_____

ANSWERS TO EXERCISES

1. population
2. immigration
3. emigration
4. biotic potential
5. environmental resistance
6. growth rate
7. exponential
8. J-curve
9. boom-and-bust cycle
10. S-curves
11. carrying capacity
12. density-independent
13. density-dependent
14. predation
15. predator
16. population cycle
17. parasitism

18. parasite
19. host
20. competition
21. interspecific competition
22. intraspecific competition
23. clumped distribution
24. uniformly distributed
25. randomly distributed
26. cultural revolution
27. agricultural revolution
28. industrial-medical revolution
29. age structure
30. replacement-level fertility
31. true
32. true
33. false, short
34. true

35. false, density-independent
36. false, more
37. true
38. true
39. false, slowly
40. false, more intense
41. true
42. true
43. false, increasing
44. true
45. true
46. e
47. c
48. d
49. b
50. a

51. Population change = (births – deaths) + (immigrants – emigrants).

52. (1) Age at which the organism first reproduces, (2) frequency with which reproduction occurs, (3) average number of offspring produced each time, (4) length of reproductive life span of an organism, and (5) death rate of individuals under ideal conditions.

53. Short-lived, rapidly reproducing organisms such as bacteria, algae, and insects have population cycles that are often dependent on amount of rainfall (flood or drought), temperature (intense heat or killing frost), or nutrient availability.

54. b
55. b
56. S
57. J
58. S

59. b
60. S
61. J
62. a
63. c

64. b
65. a
66. b
67. c

68. Introduced species often invade new habitats where conditions are favorable, food or nutrients are plentiful, and competition is scarce. Predators, parasites, or disease have little or no effect on the population of the introduced species. This leads to exponential growth of the introduced species, which may seriously damage the ecosystem by displacing, outcompeting, or preying on native species.

Chapter 28: Community Interactions

OVERVIEW

This chapter looks at the how organisms interact with members of their own species, as well as with members of different species. These interactions include mechanisms that have evolved to deal with competition for limited resources, predator-prey relationships, and symbiotic relationships. The species that are present in a community depends on the ecosystem. This chapter also deals with how an ecosytem changes over time (succession).

1) Why Are Community Interactions Important?

The interactions among populations within a **community** maintain a balance between available resources (food, water, shelter) and the number of individuals using them. As the interactions among the populations limit population size, they also lead to changes in characteristics and behaviors, increasing the fitness of the total population (evolution). When changes in one species results in adaptive changes in an interacting species, **coevolution** has occurred.

2) What Are the Effects of Competition Among Species?

Competition among species, or **interspecific competition**, has such a strong effect on the species involved that each evolves ways to reduce any overlap in needs. In other words, each species specializes within the community, developing its own well-defined, **ecological niche**, and thus **partitioning resources**. If one of the competing species is removed from the community, the other species may expand its niche because the competition pressure has been reduced.

Gause showed this **competitive exclusion principle** in his experiments with two species of *Paramecium*. Ecologist J. Connell used the barnacles *Chthamalus* and *Balanus* to study the effects of competition on population size and distribution. These species of barnacles live in the **intertidal zone**, a harsh marine environment that is either submerged by high tides or exposed by low tides. The larger *Balanus* outcompetes *Chthamalus* on the lower shore. But since *Chthamalus* tolerates drier conditions, it has the competitive advantage over *Balanus* on the upper shore.

3) What Are the Results of Interactions Between Predators and Their Prey?

Predation interactions have intense effects on the species involved. Predators have evolved ways to capture their prey; the prey have evolved mechanisms to elude their predators. This coevolution has resulted in some very complex physical characteristics and behaviors. Bats and their moth prey have developed complex "cat and mouse" behaviors. Other species **camouflage** themselves to avoid predators or detection by prey. In contrast to camouflaged species, some species stand out with bright coloration. These species advertise their presence, safe in the knowledge that they will be left alone. Their bright colors (or **warning coloration**) warn potential predators that they are poisonous or otherwise distasteful and are to be avoided.

Species with common characteristics may share warning patterns; for example, stinging insects tend to be bright yellow with black stripes, and poisonous frogs from the tropics display very colorful skin pigments. Some harmless species have evolved to **mimic** their poisonous relatives, thus taking advantage of the effect of the warning pattern on potential predators. Some stingless wasps, for example, are bright yellow with black stripes. Devious predators exists as well: In **aggressive mimicry** species that have evolved to resemble harmless species are just waiting to take a bite out of an unsuspecting prey.

Predators, however, may be caught off guard. Some prey make use of color patterns that mimic a larger organism. These species use their **startle coloration** to scare the predator and make a safe getaway. Some prey species have the ultimate defense: chemical warfare. Coevolution, however, has also led to a few predator species that are not harmed by the chemicals produced and may even use them as their own defense mechanism.

4) What Is Symbiosis?

Within a community, interacting with other species is unavoidable; however, some species have such close interactions that they have developed **symbiotic** relationships. When one species of the relationship benefits and the other is unaffected, the relationship is **commensalism**. If one species benefits and the other is harmed, the relationship is **parasitism**. If both species benefit, the relationship is **mutualism**.

5) How Do Keystone Species Influence Community Structure?

The influence of species on community structure is not necessarily equal. A species whose role is out of proportion to its population size is a **keystone species** in the community. Often, a keystone species cannot be identified until it has been removed from the community. At this point it may be too late to reduce the impact its absence will have on the community.

6) Succession: How Does a Community Change over Time?

The interactions among members of a community lead to structural changes within that community which are identified as stages in **succession** of the community. **Primary succession** begins with **pioneer** species such as lichens and mosses establishing a hold on bare rock. As soil slowly forms, additional species move into the young community in a recognizable pattern. **Secondary succession** occurs after an established community has been disturbed, perhaps by fire, windstorm, or farming.

If left undisturbed, succession will continue to a stable endpoint, the **climax**, determined in large part by the geography and climate of the area. If a community is regularly disturbed, it will be maintained at a succession point below the climax, a **subclimax**. Climax communities that cover broad geographical regions are **biomes**. Biomes are distinguished by specific climatic conditions and characterized by specific plant communities.

294 Chapter 28: Community Interactions

KEY TERMS AND CONCEPTS

Fill-In: From the following list of terms, fill in the blanks below.

aggressive mimicry
biomes
camouflaged
climax community
coevolution
commensalism
community
competitive exclusion principle
ecological niche

exotic
interspecific competition
intertidal zone
keystone species
mimicry
mutualism
parasites
pioneers

primary succession
resource partitioning
secondary succession
startle coloration
subclimax
succession
symbiosis
warning coloration

All the interacting populations within an ecosystem make up an ecological (1)_____.

In order for (2)_____ to occur, two interacting species serve as agents of natural selection on one another over evolutionary time.

When two or more species try to use the same limited resource, each species is harmed. This type of species interaction is called (3)_____.

To reduce competition among species, each species has evolved its own (4)_____; each species has its own physical environmental factors necessary for its survival, as well as a specific "occupation" within its habitat. With this in mind, the (5)_____ states that no two species can inhabit the same ecological niche; eventually one species would eliminate the other through competition. However, examples of species with very similar niche requirements exist. Through evolutionary adaptations, these organisms have reduced the overlap of their niches. This is referred to as (6)_____.

The barnacles *Chthamalus* and *Balanus* live along rocky ocean shores and are exposed to flood and drought conditions as the tide comes in and recedes. This area of the coastline is referred to as the (7)_____.

Many animals have evolved colors, patterns, or shapes to avoid a predator or to avoid being noticed by their prey. These animals are (8)_____. Other animals display bright (9)_____, announcing that they are poisonous or otherwise unpalatable. Some harmless species take full advantage of the brightly colored species by resembling them in appearance. This (10)_____ saves the harmless, tasty species from predation.

Predators may also deceive. Through (11)_____ a predator resembles a harmless species, allowing its prey to unknowingly come into range for an attack.

Certain moths and caterpillars have evolved eye-spots and other color patterns that resemble the eyes of a larger animal. When the prey uses its (12)_____, the predator is frightened, allowing the prey to escape.

(13)_____ is defined as a close interaction between members of different species for an extended period of time. In a relationship such as (14)_____, one species benefits while the other is unaffected. However, (15)_____ live on or in their hosts, usually harming the host in some way but not killing it. When both species in the relationship benefit from the interaction, the relationship is called (16)_____.

Some communities contain one species that plays a major role in determining the community's structure. If this (17)_____ is removed, the structure of the community is dramatically altered.

When a community changes structurally over time, (18)_____ is occurring. The changes begin with the first species to invade an area; these species are called the (19)_____. As time and climate allow, the community will reach a relatively stable endpoint, the (20)_____. When there has been no previous community in existence, the ecosystem begins with the process of (21)_____. If, however, an ecosystem has been disturbed by fire, storm, or farming, a new ecosystem develops through the process of (22)_____. If an ecosystem is periodically and regularly disturbed, the potential climax community may not be reached; instead, a(n) (23)_____ community is maintained. Large geographical regions consisting of climax communities and characterized by specific plant species make up the (24)_____ of the world.

The balance of a community may be severely disrupted when a(n) (25)_____ species is introduced to the community.

Key Terms and Definitions

aggressive mimicry (mim′ik-rē): the evolution of a predatory organism to resemble a harmless animal or part of the environment, thus gaining access to prey.

biome (bī′-ōm): a terrestrial ecosystem that occupies an extensive geographical area and is characterized by a specific type of plant community: for example, deserts.

camouflage (cam′-a-flaj): coloration and/or shape that renders an organism inconspicuous in its environment.

climax community: a diverse and relatively stable community that forms the end point of succession.

coevolution: the evolution of adaptations in two species due to their extensive interactions with one another, such that each species acts as a major force of natural selection on the other.

commensalism (kum-en′-sal-iz-um): a symbiotic relationship in which one species benefits while another species is neither harmed nor benefited.

community: all the interacting populations within an ecosystem.

competitive exclusion principle: the concept that no two species can simultaneously and continuously occupy the same ecological niche.

ecological niche (nitch): the role of a particular species within an ecosystem, including all aspects of its interaction with the living and nonliving environments.

exotic/exotic species: a foreign species introduced into an ecosystem where it did not evolve; such species may flourish and outcompete native species.

interspecific competition: competition among individuals of different species.

intertidal zone: an area of the ocean shore that is alternately covered and exposed by the tides.

keystone species: a species whose influence on community structure is greater than its abundance would suggest.

mimicry (mim′-ik-rē): the situation in which a species has evolved to resemble something else—typically another type of organism.

mutualism (mu′-choo-ul-iz-um): a symbiotic relationship in which both participating species benefit.

parasite (par´-uh-sīt): an organism that lives in or on a larger prey organism, called a host, weakening it.

parasitism: a symbiotic relationship in which one organism (commonly smaller and more numerous than its host) benefits by feeding on the other, which is normally harmed but not immediately killed.

pioneer: an organism that is among the first to colonize an unoccupied habitat in the first stages of succession.

primary succession: succession that occurs in an environment, such as bare rock, in which no trace of a previous community was present.

resource partitioning: the coexistence of two species with similar requirements, each occupying a smaller niche than either would if it were by itself; a means of minimizing their competitive interactions.

secondary succession: succession that occurs after an existing community is disturbed—for example, after a forest fire; much more rapid than primary succession.

startle coloration: a form of mimicry in which a color pattern (in many cases resembling large eyes) can be displayed suddenly by a prey organism when approached by a predator.

subclimax: a community in which succession is stopped before the climax community is reached and is maintained by regular disturbances—for example, tallgrass prairie maintained by periodic fires.

succession (suk-seh´-shun): a structural change in a community and its nonliving environment over time. Community changes alter the ecosystem in ways that favor competitors, and species replace one another in a somewhat predictable manner until a stable, self-sustaining climax community is reached.

symbiosis (sim´-bī-ō´sis): a close interaction between organisms of different species over an extended period. Either or both species may benefit from the association, or (in the case of parasitism) one of the participants is harmed. Symbiosis includes parasitism, mutualism, and commensalism.

symbiotic: referring to an ecological relationship based on symbiosis.

warning coloration: bright coloration that warns predators that the potential prey is distasteful or even poisonous.

THINKING THROUGH THE CONCEPTS

True or False: Determine if the statement given is true or false. If it is false, change the underlined word so that the statement reads true.

26. _____   The interacting populations of a community influence one another's ability to survive and reproduce, leading to a system that results in coevolution.

27. _____   A species' niche in the environment can be described as its occupation or role in the community.

28. _____   Species may reduce competition by partitioning the available resources with the result that each species occupies a larger niche than if there were no competition.

29. _____   Many poisonous or harmful species display bright coloration to stand out to a predator; in this way, the predator is sure to eat the bright organism.

30. _____   Common coloration patterns of equally poisonous or harmful species aid in a predator's learning to avoid these prey items.

31. _____   Prey species have evolved predator avoidance mechanisms, while predator species have responded by evolving deceptive mechanisms to catch their prey.

32. _____   Plants are defenseless against species that feed on them.

33. _____   Parasites generally do not kill their hosts.

34. _____   If elephants disappear from the African savanna, the grasslands will eventually succeed to forest. This is because the elephant is a prey species.

35. _____ After a forest fire, the new community that will develop will do so through <u>primary</u> succession.

36. _____ The organisms that invade bare rock to begin a new community are the <u>biomes</u> of the community.

37. _____ If a farmer allows a field to lie fallow, or abandons the field altogether, <u>secondary succession</u> will quickly establish a new community structure.

38. _____ A <u>pond</u> that is left undisturbed will eventually fill in with silt, forming a marsh; a meadow may eventually be formed as the marsh dries.

39. _____ Climax communities <u>undergo constant change</u>, resulting in diverse populations inhabiting numerous ecological niches.

40. _____ Fields maintained for agriculture represent communities held at a specific <u>subclimax</u> by humans.

Matching: Nature's "chemical warfare."

41. _____ grasses

42. _____ squid, octopus

43. _____ spiders, snakes

44. _____ bombardier beetle

45. _____ milkweed plants

Choices:

a. produce toxic, distasteful chemicals

b. produce silicon

c. produce a boiling hot, toxic spray

d. produce ink clouds

e. produce a paralyzing venom

Identification: Determine whether the following statements refer to **competition, parasitism, commensalism,** or **mutualism**?

46. _____ Lichens are a growth form that occurs when fungi and algae live together. The fungus absorbs nutrients for the alga while the alga photosynthesizes providing carbohydrates for the fungus.

47. _____ Bromeliads, ("air plants"), grow in the notches of tropical trees. The trees are not harmed nor do they benefit from the bromeliads; however, the bromeliads absorb water and nutrients collected in rainwater in the notch.

48. _____ Both hyenas and vultures feed from animal remains after lions have finished feeding.

49. _____ A tick that has embedded itself into the hide of a deer feeds off the deer, possibly weakening or infecting the deer.

50. _____ Egrets can often be seen following cattle through a field. As the cattle disturb insects in the grass, the egrets eat the insects; the cattle are unaffected.

51. _____ Roundworms are often found in the intestines of feral cats. The roundworm feeds off the nutrients the cat has ingested, leaving the cat malnourished.

52. _____ An oak seedling and a maple seedling are growing in an opening in the forest. They both require sunlight, water, and nutrients from their environment.

53. _____ Flowers are pollinated by insects. The insects, in turn, receive pollen and nectar for nourishment from the flowers.

Identification: Determine whether the following statements refer to **primary** or **secondary** succession.

54. _____ Large areas of Australia were burned during the Southern Hemisphere's summer season of 1997. However, new ground cover soon germinated in the open areas and rich nutrients of the fire ashes.

55. _____ When Mt. St. Helens volcano in Washington State, USA, erupted in 1980, the existing communities were destroyed. Within two years subalpine flowers could be seen blooming, and mountain meadows had formed; the communities were reforming.

56. _____ Tornadoes during theNorthern Hemisphere's spring season of 1985 leveled acres of virgin forests in northwest Pennsylvania Commonwealth, USA. This event gave researchers first-hand information on regeneration patterns in forests never touched by human development.

57. _____ As global temperatures rise and glaciers recede, the stratum left behind will be inhabited by lichens, followed by mosses. As plant matter decays and weathering continues, soil will slowly develop that will sustain tundra grasses and wildflowers.

Short Answer:

58. A predator's prey may avoid being eaten by using body parts that have evolved to camouflage it with its environment. Identify three examples of how a prey species may camouflage itself. A predator may also have evolved camouflage patterns, concealing it from its prey. Identify three examples of camouflage by predators.

    Camouflaged prey:

    _____

    _____

    _____

    Camouflaged predator:

    _____

    _____

    _____

59. Warning colorations are commonly displayed by poisonous organisms and are often mimicked by equally harmful species and by harmless species as well. Identify three toxic organisms that display warning coloration. Match these organisms with their equally distasteful or harmless mimics.

    Poisonous organism: Mimic:

    _____   _____

    _____   _____

    _____   _____

60. What is the key difference between primary succession and secondary succession?

    _____

    _____

    _____

CLUES TO APPLYING THE CONCEPTS

These practice questions are intended to sharpen your ability to apply critical thinking and analysis to the biological concepts covered in this chapter.

61. Kangaroo of Australia fill a niche very similar to that of deer in North America. If a deer population from North America were introduced to Australia, the kangaroo and deer would be in direct competition for many resources. Using what you have learned about competition, the competitive exclusion principle, and introduced species, explain what would happen between the two populations.

_____

_____

_____

_____

_____

_____

62. The organisms in a community are tied together either directly or indirectly. This is illustrated best by studying keystone species. Briefly explain how the removal of a keystone species from an ecosystem affects the balance of the communities found there.

_____

_____

_____

_____

_____

_____

63. The snowberry fly has evolved specific behavorial patterns to ward off its predator, a jumping spider. Explain how the fly's behavior is its defense against predation.

_____

_____

_____

_____

ANSWERS TO EXERCISES

1. community
2. coevolution
3. interspecific competition
4. ecological niche
5. competitive exclusion principle
6. resource partitioning
7. intertidal zone
8. camouflaged
9. warning coloration
10. mimicry
11. aggressive mimicry
12. startle coloration
13. symbiosis
14. commensalism
15. parasites
16. mutualism
17. keystone species
18. succession
19. pioneers
20. climax community

21. primary succession
22. secondary succession
23. subclimax
24. biomes
25. exotic
26. true
27. true
28. false, smaller
29. false, sure to avoid
30. true
31. true
32. false, may produce defense chemicals
33. true
34. false, keystone
35. false, secondary
36. false, pioneers
37. true
38. true
39. false, are stable

40. true
41. b
42. d
43. e
44. c
45. a
46. mutualism
47. commensalism
48. competition
49. parasitism
50. commensalism
51. parasitism
52. competition
53. mutualism
54. secondary
55. secondary
56. secondary
57. primary

58. Camouflaged prey: dappled fawns; grasshoppers; prey resembling leaves, twigs, thorns, bird droppings; plants resembling rocks. Camouflaged predators: spotted cheetah; striped tiger, frogfish resembling algae covered rocks.

59. Yellow jackets, hornets, and bees are mimicked by stingless bees; the coral snake is mimicked by the mountain king snake; the monarch butterfly is mimicked by the viceroy butterfly.

60. Primary succession begins with bare rock; secondary succession occurs when a community previously existed in the area.

61. The competitive exclusion principle states that if two species with the same niche are placed together and forced to compete for limited resources, one will outcompete the other. The deer, as the introduced species, would have few or no natural predators. Thus the deer would have a competitive edge. The deer would most likely outcompete and eventually replace the kangaroo in Australia.

62. If the keystone species is removed, the species that it preyed on will increase in number because the keystone species is no longer keeping the prey population under control. The prey species may outcompete the other species in the community, possibly eliminating them. With the species distribution altered, the balance of the community has changed.

63. When approached by a predatory jumping spider, the snowberry fly mimics the behavior and appearance of a jumping spider protecting its territory. Seeing this specific behavior pattern, the predator retreats, leaving the fly alone.

Chapter 29: How Do Ecosystems Work?

OVERVIEW

This chapter traces the pathways of energy and nutrients through ecosystems. Energy follows a one-way path through an ecosystem, passing from the sun through the organisms in a community and being lost as heat as it is transferred. Nutrients, on the other hand, cycle through ecosystems using the natural recycling properties of each community. When the cycles are influenced by humans, as is currently the case with the carbon cycle, the natural balance is disturbed. The result has led to acid deposition and global warming.

1) What Are the Pathways of Energy and Nutrients Through Ecosystems?

Energy flows through communities from the sun to the organisms inhabiting them. As the energy flows, some is lost to the environment as heat. The energy supply must be continuously replenished from the sun. Nutrients, on the other hand, are recycled; thus, they remain in the ecosystem.

2) How Does Energy Flow Through Ecosystems?

Energy enters communities through photosynthesis. Plants, algae and a few other protists, and cyano-bacteria absorb sunlight energy using light-absorbing pigments within them. Through lphotosynthesis, sunlight energy is converted to chemical energy and is stored as sugar and other molecules that make up the photosynthetic organism. These organisms are **autotrophs** and since they produce "food" for themselves, they are also called **producers**. Organisms that feed on other organisms are **heterotrophs**. Since these organisms consume other organisms, they are called **consumers**. The stored energy in photosynthetic organisms is available to the other members of a community. The amount of energy that has been stored in a given period is the **net primary productivity**. Net primary productivity is often measured as the **biomass** of the producers that is added to the ecosystem.

As energy flows through the community, it passes from one **trophic level** to the next. Trophic levels begin with producers and progress to consumers. The number of trophic levels in a system depends on the level of consumers involved. Organisms that feed directly on producers are **herbivores**, and are also called **primary consumers**; they form the second trophic level. Organisms that feed on primary consumers are **carnivores** (flesh-eaters). The carnivores are **secondary consumers**; they form the third trophic level. A fourth trophic level (the **tertiary consumers**) is formed when carnivores eat other carnivores. A **food chain** is a diagram that illustrates relationships between producers, primary consumers, secondary consumers, and tertiary consumers. In nature, however, relationships are not so simple. Instead of a food chain, a **food web** illustrates how food chains merge in complex relationships. Rounding out the food web is the group of organisms that break down and decompose plant and animal matter. **Detritus feeders**, including earthworms, centipedes, and vultures, feed on dead organic matter such as fallen leaves, cast-off exoskeletons, carcasses, and bodily wastes. **Decomposers**, such as bacteria and fungi, further break down dead organic matter, releasing any remaining nutrients.

As energy flows through the trophic levels, only about 10% is transferred from one level to the next. **Energy pyramids** are used to diagram this transfer of energy.

Harmful chemicals may flow through an ecosystem as well. A caterpillar that feeds on leaves sprayed with a pesticide may not die from ingesting the chemical. Instead, the chemical may be stored in its body. A bird that feeds on caterpillars may eat several caterpillars with the chemical stored in their bodies. Thus the bird is consuming a great deal more of the pesticide, which is also stored in the bird's body. Any organism that feeds on the bird will ingest a concentrated amount of the chemical each time it feeds on such birds. This organism will store even greater amounts of the pesticide in its body. The process by which toxic substances accumulate in increasing concentrations in progressively higher trophic levels is known as **biological magnification**. It occurs because the chemicals used are (1) not **biodegradable** (that is, they are not easily broken down by decomposers into harmless substances) and (2) are fat soluble thus accumulate in an organism rather than being excreted in urine.

3) How Do Nutrients Move Within Ecosystems?

Nutrients are elements and small molecules that are used to make the chemical building blocks of life. Molecules needed by organisms in large amounts are **macronutrients**; those needed only in very small amounts are trace nutrients or **micronutrients**. Nutrients do not flow through communities, rather they cycle through. These **nutrient cycles** are also referred to as biogeochemical cycles. The nutrients tend to be stored in nonliving, or **abiotic**, **reservoirs** such as CO_2 and nitrogen in the atmosphere and phosphorus in rocks. Other major reservoirs for CO_2 include the dissolved form in oceans and the remains of ancient plants and animals transformed by heat and pressure into **fossil fuels**.

Although the atmosphere is composed of 79% nitrogen gas, plants and animals cannot use nitrogen in its gaseous form. Atmospheric nitrogen is converted to more usable forms by bacteria and cyanobacteria that conduct **nitrogen fixation**. Plants that belong to the **legume** family play a very important role in nitrogen fixation. Bacteria that can fix nitrogen live in the roots of legumes. Thus, plants such as soybeans and clover are often planted to replace nitrogen in nutrient-poor soils. After cycling through plants and animals, nitrogen is returned to the atmosphere by **denitrifying bacteria**.

Water is also considered to be a nutrient. It cycles in the **hydrologic cycle**. The ocean serves as the major reservoir for water. Water is evaporated from the oceans and returned to land as precipitation.

4) What Is Causing Acid Rain and Global Warming?

Many of the current environmental problems are the result of human interference in the way ecosystems function. Acid rain, or **acid deposition**, occurs when nitrogen oxide and sulfur dioxide combine with water vapor in the atmosphere, forming nitric acid and sulfuric acid. The acids then come down in the form of acid rain or as dry particles interacting with the structures and organisms they touch. Acid deposition threatens (1) aquatic ecosystems (25% of the lakes in the Adirondack region of New York, USA, are lifeless), (2) growth and productivity of farms (acid rain interacts with soil nutrients and decomposers), (3) forest health (33%-50% of beech and red spruce trees in the Green Mountains of Vermont, USA, are dead), and (4) animal, and human, health (exposure to toxic metals increases)

From the start of the Industrial Revolution, carbon, stored in fossil fuels, has been released into the atmosphere. This has increased the CO_2 content of the atmosphere 25%, from 280 ppm or .028% preindustrial revolution to over 360 ppm or .036%. Carbon dioxide and other **greenhouse gases** in the atmosphere trap heat from the sun and heat radiating from Earth. The result is a natural **greenhouse effect**, keeping our atmosphere warm to sustain life. However, as the CO_2 levels increase, the warming effect increases also, leading to warmer temperatures globally, or **global warming**. Increased CO_2 levels threaten (1) coastal ecosystems, the breeding grounds for many aquatic organisms; (2) current temperature and precipitaion patterns globally; and (3) distribution and species composition of forest ecosystems.

KEY TERMS AND CONCEPTS

Fill-In: From the following list of terms, fill in the blanks below.

abiotic
acid deposition
autotrophs
biodegradable
biogeochemical cycles
biological magnification
biomass
carnivores
consumers
decomposers
deforestation
denitrifying bacteria

detritis feeders
energy pyramid
food chain
food web
fossil fuels
global warming
greenhouse effect
herbivores
heterotrophs
hydrologic cycle
legume

macronutrients
micronutrients
net primary productivity
nitrogen fixation
nutrient cycles
primary consumers
producers
reservoirs
secondary consumers
tertiary consumers
trophic level

(1)_____ are organisms that produce their own organic material using inorganic materials as their energy source. Organisms that use other living organisms as a source of energy are called (2)_____ and are also known as (3)_____.

Plants are (4)_____, using sunlight as their source of energy to make organic material. The amount of energy captured by these organisms is measured as (5)_____. If the amount of energy captured is measured in dry weight of the organisms, the (6)_____ has been determined.

Plants as producers form the first (7)_____. Organisms that ingest plant material are the (8)_____ and are also called (9)_____. Animals that eat only other animals are called (10)_____. These animals are the (11)_____, making up the third trophic level, and the (12)_____, the fourth trophic level.

Animals such as earthworms, centipedes, and termites, which feed on dead organic matter, are referred to as (13)_____. Fungi and bacteria make up the (14)_____, releasing the final nutrients.

Approximately 10% of biomass energy is passed on to the next energy level, forming a(n) (15)_____.

Some human-made chemicals are not readily broken down in the environment. These chemicals are not (16)_____. Therefore, their concentration may increase in the organisms of progressively higher trophic levels in the environment. This increase is called (17)_____.

Nutrients that are required by organisms in large amounts are (18)_____; those needed in only trace amounts are (19)_____. Within the ecosystem, nutrients are recycled in (20)_____, also called (21)_____.

In each nutrient cycle, large storage areas serve as (22)_____. These storage areas are often nonliving, or (23)_____. During the Carboniferous period, the remains of ancient plants and animals were covered with sediment. Today, these carbon stores are (24)_____, burned for electricity production.

Unusable nitrogen gas is converted to usable ammonia by bacteria living in the roots of plants in the (25)_____ family. This process is called (26)_____. After passing through organisms in the ecosystem, nitrogen is returned to the atmosphere by (27)_____.

Water evaporating from the oceans and falling back to land as rain is part of the (28)_____. When evaporated water in the atmosphere mixes with nitrogen oxide or sulfur dioxide, nitric acid or sulfuric acid, respectively, is formed. With their formation, (29)_____ follows, damaging ecosystems and human-made structures.

Atmospheric CO_2 absorbs heat, creating a natural (30)_____ around Earth. As CO_2 levels increase due to deforestation and fossil fuel burning, the average temperature of Earth is expected to increase in a phenomenon known as (31)_____.

Key Terms and Definitions

abiotic (ā-bī-ah´-tik): nonliving; the abiotic portion of an ecosystem includes soil, rock, water, and the atmosphere.

acid deposition: the deposition of nitric or sulfuric acid, either dissolved in rain (acid rain) or in the form of dry particles, as a result of the production of nitrogen oxides or sulfur dioxide through burning, primarily of fossil fuels.

autotroph (aw´-tō-trof): "self-feeder"; normally, a photosynthetic organism; a producer.

biodegradable: able to be broken down into harmless substances by decomposers.

biological magnification: the increasing accumulation of a toxic substance in progressively higher trophic levels.

biomass: the dry weight of organic material in an ecosystem.

carnivore (kar´-neh-vor): literally, "meat eater"; a predatory organism that feeds on herbivores or on other carnivores; a secondary (or higher) consumer.

consumer: an organism that eats other organisms; a heterotroph.

decomposer: an organism, normally a fungus or bacterium, that digests organic material by secreting digestive enzymes into the environment, in the process liberating nutrients into the environment.

deforestation: the excessive cutting of forests, primarily rain forests in the tropics, to clear space for agriculture.

denitrifying bacterium (dē-nī´-treh-fī-ing): a bacterium that breaks down nitrates, releasing nitrogen gas to the atmosphere.

detritus feeder (de-trī´-tus): one of a diverse group of organisms, ranging from worms to vultures, that live off the wastes and dead remains of other organisms.

energy pyramid: a graphical representation of the energy contained in succeeding trophic levels, with maximum energy at the base (primary producers) and steadily diminishing amounts at higher levels.

food chain: a linear feeding relationship in a community, using a single representative from each of the trophic levels.

food web: a representation of the complex feeding relationships (in terms of interacting food chains) within a community, including many organisms at various trophic levels, with many of the consumers occupying more than one level simultaneously.

fossil fuel: a fuel such as coal, oil, and natural gas, derived from the remains of ancient organisms.

global warming: a gradual rise in global atmospheric temperature as a result of an amplification of the natural greenhouse effect due to human activities.

greenhouse effect: the process in which certain gases such as carbon dioxide and methane trap sunlight energy in a planet's atmosphere as heat; the glass in a greenhouse does the same. The result, global warming, is being enhanced by the production of these gases by humans.

greenhouse gas: a gas, such as carbon dioxide or methane, that traps sunlight energy in a planet's atmosphere as heat; a gas that participates in the greenhouse effect.

herbivore (erb´-i-vor): literally, "plant-eater"; an organism that feeds directly and exclusively on producers; a primary consumer.

heterotroph (het´-er-ō-trōf´): literally, "other-feeder"; an organism that eats other organisms; a consumer.

hydrologic cycle: the water cycle, driven by solar energy; a nutrient cycle in which the main reservoir of water is the ocean and most of the water remains in the form of water throughout the cycle (rather than being used in the synthesis of new molecules).

legume (leg´-ūm): a member of a family of plants characterized by root swellings in which nitrogen-fixing bacteria are housed; includes soybeans, lupines, alfalfa, and clover.

macronutrient: a nutrient needed in relatively large quantities (often defined as making up more than 0.1% of an organism's body).

micronutrient: a nutrient needed only in small quantities (often defined as making up less than 0.01% of an organism's body).

net primary productivity: the energy stored in the autotrophs of an ecosystem over a given time period.

nitrogen fixation: the process that combines atmospheric nitrogen with hydrogen to form ammonium (NH_4^+).

nutrient cycle: a description of the pathways of a specific nutrient (such as carbon, nitrogen, phosphorus, or water) through the living and nonliving portions of an ecosystem.

primary consumer: an organism that feeds on producers; an herbivore.

producer: a photosynthetic organism; an autotroph.

reservoir: the major source and storage site of a nutrient in an ecosystem, normally in the abiotic portion.

secondary consumer: an organism that feeds on primary consumers; a carnivore.

tertiary consumer (ter´-shē-er-ē): a carnivore that feeds on other carnivores (secondary consumers).

trophic level: literally, "feeding level"; the categories of organisms in a community, and the position of an organism in a food chain, defined by the organism's source of energy; includes producers, primary consumers, secondary consumers, and so on.

THINKING THROUGH THE CONCEPTS

True or False: Determine if the statement given is true or false. If it is false, change the underlined word(s) so that the statement reads true.

32. _____ Almost all of the energy produced by the sun reaches Earth.

33. _____ Ecosystems that have a low producer biomass will have low productivity.

34. _____ Herbivores constitute the first trophic level.

35. _____ Omnivores consume both plant and animal material.

36. _____ A food chain can be very complex, since it considers all the feeding relationships between organisms.

37. _____ Vultures and hyenas are detritus feeders.

38. _____ The transfer of energy between trophic levels is extremely efficient.

39. _____ The most infamous chemical related to biomagnification is DDT.

40. _____ Biogeochemical cycles connect the biotic and abiotic portions of the ecosystem.

41. _____ Plants of the rose family are important because they house nitrogen-fixing bacteria in root nodules that can directly absorb and use nitrogen gas from the air, and directly convert atmospheric nitrogen into fertilizer.

42. _____ Human activities are stabilizing the balance of biogeochemical cycles.

43. _____ In the hydrologic cycle, some of the water enters the <u>living community</u> before it evaporates back into the atmosphere.

44. _____ Acid particles can fall from the atmosphere in <u>dry form</u>.

45. _____ Twenty-five percent of the Adirondack lakes are <u>dead</u>.

46. _____ Acid deposition <u>increases</u> lead and other heavy-metal poisoning in animals.

47. _____ Climate prediction for the future is <u>certain</u> in the face of global warming.

Matching: Members of the ecosystem and their trophic level.

48. _____ bracket fungus

49. _____ squirrel

50. _____ sheep

51. _____ dead leaves

52. _____ oak tree

53. _____ hawk

54. _____ mushroom

55. _____ alga

56. _____ shark

57. _____ bacterium

58. _____ earthworm

59. _____ snake skin

Choices:

a. producer

b. primary consumer

c. detritus feeder

d. detritus

e. decomposer

f. secondary consumer

True or False: Determine if the following statements regarding the phosphorus (P) cycle are true or false. You do not need to correct the statement if it is false.

60. _____ The main source of P is from rock.

61. _____ The P cycle is greatly accelerated by transport through the atmosphere.

62. _____ Organic P is transported through the food chain.

63. _____ P is the limiting nutrient in many ecosystems.

64. _____ Humans have affected the phosphorus cycle by inadvertent and undesirable fertilization of waterways, accumulation of phosphorus-rich pollutants in the atmosphere, and depletion of soil supplies by overcutting and erosion.

Short Answer.

65. Define the term *abiotic* and provide two examples of abiotic reservoirs each for the carbon, nitrogen, and phosphorus cycles.

_____

_____

_____

_____

66. Which of the following derive energy for growth *directly* from light?

autotrophs   heterotrophs   tertiary consumers

decomposers   primary consumers   producers

67. Which of the following derive energy for growth *indirectly* from light?

autotrophs   heterotrophs   tertiary consumers

decomposers   primary consumers   producers

68. Identify six trophic levels. Explain how they interact with one another.

_____

_____

_____

_____

_____

CLUES TO APPLYING THE CONCEPTS

These practice questions are intended to sharpen your ability to apply critical thinking and analysis to the biological concepts covered in this chapter.

69. Assuming typical efficiency of energy transfer from one trophic level to the next, describe how 1000 calories in producer biomass might be converted to carnivores. How many calories will a carnivore receive from the original 1000 calories?

_____

_____

_____

_____

70. Why has there been no mention in this chapter of quaternary, or fourth-level, consumers? Energetically, is a fifth trophic level possible? Why or why not?

_____

_____

_____

_____

_____

71. Using the following list, carefully trace the path of a carbon atom through the carbon cycle.

secondary consumer	fecal matter	atmosphere
sugar molecule in plant	fungus	detritus
primary consumer	plant stem	cell respiration
green leafy plant	detritus feeder	decomposer

_____

_____

_____

_____

_____

_____

_____

72. Briefly describe three ways in which humans have affected the nutrient cycles of carbon, nitrogen, and phosphorus. Do not state three examples for each cycle, rather give examples of how humans have affected the cycling of nutrients as a whole.

_____

_____

_____

_____

_____

_____

_____

_____

_____

_____

ANSWERS TO EXERCISES

1. Autotrophs	23. abiotic	44. true
2. heterotrophs	24. fossil fuels	45. true
3. consumers	25. legume	46. true
4. producers	26. nitrogen fixation	47. false, uncertain
5. net primary productivity	27. denitrifying bacteria	48. e
6. biomass	28. hydrologic cycle	49. b
7. trophic level	29. acid deposition	50. b
8. herbivores	30. greenhouse effect	51. d
9. primary consumers	31. global warming	52. a
10. carnivores	32. false, relatively little	53. f
11. secondary consumers	33. true	54. e
12. tertiary consumers	34. false, second	55. a
13. detritis feeders	35. true	56. f
14. decomposers	36. false, food web	57. e
15. energy pyramid	37. true	58. c
16. biodegradable	38. false, inefficient	59. d
17. biological magnification	39. true	60. true
18. macronutrients	40. true	61. false
19. micronutrients	41. false, legume	62. true
20. nutrient cycles	42. false, threatening	63. true
21. biogeochemical cycles	43. true	64. true
22. reservoirs		

65. *Abiotic* means nonliving. Carbon reservoirs include gas in the atmosphere, dissolved carbon in the oceans, and fossil fuels. Nitrogen reservoirs include gas in the atmosphere, nitrogen-containing molecules, and wetlands. Phosphorus reservoirs include phosphates in rock, bird guano, and animal teeth and skeletons.

66. autotrophs, producers

67. heterotrophs, primary consumers, decomposers, tertiary consumers

68. (1) Producers capture sunlight energy. (2) Primary consumers feed on producers. (3) Secondary consumers feed on primary consumers. (4) Tertiary consumers feed on secondary consumers. (5) Detritis feeders feed on dead producers, and on waste material from or dead primary, secondary, and tertiary consumers. (6) Decomposers externally digest what remains of producers, and of primary, secondary, and tertiary consumers, and release the remaining nutrients to the environment.

69. 1000 calories exists in producer biomass. If 10% of the energy is lost with each trophic level, 100 calories will be converted to herbivore (primary consumer) biomass. As a carnivore (secondary consumer) feeds on the herbivore, it will receive only 10 calories from the original 1000 in the producer biomass.

70. The existence of a quaternary consumer would indeed be very rare. Using exercise 69 and continuing to assume that 10% energy is lost with each trophic level, a tertiary consumer would receive only 1 calorie from the original 1000. If a fourth-level consumer existed, it would receive 0.1 calories from the original 1000. In order to maintain energy demands, this organism would need to consume very large quantities of food.

71. Possible scenario: Atmosphere → green leafy plant → sugar molecule in plant →
cell respiration → atmosphere → green leafy plant → plant stem → detritus → detritus feeder →
decomposer → atmosphere → green leafy plant → primary consumer → secondary consumer →
cell respiration → atmosphere → green leafy plant → primary consumer → secondary consumer →
fecal matter → decomposer → atmosphere.
*Note: the cycle always starts with and comes back to the atmosphere.

72. The carbon cycle has been affected by the burning of fossil fuels. Massive quantities of carbon were stored in plant material during the Carboniferous period, which lasted approximately 150 million years. In the roughly 150 years since the beginning of the Industrial Revolution, humans have returned much of this stored carbon to the atmosphere, at a rate that is orders of magnitude greater than the rate at which it was stored. In the meantime, deforestation and the burning of the tropical rain forests have added additional carbon to the atmosphere while at the same time removing areas that could absorb CO_2 from the atmosphere.

The nitrogen cycle has been affected by human-made nitrogen fixation: the production and overuse of fertilizer. Fertilizer runoff from farms into streams and rivers has led to massive die-offs of aquatic ecosystem life. Nitrogen oxides put into the atmosphere by the burning of fossil fuels mix with water vapor, forming nitric acid. Nitric acid is, in part, responsible for damage to crops, aquatic systems, and human-made structures.

The phosphorus cycle also has been affected, again, by the formation and overuse of fertilizer. Phosphorus-rich soil runoff into waterways stimulates the growth of producers such as algae. When the algae die, their decomposition uses oxygen at a high rate, suffocating fish and other aquatic organisms; ultimately disrupting the aquatic balance.

Chapter 30: Earth's Diverse Ecosystems

OVERVIEW

This chapter looks at how weather patterns and climate determine how the organisms on Earth are distributed. In terrestrial ecosystems, climate determines which plants inhabit an area. The plants present, in turn, determine the animal life existing there. This chapter outlines the major biomes and their characteristic plant communities. The impact humans have on each biome is addressed. Additionally, since the oceans cover 71% of Earth, aquatic life, both freshwater and marine, is discussed, and the impact humans have on aquatic ecosystems is considered.

1) What Factors Influence Earth's Climate?

Earth's **climate** is determined by the patterns of **weather** that exist in a specific region. The climate in a region is influenced by latitude, air currents, ocean currents, and the presence of mountains and irregularly shaped continents. Latitude is measured as the distance north or south of the equator. The sunlight that heats Earth's surface hits Earth at an angle; the degree of the angle determines the overall temperature for a region. Earth's rotation and temperature differences in air masses, create air currents. As warm, moist air rises, it cools causing precipitation. Ocean currents are formed from the Earth's rotation, wind, and the sun's heating of the water. The presence of continents causes the ocean currents to circulate forming **gyres**. The circular patterns generate moderate weather patterns on the coastal regions of a land mass. Different elevations within continents also generate climate variations. As moist air approaches a mountain, it rises, cools, and the moisture condenses causing precipitation. The dry air passes over the mountain, absorbing moisture as it flows, causing a **rain shadow** phenomenon on the far side of the mountain.

2) What Are the Requirements of Life?

Four basic resources are required for life: (1) Nutrients to build living tissue, (2) energy to produce tissues, and (3 & 4) liquid water and appropriate temperatures for metabolic reactions. Within diverse ecosystems, the organisms have adapted the mechanisms necessary to acquire resources and to survive.

3) How Is Life on Land Distributed?

Temperature and the availability of water determine the distribution of terrestrial organisms. Both temperature and water are unevenly distributed, and organisms have adapted various mechanisms to tolerate unfavorable temperatures and drought or flood conditions.

Terrestrial communities are defined by their plant life. Large land areas with similar environmental conditions are called **biomes**. The **tropical rain forest** biomes are dominated by a diverse population of huge, broadleaf, evergreen trees that grow well along the equator where temperatures are relatively consistent and 250 to 400 cm of rain falls. These complex ecosystems are cherished for their **biodiversity**. The soil in this biome is infertile since all the nutrients are tied up in the lush vegetation. Still, humans are deforesting the area for agriculture, inefficient in the infertile soil, causing the loss of countless species and immeasurable potential. **Tropical deciduous forests** are located slightly north and south of the equator, where rainfall is not as predictable. During the dry season, trees drop their leaves to reduce water loss.

Farther away from the equator, the grasses of the **savanna** dominate. Any trees here are scrubby, with thorns protecting their sparse foliage. The root systems of the grasses can withstand the severe droughts less (than 30 cm of rain) common to the savanna regions. Human settlements have spread into the savanna, threatening the black rhino and African elephant populations, as well as other wildlife, through poaching and habitat conversion to cattle pastures.

Where rainfall decreases below 25 cm a year, the savanna gives way to **desert**. Plants that survive in the deserts have extended root systems to quickly absorb any rain. The absorbed water is stored in fleshy stems covered with wax to prevent evaporation. The area of Earth covered by deserts is increasing as human activities (such as deforestation, soil destruction, and overuse of once productive land) cause **desertification** of the fragile habitats. Deserts that merge with a coastal region give rise to **chaparral**, a unique ecosystem found along the Mediterranean Sea and along the southern California coast.

In the centers of Eurasia and temperate North America, **prairies**, or **grasslands**, dominate. Limited rainfall and relatively frequent fires restrict the growth of trees to riverbanks while promoting the growth of the prairie grasses. Humans have used the fertile soil created by the dense grass growth for intense cereal agriculture or pastureland. Overgrazing on western prairies in the United States has lead to desertification and agriculture has left only a few, small, remnants of original prairie habitat.

As the amount of precipitation increases, trees can take root, shading out the grasses. This gives rise to the **temperate deciduous forests**. Because the trees cannot obtain water during winter, they drop their leaves to reduce moisture loss. Spring brings short-lived wildflowers to bloom before new leaves form on the trees, shading the forest floor. Along the southeastern coast of Australia, the southwestern coast of New Zealand, and the northwestern coast of North America lie very wet ecosystems called **temperate rain forests**. These rare habitats receive upward of 400 cm of rain a year, giving rise to lush plant growth of evergreen conifers, ferns, and mosses.

In the interior of northern North America and northern Eurasia, harsh temperatures and a short growing season produce the **northern coniferous forests**, or the **taiga**. Humans have clear-cut vast areas of the taiga forests for timber; however, because of the harsh climate, much has remained undisturbed. Farther north the climate becomes even more extreme. Winter temperatures of the **tundra** may drop below −55°C. A **permafrost** layer is impervious to water even when temperatures allow for the top meter or so to thaw. Thus a wet marshy expanse is formed. During the brief summer thaw, small flowering plants quickly grow, bloom, and die back until the next thaw. Because of its short growing season, the tundra is extremely fragile. Human activites leave long-lasting scars. Fortunately, impact is limited to the areas around oil-drilling sites, pipelines, mines, and military bases.

4) How Is Life in Water Distributed?

Water has unique characteristics that limit where life can or does exist in aquatic habitats. Water is a great insulator; thus it warms and cools slowly. The sunlight that penetrates water is quickly absorbed, so depths below 200 m do not receive enough light energy for photosynthesis. Any suspended sediment reduces the depth of light penetration. Available nutrients settle to the bottom of aquatic ecosystems, where light often does not reach, limiting life.

Large freshwater lake ecosystems have distinct life zones. The **littoral zone** occurs where water is shallow, light is abundant, and plants can root and find nutrients in the bottom sediments. Among the rooted plants, **plankton** drift. **Phytoplankton**, such as algae and photosynthetic bacteria, and **zooplankton**, such as protozoa and minute crustaceans, add to the diversity of this ecosystem. In deeper water, light is limited to the **limnetic zone**, where the aquatic food web is supported by abundant phytoplankton. Light does not reach the deeper depths of the **profundal zone**, and the detritus feeders and decomposers living on the lake floor receive nutrients from detritus that falls from the littoral and limnetic zones.

Lakes that are extremely nutrient poor are referred to as **oligotrophic lakes**. These lakes are often formed from deep depressions left by glaciers and fed by mountain streams. They are often clear, deep, and oxygen rich. Lakes that receive nutrients and sediments in high amounts as runoff from surrounding areas are **eutrophic lakes**. Eutrophic lakes are clouded with suspended sediment and phytoplankton. Oxygen content in the profundal zone is often limited because decomposers use any available oxygen while feeding on dead phytoplankton. Human activites have greatly increased the rate of eutrophication. The flow of nutrients from farms, feedlots, and sewage into lakes causes excessive growth of phytoplankton, which form a scum on the lake surface. The scum blocks sunlight into the lake causing the death of submerged plants and the gradual loss of higher trophic levels. In addition, acid rain has lowered the pH of lakewater, threatening the ecosystem. Acidified lakes often appear oligotrophic because of their lack of life.

Marine ecosystems are also divided into life zones based on depth and availability of light energy. The **photic zone** is the upper region where light energy supports photosynthesis. Below the photic zone is the **aphotic zone**, where nutrients settle. Nutrients from the aphotic zone rise to the photic zone during **upwelling** events caused by surface winds displacing surface water. Closer to shore, organisms of the **intertidal zone** experience alternating dehydration, as the tides recede, and rehydration, as the tides rise again. Bays and coastal wetlands make up the **near-shore zone**, which is constantly submerged. Both of these ecosystems support diverse and abundant life. Where freshwater rivers flow into the ocean, **estuaries** form. Human activities have greatly impacted the fragile coastal ecosystems. By filling in or dredging, humans have removed almost all of the world's wetlands.

Equally fragile are **coral reef** communities. Minute animals, the corals, live symbiotically with algae, building great structures out of calcium carbonate secreted from their bodies. These structures serve as habitat for unique and specialized organisms. Because of their fragility, coral reefs are extremely sensitive to human activities. As sediment and silt from nearby land areas cloud the water around a coral reef, the algae are not able to photosynthesize and provide the energy necessary for the organisms to survive. Overfishing and fishing methods also threaten their existance.

The open ocean supports free-swimming, or **pelagic** life-forms in the upper photic zone. Here, the food web is supported by phytoplankton. The aphotic zone, however, supports unique life-forms of its own. Even the open ocean has been subjected to misuse by humans. Trash, dumped by ships or blown from shore, endangers the lives of many animals in the sea as they mistake it for food. Radioactive wastes have also been dumped in the open ocean under the pretenses that it could "do no harm out there." However, unique life forms may live in undiscovered areas of the deep ocean. **Hydrothermal vent communities** represent one such example. Deep in the ocean, cracks in Earth's crust heat the surrounding water, supporting an ecosystem where 284 new species have been found. These organisms do not use the sun's energy for life support. Instead, they use hydrogen sulfide from Earth's crust in a process called chemosynthesis.

KEY TERMS AND CONCEPTS

Fill-In: From the following list of terms, fill in the blanks below.

aphotic zone
chaparral
climate
coral reefs
desert
desertification
eutrophic
grassland
gyres
hydrothermal vent communities
intertidal zone
latitude

limnetic zone
littoral zone
near-shore zone
northern coniferous forest
oligotrophic
ozone layer
pelagic
permafrost
photic zone
phytoplankton
plankton
prairie

profundal zone
rain shadow
savanna
taiga
temperate deciduous forest
temperate rain forest
tropical deciduous forest
tropical rain forest
tundra
upwelling
weather
zooplankton

Short-term changes in temperature, precipitation, or cloud cover determine the (1)_____
of an area. However, temperature or precipitation patterns over the long term determine the
(2)_____ of a region. The equator, at zero degrees (3)_____, has
consistently warm temperatures. Ocean currents occur in circular patterns called (4)_____
as determined by Earth's rotation, wind, warming of the water, and the continents.

Mountains modify precipitation patterns. As air passes over a mountain it releases precipitation. On the
far side of the mountain, then, the air is dry, creating a(n) (5)_____.

The plant life in a terrestrial biome may be determined by the amount of rainfall and the frequency with
which it occurs. In the (6)_____, temperature and rainfall averages are consistent
from year to year and the organisms found there are the most diverse. However, if rainfall were not so
consistent and there were distinct wet and dry seasons, the plants would drop their leaves during the dry
season. This pattern is more characteristic of the (7)_____. Where grasses are
dominant and very tolerant of the severe dry season, the (8)_____ exists. The
use of this biome for cattle grazing is threatening its wildlife. Where rainfall averages less than 25 cm,
water-storing cacti live, making up the flora of the (9)_____. Overuse of
land compromised by drought, deforestation, and soil destruction has led to irreversible
(10)_____ in many regions.

Coastal areas on the margins of deserts result in the unique biome of the (11)_____. In
temperate regions, as rainfall increases away from the deserts, grasses and wildflowers grow. This region
is the (12)_____ biome, more commonly referred to as the
(13)_____.

In areas that can support tree growth, grasses are shaded out and forests dominate. In regions that have
cold winters with below-freezing weather, trees drop their leaves to conserve water. This pattern
describes the (14)_____. However, if cold temperatures are moderated and heavy

rainfall occurs, as along the Olympic Peninsula, then a(n) (15)_____ exists.

The long, hard, cold winters and short springs of southern Canada result in heavy growth of evergreen conifers in the (16)_____, or (17)_____ biome. As temperature becomes even colder, the fragile (18)_____ exists, the last biome before the polar ice caps.

Aquatic ecosystems are also defined by their unique characteristics. Areas of freshwater lakes are divided into three zones. The (19)_____ has shallow water with diverse communities. Drifting among the plants in this zone are microscopic organisms, the (20)_____. If these organisms are photosynthetic bacteria or protists such as algae, they are called (21)_____. If, instead, the organisms consist of protozoa and minute crustaceans, they are called (22)_____.

Deeper open water that does not allow plants to be rooted to the bottom consists of the upper (23)_____, which allows photosynthesis to occur, and the lower (24)_____. Here, light does not penetrate to allow photosynthesis.

Lakes are also classified according to their nutrient content. (25)_____ lakes are very low in nutrients; they were formed by glaciers and are fed by mountain streams. On the other hand, (26)_____ lakes have high sediment rates and high deposition rates of organic and inorganic material from their surroundings.

Ocean ecosystems consist of the upper layer that allows light penetration for photosynthesis, the (27)_____, and the deeper, nonphotosynthetic region, the (28)_____. Nutrients from the lower oceanic regions may be brought to the surface as (29)_____ occurs.

Aquatic areas along the coast may alternately be wet and dry, a pattern that occurs at the (30)_____ as the tide rises and falls. Shallow, submerged bays and wetlands make up the (31)_____.

Offshore areas with all the right parameters allow corals and algae to build structures of calcium carbonate. The diverse habitats of these (32)_____ are extremely fragile and sensitive.

Life in the open ocean exists primarily in the upper photic zone. The life-forms here are free-swimming or (33)_____. However, new and unusual life-forms have been discovered far from the ocean surface. Deep in the ocean, extremely hot water, heated by Earth's core, supports the (34)_____.

Key Terms and Definitions

aphotic zone: the region of the ocean below 200 meters, where sunlight does not penetrate.

biodiversity: the total number of species within an ecosystem and the resulting complexity of interactions among them.

biome (bī´-ōm): a terrestrial ecosystem that occupies an extensive geographical area and is characterized by a specific type of plant community: for example, deserts.

chaparral: a biome that is located in coastal regions but has very low annual rainfall.

climate: patterns of weather that prevail from year to year and even from century to century in a given region.

coral reef: a biome created by animals (reef-building corals) and plants in warm tropical waters.

desert: a biome in which less than 25 to 50 centimeters (10 to 20 inches) of rain falls each year.

desertification: the spread of deserts by human activities.

estuary: a wetland formed where a river meets the ocean; the salinity there is quite variable but lower than in seawater and higher than in freshwater.

eutrophic lake: a lake that receives sufficiently large inputs of sediments, organic material, and inorganic nutrients from its surroundings to support dense communities; murky with poor light penetration.

grassland: a biome, located in the centers of continents, that supports grasses; also called *prairie*.

gyre (jīr): a roughly circular pattern of ocean currents, formed because continents interrupt the currents' flow; clockwise-rotating in the Northern Hemisphere and counterclockwise-rotating in the Southern Hemisphere.

hydrothermal vent community: a community of unusual organisms, living in the deep ocean near hydrothermal vents, that depends on the chemosynthetic activities of sulfur bacteria.

intertidal zone: an area of the ocean shore that is alternately covered and exposed by the tides.

limnetic zone: a lake zone in which enough light penetrates to support photosynthesis.

littoral zone: a lake zone, near the shore, in which water is shallow and plants find abundant light, anchorage, and adequate nutrients.

nearshore zone: the region of coastal water that is relatively shallow but constantly submerged; includes bays and coastal wetlands and can support large plants or seaweeds.

northern coniferous forest: a biome with long, cold winters and only a few months of warm weather; populated almost entirely by evergreen coniferous trees; also called *taiga*.

oligotrophic lake: a lake that is very low in nutrients and hence clear with extensive light penetration.

ozone layer: the ozone-enriched layer of the upper atmosphere that filters out some of the sun's ultraviolet radiation.

pelagic (puh-la´-jik): free-swimming or floating.

permafrost: a permanently frozen layer of soil in the arctic tundra that cannot support the growth of trees.

photic zone: the region of the ocean where light is strong enough to support photosynthesis.

phytoplankton (fī´-tō-plank-ten): photosynthetic protists that are abundant in marine and freshwater environments.

plankton: microscopic organisms that live in marine or freshwater environments; includes phytoplankton and zooplankton.

prairie: a biome, located in the centers of continents, that supports grasses; also called *grassland*.

profundal zone: a lake zone in which light is insufficient to support photosynthesis.

rain shadow: a local dry area created by the modification of rainfall patterns by a mountain range.

savanna: a biome that is dominated by grasses and supports scattered trees and thorny scrub forests; typically has a rainy season in which all the year's precipitation falls.

taiga (tī´-guh): a biome with long, cold winters and only a few months of warm weather; dominated by evergreen coniferous trees; also called *northern coniferous forest*.

temperate deciduous forest: a biome in which winters are cold and summer rainfall is sufficient to allow enough moisture for trees to grow and shade out grasses.

temperate rain forest: a biome in which there is no shortage of liquid water year-round and that is dominated by conifers.

tropical deciduous forest: a biome with pronounced wet and dry seasons and plants that must shed their leaves during the dry season to minimize water loss.

tropical rain forest: a biome with evenly warm, evenly moist conditions; dominated by broadleaf evergreen trees; the most diverse biome.

tundra: a biome with severe weather conditions (extreme cold and wind and little rainfall) that cannot support trees.

upwelling: an upward flow that brings cold, nutrient-laden water from the ocean depths to the surface; occurs along western coastlines.

weather: short-term fluctuations in temperature, humidity, cloud cover, wind, and precipitation in a region over periods of hours to days.

zooplankton: nonphotosynthetic protists that are abundant in marine and freshwater environments.

THINKING THROUGH THE CONCEPTS

True or False: Determine if the statement given is true or false. If it is false, change the <u>underlined</u> word(s) so that the statement reads true.

35. _____   The <u>tilt of Earth's axis</u> influences air and ocean currents.

36. _____   The <u>presence of continents</u> affects ocean currents, producing gyres.

37. _____   Deserts are often found in the <u>rain shadow</u> of a mountain range.

38. _____   The <u>specific</u> requirements of life for each organism are the same.

39. _____   Since plants are specifically adapted to their environment, <u>terrestrial communities</u> are defined by the plant life found there.

40. _____   It is possible to <u>harvest products</u> from the tropical rain forests without damaging the ecosystem.

41. _____   Grazing cattle on the rangeland of the savanna has had <u>little impact</u> on the wildlife there.

42. _____   The total area of land occupied by deserts is <u>decreasing</u> because of human activities.

43. _____   <u>Fire</u> plays an important role in the maintenance of healthy prairies.

44. _____   In the temperate rain forest, seedlings often take root in a newly fallen tree, which serves as a <u>nurse log</u>, providing nutrients and protection for the developing plant.

45. _____   Clear-cutting of forests in the <u>tundra</u> has destroyed habitat in large regions.

46. _____   The major factors that determine the quantity and type of life in aquatic ecosystems are <u>energy and nutrients</u>.

47. _____   Wastes from sewer treatment facilities and overuse of fertilizers may lead to <u>excessive amounts of nutrients</u> being washed into aquatic ecosystems.

48. _____   Coral reef ecosystems are <u>ultimately resilient</u> and therefore are <u>unaffected</u> by human activities.

49. _____   Fish populations in the ocean have <u>declined dramatically</u> as a result of overfishing practices.

Fill-In:
50. Complete the table below with characteristics of the biomes listed.

Biome	Precipitation range	Temperature range	Typical plants present	Typical animals present
tropical rain forest				
tropical deciduous forest	NA	NA		NA
savanna		NA		
desert				
chaparral		NA		NA
prairie; grassland				
temperate deciduous forest				
temperate rain forest				NA
taiga; northern coniferous forest				
tundra				

Identification: Determine whether the following statements refer to **eutrophic** lakes or **oligotrophic** lakes.

51_____ receive high inorganic material from area runoff

52. _____ contain very few nutrients

53. _____ are often clear

54. _____ profundal zones are often low in oxygen

55. _____ tend to be good trout-fishing lakes

56. _____ receive high organic material from area runoff

57. _____ are oxygen rich

58. _____ are murky with a dense phytoplankton population

59. _____ experience seasonal algal blooms

60. _____ limnetic zone may extend to the bottom

Identification: Determine whether the following statements refer to **human** impacted ecosystems or **undisturbed** ecosystems.

61. _____ animals in the highest trophic levels are rare

62. _____ species diversity is high

63. _____ fueled by sunlight

64. _____ nutrients are recycled

65. _____ fueled by fossil fuels

66. _____ fertilizers, pesticides, and topsoil pollute streams and rivers

67. _____ water is stored

68. _____ water is polluted

69. _____ water is filtered and purified

70. _____ natural predators control population growth

71. _____ crops planted close together encourages pest outbreaks

72. _____ population is expanding exponentially

73. _____ populations are relatively stable

74. _____ ecosystems are simple

Short Answer.

75. Identify the four fundamental resources necessary for life.

_____

_____

_____

CLUES TO APPLYING THE CONCEPTS

These practice questions are intended to sharpen your ability to apply critical thinking and analysis to the biological concepts covered in this chapter.

76. Discuss how the limnetic and profundal zones of freshwater lakes relate to the photic and aphotic zones of oceans.

_____

_____

_____

_____

77. Discuss how the ozone layer is formed in the stratosphere and its function. How is the layer being destroyed, and what are the possible results of this destruction?

_____

_____

_____

_____

_____

_____

_____

_____

_____

_____

_____

_____

_____

_____

78. How can humans reverse the destructive trends of our activities?

_____

_____

_____

_____

_____

_____

_____

_____

_____

_____

_____

_____

ANSWERS TO EXERCISES

1. weather
2. climate
3. latitude
4. gyres
5. rain shadow
6. tropical rain forest
7. tropical deciduous forest
8. savanna
9. desert
10. desertification
11. chaparral
12. grassland
13. prairie
14. temperate deciduous forest
15. temperate rain forest
16. northern coniferous forest
17. taiga
18. tundra

19. Littoral zone
20. plankton
21. phytoplankton
22. zooplankton
23. limnetic zone
24. profundal zone
25. oligotrophic
26. eutrophic
27. photic zone
28. aphotic zone
29. upwelling
30. intertidal zone
31. near-shore zone
32. coral reefs
33. pelagic
34. hydrothermal vent communities

35. false, rotation of Earth
36. true
37. true
38. false, general
39. true
40. true
41. false, life-threatening impact
42. false, increasing
43. true
44. true
45. false, taiga
46. true
47. true
48. false, extremely fragile, severely affected
49. true

50. Biomes table

Biome	Precipitation range	Temperature range	Typical plants present	Typical animals present
tropical rain forest	250 cm - 400 cm	20 - 25°C	broadleaf evergreens	arboreal monkeys, birds, insects
tropical deciduous forest	NA	NA	deciduous trees	NA
savanna	30 cm	NA	scrubby trees, grasses	antelope, buffalo, lions, wildebeest, elephants
desert	< 25 cm	ave 20°C	cacti, succulents	lizards, snakes, kangaroo rats
chaparral	< 25 cm	NA	small evergreen trees, bushes	NA
prairie; grassland	> 25 cm	ave 7°C, hot summers	grasses	bison, antelope
temperate deciduous forest	75 cm - 150 cm	periods of subfreezing temperatures	deciduous trees, wildflowers	black bear, deer, wolves shrews, raccoons, birds
temperate rain forest	400 cm	moderate	evergreen conifers	NA
taiga; northern coniferous forest	25 cm - 30 cm	ave -4°C	evergreen conifers	bison, grizzly bear fox, moose, wolves
tundra	< 25 cm	below -55°C	perennial wildflowers, dwarf willows	caribou, lemmings, birds mosquitos, snowy owls

51. eutrophic	59. eutrophic	67. undisturbed
52. oligotrophic	60. oligotrophic	68. human
53. oligotrophic	61. human	69. undisturbed
54. eutrophic	62. undisturbed	70. undisturbed
55. oligotrophic	63. undisturbed	71. human
56. eutrophic	64. undisturbed	72. human
57. oligotrophic	65. human	73. undisturbed
58. eutrophic	66. human	74. human

75. Nutrients to construct living tissue; energy to support the construction of living tissue; liquid water in which metabolic reactions can occur; appropriate temperatures for metabolic reations to occur.

76. In both the limnetic zone of a lake and the photic zone of the ocean, enough sunlight energy penetrates to support photosynthesis. Both areas may provide the energy to support the profundal and the aphotic zones, respectively. The profundal and the aphotic zones do not receive enough light energy to support photosynthesis, and they rely on the limnetic zone or the photic zone for energy.

77. The stratospheric ozone layer is formed by ultraviolet light striking oxygen, forming O_3. Ozone filters damaging UV radiation, greatly reducing the amount that reaches life on Earth. This layer of ozone is destroyed when CFC's (chlorofluorocarbons) are degraded by UV radiation, releasing chlorine atoms. Chlorine reacts with the O_3 molecules, breaking it into O_2 molecules. The chlorine stays in the stratosphere, reacting with ozone molecule after ozone molecule. The result of the destruction of the stratospheric ozone layer is increased UV radiation reaching Earth, which will ultimately result in increased health concerns, such as reduced immune function and increased skin cancer in humans. Globally, it will result in reduced net primary productivity and increased damage to DNA molecules in most organisms.

78. Humans can reverse the destructive trends our activities have on the ecosystem through understanding how healthy ecosystems function, educating ourselves and others about the destruction that is occurring and how it can and should be reversed, and by making a commitment, globally, to the reversal of the destruction. Through the appropriate use of technology, water and air do not have to be polluted, soil does not have to be depleted of nutrients so that artificial fertilizers are needed, and we do not have to rely on fossil fuels to provide energy for our needs. Finally, humans need to stabilize population growth to reduce the expansion of human-dominated ecosystems.